THE COBB GROUP

Windows™ 3.1

Companion

THE COBB GROUP

Windows™ 3.1

Companion

THE COBB GROUP

Lori L. Lorenz
R. Michael O'Mara
with Russell Borland

Microsoft PRESS

PUBLISHED BY
Microsoft Press
A Division of Microsoft Corporation
One Microsoft Way
Redmond, Washington 98052-6399

Library of Congress Cataloging-in-Publication Data
Lorenz, Lori, 1962–
    Windows 3.1 companion / Lori L. Lorenz, R. Michael O'Mara; with
  Russell Borland.
      p. cm.
    Includes index.
    ISBN 1-55615-372-4
    1. Windows (Computer programs) 2. Microsoft Windows (Computer
  program) I. O'Mara, R. Michael, 1951– . II. Borland, Russell, 1946– . III. Title.
  QA76.76.W56L68   1992
  005.4'3--dc20   91-40737
                                     CIP
Printed and bound in the United States of America.

1 2 3 4 5 6 7 8 9 RDRD 6 5 4 3 2 1

Distributed to the book trade in Canada by Macmillan of Canada, a division
of Canada Publishing Corporation.

Distributed to the book trade outside the United States and Canada by Penguin Books Ltd.

Penguin Books Ltd., Harmondsworth, Middlesex, England
Penguin Books Australia Ltd., Ringwood, Victoria, Australia
Penguin Books N.Z. Ltd., 182–190 Wairau Road, Auckland 10, New Zealand

British Cataloging-in-Publication Data available.

PostScript® is a registered trademark of Adobe Systems, Inc. Aldus® and PageMaker® are registered trademarks of
Aldus Corporation. Apple,® Macintosh,® and TrueType® are registered trademarks of Apple Computer, Inc. dBase
IV® is a registered trademark of Ashton-Tate Corporation. ToolBook® is a registered trademark of Asymetrix Corporation. PC Tools™ is a trademark of Central Point Software, Inc. CompuServe® is a registered trademark of
CompuServe, Inc. Crosstalk® is a registered trademark of Digital Communications Associates, Inc. Hayes® is a
registered trademark of Hayes Microcomputer Products, Inc. HP,® LaserJet,® and Scanjet® are registered trademarks of Hewlett-Packard Company. Intel® is a registered trademark of Intel Corporation. AT,® IBM,® and PS/2®
are registered trademarks and PC XT™ is a trademark of International Business Machines Corporation. Lotus® and
1-2-3® are registered trademarks of Lotus Development Corporation. MCI Mail® is a registered servicemark of
MCI Communications Corporation. WordStar® is a registered trademark of MicroPro International. MS® and
MS-DOS® are registered trademarks and Windows™ is a trademark of Microsoft Corporation. QMS-Color
Script® and QMS-PS® are registered trademarks of QMS, Inc. Epson® is a registered trademark of Seiko Epson
Corporation. Ventura Publisher® is a registered trademark of Ventura Software, Inc. WordPerfect® is a registered
trademark of WordPerfect Corporation.

Acquisitions Editor: Marjorie Schlaikjer
Project Editor: Mary Renaud
Manuscript Editor: Barbara Browne
Technical Editors: Jim Fuchs, James Johnson

Contents

SECTION 2: USING PROGRAM MANAGER APPLICATIONS

SECTION 3: BEYOND THE BASICS

SECTION 4: APPENDIXES

The section "Windows in Color" follows page 274

Acknowledgments

This book, like all others at Microsoft Press, required a team effort. Though I get my name on the cover and thus am entitled to keep all the blame for deficiencies, I gladly acknowledge the contributions of the team that made this book better than I could have alone: Mary Renaud, project editor, who miraculously stayed sane; Jim Fuchs and James Johnson, technical editors, who skillfully kept up with software changes; Connie Little, compositor, who mastered Aldus PageMaker; Peggy Herman, who designed and assembled the color section; Kathleen Atkins, who ably proofread chapter after chapter; and Kim Eggleston and Lisa Sandburg, who handled design coordination.

I also thank many unnamed members of the team for handling printing, manufacturing, distribution, marketing, and sales. No book ever gets to you without these people, who toil, mostly anonymously, for the greater good of the general reading public.

–Russell Borland

Introduction

*M*icrosoft Windows helps personal-computer users work in a more natural, intuitive fashion. Windows replaces the sparse and sometimes intimidating MS-DOS command line with a visually pleasing and richly featured graphical user interface. You interact with the computer by selecting commands from easy-to-use menus or by double-clicking on icons instead of typing terse instructions at the C:\> prompt. Your mouse replaces the keyboard as your primary means of communication with the computer.

Windows offers the advantages of a consistent, predictable interface for all Windows-based applications. This common interface makes learning to use new applications easy. Whether you are using a spreadsheet, a word processor, or a desktop publishing application, you always open a file or print a document the same way. Each application appears in a rectangular window on your screen. You can view the contents of several windows at a time, copy information between the windows, and switch from one application to another by clicking a mouse button—without exiting one application and loading another. In addition, Windows provides common access to your display, printers, and other system peripherals for all your Windows-based applications.

Windows' program execution shell—the Program Manager—presents your applications as icons, organized into groups, ready for you to select and run with a double-click of your mouse. With the File Manager, you can copy a file by dragging its icon to the icon for a different drive, move a file by dragging its icon to a different directory on the same drive, open a file by double-clicking on its icon, and print a file by dragging its icon onto the minimized Print Manager icon. The Task Manager makes it simple to switch between applications; and Control Panel allows you to control your Windows environment with ease.

With the introduction of Windows 3.0, your 80286-, 80386-, or 80486-based computer was released from the confines of the DOS 640-kilobyte (KB) barrier. Now, Windows can use the full potential of your 286, 386, or 486 computer's protected mode to bring advanced memory management and true multitasking to all your Windows applications. With a 386 or 486 computer, you can even run DOS applications and Windows applications simultaneously.

NEW FEATURES

Windows 3.1, the latest version of the Windows operating environment, contains some important new features:

- A new File Manager that combines the directory tree and the directory contents listing in one window

- A new StartUp program group in the Program Manager

- The inclusion of TrueType fonts for crisper display and printing of text

- A shortcut that allows you to drag files to the Print Manager and drop them for printing as if they were being printed by the files' application

- A new accessory called Character Map, which lets you easily insert special symbols and foreign-language characters into your Windows applications

- A new accessory called Object Packager, which lets you create an icon representing an embedded or linked object and then insert the icon into a document

- The Media Player accessory, which you can use to play animation, sound, and MIDI sequencer files and to control hardware such as CD-ROM drives and videodisc players

- The Sound Recorder accessory, which allows you to play, record, and edit sound files if you have installed a sound card

- The inclusion of Microsoft OLE (Object Linking and Embedding) technology in the Write, Paintbrush, and Cardfile applications and in the new accessories Object Packager, Media Player, and Sound Recorder

ABOUT THIS BOOK

All of this computing power is not without a price, however—Windows is a very complex environment. Even with its user-friendly features, learning Windows is a big job.

We wrote *Windows 3.1 Companion* to help make Windows 3.1 easier to learn and use. If you are new to the Windows operating environment, you can use this book as a tutorial to help you get started. If you're already familiar with Windows, you can use the book as a reference guide to help you fully utilize the new capabilities of Windows 3.1.

We had two goals in mind as we created this book. First, we wanted to show you how to use Windows efficiently—after all, one of Windows' strongest selling points is that it saves time. Second, we wanted to provide Windows information in a format that you can return to time and time again, whether you're a Windows novice or an expert.

We designed the various sections of the book to let you quickly find the information you need. Section 1 covers the basics. Even if you've worked with earlier releases of Windows, you'll want to review the chapters in this section to learn how to use many of the new features of Windows 3.1. In Section 2, we show you how to work with Windows' built-in applications, such as Write, Paintbrush, Terminal, and Recorder. We also explain the workings of the desktop accessories and even provide tips for improving your skills with Windows' games. Section 3 explains Windows' operating modes and includes a chapter describing PIFs (program information files), which you'll find extremely useful if you plan to work with both Windows and non-Windows applications. In addition, because Windows relies heavily on color to communicate, we've assembled a color section that displays some of the color options and graphics you can work with.

Finally, Appendix A discusses installation procedures in detail, and Appendix B provides a glossary of Windows terms. A thorough index will help you locate or return to topics of interest. And, at the end of the book, you'll find a set of detachable Quick Reference Cards that list keyboard shortcuts you can use in Windows 3.1.

Section 1
Using Microsoft Windows

In this chapter

Getting Started 1

*I*n this chapter, we'll review what you need to install and run Microsoft Windows 3.1. (If you are installing Windows yourself, you'll want to refer to the complete installation procedure outlined in Appendix A.) We'll explain how to start Windows in each of its operating modes and how to exit Windows and return to the MS-DOS prompt. Then we'll list your options for tailoring Windows to suit your needs and explain where to find more information on customizing Windows.

To install and run Windows, your computer system must meet certain specifications. We assume that you are familiar with the concepts and terms involved in software installation. If you are a novice, we suggest that you consult your local computer guru or vendor to obtain a clearer understanding of these concepts.

SYSTEM SPECIFICATIONS

Windows 3.1 requires at least an IBM PC AT or compatible computer with a minimum of 1 MB (megabyte) of RAM, a hard drive, and a monitor. In addition, you'll want a mouse and a printer, plus a modem if you want to use Windows' Terminal application. You'll need a 386 or 486 computer with extended memory and a VGA monitor and graphics display adapter to use all the features of Windows 3.1. You'll see a noticeable difference in Windows' performance on faster machines.

Hardware

- 286/386/486-based computer—You'll need a computer based on the Intel 80286, 80386, or 80486 chip (such as an IBM PC AT, IBM PS/2 model 25 286 or higher, or a compatible). Windows' 386 enhanced mode is

3

available only if you have a 386 or 486 computer with sufficient extended memory. Computers based on the Intel 8088 or 8086 chip (such as the IBM PC, IBM XT, IBM PS/2 models 25 and 30, and their compatibles) cannot run Windows 3.1.

- 1 MB or more of RAM—Windows 3.1 requires that your computer have at least 1 MB of total memory (640 KB conventional, plus 384 KB extended). You should configure any memory above 1 MB as extended memory for Windows. You'll want 2 MB (or more) of extended memory if you plan to use Windows' multitasking capabilities with large applications. Windows' 386 enhanced mode requires at least 2 MB of memory. Windows 3.1 will not run if your computer has less than 1 MB of memory.

- A hard drive—You need a hard drive with 6 MB to 8 MB free and at least one floppy drive to install Windows.

- Monitor and graphics display adapter—Windows will work with many of the common video graphics adapters and monitors. If your specific display is not on Windows' list of supported devices, consult the manufacturer of your equipment. Many manufacturers offer special drivers that allow you to use their equipment with Windows. Your other option is to select one of Windows' generic drivers, which, although it probably won't make optimal use of your display, will probably allow you to use Windows on your equipment. A graphical user interface really comes into its own on a high-resolution display. Thus we strongly recommend at least a VGA display—preferably in color.

- Mouse—You can operate Windows solely with the keyboard, but you need a mouse to realize the full benefit of the graphical user interface.

- Optional hardware—You'll need a Hayes-compatible modem if you plan to use Windows' Terminal application for communications. For printing, you'll need one of the printers Windows supports. As with displays, the manufacturer of your printer may have a driver available that will allow you to use your printer with Windows, even if the printer does not appear on Windows' standard list of supported devices.

MS-DOS requirements

To run Windows, you must have MS-DOS version 3.1 or later (or a comparable version of another disk operating system such as PC-DOS) installed on your computer. Although Windows' environment may seem to be a separate operating system, it is not. Windows adds to and expands—but does not replace—the MS-DOS operating system. You need them both.

To get the maximum benefit from your Windows environment, you'll need to use applications created specifically for Windows, such as Microsoft Excel, Microsoft Word for Windows, and Aldus PageMaker. Windows-based applications will have a consistent user interface and the ability to smoothly integrate with the other Windows applications on your desktop. They will all share the same printers and other system resources under Windows' direction and can pass information back and forth through Windows' Clipboard. Some applications can share information through Microsoft's Object Linking and Embedding (OLE) technology. The Object Packager program provides an alternative way to share information in the form of icons. (See Chapter 14 for details.) **Compatible software**

Initially, a few older Windows applications may not be fully compatible with the memory management and fonts of Windows 3.1. If you get an error message when you try to run an older Windows application in Windows 3.1, you need to check with the software manufacturer to see if an update is available.

However, you aren't limited to running Windows-based applications. You can launch many of your favorite DOS-based (non-Windows) applications from within Windows. Some of these applications will run in a window on your desktop alongside your Windows applications and will retain at least some of the advantages of the Windows environment. Others require the full screen.

Applications that use "DOS extenders" to address memory beyond the 640 KB of conventional memory may conflict with Windows 3.1 in some operating modes. Lotus 1-2-3 release 3 and dBase IV are examples of large, complex applications that use this technology. As this book goes to press, we expect most major applications using DOS extenders to run in Windows. **Incompatibilities**

A more common form of incompatibility is a "pop-up" or TSR (terminate-and-stay-resident) program. Although some TSRs—such as most networks—will work just fine with Windows, many pop-up utilities won't be available while you are operating in the Windows environment.

An outstanding Setup utility program is included to install Windows on your computer. Windows is a complex product, and installing it can be a lengthy process, but the Setup utility program leads you painlessly through the entire installation procedure. You've probably learned to expect an installation program to automatically copy files from the installation disks to your hard drive. But Setup doesn't stop there. It examines your system and configures Windows to work with the hardware it finds, modifies both your AUTOEXEC.BAT and CONFIG.SYS files, allows you to install and configure your printer, and searches your hard drive for existing applications and installs them in Windows' Program Manager. The Setup utility program allows you the option of controlling **INSTALLING WINDOWS** each step of your Windows installation, and it even has its own Help system. After you have run the Setup utility program and rebooted your computer, Windows will be ready to run. See Appendix A for more complete information on installing Windows.

Upgrading

If you have a previous version of Windows installed on your computer, the Setup program will automatically save some of your preferences and system information for use in Windows 3.1. Upgrading from Windows 3.0 is especially easy and requires no changes to your Windows applications.

**WINDOWS'
OPERATING
MODES**

Windows 3.1 has two operating modes. These two modes—standard and 386 enhanced—take advantage of the protected modes of 286, 386, and 486 chips to add extended memory management and improved multitasking capabilities to Windows. Windows no longer comes in different versions for different computers. Both operating modes are integrated into a single package, and Windows will even sense automatically which mode is appropriate for your hardware. (Windows 3.0 included real mode, a less powerful mode for 8088 computers and 286 computers that use expanded memory. Windows 3.1 does not operate in real mode.)

In standard mode, Windows can access the 16 MB of extended memory addressable by the 80286 chip and can multitask Windows applications. But DOS applications will be suspended while you are working in the Windows environment, and Windows applications will be suspended while a DOS application is active.

Windows' most powerful operating mode is 386 enhanced mode, which uses the protected mode of the 80386 or 80486 processor to maximize your computer's memory management and multitasking capabilities. On an 80386- or 80486-based computer, Windows can address the maximum amount of extended memory and can reallocate memory to the various tasks it runs. It can even create virtual 8088 machines in memory so that each application thinks that it is running on its own computer. In its 386 enhanced mode, and with the appropriate program information file (PIF) settings, Windows can implement multitasking for some of your DOS applications so that they can continue to run in the background, even while you work with another Windows application in the foreground.

**STARTING
WINDOWS**

To start Windows, simply type *WIN* at the MS-DOS prompt and press the [Enter] key. Windows will start in the default operating mode for your machine and will immediately open the Program Manager, from which you'll be able to launch your applications. You can add switches to the basic Windows startup command to invoke a different operating mode, to fine-tune Windows' use of expanded memory, or to run a specified application or open a document immediately upon entering the Windows environment.

By default, Windows starts in the most powerful operating mode supported by your hardware. If you have an 80386- or 80486-based computer with at least 2 MB of extended memory, Windows will start in 386 enhanced mode. If your computer is an 80286 (IBM PC AT, IBM PS/2 25 286 through PS/2 60, or a compatible) with at least 1 MB of memory or an 80386 or 80486 with less than 2 MB of extended memory, Windows will start in standard mode.

The Windows mode switch

Occasionally, you may need to override Windows' default operating mode for your machine. For example, you might want to run standard mode on a 386 or 486 machine. You can add a command-line switch to the starting command to specify Windows' operating mode.

If you start Windows with the command *WIN /S*, you force Windows to start in standard mode on a 386- or 486-based computer. You don't need to explicitly invoke standard mode on a 286-based computer, since Windows will recognize the 80286 processor and will accordingly use that mode as the default when you start Windows with the *WIN* command.

Standard mode

On a 386 or 486 machine with at least 2 MB of RAM, 386 enhanced mode is the default, so you shouldn't need to use the *WIN /3* command to explicitly invoke 386 enhanced mode on one of these computers.

386 enhanced mode

If you usually start specific programs every time you start Windows, you'll want to take advantage of Windows' StartUp group in the Program Manager. Consider adding to the StartUp group the icons of the programs you always run under Windows. See Chapter 5 for information about adding icons to an existing group window.

Starting Windows and applications together

If you occasionally want to run an application as soon as you enter the Windows environment, you can specify its file name as part of the Windows startup command. For example, entering the command *WIN CALENDAR.EXE* will start Windows and immediately run the Calendar application. The Program Manager will appear as an icon on your desktop instead of taking its usual place as the active window. If the application you want to run is in a drive or directory that is not part of your MS-DOS search path, you must supply a full path name in addition to the file name of the application you want to run.

You can go a step further with the Windows startup command. You can also supply the name of a document or a data file that you want the application to open as soon as it begins running. Just add the file name to the Windows startup command line, following the file name for the application. For example, if you type the command line *WIN C:\EXCEL\EXCEL.EXE B:\CHECKBK.XLS,* Windows will start, automatically run Microsoft Excel (which is in the \EXCEL directory of the C drive), and then immediately open the CHECKBK.XLS spreadsheet file from the disk in the B drive. As a shortcut, you can omit the name of the application: Entering the command line *WIN B:\CHECKBK.XLS* will start Windows and Microsoft Excel and will open the spreadsheet file.

EXITING WINDOWS

The safest way to end a Windows session and return to the MS-DOS prompt is to select Exit Windows from the File menu in the Program Manager. Always returning to the Program Manager and using the Exit Windows command is the best way to ensure that Windows will close all open files and take care of other housekeeping chores before you leave the Windows environment.

TAILORING WINDOWS TO YOUR NEEDS

You can control the look and feel of Windows as you install printers, fonts, and applications. You can also change your initial choices, and many other aspects of the Windows environment, from within Windows—without reinstalling the software. The Control Panel and Windows Setup applications allow you to modify your Windows environment to accommodate changes in your computer equipment, your current needs, or your changing preferences.

Control Panel options

The Control Panel application offers extensive opportunities to customize your Windows environment to fit your own needs and style. You can make most of the changes "on the fly" while you work with Windows. You have the option to keep the changes you've made as the new defaults or to discard them when your Windows session ends. Occasionally, you'll have to restart Windows to implement a major change.

With Control Panel, you can configure your computer's ports and install, remove, configure, and select printers. You can control international settings such as date or currency formats and set your keyboard for foreign-language characters. You will be able to delete, add, and size the fonts you employ for more appealing and effective communication. The Color and Desktop commands allow you to customize Windows' appearance to your own personal taste. The Mouse command can switch your mouse buttons and adjust tracking sensitivity. You can change your system date and time, and you can even disable the sound if you find the computer's beeps annoying. (If you have a sound card installed in your computer, you can set up specific sounds to signal various

Windows events.) Control Panel also includes controls for installing and setting multimedia devices such as sound cards, compact-disc players, and MIDI instruments, plus special settings for the multitasking functions of 386 enhanced mode. We'll cover Control Panel and its many options in Chapter 3.

The Windows Setup application allows you to restructure Windows to reflect changes in your display, keyboard, mouse, or network. However, you probably won't need to change any of these settings unless you physically change your computer hardware.

Windows Setup

The portion of Windows Setup that you are likely to use is its Set Up Applications command. After you install new Windows-based applications on your computer, you can instruct Windows Setup to search your disk drives for the applications and install them in the Program Manager (if the applications haven't already installed themselves in the Program Manager).

You also can add applications directly to the Program Manager. In fact, you can create and remove group windows and arrange your applications to appear any way you like. As soon as you finish installing Windows, you'll probably need to go to the Program Manager to add some of your non-Windows applications that Windows Setup didn't recognize. Chapter 5 will help you explore the power of the Program Manager.

Another way to add applications

Windows needs to know a number of technical details about the applications it runs. Windows-based applications are designed to automatically supply Windows with the information it needs. For non-Windows applications, the necessary information goes into a separate program information file. Often, software developers will supply a PIF to facilitate the use of their application with Windows. But you may need to create or edit a PIF to allow some of your non-Windows applications to run well in Windows. Chapter 17 explains the PIF Editor.

The preferences and configuration information for Windows is stored in special files (WIN.INI, SYSTEM.INI, and others) on your hard drive. After you use the Windows Setup and Control Panel applications to change the Windows environment, Windows records those changes in the .INI files. Some older versions of Windows required you to modify those files directly to control some features—a tedious and confusing procedure filled with the potential for mistakes. Although you can read and edit the information in these files with Notepad (or any ASCII text editor), doing so will seldom be necessary.

WIN.INI and friends

In this chapter

Windows Fundamentals 2

*W*indows offers something special for everyone who uses it. Perhaps its most powerful feature is its ability to address 16 MB of memory or more for Windows applications, allowing the applications to run quickly and implement a wide range of services. In addition to its advanced memory management capabilities, Windows also sports an attractive graphical user interface that makes all Windows applications easy to learn and fun to use.

You may be surprised to know that Windows will let you load several non-Windows applications at once (even if your machine has only 1 MB of memory) and will allow you to switch between them without returning to the MS-DOS prompt. On a 386- or 486-based computer, Windows will even let you run multiple non-Windows applications simultaneously.

In this chapter, we'll introduce you to the feature you'll probably care about the most—Windows' graphical environment, which is also known as Windows' graphical user interface (GUI). If you're already familiar with working in a graphical environment or with an earlier version of Windows, we suggest you skim this chapter just to be sure you're familiar with our terminology. If you've worked only in a character-based environment, however, you'll want to read this chapter carefully—it lays the groundwork for everything to follow.

If you've never worked in a graphical environment before, you'll find that working in Windows is much easier (and more fun) than working in a character-based environment. One reason you'll enjoy Windows' graphical environment is that you can do much of your work with the mouse instead of the keyboard. By using the mouse to manipulate various elements on the screen directly, you can quickly perform tasks that would otherwise require dozens of keystrokes.

UNDERSTANDING THE ENVIRONMENT

If you haven't installed a mouse on your computer (or if you're a keyboard fanatic), you'll be relieved to know that most Windows applications will let you use both the keyboard and the mouse.

Windows' graphical environment also provides three key features you'll find in nearly all Windows applications: icons, drop-down menus, and dialog boxes. As you'll discover later in this chapter, these three elements are the primary reasons Windows applications are easy to learn and use. Once you've learned to use your first application, you can come up to speed on a new application quickly because these graphical elements give all Windows applications a similar look and feel.

Another benefit to working in Windows' graphical environment is that it allows you to easily exchange information between applications. In fact, you can either dynamically link applications so that data is automatically updated as it changes, or you can copy and paste data from one application to another without establishing a dynamic link.

Finally, Windows' graphical environment allows you to see on the screen an exact representation of an application's printed output. For example, if you're using a word processor to create a report that uses a variety of type styles, Windows will let you see on the screen how the report will appear when you print it. In addition, if you want to integrate text and graphics on a single page, Windows will allow you to view both the text and the graphics on the screen simultaneously. This ability to see on the screen what will appear in the printed output is referred to as WYSIWYG (What You See Is What You Get) capability.

Before we move on, keep in mind that there is a fundamental difference between the way you'll approach commands in a graphical environment as opposed to a character-based environment. Instead of selecting a command and indicating what you want that command to act upon, Windows applications require that you first indicate what material you want the command to affect and then select the command. For example, to assign boldface to some text in a document, you would first highlight the text you want to make bold and then issue the command that assigns boldface. You'll see many examples of this approach throughout this book.

USING THE POINTER

The pointer, a floating graphic on your screen that represents the actions of your mouse, will let you interact with Windows. The pointer can assume various shapes, depending on its current function. Table 2-1 shows an assortment of the pointers you'll use in Windows. You'll see the pointer change into a different shape when you start an application, move objects on the desktop, or use a Paintbrush tool.

Table 2-1

Pointer	Name	Definition
⌖	Arrow pointer	The "mouse" pointer for all Windows applications is used for selecting commands, activating applications, and moving windows.
⤢ ⇕ ⇔	Sizing pointers	These pointers adjust the size of a window on the desktop.
✜	Move pointer	This pointer lets you move a window with the arrow keys to a new location on the desktop.
+	Crosshair pointer	Whenever you work with graphics, you'll see the crosshair pointer or a variation of it. This pointer is often found in Windows' drawing application, Paintbrush.
🖑	Hand pointer	The Help application uses the hand pointer to let you select Help topics.
⧗	Hourglass pointer	The hourglass pointer indicates that Windows is working to complete the command you issued. While the hourglass is on the desktop, you can't issue any other commands or select desktop elements. When the pointer returns to its previous shape, you can go to the next task.
I	I-beam pointer	The default arrow pointer changes into an I-beam shape whenever you point to a desktop element that works with text. You'll also see a blinking vertical line, or cursor, in that desktop element. The cursor is sometimes called an insertion-point marker.
⊘	Prevent pointer	The prevent pointer indicates that you can't relocate a desktop element to the spot where you're pointing.

You'll see these pointers throughout Windows.

The pointer's shape is directly related to what you're doing with Windows. For example, if you start an application and are waiting for it to open, you'll see the pointer turn into an hourglass. Because some pointers have an active area that does all the work, you must have the active area of the pointer on top of an item or pointing to a specific spot in order for the pointer to accomplish its task. For example, the I-beam pointer must be positioned on the text you want to manipulate.

Navigating

Pointer movements correspond to the movements you make with the mouse. If you move the mouse to the right, the pointer moves to the right. The mouse buttons enable you to perform Windows functions. The left mouse button is the primary button. The right mouse button is used for special functions, which we'll point out as we discuss Windows applications. If you'd prefer to use the right mouse button as your primary button, use Windows' Control Panel to swap the functions of the left and right mouse buttons. Chapter 3 explains this process.

When you're navigating with the keyboard, you'll use the direction keys ([Page Up], [Page Down], [Home], [End], ↑, ↓, ←, and →) to move through selections or text. You'll also use the [Tab] key to move between elements in a dialog box.

Selecting

When you want to run an application or choose a command, you can use the mouse to issue your instructions. Windows uses three main mouse actions for selecting: clicking, double-clicking, and dragging. Clicking is a single press and release of a mouse button. Double-clicking is pressing a mouse button twice in quick succession without moving the mouse. Dragging involves holding down a mouse button and moving the mouse without releasing the button. After you select a series of items or text by dragging or move an item by dragging, you release the button to complete the action. (If you want to practice these mouse actions, you can use the Windows tutorial. To run the tutorial, choose Windows Tutorial from the Program Manager's Help menu.)

Windows also uses some variations of the three main mouse actions. Later, when we discuss Windows' built-in applications, such as Write, we'll introduce functions that require simultaneous mouse and keyboard actions. Tasks that use the mouse with specific keys are secondary functions, just like the secondary functions you see on calculators or keyboards. For example, to select all the text in a Write document, you press the [Ctrl] key at the same time you click your mouse button in the selection area. You can perform other Windows functions with the mouse and the [Shift], [Alt], or [Ctrl] key.

As you work with Windows' various applications, your desktop and its elements will change. Not only will your pointer alter its shape, but other elements such as icons and windows will also change. After you select an item, it will be highlighted—that is, it will appear in inverse video (white becomes black and vice versa). Later, when you use tools in Paintbrush, you'll see guidelines (fine dashed lines) that outline the shape the pointer is creating. We'll point out these changes as you learn about the functions of Windows.

An icon is a graphical representation of an application, a document, or a program item. An icon that shows up on your desktop is like the tip of an iceberg because it is a small part of a larger program. When you activate an icon to run an application, the application appears on your desktop as a window.

An icon is made up of a graphic and a title. The graphic identifies the application with a schematic picture that represents its function. For example, the Write icon, shown in Table 2-2, contains a pen writing an *A,* indicating that this application creates text. The title, Write, is the application's name.

WORKING WITH ICONS

Table 2-2

File Manager Control Panel Print Manager Clipboard Viewer MS-DOS Prompt

Windows Setup PIF Editor Calendar Calculator Clock

Write Paintbrush Terminal Notepad Recorder

Solitaire Minesweeper Program Manager Object Packager Character Map

Dr. Watson Cardfile Read Me Media Player Sound Recorder

You'll find these application icons in Windows.

Activating an icon

You can run, or activate, an application by double-clicking on its icon. After the first click, Windows will highlight the icon's title. After the second click, Windows will change the pointer into an hourglass, indicating that you must wait for Windows to set up the application's window on the desktop.

If you are using the keyboard instead of a mouse, you can use the Program Manager's menu to open or run an application from its icon. First, move the highlight to the icon's title by using the arrow keys or by pressing the first letter of the title. After you highlight the icon, you can simply press [Enter], or you can press [Alt]F to access the File menu and press O to choose the Open command. Windows will then activate the icon and open the application's window.

Moving an icon

If you want to move an icon, you need to drag it with the mouse. When you click on an icon, Windows highlights the title. As you drag the icon, the pointer transforms into an untitled black-and-white version of the icon. When you release the mouse button, the icon returns to its normal appearance.

If you are using the keyboard, you can't move individual icons unless the icon represents a minimized window. (We'll talk about minimizing windows later in this chapter.)

WORKING WITH A WINDOW

A window is a framed area in which Windows runs an application, displays a document, or performs a task. There are several types of windows, primarily application and document windows. When you start an application by double-clicking on its icon, the application will appear in an application window on the desktop. In an application window, you can work with a specific application, such as Microsoft's word processor Word for Windows. The application window furnishes menus of commands and a work area for your data. Your data can appear in either the work area or a smaller window called a document window.

You can open several document windows as partitions of the work area when you're working with an application that allows you to do so. The various document windows can each display one file. These files themselves are often referred to as documents, even though they may be spreadsheets or graphics. However, not all Windows applications are designed to use document windows. Some of Windows' built-in applications, such as Write or Paintbrush, can't use document windows. Later in this chapter, we'll show you how to get around this limitation by using multiple application windows.

Windows also uses variations of application and document windows. A shell, which is a variation of an application window, does more than carry out regular application functions; it actually controls the applications and devices of your computer. The shell, application windows, and document windows form a hierarchy similar to the hierarchy on a ship, where the admiral, captain, and crew form the various levels. The shell starts an application when you have a job in mind, like the admiral who directs an operation to begin. The application window manipulates the data with a series of instructions, like the captain of a ship, who manipulates the crew. The document windows are like the crew stations where the work gets done.

A group window, which is a variation of a document window, groups icons inside a shell like the Program Manager. We'll talk more about group windows when we discuss the Program Manager in Chapter 5.

Before you can work with a window, you need to know what's in it. Figure 2-1 shows a Write window with labeled parts. All windows have a frame, a title bar, and a Control menu box. Application windows also contain a menu bar. The frame is the outside edge of the window that controls the size of the window. The title bar presents the name of the application and the file it's working with (if applicable). The color of the title bar indicates whether the window is active (that is, whether it's the one you're working in) or inactive. By default, an active window has a blue title bar and an inactive one has a white title bar. You can have more than one inactive window open at a time, although only one window will be active. The Control menu box, which is the box containing the dash in the upper-left corner of the window, is used predominantly by keyboard users to manipulate a window (for example, to move or size a window). With the keyboard, a Control menu box containing a long dash, usually found in application windows, is accessed by pressing [Alt][Spacebar]; a Control menu box containing a shorter dash, usually found in document windows, is accessed by pressing [Alt]- (hyphen). The menu bar, below the title bar, contains a series of menus listed by title (for example, the File menu).

Figure 2-1

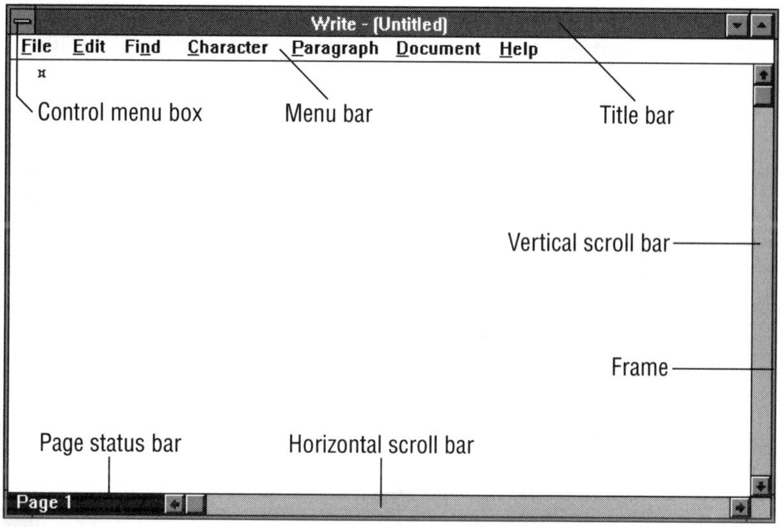

All windows contain a frame, a title bar, and a Control menu box.

**Navigating
in a window**

Windows lets you navigate within a window by using the vertical and horizontal scroll bars located at the right and bottom of a window, respectively. The vertical scroll bar advances the work area one line at a time in the direction of the arrow if you click on one of the arrow boxes at the top or bottom of the scroll bar. For example, if you need to see one line above the top line in a Write window, you would click on the top arrow box on the vertical scroll bar to move up one line. In addition, you can use the horizontal scroll bar to shift the work area to the right or left.

To move through your document at a faster rate, you can continuously select the arrow box by holding down the mouse button instead of just clicking on the arrow box. The document will scroll until you release the mouse button. If you know the approximate relative location of the information you want to scroll to, you can drag the slider (the unmarked box on the scroll bar) to quickly move to another part of the document. After you release the mouse button, Windows will display the new location. As you scroll between the pages of the document, the page status bar will change to reflect the new position.

Using the slider is fine if you know where the information appears in your document. However, if you don't know where it is, you may want to advance one screenful of information at a time. You can do this by clicking above or below the slider. If you want to bring the previous screenful of information into view, click in the vertical scroll bar above the slider. If you want to bring the following screenful of information into view, click below the slider.

To scroll through your document with the keyboard, you can use the direction keys and key combinations. You need to use the arrow keys to move up and down a line at a time. To move a screenful at a time, use the [Page Up] and [Page Down] keys. You can quickly move to the top of the work area by pressing [Ctrl][Home]. To move to the bottom of the work area, press [Ctrl][End].

Moving a window

Moving a window is necessary when you need more space or when you need to view more than one window on your desktop. To move a window, drag the title bar at the top of the window to the new location and then release the mouse button to place the window. As you drag the title bar, a guideline the shape and size of the window frame will appear so that you can find a space that is the right size for your window. Since Windows doesn't reconstruct all the complex graphics with each movement of the mouse, the process of moving a window becomes much quicker.

If you're using the keyboard, you must use the Control menu to move a window. First, you need to access the Control menu by pressing [Alt]- (hyphen) or [Alt][Spacebar]. Next, press *M* to choose the Move command, and then use the arrow keys to reposition the window. Press [Enter] to place the window.

If you want Windows to rearrange the windows on the desktop, you can use commands from the Task Manager and from the Control menu. We'll show you more about these commands later in this chapter.

Resizing a window allows you to vary your workspace and to make room for other windows. To resize a window, move the pointer over any part of the frame; the pointer will change into a double-headed arrow called a sizing pointer. When you adjust the top or bottom of a window, you'll see a vertical pointer (↕). When you adjust the sides, the pointer will look horizontal (↔). If you adjust a window from a corner, you'll see a diagonal pointer (⬦), indicating that you can change both the height and width simultaneously. After you point to any part of the window frame, drag it to change the size. You'll see guidelines similar to the ones you see when you move a window. When the window is the right size, release the mouse button to lock in the new size. As an example, Figure 2-2 shows a Write window before and after resizing.

If you are using the keyboard, you have to use a different method to resize a window. First, press [Alt][Spacebar] or [Alt]- (hyphen) to access the Control menu. Next, press *S* to choose the Size command, and then use the arrow keys to change the dimensions. The first arrow key you press determines which edge of the window is chosen for repositioning: the ↑ key selects the top of the window, the ← key selects the left edge of the window, and so forth. Once an edge is selected, other arrow keys can be used for final sizing. For example, pressing the ↓ key chooses the bottom edge of the window, which you can move up with the ↑ key. Pressing ← or → then moves the pointer to the left or the right bottom corner, where you can adjust two sides of the window simultaneously. Finally, when you have changed the dimensions to the desired size, press [Enter] to finish resizing the window.

Resizing a window

Figure 2-2

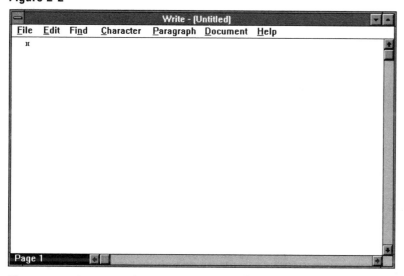
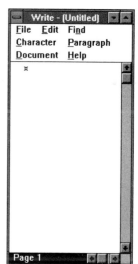

You can resize a window to use your workspace more efficiently.

Working with more than one window

Multiple windows offer an easy way to copy information between applications or documents. For example, if you are writing a report that involves statistics, you might use Word for Windows to create the report and Microsoft Excel to create the statistics. If both windows are on the desktop, you can quickly move between them to calculate the statistics and then copy the numbers into your report.

Besides using more than one application on the desktop, you can have more than one copy of the same application on the desktop. For example, for every Write document you want to open, you need a running copy of Write. Because Write has a simple application window that can have only one document in its work area at a time, you need multiple copies of Write running to have multiple documents on the desktop. Once you have multiple documents on the desktop, you can move between them just by clicking on the one you want to activate. We'll show you how to copy information between windows in Section 2 of this book, when we discuss Windows' built-in applications.

Using group windows

Group windows are variations of document windows because they are partitions of the Program Manager. Group windows don't have their own menu bars; instead, they use the Program Manager's menu bar. (Each group window does, however, have its own Control menu.) The various Windows application icons are sorted into groups when Windows is installed. You can add application icons to the group windows, and you can also add group windows to the Program Manager. You'll learn how to add these windows and icons in Chapter 5.

You can move and resize group windows just as you do application windows, but you can do so only within the space of the Program Manager window. Likewise, if you minimize a group window into an icon, Windows will place the icon at the bottom of the Program Manager window. To move or resize a group window with the keyboard, you have to access the group window's Control menu by pressing [Alt]- (hyphen). Then you can use the Control menu commands to manipulate the group window.

When you close a group window by double-clicking on its Control menu or issuing the Close command from the Control menu with the keyboard, the group window will minimize into an icon in the Program Manager window rather than disappearing from the desktop.

Using the Minimize, Maximize, and Restore boxes

In addition to resizing a window by moving its frame, you can resize a window with the Minimize, Maximize, and Restore boxes in the upper-right corner of the window. If you click on the Minimize box (the box with the down arrow), Windows will substitute an icon for the window and move the icon to the bottom of the desktop. The application will still be running, but it won't consume as much space on the desktop. If you click on the Maximize box (the box with the up arrow) in an application window, Windows will enlarge the window to fill the entire desktop. (A maximized document window will fill the application window in which it appears.) After the window is maximized, Windows will replace the Maximize box with the Restore box (the box with the double arrow). If you click on the Restore box, Windows will restore the window to its previous size. (Note that some windows—those used by Calculator or Character Map, for example—cannot be enlarged.)

To restore a minimized icon to a window, just double-click on the icon, or highlight the icon and press [Enter]. Alternatively, if you click on the icon once, its Control menu will pop up, and you can choose the Restore command.

To minimize, maximize, or restore a window's size with the keyboard, you can use the Control menu. First, press [Alt][Spacebar] or [Alt]- (hyphen) to access the Control menu of the active window. Next, press the underlined letter of the command to minimize, maximize, or restore the window.

A minimized icon remembers its location. You can move the minimized icon by dragging it or by using the Move command on its Control menu. If you move the icon on the desktop and then restore the application to its original size, the next time you minimize the icon during your Windows session, the icon will return to where it was relocated. For example, if you resize your Write document to fill all but the left edge of your screen, you can move any minimized icons to the left edge of the screen. Then, you can still access the other icons on the desktop since the application window won't cover them.

When you're working with a group window, you can use a shortcut to maximize the group window to fill the Program Manager workspace: double-click on the group window's title bar. You can use the Restore box to shrink the group window to its previous size.

Closing versus exiting

When you're finished working with an application designed to run with Windows, you can store it by closing it or exiting the application. It's always better to exit with the Exit command on the File menu so that the application's files are closed along with the data files. The Close command on the Control menu will remove the application from the desktop, but it might not clear the application from your computer's memory or, in some cases, save the file. For a shortcut, you can double-click on the Control menu box to close the window, although it's best to use the Exit command if you don't know whether the application will save your changes.

If you just want to move a window out of the way to make more room on the desktop, you can minimize the window into an icon. This way, the application will still be in memory, and you can restore it to a window more quickly than you can by restarting it from the Program Manager. Minimizing an application into an icon also leaves the file open, which saves a step when you want to use the application. (You won't have to open the file again after you restart the application.) Later in this chapter, we'll show you another safe way to exit an application with the Control menu's Switch To command, which displays the Task Manager's Task List dialog box.

**THE PROGRAM
MANAGER**

From the Program Manager, you can launch most of the applications that run in Windows. The Program Manager, which is the first application you see when you start Windows, uses a special window called a shell. A shell is a window that can start other programs. When a shell is active, it also contains an active window. For example, the Program Manager window and one of its interior, or group, windows can both be active. If all the windows inside the Program Manager window are minimized, however, an icon and the shell are active or selected. When the Program Manager window is inactive, the group window is inactive, too. Figure 2-3 displays some of the elements found in the Program Manager, including group windows and minimized group icons. In Chapter 5, we'll talk about the Program Manager in detail.

Figure 2-3

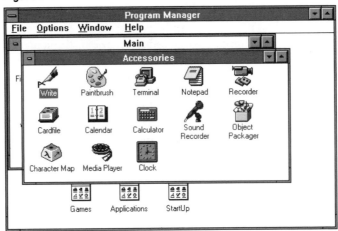

Group windows are elements of the Program Manager.

**THE FILE
MANAGER**

The File Manager, another shell, is true to its name—it manages files. It carries out many of the tasks you used to perform with MS-DOS. You can find its icon in the Main group window of the Program Manager. With the File Manager, you can format floppy disks, copy files, create directories, and rearrange the files in your directories.

Directory trees are an important part of the File Manager. As you can see in Figure 2-4, each directory has an icon next to its name in the directory tree pane. The directory tree pane is like a group window in the Program Manager. You can use more than one pane at a time, but only one can be active at a time. We'll give you all the details about the File Manager in Chapter 6.

Figure 2-4

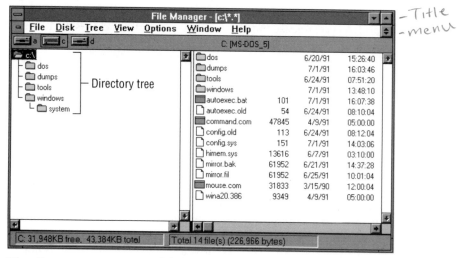

The directory tree is part of the File Manager.

**USING THE
MENU BAR**

In applications designed to run with Windows, every application window has a menu bar that provides access to the application's commands. Each application's menu bar works the same way—the commands differ, but the way you access them doesn't.

The menu bar, which always appears directly below the title bar in the application window, lists the names of the drop-down menus. For example, the File menu is the first menu listed on Write's menu bar, shown in Figure 2-5.

Figure 2-5

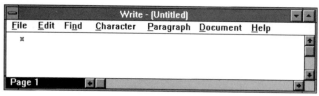

Write's menu bar contains seven menus.

Issuing commands

You can issue commands with the mouse, the keyboard, or the accelerator keys. You'll want to employ accelerator key shortcuts for the commands you use regularly.

When you click on a menu, a box containing commands drops down. To issue a command, you click on the command in the box, and the highlight moves to that command. As you release the mouse button, Windows closes the box and issues the command. You can save a step by positioning the mouse pointer on the menu, holding down the mouse button, and dragging to the command you want. When you release the button, the application executes that command.

If you're using the keyboard, you can access the menu bar by pressing the [Alt] key. Then select a menu by pressing the underlined letter in the menu name or by using the arrow keys to highlight the menu name and pressing [Enter]. Notice, for example, that the File menu has an underlined *F.* The underlined letter is the one you use with the [Alt] key to access that menu. If you then press [Alt] by itself, the menu will close. You can also use the arrow keys to move between and within the menus. To issue a command from the keyboard after a menu is displayed, type the underlined letter in the command name or use the arrow keys to move the highlight to the command you want; then, after the command is highlighted, press [Enter].

The keystroke combinations you see next to some of the command names on the menus are accelerator keys that work when the menus are closed. They offer a third and often faster way to issue a command. Only the commands used most often have accelerator key shortcuts. For example, you can issue the Undo command (from Write's Edit menu) by pressing [Ctrl]Z. As we present the various applications, we will point out the accelerator keys.

Types of commands

Each menu groups its commands differently, depending on the functions of the commands. For example, Write's Paragraph menu, shown in Figure 2-6, groups the reset (Normal) command separately from the alignment, spacing, and indenting commands.

Figure 2-6

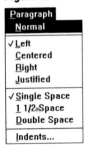

Write's Paragraph menu groups its commands.

Windows supplies many types of commands, most of which can be divided into three categories: immediate, toggle, and user input. Immediate commands, of course, work as soon as you issue them, without any request for user input. They perform a single operation. For example, in Write, the File menu's New command opens a new file. Toggle commands will keep an option turned on until you turn it off. An example is the Paragraph menu's Left command (left alignment) in Write. You can tell when a toggle command is on by the check mark next to its name. User input commands have an ellipsis (...) next to the command name to let you know that the application needs information from you before the command can work. The application requests this information by presenting a dialog box. For example, when you issue Write's Open command, you'll see an Open dialog box from which you can choose a file.

Sometimes a command name will change to fit the context of the last action you performed. The Undo command changes to let you know specifically what it will affect. For instance, if the last action you completed involved formatting, the Undo command will change to Undo Formatting on the menu. You'll find this change in a command name in special cases with most of the applications.

The Task Manager is a built-in feature of Windows that allows you to switch between multiple open applications, end tasks, and arrange the windows and icons on your desktop. Unlike the Program Manager or the File Manager, the Task Manager is not a distinct application with its own icon; it is an integral feature of Windows and is always available.

THE TASK MANAGER

When you call on the Task Manager (by pressing [Ctrl][Esc]), Windows displays the Task List dialog box, shown in Figure 2-7. This dialog box lists the applications running on the desktop in reverse order of their appearance. The active window is at the top of the list. The six buttons in the dialog box let you switch between the applications (Switch To), close an application window (End Task), exit the dialog box (Cancel), rearrange the open application windows on the desktop in a cascaded stack (Cascade), rearrange the open application windows so that each gets a portion of the desktop (Tile), and arrange the minimized icons on the desktop (Arrange Icons). To activate one of these buttons, click on it or, with the keyboard, press [Tab] to move to the button and then press [Enter].

If you want to switch between the application windows, usually you'll just click on the one you want to use. However, you can't click on something you

Figure 2-7

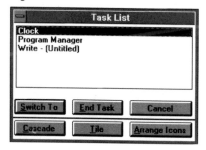

The Task List dialog box manipulates all the items on the desktop.

can't see on the desktop. To activate a window that is covered, use the Switch To command to bring the window to the top of the pile. If you use the keyboard instead of a mouse, the Switch To command provides an easy, clear way to move between the windows. You can also use [Alt][Tab] or [Alt][Esc] to move between application windows.

To move to another window, select Switch To from the Control menu or use the accelerator keys [Ctrl][Esc] to display the Task List dialog box. Mouse users can take a shortcut to the Task List dialog box by double-clicking on any vacant part of the desktop. In the Task List dialog box, you can switch to the window whose title is highlighted in the list box by clicking on the Switch To button. If you're using the keyboard, simply press [Alt]S to select the Switch To button.

The End Task button is a safe way to exit an application without losing any of the changes you made to your document. After you select one of the listed windows, choose the End Task button to exit that window. When you do, the next window on the list appears on the desktop as the active window.

If you have several windows open on the desktop and you don't want to manually resize them to fit on the desktop, you can let the Task Manager organize the desktop for you. The Cascade, Tile, and Arrange Icons buttons organize your desktop to work more efficiently by making the windows easier to find and move. The Cascade button stacks the windows diagonally so that their title bars show. Figure 2-8 shows the desktop with cascading windows. The Tile button divides the space among all the windows so that you can see the work area of each window. Figure 2-9 shows the effect of the Tile button. The Arrange Icons button is handy when you have several minimized icons that were moved but not tidied up. Figure 2-10 shows the desktop after we used the Arrange Icons button to rearrange our minimized icons.

Figure 2-8

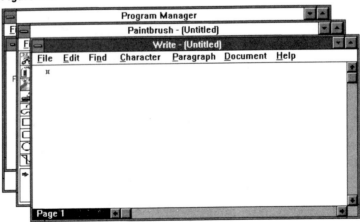

The Cascade button stacks the windows on the desktop.

Figure 2-9

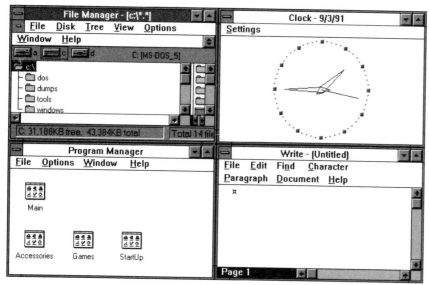

The Tile button divides the desktop among all the windows.

Figure 2-10

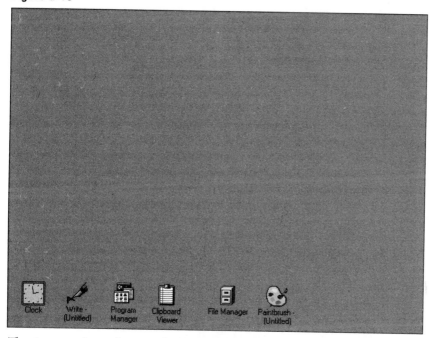

The Arrange Icons button places minimized icons in a row on the desktop.

When you've finished working with the Task List dialog box, you can close it by clicking on the Cancel button or by clicking in another window. You can also close the dialog box by double-clicking on its Control menu box or by pressing [Alt][F4] or [Esc].

WORKING WITH DIALOG BOXES

Many command names on Windows' menus are followed by an ellipsis (...). The ellipsis indicates that a second level of options is available "below" that command. These options appear in a special window called a dialog box. Dialog boxes open automatically when you issue a command that's followed by an ellipsis. When you've completed your selections in a dialog box, you can click on OK or press [Enter] to close the dialog box. To cancel your selections, click on Cancel or press [Esc]. You can also close a dialog box by opening the Control menu and selecting Close, by pressing [Alt][F4], or by double-clicking on the Control menu box.

Dialog boxes share some features with other windows. All dialog boxes have a Control menu that you can use to move and close the box. Most have OK and Cancel buttons. If you select the Open command from the File menu in Write, for example, you'll see the Open dialog box shown in Figure 2-11.

Figure 2-11

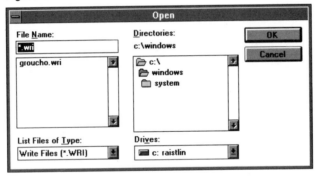

The Open dialog box includes a Control menu, a title bar, an OK button, and a Cancel button.

Navigating in a dialog box

Just as you can have only one application window active at a time, you can activate only one part of a dialog box at a time. An active dialog box element is highlighted, outlined with a dashed line, or designated by a blinking cursor.

To move to an element in a dialog box, just click on the element. To navigate in a dialog box with the keyboard, press [Tab] to move forward or [Shift][Tab] to move backward. You can also move to another element by pressing [Alt] plus the underlined character in the element's name. For example, in the Open dialog box, you would press [Alt]D to move to the Directories list box. Table 2-3 lists the keyboard shortcuts you can use in dialog boxes.

Table 2-3

Keystroke	Function
[Tab]	Move to the next element.
[Shift][Tab]	Move to the previous element.
[Alt]n	Move to the element whose title has n underlined.
↑, ↓, ←, →	Move between options in a group, or move the cursor up or down in a list or left or right in a text box.
[Home]	Move to the top item in a list box, or move to the first character in a text box.
[End]	Move to the last item in a list box, or move to the last character in a text box.
[Page Up] or [Page Down]	Scroll up or down one boxful of data at a time in a list box.
[Alt]↓	Open and display a drop-down list box.
↑ or ↓	Select an item in a drop-down list box.
[Spacebar]	Select or cancel a highlighted item in a list box, or select or clear a check box.
[Ctrl]/ (slash)	Select all items in a list box.
[Ctrl]\ (backslash)	Cancel all selections except the active item in a list box. The active item will have a dashed frame around it.
[Shift]↑ or [Shift] ↓	Extend the list box highlight in the direction of the arrow.
[Shift][Home]	Extend the text box highlight to the first character.
[Shift][End]	Extend the text box highlight to the last character.
[Enter]	Execute the active command button, or select the highlighted item and simultaneously execute the active command button.
[Esc] or [Alt][F4]	Close or exit a dialog box without completing any commands.

You can use these keys to navigate in a dialog box.

Dialog box elements

You can issue instructions from a dialog box in several ways. The elements of a dialog box are tools you can use to set options and make choices before executing the command. Dialog box elements range from simple check boxes to multiple-part scroll bars. Windows varies the basic dialog box elements to accommodate the needs of the individual commands. We'll explain basic group boxes, check boxes, radio buttons, list boxes, drop-down list boxes, scroll bars, text boxes, increment boxes, display boxes, and command buttons. As we present Windows' desktop applications, we'll point out the variations on these basic dialog box elements.

Group boxes

A group box organizes dialog box elements by function so that an option is easier to find in a busy dialog box. The group box doesn't set an option itself but simply frames a number of different options under one main heading. Group boxes contain an assortment of dialog box elements, such as text boxes, drop-down list boxes, buttons, and check boxes. For example, the International-Date Format dialog box shown in Figure 2-12 has a Short Date Format group box. This group box in turn contains a combination of radio buttons for Order, a text box for Separator, and check boxes for other details, such as leading zeros. We'll often direct you to part of a dialog box by referring to a group box title.

Figure 2-12

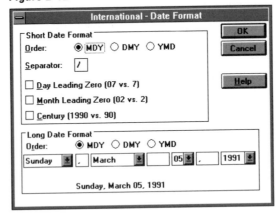

The International-Date Format dialog box has two group boxes: Short Date Format and Long Date Format.

Check boxes

A check box lets you turn a particular dialog box option on or off. To select a check box option with the mouse, just click inside the check box or on the check box's name. As soon as you select a check box option, an X will appear inside the check box to indicate that you've turned that option on. To deselect a check box option, simply choose that option a second time. As you'd expect, deselecting a check box option causes the X to disappear, indicating that you've turned that option off.

To select or deselect a check box option with the keyboard, you can use either of two techniques: You can hold down the [Alt] key while you type the underlined letter in the check box name. Or you can use the [Tab] key to activate the check box inside the dialog box (a dashed line will frame the check box name to indicate that it is currently activated). Once you've activated the check box, you can turn that option on or off by pressing [Spacebar].

For example, Write's Save As dialog box, shown in Figure 2-13, contains a check box that you can use to create a backup copy of your work. When you click on the Backup check box, an X will appear in it, indicating that you want to make a backup copy as you save a file. If you change your mind and don't want to use this option, you can turn it off by clicking on the box again.

Figure 2-13

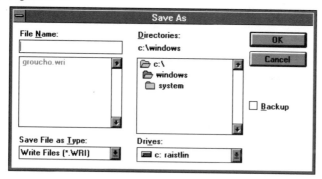

Write's Save As dialog box contains one check box.

Radio buttons allow you to choose a single option from a group of options, much as you'd choose one answer to a question on a multiple-choice exam. For example, the Dithering group box shown in Figure 2-14 (which is accessed by clicking on the Options button in the HP LaserJet Series II dialog box) presents four radio buttons that let you choose among four levels of dithering (a coloring or shading technique used with computer graphics). As you can see, the Coarse button—the default for this dialog box—is already selected. To select a different radio button with the mouse, click on either the button or the button's name. When you select a new radio button, the highlight will move from the old button to the new one.

Radio buttons

Figure 2-14

The Dithering section from a printer setup dialog box has four radio buttons.

To select a radio button with the keyboard, you can use either of two techniques: You can hold down the [Alt] key while you type the underlined character in the radio button's name. Or you can use the [Tab] key to move to the group box and then use the arrow keys to change the selection.

You may be wondering why some options are represented by radio buttons and others by check boxes. Radio buttons are used for options that are mutually exclusive. When you select an option from a group of radio buttons, the previously selected option will become deselected. Check box options, however, are independent of all other options in the dialog box. You can select or deselect any check box option without affecting any other options in a dialog box; that is, you can select more than one check box option at a time.

By the way, radio buttons are so named because early car radios had selector buttons that stayed in when you pushed them, causing the previously pushed-in button to pop out. Sometimes we will also refer to radio buttons as option buttons.

List boxes

Like radio buttons, list boxes let you choose a single option from a group of options. Windows uses list boxes instead of radio buttons when one of three conditions exist: when you must select an option from a large list, when the list of options is dynamic, or when Windows needs to save space in the dialog box.

Consider the dialog box shown in Figure 2-15, which appears when you choose the Open command from Write's File menu. This dialog box provides the File Name list box (and its associated text box) to let you specify the file you want to open. You can use the Directories, List Files of Type, and Drives list boxes to locate the file you want if it is not listed in the File Name list. (Later in this chapter, we'll show you in detail how to work with text boxes.)

To select an option from a list box with the mouse, simply click on the appropriate option. To make a selection with the keyboard, first press the [Tab] key until you've activated the list box. At this point, a dashed line will frame either the selected entry or the first entry in the list. Now, you can use the ↑ or ↓ key to highlight the appropriate option in the list.

Since list boxes can't always display the entire list of options at once, you'll occasionally need to use the scroll bars along the right side of the list box to find the option you want to choose. As we discussed earlier in this chapter, you can click on the scroll arrows or the scroll bar or drag the slider to move through the list. To scroll with the keyboard, you can use the ↑ or ↓ key to move one line at a time. Alternatively, you can use the [Page Up] and [Page Down] keys to scroll through the list a boxful at a time. To move to the top of the list, press the [Home] key. To move to the bottom of the list, press the [End] key.

Figure 2-15

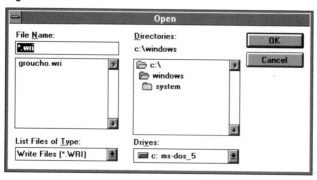

To open a file in Write, you can use the list boxes in the Open dialog box.

Sometimes a dialog box will use a text box in conjunction with a list box, as the Open dialog box in Figure 2-15 does. In these instances, you can change the dialog box's current setting by typing a new entry in the text box or by selecting a new item from the list box. In either case, the entry in the text box will change to reflect the dialog box's new setting.

Some dialog boxes allow you to select more than one option at once. If the original command can work with several options at once, you can also select more than one item from that command's dialog box. For example, if you want to add a number of applications to Windows with the Windows Setup application, you can select more than one application in the list box, as shown in Figure 2-16. You can select an adjacent or nonadjacent item simply by clicking on the item. To select an item with the keyboard, move the dashed-line frame to an application and then press [Spacebar]. To deselect an item, click on it (or press [Spacebar]) to toggle the highlight off.

Figure 2-16

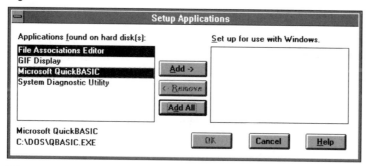

This Setup Applications dialog box from Windows Setup allows multiple selections.

**Drop-down
list boxes**

Drop-down list boxes serve the same purpose as standard list boxes. They allow you to choose a single option from a large, dynamic list. Unlike a standard list box, however, a drop-down list box does not appear on the screen at all times. Instead, you'll see only a text box containing the list box's current setting, along with the special drop-down arrow (an underlined arrow). To display the options in a drop-down list box, you must "drop down" the list from within the dialog box.

The HP LaserJet Series II dialog box, shown in Figure 2-17, contains four drop-down list boxes: Resolution, Paper Size, Paper Source, and Memory. As you might expect, you can drop down any of these list boxes with the mouse simply by clicking on the appropriate drop-down arrow or by clicking in the text box portion. For example, if you click on the arrow in the Resolution drop-down list box, the list will drop down and show you the entire range of choices, as shown in Figure 2-18.

To expand a drop-down list box with the keyboard, first use the [Tab] key to move to the appropriate drop-down list box. Once you've activated the box, press [Alt]↓ to drop down and view the entire list. You can scroll through the list by using the ↓ and ↑ keys.

Figure 2-17

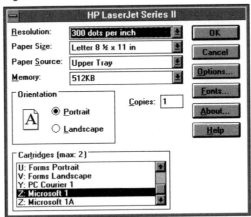

The HP LaserJet Series II dialog box contains four drop-down list boxes.

After you've expanded a drop-down list box, you can use it exactly as you use a standard list box. When you make a selection from the list, the list box will disappear, and your new selection will appear in the text box portion of the drop-down list box. If you expand a drop-down list box by mistake, simply click on a different area of the dialog box to remove the list. (With the keyboard, press [Tab].)

Figure 2-18

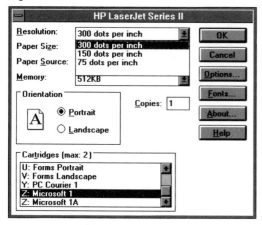

The Resolution drop-down list box expands when you click on its drop-down arrow.

Scroll bars

So far, you've seen scroll bars that can help you navigate through windows and lists. In addition to its navigational capability, a scroll bar can control the value of an option. For example, if you want to increase the double-click speed of the mouse or the pace or time between clicks that Windows recognizes as a double-click, you need to use the scroll bar in the Mouse dialog box of Control Panel to vary the speed. As you can see in Figure 2-19, the scroll bar in the Double Click Speed box represents the range of double-click speeds. As you drag the slider along the gradient, the default double-click pace of the mouse changes. Windows uses this gradient type of scroll bar in other dialog boxes to control such options as custom colors (color gradient) or key repeat rates (another speed gradient).

Windows doesn't highlight the scroll bar to show you that the bar is active as it does with other dialog box elements. Instead, when a gradient scroll bar is active, its slider will blink in alternating shades of gray.

Figure 2-19

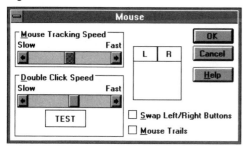

The Mouse dialog box from Control Panel uses scroll bars to control the mouse tracking speed and the double-click speed.

To control a gradient scroll bar with the keyboard, simply use the ← or → key to move the slider. Remember, you need to use either the [Tab] key or the [Alt] key plus the underlined letter in the option's name to activate the scroll bar so that you can change the option's value.

Text boxes

Text boxes allow you to answer a dialog box's "fill in the blank" questions. You can enter text, file names, directories, or drives in text boxes. For example, to rename a selected file in the File Manager, you issue the Rename command on the File menu. Then, in the Rename dialog box, shown in Figure 2-20, you type the new file name in the To text box.

Figure 2-20

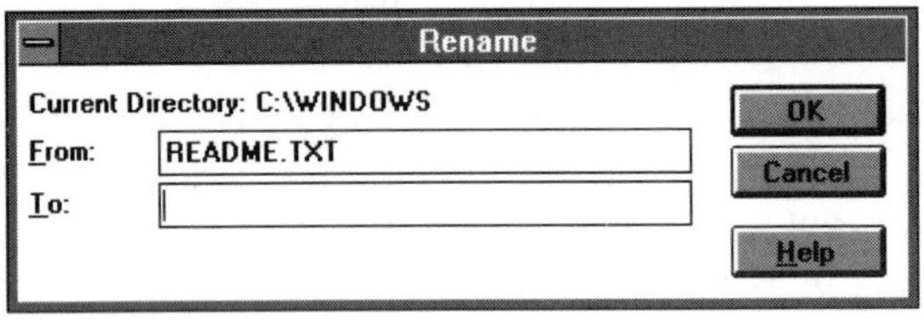

| Rename |
| Current Directory: C:\WINDOWS |
| From: README.TXT |
| To: |
| OK Cancel Help |

The File Manager's Rename dialog box contains a text box in which you can type a new file name.

To enter text in a text box with the keyboard, first either press the [Tab] key repeatedly to move to the text box or press [Alt] and the underlined letter in the text box's name. When you use the keyboard to activate a text box that contains an entry, the text box's entry will appear in highlighted type (inverse video). At this point, you can type a new entry that will replace the existing entry. If, however, you use the keyboard to activate an empty text box, a blinking cursor will appear along the left edge of the text box. As you might imagine, any new characters you type will appear just to the left of the cursor inside the text box.

Activating a text box with a mouse is a little trickier than activating a text box with the keyboard. When you move the arrow pointer inside the text box, the arrow will change to an I-beam pointer. If you press the mouse button while the I-beam is inside an empty text box, a blinking cursor will appear at the left edge of the text box. As you type, the characters will appear to the left of the cursor.

To highlight an existing entry in a text box with the mouse, first position the I-beam at the left edge of the text box. Next, drag the I-beam across the characters inside the text box. As you drag across the characters, their appearance will change from normal type to highlighted type. After you've highlighted the appropriate characters, any new entry you type will replace the highlighted characters in that text box. If the existing entry is longer than the text box, you will see the end of the entry displayed in the text box. In this case, position the I-beam at the right edge of the text box, and then drag the I-beam to the left across the characters inside the text box. A quick way of highlighting all the text in a text box is to double-click on the text.

An increment box is a text box that will accept only numbers. Windows adds a pair of arrows to the increment box that you can use with the mouse to scroll up and down the range of values for an option. For example, the Custom Color Selector from Control Panel uses increment boxes to set values for hue, saturation, and luminosity, as shown in Figure 2-21.

Increment boxes

To change a value, simply click on one of the arrows to increment or decrement the value. If you hold down the mouse button on one of the arrows, the number will continue to change until you release the button. If you are confined to the keyboard or know the number you want to enter in the increment box, you can activate the increment box area and type the new number.

Figure 2-21

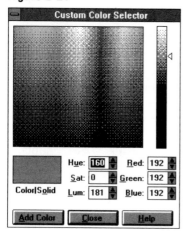

The Custom Color Selector uses increment boxes to set hue, saturation, and luminosity.

A display box or area provides a picture of the results from one or more options in the dialog box. For example, the HP LaserJet Series II dialog box from Control Panel has a display that shows you how the print will appear on a page. In the display area, a graphic of a page with the letter *A* on it changes, depending on the orientation option you select. You can see the graphics for both Portrait and Landscape orientation in Figure 2-22. Notice how the graphic changes as you change the option.

Display boxes

Figure 2-22

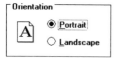 

The display reflects the Orientation setting for the printer.

Command buttons

Command buttons are the large, gray, rectangular elements with words on them. Command buttons look like 3-D buttons, with the command in black letters at the center of the button. If a command isn't available, the letters change to gray. The dialog box in Figure 2-23 contains three command buttons: OK, Cancel, and Options. The OK and Cancel command buttons appear in nearly every dialog box. The OK command button closes the dialog box and carries out the selected command; the Cancel command button also closes the dialog box but without executing the command. To select the OK command button, either use the mouse to click on OK or use the keyboard and press [Enter]. (The heavy outline around the OK button indicates that this default option will be selected when you press [Enter]. In other dialog boxes, buttons other than OK may be outlined.) To select the Cancel command button, either use the mouse to click on Cancel or press [Esc].

Figure 2-23

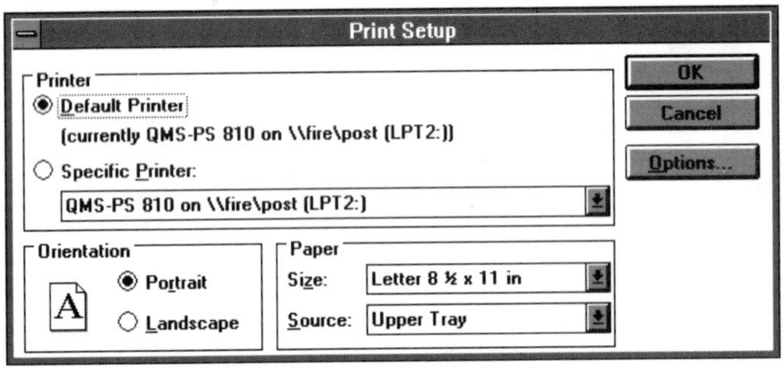

Write's Print Setup dialog box has three command buttons.

Like the Options button in the Print Setup dialog box in Figure 2-23, some command button names are followed by an ellipsis (...). Selecting one of these buttons will open another dialog box. Windows will keep the first dialog box open along with the second dialog box. Typically, when you close the second dialog box, you'll return to the first dialog box, where you can continue making selections. As you might expect, you can select a button of this type either by using the mouse to click on the button or by holding down the [Alt] key and typing the underlined letter in the button's name.

Sometimes two chevrons (>>) will follow a command button name. This type of command button is called a push button. When you choose a push button, the dialog box will expand to display additional options.

In our discussions throughout the book, we'll often refer to a push or command button simply as a button. For instance, we might instruct you to choose the Options button or the Cancel button. In addition, we'll typically instruct you to choose OK rather than to choose the OK command button. We think you'll find these conventions make our explanations more readable.

Windows uses dialog boxes for its alert messages. For example, Windows will present a message if you attempt to exit a program before saving your work. These messages range from critical Windows system messages to information messages. Windows makes the importance of a message easy to recognize by using a color icon to tell you what type of message you're reading. Figure 2-24 displays the four icons Windows uses with alert messages: a red stop sign for a critical message, a yellow circle with an exclamation point for a warning, a green circle with a question mark for a warning that requires user verification, and a blue circle with a lowercase *i* for information.

Identifying alert messages

Figure 2-24

Windows identifies alert messages with one of these four icons.

Alert messages appear in standard dialog boxes that have title bars, Control menus, and usually buttons for OK and Cancel. If you can try to fix the problem and attempt the command again, a Retry button is provided. To respond to a message with the keyboard, press [Tab] to move to the appropriate command button and then press [Enter] or [Spacebar] to choose it.

You can reposition a dialog box or a message box on your screen by dragging its title bar. When you begin to drag the title bar, you'll see guidelines that are the shape and size of the dialog box. You can move the mouse to position the guidelines where you want the dialog box to appear. When you release the mouse button, the dialog box will move to that spot.

Moving a dialog box

If you're using the keyboard, you need to use the Control menu to move the dialog box. First, press [Alt][Spacebar] to open the dialog box's Control menu. Next, press *M* to choose the Move command, and then use the arrow keys to move the dialog box. Finally, press [Enter] to complete the move.

You can click on one of the command buttons, such as OK or Cancel, to exit a dialog box. You can also double-click on the Control menu box, press [Esc], or press [Alt][F4] to close the dialog box without saving any changes. ([Esc] and [Alt][F4] do not close alert message dialog boxes.)

Exiting a dialog box

In this chapter

Setting Defaults 3

*H*ave you ever wanted to use a new color combination on your screen? Did a warning beep ever annoy you so much that you needed to turn it off? If so, you'll want to make Windows friendlier by changing some of its options, such as screen colors or the warning beep. Control Panel is the application that lets you customize Windows by altering its default settings. Windows also lets you change the defaults that govern hardware such as your monitor; to do this, you must use the Windows Setup application.

In this chapter, we'll take you on a tour of Control Panel and the Windows Setup application. We will use Control Panel to change colors, fonts, mouse capabilities, desktop patterns, international settings, keyboard options, the date and time, sound options, 386 enhanced mode features, ports, printers, and multimedia devices. Since there are so many things to look at, we'll first discuss the settings that affect the look and feel of Windows, and then we'll talk about settings that affect printers or external devices. We'll also show you how to use the Windows Setup application to change your hardware configuration and how to add application icons to the Program Manager group windows. If you are part of a network, you'll want to refer to Chapter 8, in which we cover Control Panel's Network icon.

Before you can change Windows' default settings, you must start Control Panel. To do this, click on the Main group window to access the Control Panel icon, place your pointer on the icon, and double-click. If you're running Windows in standard mode, you'll then see the Control Panel application window

CONTROL PANEL

shown in Figure 3-1. The icons in this window will help you change any Windows standard mode setting. Your changes will be incorporated in your WIN.INI file so that the next time you start Windows the changes will still be in effect. To exit Control Panel, issue the Exit command on the Settings menu.

Figure 3-1

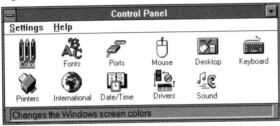

The Windows standard mode Control Panel contains these icons.

If you are running Windows in 386 enhanced mode, you'll see a Control Panel application window that contains the icons shown in Figure 3-2. The extra icon controls settings for 386 enhanced mode. You'll find yet another icon on Control Panel if your computer is running on a network with Windows. Figure 3-3 shows a Control Panel application window with the Network icon.

Figure 3-2

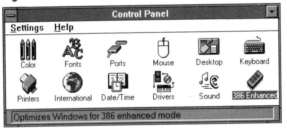

The 386 Enhanced icon on Control Panel controls the 386- and 486-based functions.

Figure 3-3

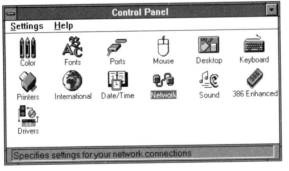

The Network icon on Control Panel lets you issue network commands or change network settings.

Windows creates a pleasant working environment with color, sound, and a mouse. Control Panel gives you easy access to these and other Windows environment options.

To activate Control Panel icons with the mouse and use the specific function you want, just double-click on the function's icon. To activate icons with the keyboard, you'll use Control Panel's Settings menu. The Settings menu has one command for each of the Control Panel icons. These commands provide access to all the Control Panel functions. If you have the 386 Enhanced icon or the Network icon on your Control Panel, Windows adds the corresponding command to your Settings menu. Simply open the Settings menu and select the command that names the application you want to use. Alternatively, you can press the key that matches the initial letter of the icon's title (or use the arrow keys) to move the highlight to the icon and then press [Enter].

SETTING ENVIRONMENT OPTIONS

Windows provides a wide variety of colors for your screen. You can choose among an assortment of built-in color schemes, or you can create an entirely new color scheme. A section of color illustrations, titled "Windows in Color," that appears later in this book offers examples of some of the color and design options that are available.

To change screen colors, double-click on Control Panel's Color icon to bring up the Color dialog box shown in Figure 3-4. Control Panel will highlight the current color scheme in the Color Schemes list box. When setting screen colors, you can use Windows' color schemes or choose your own combinations. To view the list of preformatted color schemes, click on the drop-down arrow of the Color Schemes drop-down list box. If you select one of the listed schemes, you can preview the result in the sample window in the Color dialog box.

Setting the screen colors

Figure 3-4

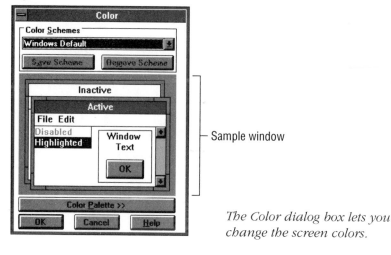

— Sample window

The Color dialog box lets you change the screen colors.

To add a color palette to the Color dialog box and to choose your own colors, select the Color Palette button. Control Panel will expand the dialog box to add two palettes (Basic Colors and Custom Colors), a Screen Element drop-down list box, and a Define Custom Colors button. Figure 3-5 shows the expanded Color dialog box.

When changing screen colors, first choose the screen element whose color you want to change, and then select a color. To select a screen element, you can either click on an area in the sample window or choose from the Screen Element drop-down list box in the upper-right corner of the expanded Color dialog box. For instance, if you click on the desktop area of the sample window, the highlighted entry in the Screen Element list box will change to Desktop. On the palette, a thick black border will surround the color that matches the current color of the selected element. At this point, you can select a new color. When you click on one of the color boxes in the Basic Colors palette, a thick black border and a dotted outline will surround your selection; the selected screen element in the sample window will automatically change to your chosen color. Note that some screen elements (for example, button faces and menu bars) use only solid colors. If the color you choose for one of these elements from the Basic Colors palette is a mixed, or dithered, color (a composite of two or more colors in a dot-pattern simulation), it may appear as a solid color.

Figure 3-5

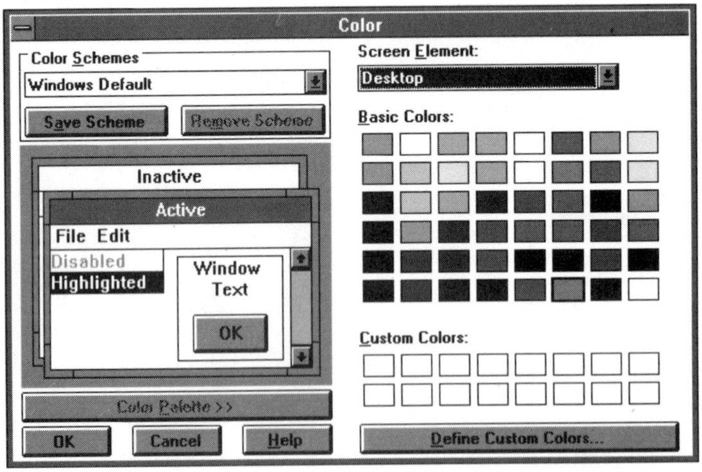

After you select the Color Palette button, the Color dialog box expands and lets you choose your own colors.

If you use the keyboard, you can press [Tab] to move forward through the Color dialog box and [Shift][Tab] to move backward. Once you arrive at the Basic Colors palette, you can navigate between the color boxes by using the arrow keys; the selection frame (a dotted outline) will move to each color in succession. When you reach the color you want to use, press [Spacebar], and the black border will then frame your selection. When you choose a color with [Spacebar], the selected screen element in the sample window will change automatically to that color. If you choose the hot pink color box, for example, the desktop element you selected earlier will become hot pink in the sample window.

After you make all your color choices, choose the OK button at the bottom of the dialog box. Windows will implement your color changes and return you to Control Panel.

If you select a preformatted color scheme and modify it but don't save it, the Color Schemes list box will be blank when you return to the Color dialog box.

Defining and using custom colors

If the Basic Colors palette doesn't offer the color you want, you can create the color with the Custom Colors palette. To do this, activate the Color dialog box, click on the Color Palette button to expand the dialog box, and then click on the Define Custom Colors button to bring up the Custom Color Selector dialog box shown in Figure 3-6 on the next page. This dialog box has an interactive color grid (color refiner box) for mouse-controlled color selection, a color scroll bar (vertical luminosity bar), a Color/Solid display box, and a series of increment boxes for fine-tuning. To use the Custom Color Selector dialog box, move the pointer to a spot on the color grid and click. Note that a dashed crosshair (color refiner cursor) moves to that spot. The color you select will appear in the Color/Solid display box as both a mixed color and a solid. If you double-click on the solid color, Windows will select the pure color your monitor supports instead of a dot-pattern simulation.

To the right of the color grid, you'll see the color scroll bar with a triangular slider. To change the brightness or intensity of the color, drag the triangular slider. Alternatively, you can point anywhere on the scroll bar and click to move the slider to that position. For finer detail, you can use the up and down arrows on the increment boxes below the color grid to increase or decrease the settings for hue, saturation, luminosity or brightness, red, green, and blue. These settings adjust automatically with the movement of the crosshair or slider.

If you are using the keyboard, press [Alt]O to select the solid color. To define custom colors with the keyboard, you must use the increment boxes. You will not be able to access the color grid or the color scroll bar with the keyboard. To change the color, press [Tab] to move to one of the increment boxes, and then type in the new value.

Figure 3-6

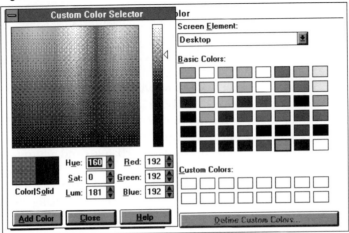

You can use the Custom Color Selector dialog box to define a custom color.

When you choose a color, you should follow a specific order in defining hue, saturation, and luminosity. Hue controls the colors you choose across the horizontal axis of the color grid. Saturation controls the vertical axis, which goes from gray to a pure color. The color bar to the right of the color grid controls the luminosity. For better control when you adjust colors, select hue first, and then select saturation and luminosity.

After you have found the right color, you can add it to the Custom Colors palette by selecting the Add Color button. You can add a color to each of the 16 selection boxes in the Custom Colors palette.

To remove a color from the Custom Colors palette, you have to replace it with another color. To do this, first click on the color you want to replace. (Note that you can use the Custom Color Selector dialog box simultaneously with the Custom Colors palette.) Next, choose a custom color from the color grid, and click on the Add Color button to replace the custom color.

If you want a Custom Colors palette box to appear blank, select that box and fill it with white. To select white, move the slider to the top of the color scroll bar and select the solid color either by double-clicking on it or by pressing [Alt]O. When you click on the Add Color button, the designated box in the Custom Colors palette will appear blank. After you've defined the custom colors, select the Close button to return to the Color dialog box.

Saving color schemes

You can save your new color scheme by selecting the Save Scheme button in the Color dialog box. A Save Scheme dialog box will appear, prompting you to name your color scheme. You can use any characters, including spaces, in the color scheme's name.

To save your changes in the Color dialog box and return to Control Panel, click on OK. Choosing Cancel or double-clicking on the Control menu will close the dialog box without changing your screen.

You don't have to save and name a color scheme in order to use it. You can click on OK in the lower-left corner of the Color dialog box, and Windows will repaint the screen with the new colors. If the colors clash or aren't satisfactory, reselect the Color icon and create another scheme. As we indicated earlier, you can also choose one of the schemes in the Color Schemes drop-down list box and click on OK to activate that selection.

Activating a color scheme

If you don't want to keep one of your custom color schemes, you can remove it from the Color Schemes list. Simply open the Color Schemes drop-down list box, highlight the named color scheme, and click on the Remove Scheme button. Be careful—if you remove a color scheme that came with Windows, you can retrieve it only by reinstalling Windows or by re-creating the color scheme yourself. You cannot delete the Windows Default color scheme.

Removing a color scheme

If you use a computer with an LCD (liquid crystal display) overlay to give presentations, you may want to select one of the LCD color schemes, which are provided especially for such presentations. Because colors have varying brightness when translated into monochrome, you might want to experiment with the three LCD choices: LCD Default Screen Settings, LCD Reversed–Dark, and LCD Reversed–Light. Sometimes, parts of the image, such as similar shades of gray, are not displayed uniquely and blend together. A good way to find out which colors translate to which monochrome patterns is to bring up the Color dialog box and then turn on your LCD overlay. Select an LCD color scheme and check the display.

A presentation tip

When you double-click on the Fonts icon on Control Panel, you'll see the dialog box shown in Figure 3-7 on the next page. With the Fonts dialog box, you can define the default fonts for the screen and printer and add fonts from floppy disks or hard disks. The Installed Fonts list box highlights the current font. For TrueType fonts, the Sample display box shows only one sample size because these fonts can be scaled to any size; for non-TrueType fonts, the display box shows a brief line of text in each available point size for the selected font. The dialog box also indicates the file size for each font. You have a choice of using raster fonts (the fonts used by Windows 3.0), TrueType fonts, or both. To use TrueType fonts, click on the TrueType button and, in the TrueType dialog box that appears, be sure that the Enable TrueType Fonts check box is turned on. To use raster fonts, be sure that the Show Only TrueType Fonts in Applications check box in the TrueType dialog box is turned off. Control Panel makes the installed list of fonts available to all Windows applications that can use them.

Using fonts

Figure 3-7

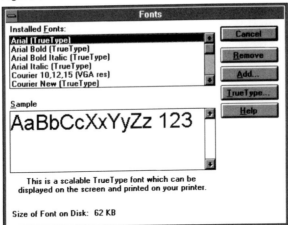

The Fonts dialog box displays a list of installed fonts.

Adding fonts

To add a font, click on the Add button in the Fonts dialog box to bring up the Add Fonts dialog box shown in Figure 3-8. Select a drive ID, usually to indicate a floppy disk in drive A or B. (The drives appear in the Drives drop-down list box, and directories appear as folders in the Directories list box.) Windows looks at the disk drive for any font file ending with the extension .FON or .TTF and displays in the List of Fonts list box the available fonts it finds. You choose a font by clicking on the name in the List of Fonts box. You can click on the Select All button to select all the listed fonts. The Copy Fonts to Windows Directory check box controls whether or not Windows will install font files on your hard

Figure 3-8

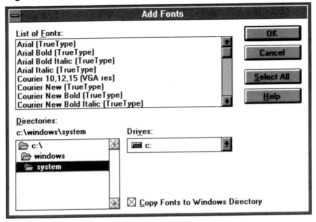

The Add Fonts dialog box provides a list of fonts you can install.

disk. Turn off this check box only if the font files are already stored on your hard disk and disk space is low. Leave this check box turned on if you are installing fonts from a network or from a floppy disk.

After you have selected the fonts, click on OK. Windows will copy the files onto your hard disk. The Fonts dialog box will remain open so that you can add or remove other fonts.

You can select fonts more efficiently by using the keyboard simultaneously with your mouse. To highlight several fonts at once, hold down the [Ctrl] key and click the mouse button on each item you want to select from the List of Fonts list box in the Add Fonts dialog box.

To select adjacent items, click on the first font name and then drag the mouse pointer to the last font name you want to select. To select several fonts with the keyboard, press the [Tab] key to reach the first font name, and then hold down the [Shift] key while you highlight adjacent fonts by pressing an arrow key. (You cannot select multiple nonadjacent font files with the keyboard.)

A quicker way

To install fonts from a floppy disk, highlight the drive you want to use from the Drives drop-down list box in the Add Fonts dialog box. Windows will display in the List of Fonts list box all the fonts available from the disk. Make your selection using any of the techniques we've explained, and then click on OK.

Suppose you have the Gothic font on a floppy disk in drive A and you want to install the font on your hard disk. To do this, follow these steps:

Installing fonts from a floppy disk

- In Control Panel, activate the Fonts icon.

- Select the Add button in the Fonts dialog box.

- When the Add Fonts dialog box appears, select drive A in the Drives drop-down list box.

- Select all Gothic files in the List of Fonts list box by highlighting them.

- Click on OK or press [Enter].

- To verify the addition, highlight the Gothic font in the Installed Fonts list box. The sample font will be displayed.

- Finally, click on the Close button to close the Fonts dialog box and return to Control Panel. (The Cancel button in the Fonts dialog box becomes the Close button after fonts have been added or deleted.)

Since you will use some fonts more than others, you can delete those fonts you don't need or want. Remember that fonts consume memory and hard-drive space; if you are running out of memory, don't keep unnecessary fonts on your

Removing font files

computer. The Remove button in the Fonts dialog box deletes a selected font file from Windows' repertoire. To remove an unwanted font, highlight a selection from the Installed Fonts list box, and then click on the Remove button. A warning dialog box appears, requiring you to verify that you want to remove the font. Click on Yes to delete the font and continue, or click on Cancel to cancel the deletion and return to the Fonts dialog box.

A word of advice: You should avoid deleting the MS Sans Serif font. Because Windows 3.1 uses MS Sans Serif for its system font, removing this font would make dialog boxes and windows difficult to read.

Controlling the mouse

The Mouse icon on Control Panel allows you to set the tracking speed, the clicking speed, the primary button, and the mouse trails display for your mouse. You can adjust these settings to match your skill level or preference. Let's activate the Mouse icon and explore the options available in the Mouse dialog box, shown in Figure 3-9.

Figure 3-9

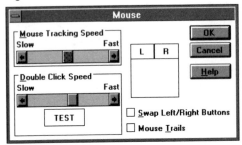

The Mouse dialog box lets you control tracking and clicking speeds, the primary button, and the mouse trails display for your mouse.

Setting the mouse tracking speed

The Mouse Tracking Speed section of the Mouse dialog box has a horizontal scroll bar that controls the speed gradient of the mouse. Tracking speed refers to the pace of Windows' efforts to keep up with you when you drag the mouse. If you'd like to speed up the response time for dragging, drag the slider toward the Fast end of the scroll bar.

Setting the double-click speed

The horizontal scroll bar in the Double Click Speed section of the Mouse dialog box controls the minimum double-clicking speed of the mouse. The faster the setting, the faster you must double-click to initiate Windows' response to the action. By double-clicking on the TEST block, you can determine whether your setting is comfortable. The highlight in the TEST block changes when Windows recognizes a double-click.

To the right of the Mouse Tracking Speed and Double Click Speed sections in the Mouse dialog box is a schematic representation of the mouse, with left and right buttons. When you press your left or right mouse button while the mouse pointer is in this dialog box, the corresponding button (L or R) on the mouse representation becomes highlighted. The schematic mouse will help you tell which button is designated as the primary (L) position and which is the secondary (R) position. Windows uses the left mouse button as the default primary button. With the Swap Left/Right Buttons check box, however, you can change the primary mouse button from the left to the right position. This swapping of primary and secondary button positions accommodates left-handed users who prefer to use the index finger to press the primary button. Go ahead and click on the check box, and then try using the mouse buttons. Notice the change in the location of the letters L and R. The L is now on the right side of the schematic mouse. To change it back to its original state, you'll have to turn off the Swap Left/Right Buttons check box by using the right mouse button (now the primary one). If you don't turn off the check box, remember to select with the right button since it is now the primary button.

Choosing the primary mouse button

Turn on the Mouse Trails check box if you want to see an "afterimage" of the mouse pointer as you move the mouse. This feature can be useful for demonstrations you set up with Recorder (discussed in Chapter 13), to show the path the mouse pointer is taking. Also, if you are working on an LCD screen, using Mouse Trails can help you see and follow the mouse pointer. For everyday operations on standard color and monochrome screens, however, you'll probably want to leave this check box turned off. (Note, too, that the Mouse Trails feature is not available on some screens.)

Displaying the mouse trails

When you activate the Desktop icon on Control Panel, you'll see the Desktop dialog box, shown in Figure 3-10 on the following page, which allows you to change some aspects of your desktop. Some of these aspects, such as window border width, are pragmatic and facilitate your work. Others, such as wallpaper, are decorative and allow you to alter the ambiance of your working environment. As you gain confidence and skill working in Windows, you might even want to create your own wallpaper (using the Paintbrush application) and copy it onto your desktop. We will show you how to change the desktop pattern or select a wallpaper image for the desktop. You also can use the Desktop dialog box to set up and test a selected screen saver display, activate a shortcut for switching between applications, change the cursor blink rate, size the icon-placement grid (granularity), change the width of window borders, and display icon titles on two or more lines.

Setting up the desktop

Figure 3-10

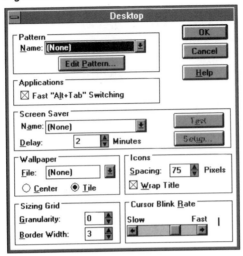

The Desktop dialog box lets you change the look and layout of the desktop.

Picking a pattern

The Pattern section of the Desktop dialog box lets you choose a pattern for your desktop or even design your own pattern. The Name drop-down list box provides a selection of patterns. Rather than choosing a pattern for your desktop sight unseen, you can preview the pattern by selecting the Edit Pattern button. Your chosen pattern will be displayed in the Sample box in the Desktop-Edit Pattern dialog box, shown in Figure 3-11. The background color will be the desktop color you previously selected in the Color dialog box; the pattern itself will be the color of the window text from your color scheme. The Name drop-down list box allows you to continue previewing patterns. Figure 3-12 shows the available patterns that come with Windows.

Figure 3-11

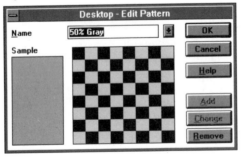

The Desktop-Edit Pattern dialog box displays available patterns.

Figure 3-12

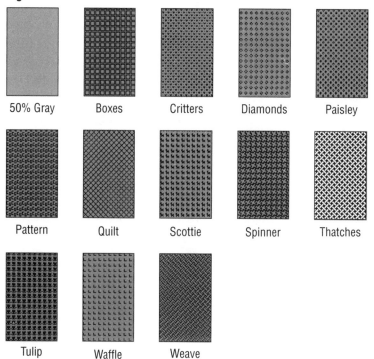

50% Gray	Boxes	Critters	Diamonds	Paisley
Pattern	Quilt	Scottie	Spinner	Thatches
Tulip	Waffle	Weave		

The installed patterns that you can use on the desktop are displayed here.

You may want to create your own desktop pattern. First, highlight (None) from the Name drop-down list box in the Pattern section of the Desktop dialog box, and then click on the Edit Pattern button to bring up the Desktop-Edit Pattern dialog box, shown in Figure 3-13 on the next page. To create a pattern, move your pointer to the center box and click anywhere. A black square will appear, representing a bit on a bit map. Click on that spot again, and the black square will disappear. The bits toggle on and off in this fashion, allowing you to change the pattern. Notice that the Sample display box to the left reflects the changes you make on the bit map. When you are satisfied with your new pattern, type a name in the Name text box, and then click on the Add button. When you finish adding patterns, click on OK to return to the Desktop dialog box. (If you click on Cancel instead of OK, the changes you made will be deleted, and Windows will return you to the Desktop dialog box.) To see how the new pattern looks on the desktop, choose OK in the Desktop dialog box.

Creating new patterns

Figure 3-13

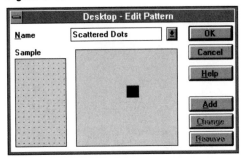

The Desktop-Edit Pattern dialog box displays a bit map that you can change.

Changing patterns

You can save time by modifying an established pattern instead of starting from scratch. Initially, you need to select the pattern from the Name drop-down list box in the Desktop-Edit Pattern dialog box. Then, change the bit map by toggling the bits on or off until you've altered the pattern to your satisfaction. Select the Change button to replace the existing desktop pattern, or type a new name in the Name text box, and then click on Add to add another pattern.

Removing patterns

If a pattern you create isn't what you had in mind, don't worry; you can remove it. Open the Desktop dialog box, and click on the Edit Pattern button. In the Desktop-Edit Pattern dialog box, select the name of the pattern you want to remove in the Name drop-down list box, and click on the Remove button. Windows will then present a warning dialog box, asking you to verify the deletion. Click on Yes to remove the pattern. Click on OK in the Desktop-Edit Pattern dialog box to return to the Desktop dialog box.

Putting up wallpaper

In addition to using bit map patterns, you can use wallpaper to customize your desktop. The File drop-down list box in the Wallpaper section of the Desktop dialog box contains the file names of several striking images whose colored graphics will be an impressive addition to your desktop. You can see a sample of the wallpaper patterns in "Windows in Color," the section of color illustrations included in this book.

Wallpaper is a detailed Paintbrush image that can be centered on your screen for a single image or tiled in a pattern of multiple smaller images. If you want to leave an *Out To Lunch* message or put your company logo on your Windows desktop, you can create your own wallpaper with the Paintbrush application. You'll need to save your Paintbrush file with a .BMP extension and be sure it's in the Windows directory so that Windows can find it again. (In Chapter 11, we will provide more information about creating wallpaper files.) Remember that wallpaper uses more memory than a pattern does; you may want to avoid using wallpaper if your computer is short of memory.

To select a wallpaper pattern, click on the File drop-down list box in the Wallpaper section of the Desktop dialog box, and then click on the file name of the wallpaper you want to use. By default, the wallpaper fills the desktop. If you would rather have the wallpaper appear only in a space in the center of the screen, you can click on the Center radio button. Some wallpaper images are very small; others fill about a quarter of the screen.

If you use both a desktop pattern and wallpaper, wallpaper will overlay the pattern. If you tile the wallpaper, the pattern will be completely covered up. If you choose centered wallpaper, the pattern will be visible only between the wallpaper and the edges of the screen. When wallpaper fills the screen, the pattern will remain visible as the background in inactive icon titles.

If you don't want to use a wallpaper file anymore, or if your file was damaged and you can't use it, you need to remove the file from your hard drive with the File Manager. (You can learn how to delete files in Chapter 6.) If you simply want to revert to a desktop without a wallpaper background, choose (None) from the File drop-down list box in the Wallpaper section of the Desktop dialog box and then click on OK.

Removing wallpaper

Throughout your work day, you might leave your computer inactive from time to time, while you are busy with phone calls, meetings, paperwork, breaks, or lunch. Darkening the monitor while the computer is inactive "saves" the screen life. Windows' built-in screen savers give you a way to automatically darken the display when you are not using the computer for a time. Later, when you move the mouse, click a mouse button, or press a key, the screen reappears as it was before the screen saver started running.

Selecting a screen saver

In the Screen Saver section of the Desktop dialog box, you can select a screen saver display and set the delay (how long the computer must be inactive before the screen darkens automatically). You can test the various displays so that you can choose the one that suits you.

The Name drop-down list box in the Screen Saver section lists the available screen saver displays. The default (None) turns off the screen saver. When you select a display from the Name drop-down list box, you can see it by clicking on the Test button. To return to the dialog box, move the mouse or press a key. Test all of the displays, and select the one you like best.

In the Delay list box, select the length of time you want Windows to wait before darkening the display. Windows starts counting time when all activities have stopped—that is, no keys have been pressed, no mouse buttons have been clicked, the mouse has not been moved, and no foreground activities have occurred in any running application. The default is 2 minutes. The up and down arrows increase or decrease the delay in 1-minute increments, with 1 minute as the minimum delay and 99 minutes as the maximum delay.

The Setup button displays the particular dialog box associated with each screen saver. (If you choose Blank Screen as your screen saver, no setup options are available.) The Marquee screen saver displays a line of text moving across the screen. You can set up the font, size, and color of the text; the background color; the text you want to display; the speed at which the text moves across the screen; and the text position. The Starfield Simulation screen saver simulates travel through a star field; you can set the speed of travel and the number of stars in the field. The Mystify screen saver displays colored lines in one of two polygon (multiple-sided) shapes; you can set the number of lines and their colors. This screen saver's dialog box contains a check box called Clear Screen, which is turned on by default. If you turn this check box off, your screen is not cleared as the screen saver starts. Instead, as each pixel is "painted" by the screen saver, it is turned off, slowly erasing the old screen and replacing it with the moving polygons on a black background.

For all the screen savers that have setup options, you can add password protection to prevent access to your screen after the screen saver starts running. Then, when you try to return to your work, Windows displays a dialog box asking for the password before restoring your screen.

Switching between applications

Fast "Alt+Tab" Switching is a method of using the keyboard to quickly move between applications. This feature is enabled when the Fast "Alt+Tab" Switching check box in the Applications section of the Desktop dialog box is turned on (contains an X). You can click on the check box or press [Alt]L to toggle the feature on or off.

To use Fast "Alt+Tab" Switching when this feature is turned on, hold down the [Alt] key and press [Tab] without releasing [Alt]. Windows will display a box in the middle of the screen containing the icon and name of a running application. Press [Tab] again (while continuing to hold down [Alt]) to see the icon and name of the next running application. Continue pressing [Tab] until you see the name of the application you want, and then release [Alt] to open that application. To cancel the move, press [Esc].

Controlling the cursor blink rate

The Cursor Blink Rate section of the Desktop dialog box has a horizontal scroll bar. You can drag the slider toward the Slow or Fast end of the scroll bar to change the blink rate. Note that a blinking cursor to the right of the scroll bar indicates the new blink rate you've selected.

Creating a placement grid for desktop elements

In its Sizing Grid section, the Desktop dialog box provides the Granularity increment box to create an invisible grid of guidelines on which Windows arranges your desktop elements. By default, granularity is set to 0 (no grid). If you enter a value for granularity, Control Panel will set up the grid. Then, whenever you drag the title bar of a window to a new position on your desktop, the window will line up using the grid.

What do the granularity values mean? Each value increases the space between guides by 8 pixels. The values range from 0 to 49. The larger the value, the farther a desktop element will jump each time it is moved.

If you have trouble sizing windows because the frame area is too narrow, you can increase the width of the border. The Border Width setting in the Sizing Grid section of the Desktop dialog box varies the width of the window border and ranges from 1 to 50 pixels. By default, the border width equals 3. The narrowest border has a width of 1. You can use the arrows in the increment box to change the width value the same way you can change the granularity value.

Setting border width

As you work with applications, you'll find situations in which the title of a minimized icon is wider than the icon. If this happens when you have several icons on your desktop, the titles will overlap. You'll need to use the Spacing increment box in the Icons section of the Desktop dialog box to solve this problem. When you increase the value in this increment box to allot more space for each icon, the icons will be positioned farther apart as they are created. You'll see a difference in spacing if you change the Spacing value in increments of 10 pixels. By default, spacing is a little more than an inch. The value in pixels will vary, depending on the size and resolution of your display.

Allotting space for an icon

You can also turn on the Wrap Title check box to reduce the space that an icon title takes up on the screen. A Windows application shows its name and the title of the current document under the application's icon. In some cases, the titles are very long and extend over the titles of icons to the right. By turning on the Wrap Title check box, you tell Windows to display icon titles on two or more lines, which reduces the amount of horizontal space the title needs. Wrapping icon titles does increase the amount of vertical space the icon takes up.

You can change basic formats such as keyboard layout, date, and time by using the International dialog box. To access the dialog box, double-click on the International icon in the Control Panel window. As you can see in Figure 3-14 on the following page, this dialog box contains four drop-down list boxes, a text box, four format boxes, and the default settings for the United States. The Country setting controls many of the other settings. If you change the Country setting, the other settings (except Language and Keyboard Layout) will follow suit. You can still make changes in any of those specific areas to override the global changes if you wish.

Changing international settings

Figure 3-14

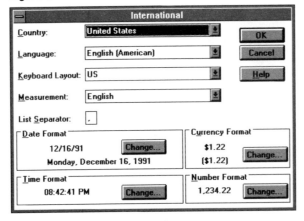

The International dialog box lets you make changes to basic formats such as date and time.

Picking a country

The Country drop-down list box will let you choose a country on which to base your various formats. For instance, if you change the country from the United States to Italy, as shown in Figure 3-15, the Currency Format setting will change from dollars to lire. The Date Format section will change from month-day-year to the European day-month-year format. The changes in the Country setting will also affect the Measurement, List Separator, and Number Format settings. For example, Italians use commas for decimal points and separate thousands with periods. As we mentioned earlier, the Country setting doesn't affect the Language or the Keyboard Layout settings, which must be changed individually.

Figure 3-15

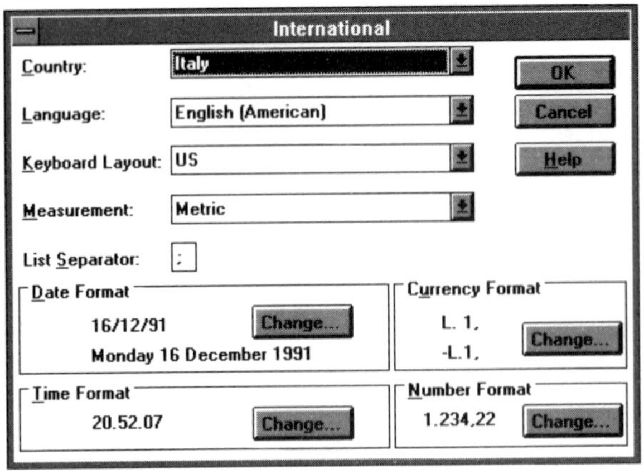

When you change the country to Italy, Control Panel automatically adjusts certain other settings.

Windows comes with many language formats. You can use the Language drop-down list box in the International dialog box to choose among the available formats. By default, English (American) appears in the list box to match the default nation in the Country list box.

Choosing a language

The keyboard layout determines which characters use which keys on the keyboard. Windows lets you choose among several keyboard layouts because many languages contain special characters that require a unique layout. The default keyboard layout is US.

Changing the keyboard layout

The Measurement option in the International dialog box lets you select the way Windows will display measurements. The Measurement drop-down list box offers two options: English and Metric. As you might expect, the default in the United States is the English system of measurement.

Metric versus English

You can change the date format manually in the Date Format section of the International dialog box or automatically by changing the Country setting. The Date Format section displays the format currently in use. To alter the current date format, click on that section's Change button. In the International-Date Format dialog box, which is shown in Figure 3-16 on the following page, you can specify the short and long date formats.

Date format

You'll use the Short Date Format group box to determine the order of the month-day-year sequence and the type of separator character you want. When you select a date order from the Order options, you'll see a border around that order pattern. If you want a different separator character, select the Separator text box and type the new character. Notice that the pointer changes to an I-beam when it's in the text box. The three check boxes in the Short Date Format group box control the format of the numbers in a date. You can choose whether single-digit day and month values will be preceded by a zero and whether year values will be preceded by a two-digit century identifier. Selecting a check box activates the first choice in the parentheses next to the box's name.

The Long Date Format group box sets the order and the format for a completely spelled-out date. First, establish the date order by selecting one of the Order radio buttons. Notice that both the displayed date and the list and text boxes above the date change their order to match your choice. Now you can format the date elements, like the day of the week, to a short or long version. For instance, Sunday can be displayed as *Sun* or *Sunday*. To display the list of choices, click on the drop-down arrow. You can also modify the punctuation and spacing of the date with the text boxes located between the date elements. Click in the text box to place a cursor inside it, and then either type in the punctuation and spacing you want (for a total of five character positions) or leave the text box blank for no punctuation and a default of one space.

Figure 3-16

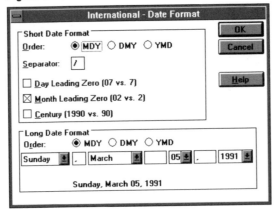

The International-Date Format dialog box sets the short and long date formats.

Currency format

The Currency Format section of the International dialog box lets you change the way Windows displays currency. When you click on the Change button in this section, you'll see the International-Currency Format dialog box, shown in Figure 3-17. In the Symbol Placement and Negative drop-down list boxes, you can tell Windows where to place currency symbols and how to display negative values. You can change the currency denomination symbol by highlighting the current symbol in the Symbol text box and typing in a new one. The Decimal Digits box is a single-character text box that allows you to change the number of decimal digits you want, up to a value of 9.

Figure 3-17

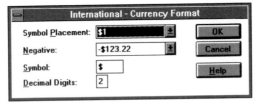

The International-Currency Format dialog box controls the appearance of symbols, negative values, and decimals.

Time format

You can change the time format by clicking on the Change button in the Time Format section of the International dialog box. You can choose either the 12-hour or 24-hour time system in the International-Time Format dialog box, shown in Figure 3-18. The text boxes to the right of the hour system radio buttons allow you to set AM or PM notation. When you select the 24-hour radio button, the text and text box to the right of the 12-hour radio button disappear because AM and PM have no meaning in 24-hour format. The Separator text box lets you type in the separator character of your choice. The Leading Zero radio buttons give you the option of adding a leading zero to single-digit hours in the displayed time.

Figure 3-18

The International-Time Format dialog box lets you set the 12-hour or 24-hour system, the separator character, and the leading zero.

You can change the number format by selecting the Change button in the Number Format section of the International dialog box. In the International-Number Format dialog box, shown in Figure 3-19, you can enter in the respective text boxes a thousands separator, a decimal separator, and the number of decimal digits. You can also indicate whether a leading zero should be used. The defaults for the number format are governed by the Country setting in the International dialog box. By default in the United States, Windows uses a comma for the thousands separator, a period for the decimal separator, two decimal digits, and no leading zero. To change one of the separator formats, double-click in the text box and enter the change. When you want to change the Leading Zero option, choose the radio button beside the format you want to use.

Number format

Figure 3-19

The International-Number Format dialog box allows you to set the numerical formatting to reflect a particular nation's preferences.

When you double-click on the Keyboard icon on Control Panel, you'll activate the Keyboard dialog box, shown in Figure 3-20 on the following page. This dialog box lets you set and test the key repeat rate. You can increase or decrease the rate at which a key will repeat by moving the slider on the Repeat Rate scroll bar toward the Slow end or the Fast end. You can test the new rate by clicking in the Test box and then holding down a character key. As you continue to hold down the key, the typed characters will be displayed in the Test box at the rate you've set.

You can also set the delay time in this dialog box. The delay time is the minimum time you must hold down a key before it begins to repeat. A short delay means that the repeat will begin right away; a long delay means that you must hold down the key for a longer time before the repeat starts. If you find that characters are repeating when you don't want them to, move the Delay Before First Repeat slider toward Long. You can check the delay time in the Test box.

Setting keyboard options

Figure 3-20

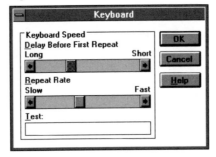

The Keyboard dialog box lets you set and test the key repeat rate and the delay time.

Setting the date and time

In addition to changing the date and time format, you can change the actual date and time within your system. Any alterations you make to the date and time will affect Windows' Clock and Calendar applications as well as your system clock. To change the date or time, double-click on the Date/Time icon in the Control Panel window. When you do, you'll see the Date & Time dialog box shown in Figure 3-21, which contains sections for setting the date and time. You can set the numbers in each section by highlighting a portion of the date or time and then typing your entry.

If you double-click on the month portion of the Date section in the dialog box, the month will be highlighted, and you can enter new text or click on one of the arrows in the increment box to change the number. You can also change your date and time by first placing the cursor in any portion of the date or time. Then, when you click on one of the arrows, Windows will automatically highlight and change the section of the date or time you've chosen.

Figure 3-21

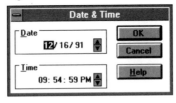

The Date & Time dialog box lets you change the date and time for your system.

Using sound

Double-clicking on Control Panel's Sound icon displays the Sound dialog box. As you can see in Figure 3-22, the Enable System Sounds check box is turned on by default. You can toggle the warning beep off by clicking on the check box to remove the X.

Figure 3-22

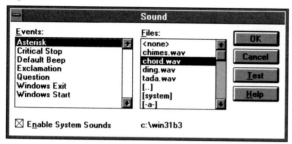

The Sound dialog box lets you turn the warning beep on or off and assign sounds to Windows events (if you have a sound card installed).

If you have a sound card installed in your computer, the Events and Files list boxes in the Sound dialog box will become active. (To install a sound card in Windows, you use the Drivers icon on Control Panel; we'll discuss this icon later in the chapter.) By default, Windows assigns the chord sound to the Windows events that cause messages to appear, the ding sound to events that cause a beep if you don't have a sound card, the chimes sound to exiting Windows, and the "ta-da" sound to starting Windows.

You can change any of these assignments by selecting an event from the Events list box, selecting the name of the sound you want to hear when the event occurs from the Files list box, and then clicking on OK. Notice that you can assign the option <none> to any event to turn off sound for that event. (Assigning <none> to all events is the same as turning off the Enable System Sounds check box.)

To hear the sound assigned to an event, you can either double-click on the event name or select the event and click on the Test button in the Sound dialog box. To hear a sound regardless of its assignment, double-click on the sound name in the Files list box, or select the sound name and click on the Test button. Be aware that testing a sound also assigns that sound to the selected event.

You can use the Files list box to select sound files from different directories and drives. Sound files, which have the .WAV file name extension, are stored in the WAVE sound file format.

If you are running Windows on a 386- or 486-based computer with more than 2 MB of memory, you will see an additional icon on Control Panel that looks like a computer chip with the number 386 on top. When you activate the 386 Enhanced icon, you'll see the 386 Enhanced dialog box, which is shown in

Using 386 Enhanced settings

Figure 3-23. This dialog box lets you control access to a device, such as a printer, and determine which window gets more processor time. Only non-Windows-based applications and earlier versions of Windows applications will need to use the settings in the 386 Enhanced dialog box. Applications based on Windows 3.0 and 3.1 already have these settings built in. In this dialog box, you can also set up or adjust a hard-disk swap file to act as virtual memory. (See Appendix A for more information about setting up or adjusting a swap file.)

Figure 3-23

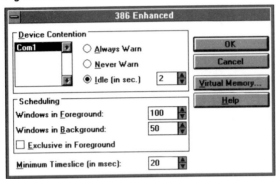

The 386 Enhanced dialog box controls access to devices and processing time.

Waiting for a device

     All application windows on the desktop can access devices, and sometimes they compete for the same device, such as a printer. If this happens, Windows can make the applications take turns. You can use the radio buttons in the Device Contention section of the 386 Enhanced dialog box to control when applications access a device or to warn you with a message box so that you can set the access manually. To set the access manually, you specify in the message box which application receives control. For example, to set the option for COM1, you can click on COM1 and then on Always Warn to warn you if two applications are trying to access the device simultaneously. A better way is to click on COM1 and then on Idle so that an application will wait a couple of seconds after COM1 is available again before trying to use it.

Sharing computer time

     Multiple application windows not only must share devices but also must share the computer's processing time. A unit of the processing time is called a time slice, which is defined in milliseconds. A Windows application gets to use the computer's processor for a portion of the time slice. All Windows applications share one time slice, but non-Windows applications use a separate time slice. You can set the time slice in the Minimum Timeslice text box to a value between 1 and 10,000 milliseconds. By default, the minimum time slice is 20 milliseconds.

Besides setting the duration of a time slice, establishing the priority for getting a time slice is also an important multitasking choice. An application can process information while it's active in the foreground or while it's inactive in the background. Normally, you give processing priority to a foreground application because you are currently interacting with it. However, if you have a communications program or major process working in the background, you should give the background application a higher priority than the foreground application so that it won't be interrupted.

There is a fine distinction between foreground and background processing selections in the Scheduling group box. Note that the foreground selection is labeled Windows in Foreground and the background selection is labeled Windows in Background. These settings are used only if a non-Windows application is active—for example, a non-Windows application in the foreground and a Windows application in the background.

You can weight the priority given to foreground and background processes by changing the values in the increment boxes. These numbers range from 1 to 10,000 and represent the total number of time slices normally shared by all Windows applications when a Windows application is active. As you define your needs, and as your knowledge of Windows deepens, you can use a variety of scheduling ratios. By default, the foreground is 100 and the background is 50.

If you don't want a non-Windows application to run when Windows applications are running, you can check the Exclusive in Foreground check box. When this check box is selected, Control Panel will reserve 100% of the processing time for Windows applications when one Windows application is active. This means that a non-Windows application cannot be processed in the background.

CONTROLLING PRINTERS AND DEVICES

You can provide Windows with more tools, such as printers, modems, and compact-disc players, but you must tell Windows what external devices are available. Typically, you'll report your hardware to Windows by configuring ports, installing drivers, and assigning ports to the installed devices.

Controlling ports

Your computer's communication ports, named COM1, COM2, COM3, and COM4, are serial ports. To configure these ports for use with a printer, you will probably need to refer to your printer manual to find out the default settings. You'll also need a manual if you want to set up a modem on your computer through Windows. You can perform the configuration with MS-DOS, but it will be easier to use Windows.

Configuring a port

To configure a port, activate the Ports icon on Control Panel. You'll then see the Ports dialog box, shown in Figure 3-24 on the following page. The Ports dialog box contains four COM icons that represent the serial ports. If you want to configure a port, you can either double-click on one of the COM icons, or you can select the icon and choose the Settings button in the Ports dialog box. Either method will produce the Settings dialog box, shown in Figure 3-25. In this dialog box, you set the various parameters, such as data bits and parity, and then click on OK. The default settings are 9600 baud rate, 8 data bits, no parity, 1 stop bit, and Xon/Xoff for flow control. Table 3-1 describes the settings and their alternatives. For further details on modems and communications settings, read Chapter 12.

Figure 3-24

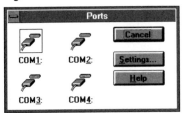

The Ports dialog box lets you set each of the four COM ports.

Figure 3-25

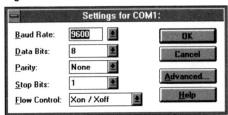

The Settings dialog box sets the parameters of a COM port.

In the Settings dialog box, you can choose the Advanced button to display the Advanced Settings dialog box for the selected COM port. In this dialog box, you can choose the Base I/O Port Address and the Interrupt Request Line settings. An I/O address is a location within the input/output address space of your computer, used by a device such as a printer or a modem. Selecting an I/O address lets you use ports with Windows that are not normally recognized by your computer. Interrupt request lines are signals used by a device to get the attention of the processor when the device is ready to accept or send information. By assigning a unique interrupt request line for each communications port, you can use ports 1 and 3 as well as ports 2 and 4 simultaneously.

Controlling printers

Control Panel will make choosing a printer an easy decision by providing a Printers dialog box when you activate the Printers icon. From a dialog box like the one shown in Figure 3-26, you can select, set up, or install a new printer. To select a printer listed in the Installed Printers list box, highlight the one you want. Windows will select only one printer at a time.

Table 3-1

Parameter	Definition	Common Setting
Baud rate	The data transfer speed between a device and a computer.	9600 for printers; 1200 or 2400 for modems
Data bits	The number of bits sent in a computer word.	7 or 8
Parity	A verification bit. It can be even, odd, not used, mark, or space. If a 7 data bits setting is used, parity is usually even. If an 8 data bits setting is used, parity is not used.	Even or None
Stop bits	The separators between computer words.	1
Flow control	The interaction between a device and a computer. The hardware needs to tell the computer when it's ready for more data. Xon/Xoff is a message sent back to the computer telling it to send more data. The Hardware setting refers to hardware handshaking that's conducted over one of the wires in the cable. The None setting means that handshaking isn't necessary.	Xon/Xoff

You'll use these communications settings to configure a port.

Figure 3-26

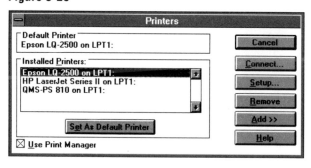

The Printers dialog box lets you select from among several installed printers.

**Choosing a
default printer**

If you begin printing before you've chosen a printer, Windows will send the output to the printer listed in the Default Printer box in the Printers dialog box. You can change the default printer by selecting a printer from the Installed Printers list box and then clicking on the Set As Default Printer button. Or, as an alternative, you can double-click on a printer in the Installed Printers list.

**Configuring
a printer**

The Connect dialog box, shown in Figure 3-27, will let you select a port. You can also use this dialog box to change the port assigned to a printer. To access this dialog box, select the Connect button in the Printers dialog box. By default, the LPT1 port is selected in the Ports list box. You can, however, choose any port from this list box.

Figure 3-27

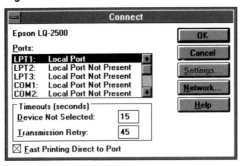

*The Connect dialog box is
useful primarily for arranging
links between printers and ports.*

In the Connect dialog box, the Timeouts section sets time limits in seconds. Before Windows sends data to a printer, it asks for a ready signal. If Windows doesn't get the signal before the Device Not Selected time limit runs out, it sends you a message that the printer is not available. When Windows is able to send data to the printer, you may run into a different problem. The printer processes data in chunks, or batches. If it doesn't ask for the next batch of data before the Transmission Retry time limit runs out, Windows will send the data again. If that doesn't work, Windows will display an error message. The default values for the time limits in the Timeouts section will work in most cases. However, if you get many error messages, you may need to increase the time limit allotted. All you need to do is double-click in the Device Not Selected or the Transmission Retry text box and then type the desired time limit, which will replace the old setting automatically.

Turn off the Fast Printing Direct to Port check box in the Connect dialog box if your application prints using MS-DOS interrupts. (Consult the application's manual if you have questions about this.) Leave this check box turned on to print through Windows, which is faster.

If you want to queue printing—that is, to print a file while working on something else—you need to be sure that the Use Print Manager check box in the Printers dialog box is selected. The Print Manager controls the queuing of your print jobs from an application, as you'll learn in Chapter 7.

Using the
Print Manager

Windows lets you install more than one printer. To add a printer, first select the Add button in the Printers dialog box. As you can see in Figure 3-28, the dialog box will expand to include a printer installation section, which contains a list of available printers and an Install button.

Adding a printer

After you choose a printer from the List of Printers list box and select the Install button, an Install Driver dialog box, like the one shown in Figure 3-29 on the next page, will prompt you to insert a floppy disk containing printer drivers into a disk drive. The printer driver will tell Windows how to use the printer and which fonts it can use. If the appropriate fonts haven't been previously installed, Windows will copy them onto the hard disk, prompting you to insert disks as necessary. If you have already copied all the printer files onto the hard disk, just type the full path name into the text box so that Windows can locate the necessary files. Select OK to continue, or choose Cancel, which will return you to the Printers dialog box without making any changes. To install a printer driver for a printer that doesn't appear in the list or to install a new printer driver for a printer that is already listed, select the entry Install Unlisted or Updated Printer from the list. After the files for a new printer are copied, the new printer will appear on the Installed Printers list. In all cases, you need to go through the configuration procedure to set any customized parameters.

Figure 3-28

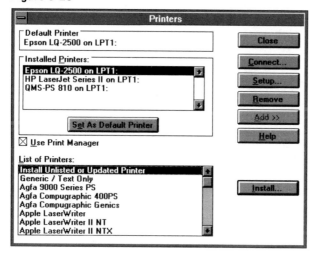

The Printers dialog box expands to include a printer installation section.

Figure 3-29

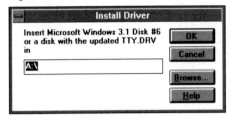

*The Install Driver dialog box copies
printer drivers to your hard disk.*

If you try to install a printer that is already installed, Windows will add
another entry to the Installed Printers list. If you want to update an existing
driver, select Install Unlisted or Updated Printer from the List of Printers list box,
and click on the Install button.

Removing an installed printer

Later on, you may find that you no longer need a printer you originally
installed for Windows. For example, you may upgrade a printer or trade one in.
You can remove a printer by using the Printers dialog box. To do this, first click
on the name of the printer in the Installed Printers list box. Then click on the
Remove button to delete the printer name. When Windows presents a warning
dialog box asking for verification, click on Yes. After you click on Yes, Control
Panel will delete the printer name from the Installed Printers list; it won't delete
the printer driver files or the font files from your hard disk. Later, if you want to
reinstall the printer, Control Panel will add the printer's name to the list, but you
won't have to copy any files onto your hard disk.

Setting up printers

Each printer has different setup options. Windows supports many printers,
but we'll limit our discussion to three common printer types: the HP LaserJet
Series II, the Epson LQ-2500, and the QMS-PS 810. After you click on the Setup
button in the Printers dialog box, you can choose paper size and number of
copies. Other options, such as orientation, memory, color, scaling (enlarging or
reducing an image), or duplexing (printing both sides of a page), depend on the
capabilities of the printer. If the printer doesn't offer a particular option, you
won't see that option in the printer's dialog box. If the option is installed in your
printer but dimmed (not available) in the dialog box, you didn't choose the
correct printer in the List of Printers list box.

Setting up the HP LaserJet Series II

Let's look at the HP LaserJet Series II setup process. In the Printers dialog
box, choose HP LaserJet Series II on LPT1: from the Installed Printers list box,
and then click on the Connect button. In the Connect dialog box, select the

appropriate port. It is important to do this before installing any soft or cartridge fonts, because font information is associated with the port to which your printer is connected. Click on OK to exit the Connect dialog box, and then click on the Setup button. The HP LaserJet Series II dialog box will appear, as shown in Figure 3-30. Note that the title bar of this dialog box contains the name of the printer you are setting up.

As you can see, the dialog box for this printer contains four drop-down list boxes that let you specify the resolution, paper size, paper source, and installed memory size of your printer.

Figure 3-30

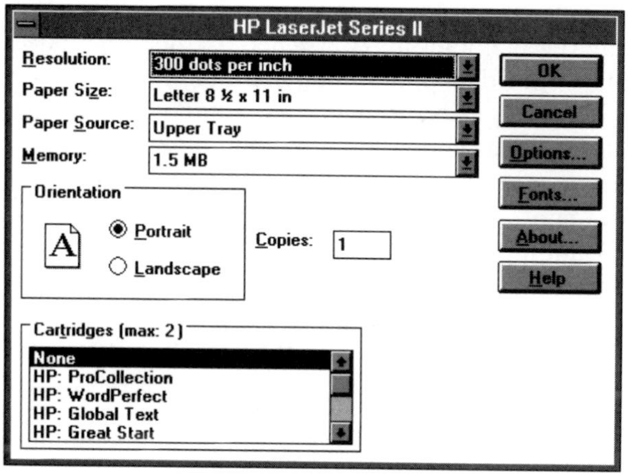

A printer-specific dialog box outlines detailed setup functions.

Resolution determines the quality of the output by setting the number of dots per inch (dpi). The higher the dpi, the crisper the image, but the greater the memory consumption. If you're printing large documents, your printer could run out of memory. If you get the error message *Out of memory*, you should install more memory in your printer. If more memory isn't available, you can select a reduced dots-per-inch setting in the Resolution drop-down list box to free up some memory. If your printout shows only half an image, your printer has a memory shortage—the printer's memory just can't hold more than half the picture.

The Orientation section of the dialog box allows you to tell the printer whether you want to print across the width or the length of the page. Notice that when you select one of the two orientations, the sample page display changes to match your selection. Normally, you will use Portrait.

The Cartridges section provides a list of available font cartridges. A cartridge, which is inserted in the printer, contains fonts on a chip. Windows can look at the printer to determine which cartridges are in the printer's cartridge slots. Windows also knows how many cartridges the printer can use at one time and displays the maximum number at the top of the Cartridges section. The HP LaserJet Series II can use two.

You can set the number of copies you want to print by changing the number in the Copies text box. Simply double-click on the text box to highlight the current number, and then type in the new number of copies. The default setting tells Windows to print one copy.

Most applications designed for Windows (such as Microsoft Excel or Word for Windows) provide a Copies option in their own Print dialog boxes. This means that you can set the number of copies in two places—in the Print dialog box and in the printer-specific setup dialog box. The number of copies your printer returns might occasionally be greater than you expect. For example, if you specify two copies in the Print dialog box in Word for Windows and two copies in the printer-specific setup dialog box, you will actually receive four copies. To avoid printing extra copies, keep your printer set up for the default (one copy), and let the application specify the number of additional copies, unless you want the same number of multiple copies printed from every application. Some Windows applications—Write, for example—copy the number from the printer-specific dialog box and use that number as the default in their own Print dialog boxes; you can then alter the number of copies in the application's dialog box when necessary for a specific printing job. Paintbrush, however, uses its own default of one copy and ignores the printer-specific number. Notepad, Calendar, and Cardfile all use the number indicated in the printer-specific dialog box; you cannot choose a different number of copies with the Print command in these applications.

Working with printer fonts

To work with printer fonts, click on the Fonts button in the HP LaserJet Series II dialog box to activate the HP Font Installer dialog box shown in Figure 3-31. The left list box displays the currently installed fonts. The right list box is available to list fonts that you can add from a disk or copy or move from another printer port. The radio buttons under the left list box designate selected fonts as permanent or temporary. Files marked as permanent have an asterisk next to their name. Windows loads a permanent font when you select the printer and a temporary font when you select the font. The buttons between these two list boxes allow you to exchange files between the boxes. At the bottom of the dialog box, below the heavy line, is a status display area where Control Panel displays file names as you add or delete them.

Figure 3-31

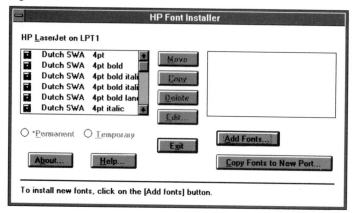

The HP Font Installer dialog box lets you add printer fonts to your hard disk.

The Add Fonts button in the HP Font Installer dialog box copies font files onto your hard disk. If you click on it, Windows displays the dialog box shown in Figure 3-32, which prompts you for a floppy disk. If you don't want to access a floppy disk in drive A, enter a new drive ID and path name in the text box.

Adding a font

Figure 3-32

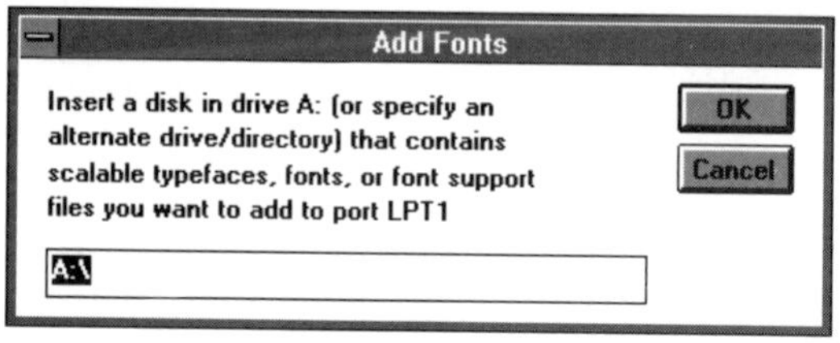

The Add Fonts dialog box copies font files onto your hard disk.

After you click on OK, the fonts appear in the list box on the right side of the HP Font Installer dialog box. The Add Fonts button changes to a Close Drive button, and the Move button becomes the Add button. Once you have established the correct drive from which to add fonts, highlight the fonts you want to add and click on the Add button. Windows will copy the fonts onto your hard disk. If you then click on the Close Drive button, the listed fonts will disappear, and Windows will reset the path to its default (C:\WINDOWS). If you don't click on Close Drive, Windows will continue to prompt you for a disk (if fonts were added from a disk) whenever it wants to issue a command.

Copying or moving fonts between ports

The Copy Fonts to New Port button in the HP Font Installer dialog box lets you copy or move fonts between printers. Windows lets you select a second port by using the Copy Fonts to New Port dialog box shown in Figure 3-33. Click on the second port, and then click on the OK button. Windows adds a printer name with that port designation above the list box on the right side of the HP Font Installer dialog box. Now you can move or copy fonts from either printer to the other printer.

Figure 3-33

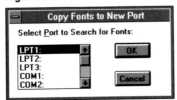

The Copy Fonts to New Port dialog box allows you to transfer fonts.

After you choose the fonts to install in one list box and click on the Move or Copy button of the HP Font Installer dialog box, Windows will transfer the fonts to the other printer. (Clicking on Move transfers a font from one list box to the other, deleting the font from its original location; clicking on Copy transfers the font but does not delete the original entry.) Then click on the End between Ports button to complete the copy. Finally, close the dialog box or click on the Exit button to return to the HP LaserJet Series II dialog box.

Editing font settings

If your printer supports soft fonts (fonts that can be downloaded into your printer's memory), then you can edit the soft font settings when you set up the printer. For example, if you want to add an HP LaserJet Series II soft font to Windows, you need to select HP LaserJet Series II on LPT1: (or another port) in the Printers dialog box, click on Setup, and then click on Fonts to access the HP Font Installer dialog box. Finally, select a font and click on Edit to display an Edit dialog box similar to the one shown in Figure 3-34. You can change the font name (in case different brands of soft fonts have the same name) and the method of downloading.

The top two lines of the dialog box display the soft font official description (which appears in the HP Font Installer dialog box) and the file name. On the next line is a Name text box where you can alter the name that appears in font listings in applications (the unofficial description).

Figure 3-34

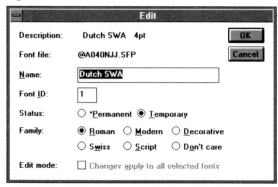

The Edit dialog box allows you to edit soft font settings such as the font name or download capabilities.

By choosing one of the Status radio buttons, you can specify whether the soft font is downloaded when you select the printer (permanent status) or when you select the font (temporary status). You can designate only one font on the list as permanent. When you designate a font as permanent, or when you exit the HP Font Installer dialog box, Windows will present the dialog box shown in Figure 3-35, asking if you want the font downloaded immediately and/or automatically each time you turn on your computer. Turn on the Download at Startup check box in the Download Options dialog box if you want Windows to modify your AUTOEXEC.BAT file to download the font when you turn on your computer or reboot it. (Rebooting means restarting the computer without turning it off, by pressing [Ctrl][Alt][Delete].) A word of caution: It will take longer to start working on your computer when you boot your system, because downloading takes a long time (how long depends on how much memory the font uses). However, your computer will prompt you with a message like *Download PCL fonts (y/n)?* so that you don't have to download the fonts every time. If you need to download fonts, you'll see the Download Options dialog box.

Figure 3-35

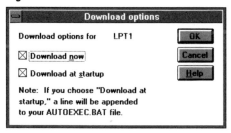

The Download Now check box in the Download Options dialog box modifies your AUTOEXEC.BAT file to load fonts to the printer.

After you have set all the options in the Edit dialog box, click on OK to return to the HP Font Installer dialog box. The status area at the bottom of the dialog box will let you know how many fonts were edited, displaying a message such as *3 font(s) edited.*

Warning: Unless you are creating and manually downloading your own fonts, do not make any other changes in the Edit dialog box. If you need more information about the other options in this dialog box, consult Windows Help by clicking on the Help button in the HP Font Installer dialog box.

What is the Options button?

You may have noticed the Options button in the HP LaserJet Series II dialog box. You can click on the Options button to see more settings for your printer, if any are available. For example, when you use the HP LaserJet Series II, you can set the intensity of print to darker or lighter with the Intensity Control section of the Options dialog box shown in Figure 3-36. Slide the control to the right to print lighter or to the left to print darker. You can change the level of dithering (which controls the number of colors or gray shades used during printing) by choosing one of the radio buttons in the Dithering section. Also, with the HP LaserJet Series II and compatible printers, you can print graphics that are positioned over text without having the text show through in your printout by turning on the Print TrueType as Graphics check box. This option will send the entire page to the printer as a graphic.

Figure 3-36

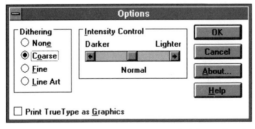

The Options dialog box is available only if the selected printer supports any additional options.

Setting up the Epson LQ-2500

If you use a dot matrix printer instead of a laser printer, you will see different options when you install the printer and set up its options. For example, when you select Setup after installing an Epson LQ-2500, which is a near-letter-quality printer, you will see a dialog box similar to the one shown in Figure 3-37. In the Epson LQ-2500 dialog box, you can set resolution, paper size, paper source, and orientation; and you can select up to two font cartridges.

Figure 3-37

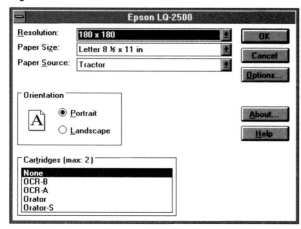

*The Epson LQ-2500
dialog box sets up
a high-end dot
matrix printer.*

You can change the resolution (density of dots) of the output. The highest
quality of printing is the slowest because a high-resolution output uses more
dots to form the characters or graphics and therefore takes more time to print.
The Resolution drop-down list box has three choices for three quality levels. By
default, Windows uses the intermediate setting, which is best for printing text.

Because dot matrix printers use an adjustable tractor feed and aren't confined to a paper tray, they can use many sizes of paper. The default size is Letter
8½ x 11 in. To set a custom paper width, select User Defined Size from the
Paper Size drop-down list box. Windows will display the dialog box shown in
Figure 3-38. Select the unit of measurement (millimeters or inches), and then
type the width and length measurements in the text boxes. The numbers you
type should be 100 times the actual size for inch measurements or 10 times the
actual size for millimeter measurements. For example, enter a 6.75" measurement as 675 or a 50 mm measurement as 500. Then select OK to return to the first
Epson LQ-2500 dialog box.

Figure 3-38

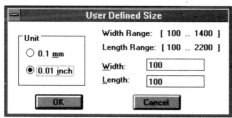

*You can set custom paper
sizes in this dialog box.*

If you want to print a spreadsheet that exceeds the width of the paper, you'll need to turn the printing sideways (to Landscape orientation) to use the length of the page and gain more space. Not all printers have this capability, but the Epson LQ-2500 does. To set the page orientation sideways, simply click on the Landscape radio button in the Orientation group box. Windows uses Portrait orientation by default.

If your printer came with several font cartridges, you'll also want to click on one or two of the names in the Cartridges list box so that you can have access to the fonts in those cartridges.

After you choose the resolution, paper size, paper source, orientation, and cartridges, you can use the Options button to display the Options dialog box, where you can set dithering, the printing intensity, and the print quality (letter or draft). If you didn't install the color option kit on your Epson LQ-2500, you can click on the Color check box to prevent applications from trying to print in color. (Note that the application, as well as Windows, needs to support the printer.)

Setting up PostScript printers

PostScript printers are similar to HP LaserJet printers, but they have more options because they have more capabilities. When you select a PostScript printer in the first Printers dialog box and then configure it, you'll see a dialog box like the one shown in Figure 3-39. You can select the paper source, paper size, orientation, and number of copies, just as you did for the HP LaserJet Series II. You don't need to install fonts. PostScript printers come with their own outline fonts to create fonts of varying sizes. You can install screen fonts with Control Panel's Fonts feature, but you don't have to install printer fonts using Control Panel. The PostScript printer also offers some options that we haven't discussed previously, including scaling, color, and printer communication options.

The Options button in the QMS-PS 810 on LPT1: dialog box directs you to more setup details. In the Options dialog box shown in Figure 3-40, you can set scaling, turn on color printing (if it is available on your printer), and send output to a file by changing the selection in the Print To section.

Figure 3-39

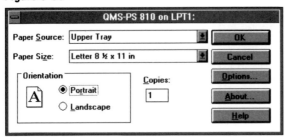

In a dialog box like this one, you can set PostScript printer options.

Figure 3-40

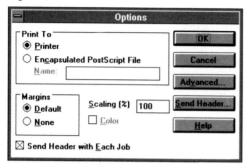

The Options dialog box sets printer-specific parameters.

Scaling will enlarge or reduce the images sent to your printer. For example, a setting of 50 percent will cut the size of the image by half, and a setting of 200 percent will double the size. You should set scaling to 100 percent to print the image at its current size.

Color is available for specific PostScript printers such as the QMS Color Script 100. If your printer is not able to print in color, the Color check box in the Options dialog box will be dimmed.

Some applications, such as PageMaker, are able to use an Encapsulated PostScript (EPS) file format. You can choose this file format by clicking on the Encapsulated PostScript File radio button. Normally, you will use Clipboard to transfer bit map graphics to another application, but bit map graphics take longer to print than EPS files. To speed printing, you can use the Encapsulated PostScript file to place the figure in PageMaker. In the Print To section of the Options dialog box, you can enter the name of the output target file. If you select the Encapsulated PostScript File radio button, the Name text box will become available, and you can enter the file name.

If you are sending the information directly to the printer, the Margins section of the Options dialog box will let you disable the default margins set up by the printer. This is especially useful if you are trying to print labels that have no top or bottom margin.

You'll also find the Send Header with Each Job check box in the Options dialog box. A header is unique to PostScript printers. A header is information sent to the printer to set up the printer with the correct page formatting and fonts. When the check box is turned on, a header is automatically sent each time a file prints; when the check box is turned off, you must specifically send the header to the printer at least once before you print. If the check box is turned off and you want to send the header to a file or a printer, choose the Send Header button in the Options dialog box to open the Send Header dialog box shown in Figure 3-41. The Send Header dialog box lets you choose to send the header information to a file or to a printer. To download to a file, select the File radio button, type a file name in the Name text box, and choose Send Now. Windows downloads the header information as soon as you choose the Send Now button. (As you may know, PostScript files are more portable than application-specific files—that is, you can use them across applications.)

Figure 3-41

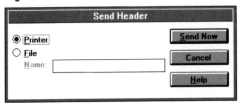

The Send Header dialog box lets you send header information to either a printer or a file.

Controlling multimedia devices

Windows 3.1 has the ability to install, set up, and remove multimedia devices such as sound cards, video players, and compact-disc players. Of course, to use these devices you must first add the necessary cards and equipment to your computer. Then, to install and set up the device in Windows, you can double-click on the Drivers icon found in the Control Panel window to display the Drivers dialog box shown in Figure 3-42.

Figure 3-42

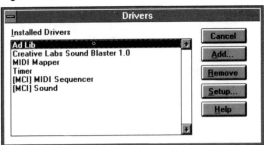

You can install and set up multimedia devices in Windows 3.1.

During Windows Setup, the basic drivers shown in the Installed Drivers list box are installed. For these drivers, you add a specific device. For a sound card, for example, select [MCI] MIDI Sequencer, and then click on the Add button to display the Add dialog box shown in Figure 3-43.

In the List of Drivers list box, select the name of the device you want to add and then click on OK. Windows asks for one of its disks so that it can copy the necessary files to your hard disk. After this, a Setup dialog box similar to the one shown in Figure 3-44 might appear if you need to adjust any settings.

Figure 3-43

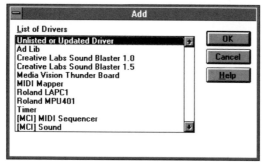

In the Add dialog box, you can select the device you want to add.

Figure 3-44

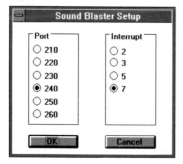

A Setup dialog box allows you to change settings to fit the device you are adding.

Check the manual for the device to find the proper settings for the device. When the device is installed and set up, Windows displays a System Setting Change message box. If you have more devices to install, click on the Don't Restart Now button in the message box. If you have installed all the devices you intend to, click on the Restart Now button. Windows must restart in order to use the multimedia device drivers.

After Windows starts again, you can play the multimedia devices you have installed. Windows 3.1 provides four sound files (described earlier in this chapter) and two MIDI sequencer files (music). See Chapter 14 for a description of the Media Player accessory, which can play sound and MIDI files.

Changing a device's setup

If for some reason you need to change the setup of a device after you have installed it, double-click on the Drivers icon, select the device from the Installed Drivers list box, and then choose the Setup button. Make the necessary changes in the Setup dialog box, and then choose OK.

Removing a device

If you no longer need a device driver (because the device is no longer connected to your computer), you can remove the device driver by double-clicking on the Drivers icon, selecting the device from the Installed Drivers list box, and then clicking on the Remove button. Windows asks you to confirm the deletion; choose Yes to remove the device driver. To completely remove the effect of the driver, you need to quit and then restart Windows.

What is MIDI Mapper?

After you install a specific multimedia device, you'll notice a new icon called MIDI Mapper in the Control Panel window. You can use the MIDI Mapper to select a MIDI setup for a sound device, to create a new setup, or to edit existing key maps, patch maps, and channel mappings. Windows supplies MIDI setups for the sound devices it supports. Unless you connect a synthesizer to the MIDI output port of your computer, you will not need to use the MIDI Mapper to create or edit a MIDI setup. See the manual that accompanied your sound device for further details.

A word of caution: Do not use the MIDI Mapper to create or edit MIDI setups unless you have some basic knowledge of MIDI concepts and terminology and understand the results of the changes you make.

WINDOWS SETUP

The Windows Setup application makes it easy to recustomize Windows whenever you change your computer's hardware or add new applications. Any changes you make with Windows Setup are reflected in your WIN.INI and SYSTEM.INI files. The options you can change include the settings for your computer's display, keyboard, mouse, and network (if applicable).

To start Windows Setup, click on the Program Manager's Main group window, and then double-click on the Windows Setup icon. A Windows Setup window, like the one shown in Figure 3-45, will appear. This window displays all your current hardware settings. You'll need to use the commands on the Options menu to change hardware settings or install applications.

To exit Windows Setup, choose the Exit command from the Options menu.

Figure 3-45

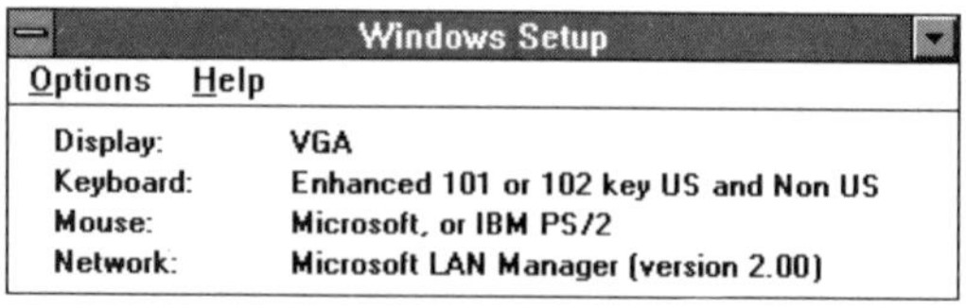

Windows Setup	
Options Help	
Display:	VGA
Keyboard:	Enhanced 101 or 102 key US and Non US
Mouse:	Microsoft, or IBM PS/2
Network:	Microsoft LAN Manager (version 2.00)

*The Windows Setup window displays the current
hardware settings.*

If you change any of your hardware—for instance, if you upgrade to a VGA
monitor—you'll need to change the hardware settings in Windows. To do this,
choose the Change System Settings command on the Options menu, and Windows Setup will display a Change System Settings dialog box, like the one shown
in Figure 3-46. This dialog box provides drop-down list boxes to let you choose
the display (monitor), keyboard, mouse, and network. These list boxes present
the current settings for the various hardware categories. To change one of these
settings, simply click on the list box's drop-down arrow, and click on a new
setting. For example, if you currently have a Hercules Monochrome interface
card and monochrome monitor and want to upgrade to a VGA interface card and
VGA color monitor, click on VGA in the Display drop-down list box. Of course,
you need to change your hardware by installing the new card and monitor so
that when you start your next Windows session, you can use the new hardware.
Note that if you change your hardware before you change the appropriate
settings with Windows Setup, you may not be able to see the desktop, since
Windows will still present it as if you had a monochrome monitor. To correct this
problem, run the Setup program in your Windows directory before restarting
Windows. Note also that the changes you have made to Windows settings are
not implemented until you restart Windows.

Figure 3-46

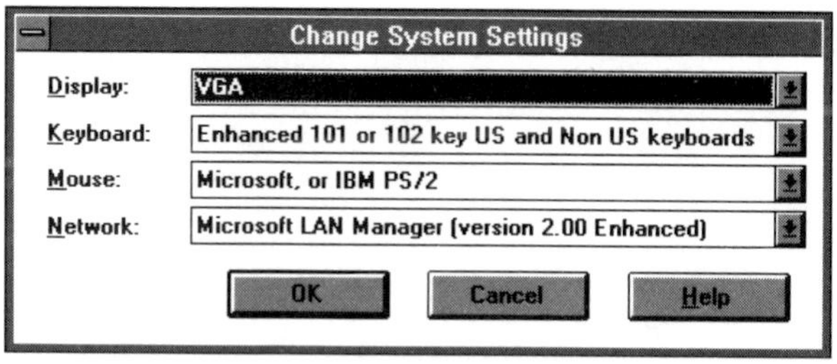

Change System Settings	
Display:	VGA
Keyboard:	Enhanced 101 or 102 key US and Non US keyboards
Mouse:	Microsoft, or IBM PS/2
Network:	Microsoft LAN Manager (version 2.00 Enhanced)

OK   Cancel   Help

*The Change System Settings dialog box lets you change
the current hardware and network settings.*

The keyboard and mouse system settings are similar to the display settings because they all depend on a type of hardware, but the network settings relate to a type of network software. As you can see in Figure 3-47, the Network list box provides a list of network software packages, such as Microsoft's LAN Manager. If you have removed your computer from a network and don't want to see the *Connect to Network* prompt as you begin each Windows session, choose the No Network Installed option to cancel that connect prompt.

Figure 3-47

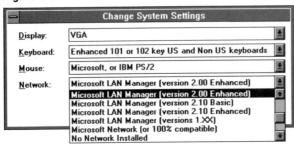

The Network drop-down list box displays network software packages.

Each drop-down list for each device includes an Other item. When you select Other, Setup displays a dialog box that prompts you to insert the device driver disk in drive A. Insert the disk, and either accept the drive and path shown or type a new one. Then click on OK. Setup reads the disk and displays a list of devices supported by the drivers on the disk. Select the device from the list, and click on OK. Setup adds the device to the appropriate drop-down list in the Change System Settings dialog box.

After you've changed any hardware settings, click on OK to save your changes. Windows will then display the Exit Windows Setup dialog box. Choose the appropriate button in this dialog box to exit Windows. When you start Windows again, the new settings will be in effect.

Adding applications to the desktop

Software packages that are designed as Windows applications should be installed according to the product's instructions. This procedure will correctly update your WIN.INI and SYSTEM.INI files, will place the appropriate icon in the Program Manager group window, and will even generate a new group window if necessary.

When you buy a new non-Windows application software package to use with Windows, you'll need to add it to a Program Manager group window with Windows Setup. Before you can run Windows Setup, you must install the application on your hard disk according to the instructions in the application's documentation. After the application is correctly installed on your hard disk, start Windows and then double-click on the Windows Setup icon. When the Windows Setup application window appears, choose the Set Up Applications command from the Options menu.

Setup displays the dialog box shown in Figure 3-48, which will search for all the applications that Setup recognizes or for a particular application that you specify. (If you want Setup to locate a specific application, choose the radio button labeled *Ask you to specify an application*; more on this in a moment.) When you choose the radio button labeled *Search for applications* and then choose OK, Setup displays the dialog box shown in Figure 3-49. Although Setup can look for applications on all drives, you can tell Setup to look at only one drive in order to speed up the process. For example, if the application you just installed was copied onto drive C, you would choose the entry for drive C in the list box. Then, after you click on the OK button, Setup would search for applications on drive C. If drive C is loaded with applications, this search could take a long time. By default, Setup will search the path you specified in your AUTOEXEC.BAT file, which lists the directories of all the major applications. To search the path, be sure that the Path entry in the list box is selected, and then click on the OK button.

Figure 3-48

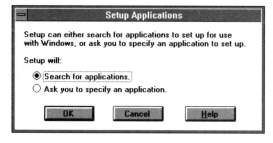

In this dialog box, you can ask Setup to search for all applications or for a specific application.

Figure 3-49

This Setup Applications dialog box starts a search for applications on your hard disk.

After you click on Search Now in the second dialog box, Setup will display a Windows Setup message box that indicates the status of the search and tells you which drive and path Setup is currently searching. If you've selected your hard disk, Setup looks at each directory on your hard disk. The last line of text lists the name of the application that Setup finds. This line changes each time Setup locates a new application. The display bar at the bottom of the dialog box shows you how much of the search Setup has completed. When the bar is all blue, the search is 100% complete. If you want to cancel the search, choose the Cancel Search button.

As soon as the search is complete, another Setup Applications dialog box will appear, like the one shown in Figure 3-50. Setup will list the applications it found in the left list box. To select an application, click on it. Setup will highlight the application name and frame it. (If you want to remove the highlight and deselect an application, click on it again.) After you select the applications you want to add to the Program Manager, click on the Add button. Now all the highlighted applications will appear in the list box on the right. If you added an application by mistake, you can use the Remove button to return it to the left list box. If you want to add all the items in the left list box and don't want to bother clicking on each one, you can simply click on the Add All button.

Figure 3-50

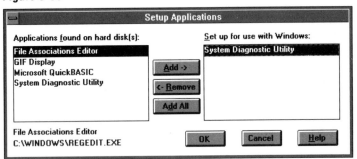

Another Setup Applications dialog box lists the applications
Setup found and allows you to choose which ones to add.

As you click on application names, the lower-left corner of the dialog box displays the application name and its path. This display lets you verify which application is being added, in case you have installed different versions of software under the same name; the path information in the display area will help to distinguish one software version from another. When you've added the application names to the right list box, click on OK.

Let's return briefly to the first Setup Applications dialog box (Figure 3-48) and see what happens when you ask Setup to locate a single application. When you choose the radio button labeled *Ask you to specify an application* and click on OK, you see the dialog box shown in Figure 3-51. In the Application Path and Filename text box, type the drive, directory path name, and application file name (including the period and the three-character extension). Or click on the Browse button to see a dialog box that helps you locate the application. From the Add to Program Group drop-down list box, select the group to which you want to add the application. Then click on OK.

Figure 3-51

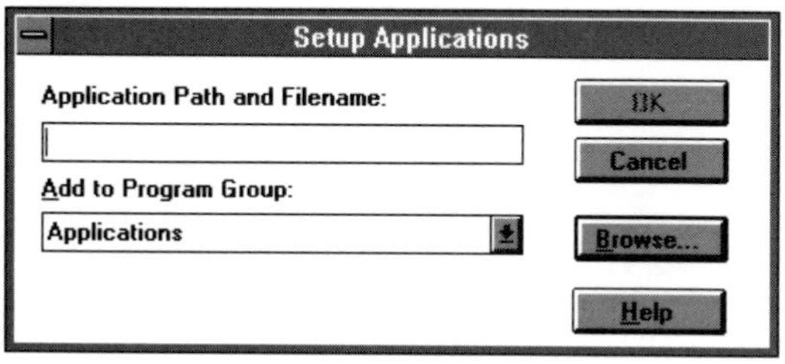

In this dialog box, you specify the single application
you want to add to a group in the Program Manager.

Whether you've chosen a single application or multiple applications, Windows will now add the application(s) to the Program Manager in the appropriate group window. It also will keep you informed of its progress in adding the application with a Windows Setup message box like the one you saw when Windows searched the drives for applications. This time, the message box will have three lines of text to tell you that Windows is *Adding item(s) to Program Manager Group...*, which group it is, and the name of the application. After you exit Windows Setup, you'll see the new icon when you activate the group window. If the application wasn't originally designed for Windows, but Windows recognizes it as compatible, Windows will write a PIF (program information file) so that it can start the application correctly later. You can read more about PIFs in Chapter 17.

If you prefer to add applications to other groups, see Chapter 5 for information about how to create new group windows and how to edit group windows in the Program Manager. Chapter 6 contains information about how to add applications to a group by dragging their file icons with the mouse from the File Manager to the Program Manager group window.

Adding and removing Windows components

As you install Windows, you can choose either Express Setup or Custom Setup. After choosing Express Setup, you might find later on that you never use certain components of Windows. Or, if you choose Custom Setup, you might discover later that you omitted some Windows components that you now want to use. To add or delete components, choose the Add/Remove Windows Components command from the Windows Setup Options menu. A Windows Setup dialog box like the one shown in Figure 3-52 will be displayed.

Figure 3-52

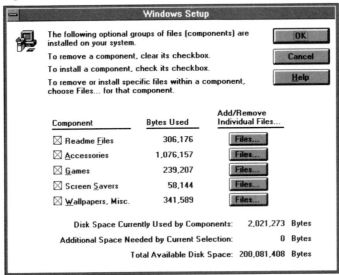

In this Windows Setup dialog box, you can add and remove Windows components.

As the text in this dialog box states, you turn on (check) a check box to add a category of components and turn off (clear) a check box to remove a category. To add or remove only certain items in a category, click on the Files button to the right of the category. For example, to remove certain accessories that you do not use—for example, Windows Notepad—click on the Files button for accessories to display the Accessories dialog box shown in Figure 3-53.

To remove an item, select it in the list box on the right. (This list box allows multiple selections. Click on every item you want to remove. If you incorrectly click on an item, click on it again to deselect it.) After you've made your selection, click on the Remove button. Then click on OK to close the dialog box and return to the Windows Setup dialog box.

Figure 3-53

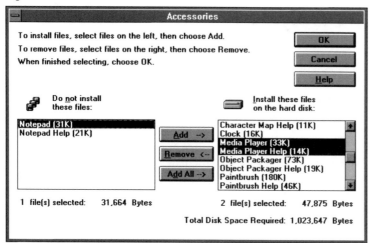

Specific accessories can be removed or added in this dialog box.

To add an item in the Accessories dialog box, select the item from the left list box. (This list box also allows multiple selections.) Then click on the Add button to move the item from the left list box to the right list box. Click on OK to return to the Windows Setup dialog box.

When you've made all your choices for additions and removals, click on OK in the Windows Setup dialog box to continue the process. For added items, Windows will ask for the appropriate disk. For both adding and removing, Windows Setup displays a message dialog box that shows your progress toward completion.

In this chapter

Getting Help 4

*S*ome programs offer so little assistance that you may feel stranded when you encounter a problem. Windows Help is determined to change that feeling by offering a new and comprehensive approach to the standard Help feature.

In DOS-based applications, Help is part of the application you are running. In Windows, Help is a separate application that is devoted to providing information about Windows. Some applications written to work with Windows will use the Help application too, but with their own data files. The installed application will supply the information, and Windows will present it to you in the Help window. Applications that weren't designed to work with Windows have their own isolated Help systems, not the advanced and easily accessible Help system Windows provides.

WINDOWS HELP

As you work with the various Windows applications, you'll see a Help menu on almost every menu bar. Because Help works the same way for all Windows applications, we will explain how to use Help only in this chapter, to avoid repetition as we explore the many applications. You'll notice Help buttons in numerous dialog boxes throughout the book, however, and we will detail their uses and functions as necessary.

In this chapter, we will show you how to start Help and how to use all its features. For instance, you can get help on a specific topic by clicking on the topic in a Help Contents window. You can even print a particular topic or add notes to it. Finally, we'll show you how to exit Help and return to the application you're working with.

Starting Help

Windows provides many avenues by which you can reach its internal Help application. You can use the Help menu on an application's menu bar, choose a Help button in a dialog box, or press [F1]. Some applications, such as the PIF Editor, Control Panel, and Windows Setup, even provide context-sensitive help.

You can access Help from within an application by choosing commands on the application's Help menu. This menu features a list of commands that will generally include Contents, Search for Help On, How to Use Help, and About, as well as commands specific to the application. For instance, the PIF Editor Help menu adds several Options commands.

When you choose one of the commands from the Help menu, Help will open a window on your desktop for the specified category. For example, if you want to see all the Help categories for the Program Manager, select the Contents command from the Help menu on the Program Manager's menu bar. The Contents for Program Manager Help window lists the available topics grouped by category, as shown in Figure 4-1.

Figure 4-1

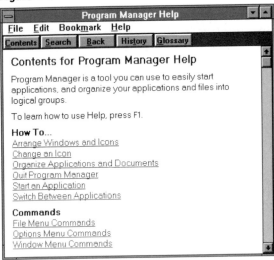

Help displays a list of available topics when you select the Contents command from the Help menu.

If you choose a Help button in a dialog box, you'll see a topic related to the functions of that dialog box. (Note that you can still use the Help menu to view the same information.) For example, when you click on the Help button in the HP Font Installer dialog box, shown in Figure 4-2, Help will open a window like the one shown in Figure 4-3 to display a list of topics related to installing fonts. After you exit the Help window, you'll return to the dialog box.

Figure 4-2

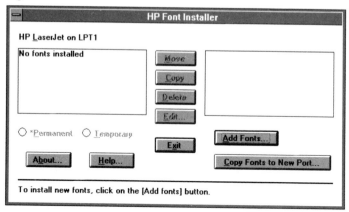

*The Help button in the HP Font Installer dialog box leads to
a list of topics related to installing fonts.*

Figure 4-3

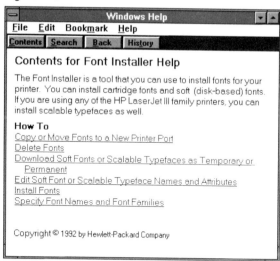

*Help displays a list of
topics that can help you
with font installation.*

In applications that do not provide context-sensitive help, Help will display
a Contents listing for the active application (the window you're currently working with) when you press [F1]. This is the same information you can reach with
the Contents command on the Help menu.

When you initially set up Windows, when the Control Panel window is
active, or when you're working with the PIF Editor, you can get context-sensitive
help without using the Contents command. If you press [F1], Help will display

information about the highlighted portion of the window. You can press [F1] to get context-sensitive help for any Windows message box. Many applications upgraded for Windows 3.1 also offer similar access to context-sensitive help for dialog boxes and message boxes.

Sizing Help

You can resize the Help window in order to work with multiple windows, to use space more efficiently, or for easier viewing. You can adjust the size of your windows by dragging the window frame or by clicking on the Minimize or Maximize box. As we showed you in Chapter 2, dragging the frame to a custom size allows you to use the rest of the desktop to display several windows simultaneously. If you click on the Minimize box, you gain the most desktop space because Windows shrinks Help into an icon, as shown in Figure 4-4, and places it at the bottom of the desktop. Clicking on the Maximize box expands the Help window to fill the entire desktop, making the topics easier to read.

Figure 4-4

You can minimize Help into an icon to save desktop space.

HELP FUNCTIONS

The Help application supplies built-in tools that allow you to access information easily. Figure 4-5 shows Help's standard window controls, menu bar, and a row of function buttons. Five function buttons are available. These buttons—Contents, Search, Back, History, and Glossary—will move you around the available Help topics or provide definitions of Windows terminology. For some lengthy topics, you might also see two Browse buttons (backward and forward, indicated by double chevrons pointing in the appropriate direction, << and >>).

As you navigate through the Help information using the function buttons, you'll notice an occasional green keyword with a dotted underline in the text. If you move the mouse pointer to the green keyword, the arrow will turn into a hand pointer. When you click on the keyword, Help will display a glossary definition for that term. For example, if you want to know the definition of the term *scroll bar* in the Window Menu Commands section of Help (a Program Manager Help topic), move the pointer to the keyword *scroll bar* and click the mouse button. Help will then display a box containing the definition, as shown in Figure 4-6. Click the mouse button again to close the definition box. To display a definition with the keyboard, press [Tab] to highlight the term, and press the [Enter] key. Press [Enter] again to close the definition box.

Figure 4-5

*The Help window
provides five
function buttons.*

Figure 4-6

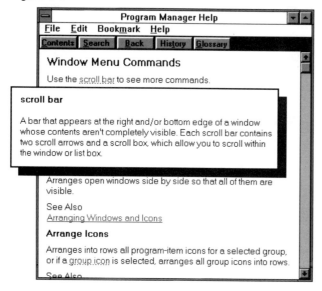

*Help defines
keywords when
you click on them.*

The Contents button takes you to the list of general categories in Help. The listed topics are green and underlined with a solid underline to indicate that you can click on them to display related information. With the keyboard, press [Tab] to highlight a topic, and then press [Enter] to display related information. Help organizes the topics within each category. When there are many topics, you may need to use the scroll bar to see them all.

If you move the pointer over one of the green underlined topics, the pointer will change from an arrow into a hand pointer. The change in the pointer is another clue that Help offers more information about that topic. For example, if you want to know more about the Program Manager's File menu commands, move the pointer to the File Menu Commands topic in the Contents for Program Manager Help window and select that topic.

**Using the
Contents button**

When you select the Search button (or press [Alt]S) in a Help window, Help displays the Search dialog box, shown in Figure 4-7 on the next page. (You can also produce this dialog box by choosing Search for Help On from the application's Help menu.) The Search dialog box makes it easy to locate Help information on specific topics. For your search text, decide on a word or phrase that

**Using the
Search button**

describes the information you want. As you type the search text in the text box (in either uppercase or lowercase letters), Help will automatically highlight in the list box the topic alphabetically closest to your entry. Or, instead of typing in your own search text, you can click on one of the keywords or keyword phrases from the list box to have it appear in the text box as the search text.

After you have entered your search text, click on the Show Topics button. Windows will find the information and will display the related topics in the lower list box, as shown in Figure 4-8. In this list box, highlight the topic you want to see, and select the Go To button to display the information. In some cases, topics with similar names might not yield the results you want, so you might need a bit of persistence.

Figure 4-7

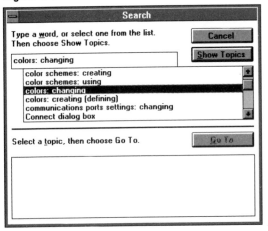

The Search dialog box finds words or phrases, whether you enter the search text in uppercase or lowercase letters.

Figure 4-8

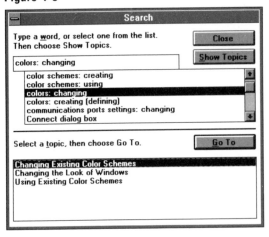

In the lower list box, the Search dialog box displays topics related to the search text.

The first time you choose Help in your Windows session, the Back button is inactive. But once Help advances to a new screen, the Back button becomes available in the Help window.

When you click on the Back button (or press [Alt]B), Help takes you to the previous screen and will backtrack through the topics in reverse order of how you originally chose them. Each time you select Back, the preceding Help screen is displayed. When you return to the category from which you started Help, the Back button will again become inactive. Obviously, this can be a handy tool for quick referral to earlier information.

Using the Back button

As you view topics in Help, Help builds a list of all the Help topics you have seen in that Windows session. When you click on the History button (or press [Alt]T), Help produces a window that displays the list of topics you've seen; an example is shown in Figure 4-9. The History window lists both the applications and the specific topics you've seen. To return to one of the Help topics listed in the History window, double-click on the topic or highlight it with the arrow keys and press the [Enter] key. Note that the History window does not list the program name for the active Help file.

Using the History button

Figure 4-9

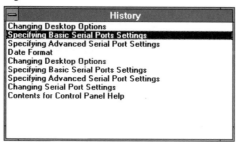

The History window lists all the Help topics you have seen in the current Windows session.

Besides clicking on keywords in Help text, you can also find definitions of Windows terminology by using the Glossary button. To see the definition of a term used in a program, click on the Glossary button (or press [Alt]G) to display the Glossary window, shown in Figure 4-10 on the next page. You can use the scroll bar or the arrow keys to scroll through the alphabetical list of terms in the Windows Help Glossary until you find the term you want. The mouse pointer will change from an arrow to a hand pointer when you move it to a term—try

Using the Glossary button

check box, for example. When you click on the term (or use the [Tab] key to move the highlight to the term and then press [Enter]), Help will display a box containing the term's glossary definition, which may also include a small illustration or a visual example. Click the mouse button again or press [Enter] to close the definition box. To close the Glossary window, double-click on the Control menu box or press [Alt]F4.

Figure 4-10

When you click on a term listed in the Windows Help Glossary, Help displays its definition.

Using the Browse buttons

In some applications, you can browse forward or backward through a series of Help categories. To browse forward through successive categories, click on the Browse forward button (>>) or, with the keyboard, press [Alt]>. Help will display the topics for each category as you repeatedly click on the >> button and move forward in the Help file. You can click on << or press [Alt]< to go back through the categories and return to the beginning.

To browse through Help topics within a category, you must click on one of the category's topics before you click on the >> button. That way, you'll start browsing within a category rather than across categories.

GETTING HELP FOR HELP

Windows provides help for all applications, including Help itself. When you choose How to Use Help from the Help menu or press [F1] while in a Help window, a window called Contents for How to Use Help, shown in Figure 4-11, will appear. You will see listings for such topics as Help Basics, How to Annotate a Help Topic, How to Define and Use Bookmarks, and How to Move Around in Help. To return to the original Help screen for the application in which you've been working, choose the Back button.

Figure 4-11

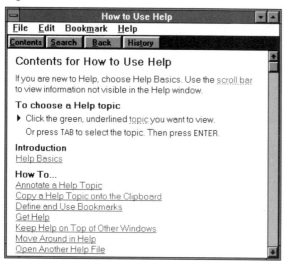

When getting help for Help, you can refer to this window.

In most applications, you probably won't use the About command on the Help menu. The About dialog box that appears when you issue this command provides information you usually don't need—the application's name, version number, copyright date, and, occasionally, the name of the contributing programmer. However, many of the Windows 3.1 About dialog boxes do contain some additional and potentially very useful pieces of information: the amount of unused RAM and the percentage of free system resources. You'll find this information helpful when you're trying to diagnose problems in which memory is a factor. These dialog boxes also display the user name and the company name you entered during setup as well as the serial number of the Windows package you installed.

Using the About command

Help's advanced features include the ability to open Help topics for applications other than the one you're currently using, to keep a Help window open on top of other windows, and to transfer Help topics to a word processor, like Notepad. You can also define bookmarks and customize Help to add or find information within a Help topic.

ADVANCED FEATURES

From the File menu of your Help application, you can open Help files for other applications. For instance, suppose you're working in Write and need to know how to paste a Paintbrush file into your Write document. When you select the Open command from the File menu in Write's Help, the Open dialog box

Opening other Help files

shown in Figure 4-12 will display all available Help files in the File Name list box. All Help files have a .HLP extension. If the file you need isn't listed, you can look in other subdirectories of your hard disk by selecting one of the directories listed in the Directories list box, or you can switch to a different drive by using the Drives drop-down list box.

Figure 4-12

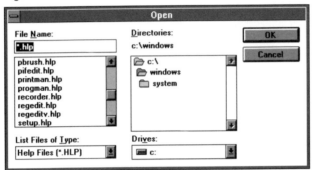

The Open dialog box displays the available Help files.

To select the Paintbrush application's Help file, either double-click on the file name (PBRUSH.HLP) from the File Name list box or type the name in the File Name text box and select OK. The Help title bar will change to *Paintbrush Help.* When the new file appears on the screen, notice that the Back button is active. Windows 3.1 will allow you to retrace your steps between files.

Using Help information in other applications

If you are using Help to learn a new technique in one of your Windows applications, you can have the open Help window remain on top of any other windows, with all its information easily accessible, even when you switch to another application. Just choose the Always on Top command from the Help menu in the Help window. A check mark will appear next to the command name to indicate that the feature is turned on. To turn it off, simply choose the command again.

You can also use the Copy command on Help's Edit menu to copy Help information to another document. For instance, to copy a Help topic to a Notepad document, first select the topic from the Help window and select Copy from the Edit menu. Then select the text you want to copy in the Copy dialog box, shown in Figure 4-13, and click on the Copy button. If you don't select any text, Help copies the entire topic and stores it in Clipboard. Exit Help by choosing the Exit command from Help's File menu. To complete the copy, double-click on the Notepad icon in the Accessories group window. Then select Paste from the Edit menu to place the topic in the new Notepad file. If both a

Notepad file and a Help window are already on the desktop, you can save a few steps. After you have selected and copied the Help topic, click on the Notepad window to make it active, and then use the Paste command. Now return to Help by clicking on the Help window, and you are ready to look at the next topic.

Figure 4-13

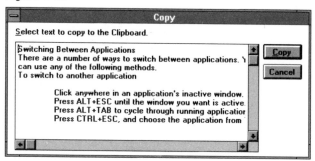

You can copy entire Help topics or selected text into other applications.

A bookmark in Windows serves the same purpose as an actual bookmark— it lets you quickly return to a specific location. The Bookmark menu in Help lets you define shortcuts to a Help topic. Instead of threading through two or three levels to find a related topic, you can simply use a bookmark to return to the topic. For example, if you are working in Notepad and find that you frequently look up the Create Time-Log Documents topic, you could set up a bookmark for that topic instead of looking through the Contents to choose it.

Defining bookmarks

Defining a bookmark is very simple. From within Help, select and display the topic on which you want to place a bookmark, and then choose Define from the Bookmark menu. When you do this, the Bookmark Define dialog box, shown in Figure 4-14, will appear. Help automatically accommodates as much of the topic name in the Bookmark Name text box as it can. You can edit the name if it is cryptic or too long. (You will want to be able to identify it easily, especially if your list of bookmarks contains more than a few names.)

Figure 4-14

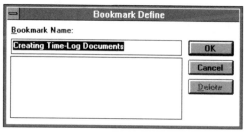

The Bookmark Define dialog box lets you type a name to be added to the Bookmark menu.

When you're satisfied with the name, click on OK to add it to the list of bookmarks at the bottom of the Bookmark menu. Help adds a number next to each bookmark for quick keyboard access. It will also truncate the bookmark's name if necessary to fit it on the Bookmark menu. To return to a topic that you've marked with a bookmark, open the Bookmark menu and click on the defined bookmark name (or type the number that's next to the bookmark). When you do, Help will display your topic.

If you no longer need a particular bookmark, you can delete it. To do this, open Help for the program in which you defined the bookmark, and select the Define command from the Bookmark menu to activate the Bookmark Define dialog box. Select the bookmark you no longer need from the list of bookmarks below the Bookmark Name text box, and click on the Delete button. Then click on OK to return to the Help topic.

Customizing Help with Annotate

You can make Help a little less generic by customizing it with the Annotate command on the Edit menu. You can add a note to a selected topic to relate the command or function to specific tasks that you need to accomplish. For example, if you want a reminder that you can use the Paste command to paste weather reports in a newsletter you've created, all you have to do is display the pertinent Help information and then select Annotate from the Edit menu. As you can see in Figure 4-15, the Annotate dialog box contains a large text box with a scroll bar. You can begin typing the desired text into this text box. As you type, Help will automatically wrap your text onto subsequent lines. If you want to force a line break before the end of a line, press [Enter]. After you finish typing, click on Save to have Help add your note to the topic. You can have only one annotation for each Help topic.

Figure 4-15

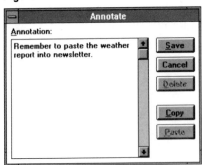

The Annotate dialog box includes a large text box in which you can type a note.

You can determine whether a topic contains an attached note by looking for the Paper Clip icon. In the Help window, the Paper Clip icon will appear at the top-left corner of the topic, as shown in Figure 4-16. The pointer will turn into a hand pointer when you move it over the icon, letting you click on the icon and open the note.

Figure 4-16

The Paper Clip icon reminds you that a note is attached to a particular Help topic.

If you want to add the same annotation to several topics, select the topic that currently has the annotation attached to it. Choose the Annotate command from the Edit menu or click on the Paper Clip icon, click on the Copy button in the Annotate dialog box, and then click on the Cancel button. Now move to the topic that should share the copied annotation. Choose the Annotate command from the Edit menu, click on the Paste button in the Annotate dialog box, and then click on the Save button.

While you're using Help to learn a new technique, you can print the accompanying Help topic so that you don't have to keep Help open while you work. Printing a topic is a two-stage process. First you need to set up your printer, and then you need to issue the Print Topic command.

PRINTING

**Setting up
the printer**

To prepare to print a Help topic, you must make sure you have set up the printer correctly. If you're not sure about your printer setup, the Print Setup command on the File menu allows you to make adjustments to most of the printer's settings. The Print Setup dialog box, shown in Figure 4-17, displays a default printer and a list of other available printers. Just click on the printer you want to use, and then click on OK. If you need to change the orientation, the paper size, or the paper source, change those settings before you click on OK. (If you need more information about printer settings, see Chapter 3.) When you click on OK, you'll return to the Help window.

Figure 4-17

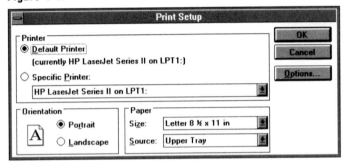

*The Print Setup dialog box allows you to select a printer from
a list of installed printers.*

Printing a topic

After the printer is set up, you can print a chosen Help topic by displaying it and then selecting Print Topic from the File menu. A Help message box like the one shown in Figure 4-18 notifies you that the topic is printing. If you change your mind and want to cancel the Print Topic command, simply click on the Cancel button in the dialog box or press the [Esc] key.

If your printed topic is misaligned or doesn't look like the topic on your screen, it's because your printer font isn't the same font that Help uses. When Help prints, it will use the fonts in your printer that are similar to the ones it was set up to use. Optimally, Help uses the Microsoft 1A font cartridge for an HP LaserJet. If you have this font cartridge and printer installed, what you see on a maximized window will be exactly what you see when Help prints the topic.

Figure 4-18

*A Help message box notifies you that
the topic is printing and allows you
to click on Cancel to stop printing.*

To exit Help, choose the Exit command from the File menu. This command closes any open Help files and returns you to the point at which you started Help. For instance, suppose you started Help from Windows' Notepad application, where you were working on a document about weather reports. When you exit Help, you will return to the place where you were last working in your weather report document.

EXITING HELP

In this chapter

Program Manager 5

The Program Manager lets you use Windows to find the right application for your job. Like the display windows of a department store, each window of the Program Manager colorfully presents the available applications. If one window doesn't have what you need, the next one probably will.

The Program Manager's series of internal windows (group windows) organizes all the application icons. Each icon is a colorful graphic with a title to remind you of the application it represents. All you need to do is double-click on the icon whose application you want to use, and the Program Manager opens the application for you.

Just as you can customize store windows, you can customize application icons and their group windows. In this chapter, we'll show you how to manipulate icons and their windows as we focus on how to move, add, delete, and edit them. You'll also learn about representing documents as icons.

You don't need to click on an icon to open the Program Manager; when you begin a new Windows session, the Program Manager appears automatically. To start Windows, type *WIN* at the MS-DOS prompt (C:\>) and press the [Enter] key. (Chapter 1 explains more about starting Windows.) The first window you see is called the Program Manager.

The Program Manager is not a typical window. As you can see in Figure 5-1 on the next page, the Program Manager consists of a window framing a series of smaller windows. The Program Manager window is a shell, which is a variation of an application window. The smaller windows, called group windows, are variations of document windows.

THE PROGRAM MANAGER

Starting the Program Manager

Figure 5-1

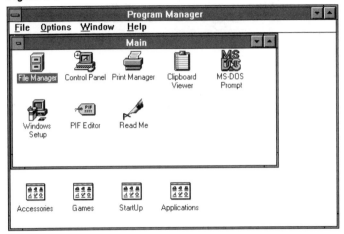

*Here the Program Manager displays its Main group window
and a series of minimized group windows.*

Group windows organize the application icons that the Program Manager
launches. Just because Windows automatically puts the icons in certain groups
doesn't mean they have to stay there. You can move the icons between the
groups to sort them in any order you want. You can add applications to the
groups by adding their icons, and you can also delete those icons later on. You
can edit group window titles and the titles that appear with the icons. And you
can even convert a document into a launchable icon.

When you minimize a group window by clicking on the Minimize box in its
upper-right corner, the group window will turn into an icon, just as an application window does. The Program Manager will place the icon at the bottom of its
window. To restore the group window to its previous size, simply double-click
on its icon.

Minimizing group windows is a handy feature for keeping your desktop
uncluttered. For example, if you seldom use the Main group window, you can
minimize it and keep other group windows open for easy access to the applications they contain.

**Minimizing the
Program Manager**

When you minimize the Program Manager, Windows will convert it into an
icon and place it at the bottom of the desktop. There's even a way to set up
Windows so that the Program Manager is minimized into an icon for easy access
every time you start an application. We'll talk about that later in this chapter.

As you work with the Program Manager, you'll need to move among its elements—such as menus, group windows, and icons—in order to use their functions. For example, if you want to start an application, you need to move to a group window. If you want to use the Program Manager's commands, you need to access the menus on the menu bar. Although you can access group windows and menus with either the mouse or the keyboard, navigating in the Program Manager is easiest when you use a mouse.

NAVIGATION

If you want to use a group window, click inside the window or double-click on its icon. When you do, the group window will become active and move to the front of the stack so that you can open the applications you need.

Mouse navigation

To use the Program Manager's menus, you can click on a menu name to access the drop-down list of commands. You can also drag down the menu to quickly choose a command. To open the Program Manager's Control menu (the box in the upper-left corner), simply click on it. Be careful not to double-click, because doing so will produce an Exit Windows dialog box that can close the window and end your Windows session. (Select the Cancel button in this dialog box if you don't want to leave Windows.) Group windows also have Control menus that you can open by clicking on them.

You can accomplish the same tasks (access the Program Manager menu bar, move between group windows, and open the Control menu) with the keyboard. You access the menu bar with the keyboard the same way you do in any other application—by pressing [Alt] and the underlined letter of the menu name. For example, to open the File menu, you press [Alt]F; F is the underlined letter. Once the drop-down list of commands is open, you can use the arrow keys to move the highlight to the command you need and then press [Enter] to issue the command. Or, when a menu is open, you can instead simply press the key for the underlined letter in the command name.

Keyboard navigation

To move between group windows with the keyboard, you can use the Window menu. When you press [Alt]W to drop down the Window menu, you will see a numbered list of the group windows in the Program Manager window. Type the number of the group window you want to use. When you choose a number, the group window will become active. The next time you open the Window menu, a check mark will appear on the menu next to the number of the active group window. You can also use the keyboard shortcuts [Ctrl][Tab] or [Ctrl][F6] to move between group windows.

To open the Program Manager's Control menu with the keyboard, press [Alt][Spacebar]; to close it, press [Alt]. To open the active group window's Control menu, you need to use a different key combination, [Alt]- (hyphen).

MANIPULATING ICONS

Icons are the most important part of the Program Manager because they allow you to start your applications. As its name implies, the Program Manager controls how applications or programs are started and how their icons are organized on your desktop. The Program Manager also allows you to add or delete application icons from the various groups, to edit the icon titles, and to change icon graphics. You can even control the way an application starts.

Starting applications

You can use several methods to start an application. With the mouse, you can click on an icon to select it and then choose the Open command from the File menu. Or you can simply double-click on the icon. If you're using the keyboard, you need to highlight the correct icon with the arrow keys or by pressing the initial letter of the icon title. (If several icon titles begin with the same letter, continue pressing the letter until the highlight reaches the icon you want to select.) Then simply press [Enter], or press [Alt]F to access the File menu and press O to issue the Open command. As you can see, double-clicking is easier and quicker. You can also drag an application's icon to the StartUp group to have the application start automatically when you start Windows.

Minimizing the Program Manager automatically

If you often return to the Program Manager to start other applications during your Windows session, you'll want to select the Minimize on Use option, which turns the Program Manager into an icon whenever you start an application. To turn this option on, choose the Minimize on Use command from the Options menu. A check mark will appear next to the command, indicating that the option is turned on. Now, every time you start an application, Windows will automatically minimize the Program Manager and place its icon at the bottom of the desktop. If you keep all the application windows sized so that the lower portion of the desktop is visible, you will be able to return to the Program Manager by double-clicking on its icon.

Moving application icons

You can reorganize your application icons simply by dragging them to different windows. For example, if you add a new group window, you can put your favorite applications, such as Word for Windows and ToolBook, in it. To do this, click on the Applications group window, and then drag the icon that represents Word for Windows to the new group window. Release the mouse button to finish placing the icon. Next, drag the ToolBook icon to the new group window. If you try to place an icon outside a group window, the pointer will change into a circle with a slash through it (the prevent pointer). The slashed circle means that the action you attempted is prohibited.

To reorganize icons with the keyboard, you need to use the Move command on the File menu to move them from one group window to another. To move an icon, use the arrow keys or press the initial letter of the icon title to highlight the icon, and then choose the Move command. When you do this, a Move Program

Item dialog box, like the one shown in Figure 5-2, will appear. The dialog box displays the program item name, the source group window, and a drop-down list box containing the available destinations. Press [Alt]↓ to drop down the list box. Then use the arrow keys to select the group window to which you want to move the icon, and press [Enter].

Figure 5-2

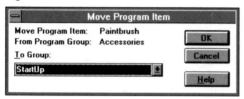

The Move Program Item dialog box lets you move icons between group windows.

Copying icons

Suppose you have an application, such as Paintbrush, that you customize for a specific job. If you have multiple copies of Paintbrush, each uniquely customized, you can place a separate Paintbrush icon on the desktop for each customized version. To make a copy of an icon with the mouse, hold down the [Ctrl] key as you drag the icon to another window or drag it to a new position in the same group window. The Program Manager will then create an identical Paintbrush icon. You can edit the new icon to change the path, the startup command, or the title so that it matches your customized version of Paintbrush. (Later, we'll show you how to use the Properties command to change an icon's startup command and title.)

To copy an icon with the keyboard, you need to use the Copy command on the File menu. Highlight the icon you want to copy, press [Alt]F to open the File menu, and then press *C* to issue the Copy command. A Copy Program Item dialog box, like the one shown in Figure 5-3, will appear. The dialog box displays the name of the icon to be copied and its current group window location. Press [Alt]↓ to open the To Group drop-down list box, and highlight the name of the group window in which you want to place a copy of the icon. Then press [Enter] to close the dialog box and have Windows immediately issue the command. The destination group window will become active as the Program Manager adds the copied icon.

Figure 5-3

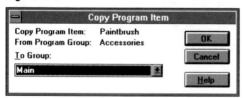

The Copy Program Item dialog box lets you copy icons from one group window to another.

**Adding
applications**

You can add installed applications at any time by using the Windows Setup application or the Program Manager. In Chapter 3, we showed you how the Windows Setup application works. Now, we'll show you how to add an application with the Program Manager.

First, of course, you must install the application on your hard disk according to the application's documentation. Then, before you can add the application to the Program Manager, you need to know which group you want to add it to, what you're going to name the icon, and which directory contains the application's program files so that you can find its startup command. When you have this information, click on the group window to which the icon should be added. Next, choose the New command from the File menu. When the New Program Object dialog box appears, just click on OK. You don't have to select anything because Program Item, the option that lets you add an icon, is the default and is already selected, as shown in Figure 5-4.

Figure 5-4

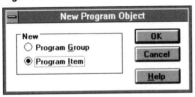

*The New Program Object dialog
box provides an option for adding
items to a group window.*

After you click on OK in the New Program Object dialog box, the Program Item Properties dialog box appears, as shown in Figure 5-5. In this dialog box, enter the title for the icon in the Description text box. Then enter the startup command (the application's executable file name, including the drive, path, and file name extension) in the Command Line text box. (We'll explain the rest of the dialog box in a moment.)

Figure 5-5

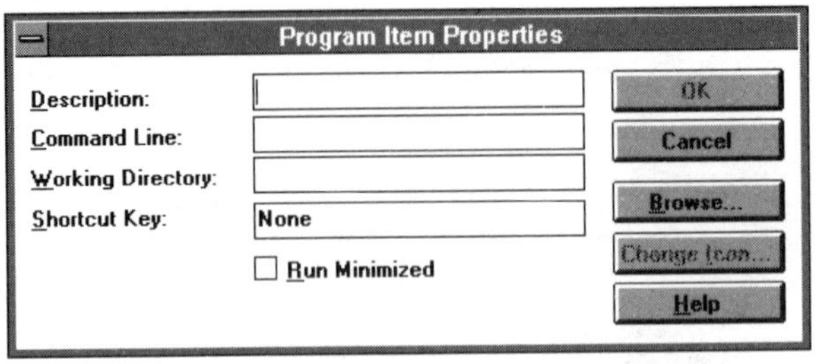

Program Item Properties
Description:
Command Line:
Working Directory:
Shortcut Key: None
☐ Run Minimized
OK · Cancel · Browse... · Change Icon... · Help

*The Program Item Properties dialog box lets you name
an icon and specify the application's startup command.*

If you need help locating the path and the startup command for the application, the Program Manager will help when you click on the Browse button. After you click on this button, you'll see a list of available program files in the Browse dialog box, shown in Figure 5-6. (By default, Windows will search for files with the .EXE, .PIF, .COM, and .BAT file name extensions.) Table 5-1 on the following page lists the Windows program files and the applications to which they belong. You can either enter the file name in the File Name text box or click on a file in the File Name list box. If you need to look in a different directory, use the Directories list box to change directories. If you need to look in a different drive, choose the new drive in the Drives drop-down list box. After you find the file and select it, click on OK to continue.

Figure 5-6

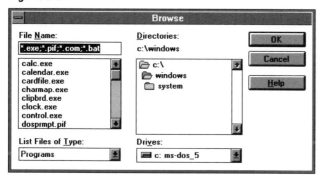

This Browse dialog box helps you find the right program file for the application.

After you click on OK in the Browse dialog box, the Program Manager will return you to the Program Item Properties dialog box (Figure 5-5) so that you can finish entering any parameters or options for your application's startup command in the Command Line text box. A parameter is any character or combination of characters that modifies how a program application runs. You can find these parameters in your application documentation. For example, with Windows, you type /3 after the word *WIN* to start Windows in 386 enhanced mode. Be sure to type a space between the file name and the parameters; otherwise, Windows will interpret the parameters as part of the file name. If you add the full path name to the Command Line text box, the Program Manager will start the program from the directory shown in this text box. This feature is especially important for programs that look for additional files in the current directory.

In the Working Directory text box of the Program Item Properties dialog box, type the path name for the directory where you usually save documents for this application. Whenever you start the application, it will use this directory as its default directory for opening and saving documents.

Table 5-1

Program File	Application
CALC.EXE	Calculator
CALENDAR.EXE	Calendar
CARDFILE.EXE	Cardfile
CHARMAP.EXE	Character Map
CLIPBRD.EXE	Clipboard Viewer
CLOCK.EXE	Clock
CONTROL.EXE	Control Panel
MPLAYER.EXE	Media Player
NOTEPAD.EXE	Notepad
PACKAGER.EXE	Object Packager
PBRUSH.EXE	Paintbrush
PIFEDIT.EXE	PIF Editor
PRINTMAN.EXE	Print Manager
PROGMAN.EXE	Program Manager
RECORDER.EXE	Recorder
SETUP.EXE	Windows Setup
SOL.EXE	Solitaire
SOUNDREC.EXE	Sound Recorder
TASKMAN.EXE	Task Manager
TERMINAL.EXE	Terminal
WINFILE.EXE	File Manager
WINHELP.EXE	Help
WINMINE.EXE	Minesweeper
WINTUTOR.EXE	Windows Tutorial
WINVER.EXE	About commands
WRITE.EXE	Write

Each Windows application has a program file.

In the Shortcut Key text box of the Program Item Properties dialog box, you can enter a key combination that will let you quickly start or switch to this application. For example, to be able to start or switch to Write with the shortcut key combination [Alt][Ctrl]W, type *W* in the Shortcut Key text box; Windows will display the text string *Ctrl + Alt + W*. Unless the current application uses this key combination within itself, pressing [Alt][Ctrl]W will now start Write.

The Run Minimized check box tells Windows to start the application as an icon. This setting can be especially important for programs you have added to the StartUp group. If this check box is turned on for a program in the StartUp group, Windows automatically starts the application as an icon when you start your Windows session.

Finally, you're ready to click on OK in this dialog box and add the application to the group window. (For an alternative way to add new program items with the mouse, refer to "Copying directories and files" in Chapter 6.)

If the application doesn't have an icon designed for it by the software company, Windows uses an MS-DOS icon resembling the one shown in Figure 5-7. For instance, applications that weren't designed for Windows won't have their own icons. If you'd rather use a different icon, you can easily change the icon assigned to an application, as we'll explain later.

Figure 5-7

Windows uses this MS-DOS icon as a default when an application doesn't come with its own icon.

Deleting application icons

You can delete an icon from the Program Manager if you no longer need an application or don't use it often. Deleting an icon doesn't mean that you delete the application; it's just a form of housekeeping to remove clutter from your desktop. You can use the application without the icon (as we'll show you later in this chapter). To delete an icon, select it and then either choose the Delete command from the File menu or press [Delete]. Windows will display a dialog box like the one shown in Figure 5-8, asking you to verify the deletion.

Figure 5-8

This dialog box asks you to verify that you want to delete an icon from a group window.

Editing icon properties

If an icon doesn't start an application the way you want it to, or if its title is wrong, don't worry. You can always modify an icon's startup command, its title, its working directory, or its shortcut key by using the Properties command on the File menu. When you select an icon and choose this command, the Program Item Properties dialog box will appear with the current information displayed. For example, when you highlight the Write icon, the Program Item Properties dialog box displays *Write* as the icon title (in the Description text box) and WRITE.EXE as the program file name, as you can see in Figure 5-9. When you upgrade application software, you'll often have to change the icon's properties. For instance, if you put the version number in the icon title, you'll need to edit it. You can edit or replace information as needed in the dialog box. When you're satisfied with your changes, click on the OK button, and the Program Manager will put those changes in place.

Figure 5-9

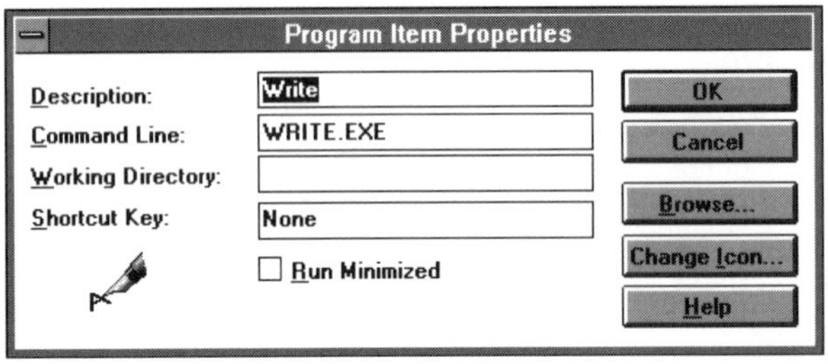

You can use the Program Item Properties dialog box to edit icon properties.

Changing icon graphics

If you add a DOS-based application to a group window and want to change the icon graphic to something other than the default MS-DOS graphic, you can use the Properties command to switch to another graphic. For example, if you are using a spreadsheet program that doesn't have a predefined Windows icon, you can choose a graphic that represents a spreadsheet to replace the MS-DOS graphic.

To change a graphic, first click on the icon that you want to modify. Next, choose the Properties command from the File menu. When the Program Item Properties dialog box appears, choose the Change Icon button to display the Change Icon dialog box. (For some applications, Windows will first display a dialog box telling you that the application has no available icons and that you can choose one of the Program Manager's built-in icons. Choose OK in this dialog box to produce the Change Icon dialog box.) In the Change Icon dialog box, the current graphic will be highlighted in the horizontal scroll list, as shown in Figure 5-10. If you click on the scroll arrows (or press the right or left arrow key), Windows will scroll through a series of graphics. When the graphic you want to use appears highlighted in the dialog box, click on OK to return to the Program Item Properties dialog box. When you click on OK in the Program Item Properties dialog box, Windows will swap the icon graphics.

Figure 5-10

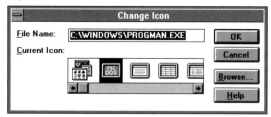

The Change Icon dialog box allows you to change icon graphics.

For a wider selection of icons, you can click on the Browse button in the Change Icon dialog box to display the dialog box shown in Figure 5-11. In this dialog box, you can select a different icon file to open. Click on OK to return to the Change Icon dialog box, and then select a new icon graphic from the new list shown in the horizontal scroll list. You might be especially interested in the file MORICONS.DLL, which contains more than 100 icons, many of them designed to represent popular programs.

Figure 5-11

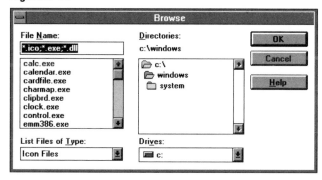

In this Browse dialog box, you can select a different icon file to open.

MANIPULATING GROUP WINDOWS

Group windows operate very much the same way that application windows do, except that they allow you to customize Windows. In this section, we'll show you how to manipulate group windows, and then we'll cover the more complex process of adding new groups, deleting old groups, and editing their properties. The basic operations include moving, resizing, and displaying group windows and arranging their icons. You can move and resize group windows in the same way you move and resize document windows.

Moving and resizing group windows

To move a group window, you can drag its title bar to a new location. Alternatively, you can press [Alt]- (hyphen) to access the active group window's Control menu, and then press *M* to use the Move command. Resizing is just as easy. Simply drag the group window's frame to a new size. Keyboard users can take the Control menu route and use the Size command and the arrow keys to resize the group window. (Refer to Chapter 2 for more detailed information on moving and resizing windows.)

Whenever you move or resize a group window, you must remain within the boundary of the Program Manager window. If you try to move the group window outside this boundary, scroll bars will appear on the Program Manager window to let you pull the group window back into view in the work area. If you want to avoid using the scroll bars, resize the group windows so that they will fit into the workspace.

Displaying group windows

There are two ways to automatically arrange open group windows to fit in the Program Manager's workspace: by cascading or by tiling. You can also realign the icons in a group window. The Program Manager provides Cascade, Tile, and Arrange Icons commands on the Window menu to let you rearrange the group windows and their icons.

Cascading group windows

To cascade the group windows as a stack with the title bars visible, as shown in Figure 5-12, click on the Cascade command on the Window menu or press [Shift][F5] to resize all the group windows and reposition them. By default, the Program Manager automatically cascades the group windows when you start Windows for the first time. The active group window appears in the front of the stack. If you click on one of the title bars in the stack, that window will become active and appear in front of the others. To view all the title bars again, you must reissue the Cascade command.

Figure 5-12

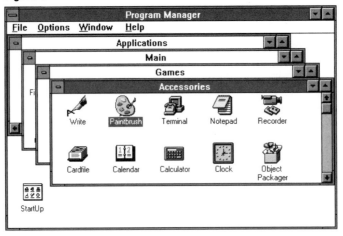

The Cascade command stacks the group windows so that the title bars show.

If you have more than a few open group windows, or if you have reduced the size of the Program Manager window, rearranging the windows will create layers. For example, suppose you cascade five group windows into a small Program Manager window like the one shown in Figure 5-13. After four levels, the remaining group window will be stacked in the upper-left corner over the other windows, beginning a second layer.

Figure 5-13

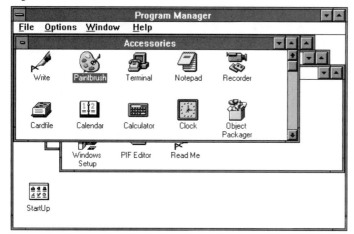

If the Program Manager window is too small, cascaded windows will begin layering.

Tiling group windows

When you want to see more of open group windows than their title bars, you can tile the windows. The Tile command ([Shift][F4]) on the Window menu divides the workspace among the different group windows, as shown in Figure 5-14 on the next page. The Tile command places the active group window in the upper-left corner when it rearranges the groups. When you click on another group window to make it active, its title bar will become highlighted, but its position will not change.

Tiled windows can overlap but only in conditions more cramped than those in which cascaded windows will overlap. After you open several group windows, it's better to tile them, because cascading will create covering layers and prevent you from viewing all the group windows.

Windows that have been minimized to icons are not affected by the Tile or the Cascade command. If you minimize some windows from a tiled Program Manager frame, cascade the remaining windows, and then maximize the icons, the screen will display tiled windows on top of cascaded windows.

Figure 5-14

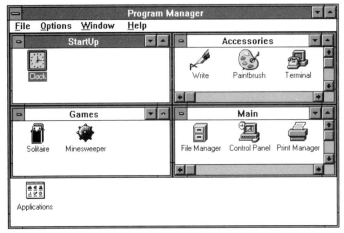

The Tile command divides the workspace among the open group windows.

Arranging icons in group windows

After you tile the windows, you'll probably want to rearrange the icons for easier access. You can make the icons in the active window more accessible by using the Arrange Icons command from the Window menu. For example, in Figure 5-15, four open windows were tiled. Before we tiled the windows, the icons in the Main group window were arranged in two rows; after we tiled the windows, we could view all the icons in this smaller, tiled window only by using both the horizontal and vertical scroll bars. But when we issued the Arrange Icons command, the Program Manager organized the icons into three columns, a configuration that better fits the shape of the window. As you can see in Figure 5-16, you would now need only one scroll bar to access all the icons. This rearrangement results in less work for you, and it also conserves space, because Windows removes the unneeded scroll bar.

Instead of selecting each group window and choosing the Arrange Icons command for each one, you can turn on the Auto Arrange option by choosing the Auto Arrange command on the Options menu. When Auto Arrange is active (a check mark will appear beside the command name the next time you open the menu), the Program Manager will rearrange the icons as it repaints the screen every time you use the Cascade command or the Tile command. If you maximize a tiled group window when the Auto Arrange option is active, the Program Manager will rearrange the icons to fill the horizontal dimension of the maximized window.

Figure 5-15

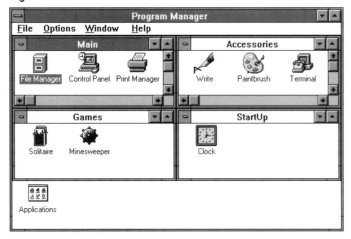

After we rearrange the windows with the Tile command,
the icons are still configured for a larger window.

Figure 5-16

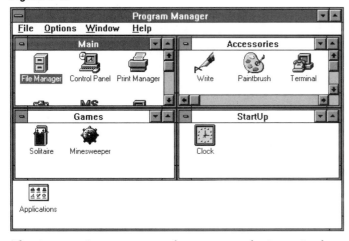

The Arrange Icons command rearranges the icons in the
active tiled window.

Windows allows you to customize the Program Manager by adding group windows. For example, if you use the applications Word for Windows and ToolBook exclusively, you'll want to add a group window that contains only those two application icons. Then, when you start Windows, you will immediately be able to use both applications.

Adding group windows

To add a group window, select the New command from the File menu. When Windows displays the New Program Object dialog box shown in Figure 5-17, choose the Program Group radio button and click on OK. The Program Manager will then bring up a Program Group Properties dialog box like the one shown in Figure 5-18. Enter the title for the new group window in the Description text box. You can enter a file name in the Group File text box, or you can leave it blank and let Windows name the file for you. If you assign the file name, you must limit the name to eight characters and use a .GRP extension. When you click on OK to add the group window, the Program Manager will place the new group window.

Figure 5-17

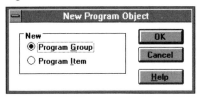

The New Program Object dialog box lets you customize the Program Manager with new group windows.

Figure 5-18

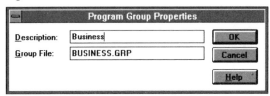

The Program Group Properties dialog box lets you name a new group window.

Let's go through the steps necessary to add a group window called *Business* to the Program Manager:

- Choose the New command from the File menu.

- Choose the Program Group radio button from the New Program Object dialog box and click on OK.

- Enter the title *Business* in the Description text box of the Program Group Properties dialog box.

- Leave the Group File text box blank so that Windows will provide the file name, and click on OK. Windows will name the file BUSINESS.GRP.

- The Program Manager will add the group window.

Deleting group windows is another aspect of customizing the Program Manager. When you reorganize the Program Manager by moving your application icons, you occasionally will empty a group window. If you're not going to use that window, you might as well remove it.

Deleting group windows

You can delete a group window by minimizing the window to an icon, selecting the icon, and then either choosing the Delete command from the File menu or pressing the [Delete] key. Windows will then present a warning message (for example, *Are you sure you want to delete group 'Business'?*) to have you verify that you want to delete the group window.

If you inherit someone else's computer and discover that it contains a lot of bizarre group window titles that you don't want to keep, you can retitle the windows. Before you can change a group window's title, you must minimize the group window to an icon and highlight the icon. Then choose the Properties command from the File menu. The Program Group Properties dialog box will appear, displaying the current information for that particular group. Now you can click on the Description text box and edit the title. You can also change the file name. After you've edited the information in the dialog box, click on the OK button to save and implement the changes.

Editing group properties

So far, you've seen the Program Manager work with application icons. In this section, we'll show you how to use the Run command to start applications that are not represented by icons. The Program Manager can also start an application with a specified document already open. It can even turn a document into an icon and launch it, just as it launches an application icon.

ADVANCED FEATURES

You can launch any application from the Program Manager, even if it doesn't have an icon. For example, if you want to use a program that you don't work with very often (and consequently haven't added to a group window), you can start it with the Run command on the File menu. This command allows you to start an application by giving the Program Manager the details it needs. To begin, select the Run command to display the Run dialog box, shown in Figure 5-19 on the next page.

Using the Run command

When you use the Run command, you'll need to know where the application is stored on your hard disk (in other words, you'll need to know the application's path) and the command that starts the application. For example, if you've installed Microsoft Excel in the directory C:\EXCEL and the command that starts this application is simply EXCEL, you would type *C:\EXCEL\EXCEL* in the Command Line text box in the Run dialog box, as we've done in Figure 5-19, and then click on OK. Immediately, the Program Manager will start Microsoft Excel. When you exit Excel, you'll return to the Program Manager.

Figure 5-19

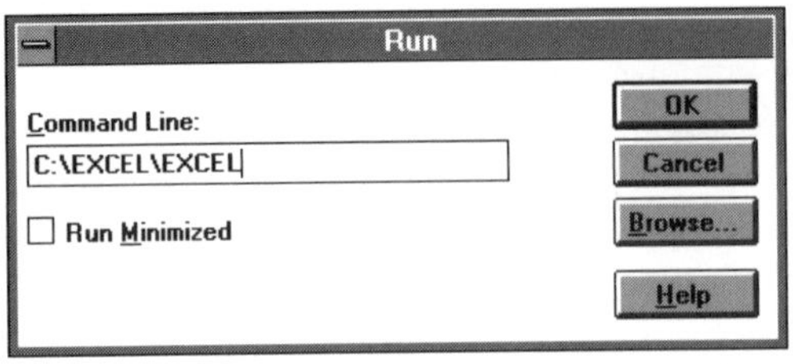

The Run dialog box lets you start applications that aren't represented by icons.

Starting an application as a minimized icon

If you want an application to have a temporary icon for a Windows session, you can use the Run Minimized check box in the Run dialog box. Windows will minimize the application into an icon as soon as it appears on the desktop. This is a good way to add an icon temporarily to the desktop instead of making it a permanent application icon in a group window. To open the application, double-click on the icon. If you exit the application, its icon will not appear on the desktop again. If you want to keep using the application during your Windows session, it's a good idea to minimize the application window before you switch to another program so that you won't lose the icon. If you exit the application and need to recreate the icon, you can reissue the Run command and select Run Minimized again.

Starting an application with a document open

If you use a document frequently, such as a Write memo template or a Microsoft Excel spreadsheet of your combined monthly sales, you can customize Windows to open a document as soon as you start the application. All you need to do is add a space and the document name after the startup command that's already in the Command Line text box in the Run dialog box. That way, every time you start the application, Windows will open that document. (If this doesn't work for you, your application may not have the capability to open a document on startup.)

Setting up a document as an icon

One of the Program Manager's most powerful features is its ability to transform a document into an icon so that you can activate the document from a group window. That way, you can double-click on the icon to start your application and immediately open a document. You can create a separate icon for each document. This will allow you to access a specific document without having to open the application separately first.

To create a document icon, you'll need to modify the properties of an application icon by adding the document name to the end of the entry in the

Command Line text box of the Program Item Properties dialog box and then changing the title in the Description text box. If you're creating a new icon instead of modifying an old one, you'll need to add both the startup command and the document name to the Command Line text box. Application icons have default titles, but you can change the default and enter a unique title for the document icon. After you click on OK, the Program Manager adds the modified icon to the desktop.

For example, if you want to add an existing Write report document to your Business group so that you can use it as a template for other reports, you need to follow these steps:

- Activate the Business group window.

- Choose the New command on the File menu, select Program Item in the New Program Object dialog box, and then click on OK.

- Enter the title of the report—*Monthly Report,* for example—in the Description text box of the Program Item Properties dialog box, as shown in Figure 5-20 on the following page.

- Click on the Command Line text box to make it active, and then click on the Browse button to display the list of Windows file names that can be used as command lines.

- In the Browse dialog box, select the file name WRITE.EXE from the File Name list and click on OK to return to the Program Item Properties dialog box. If necessary, you can use the Directories list box to look in other areas of the active drive for the file you want. To look in a different drive, use the Drives drop-down list box to change drives.

- Click on the right half of the Command Line text box, and type the file name for the Write file you want to open automatically with this icon. Leave a space between the program file name and the document file name. If the document file is not in the same directory as WRITE.EXE, you'll need to provide the drive and path for the document file in the Working Directory text box, as shown in Figure 5-20.

- Finally, click on OK to add the icon to the active group window. The graphic in the new icon will look like the one used in the Write application icon, but the new icon will be titled *Monthly Report* instead of *Write*, as shown in Figure 5-21 on the following page.

Figure 5-20

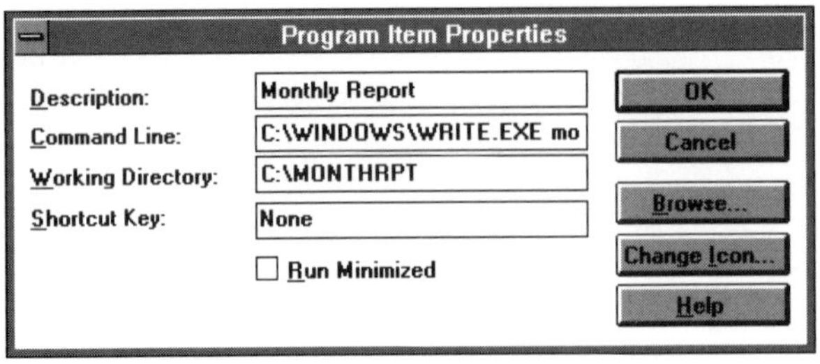

*The Program Item Properties dialog box lets you enter
a customized title, like* Monthly Report, *for an icon.*

Figure 5-21

*The Write graphic and a custom title form the
Monthly Report icon.*

**EXITING THE
PROGRAM
MANAGER AND
WINDOWS**

When you exit the Program Manager, you exit Windows and end your
Windows session. When you are ready to leave Windows, choose the Exit
Windows command from the Program Manager's File menu or double-click on
the Program Manager's Control menu box. Windows will display the Exit Windows dialog box shown in Figure 5-22. When you click on OK, Windows will
return you to the MS-DOS prompt. Click on Cancel if you decide to return to
Windows instead.

Figure 5-22

Exit Windows

This will end your Windows session.

    OK   Cancel

*Choosing OK in the Exit Windows
dialog box returns you to MS-DOS.*

The Program Manager's Options menu contains a Save Settings on Exit command, which is turned on by default. This command instructs Windows to save the sizes and positions of windows and icons and the group file changes. Changes to menus, such as turning off Save Settings on Exit, are saved automatically, regardless of the Save Settings on Exit command's settings. Turn off this command before quitting Windows if you don't want to save the window, icon, and group changes you made in the Program Manager.

In this chapter

File Manager 6

To many personal-computer users, the "basic" tasks of file management can seem complicated: moving a file or a directory, locating an application, browsing through directories and their subdirectories. Now, however, you can use Windows' File Manager to perform all file management tasks. The File Manager uses Windows' graphical user interface to make it all seem easy.

THE FILE MANAGER

The File Manager, like the Program Manager, is a shell that creates a friendly interface that you can use to access MS-DOS capabilities. You can use the File Manager to modify your files and their organization on your hard drive and to launch applications. In a single step, the File Manager lets you move a directory, with all its files and subdirectories, into another directory. You can even use the File Manager to rename your hard drive or a floppy disk. The File Manager can also display more than one directory at a time, making it easy to see how your files are organized.

An important element of the File Manager is the directory tree, a visual representation of a directory system, which you can use to manipulate directories and files on a floppy, hard, or network drive. If you apply the tree analogy, the root directory of a drive is like the trunk of a tree in that it provides a base from which subdirectories branch. Subdirectories are like limbs because they branch outward from the root directory. Files, which are attached to the directories, are like leaves on the tree. Every branch can have its own branches and leaves.

In this chapter, we'll show you how to start the File Manager, set up its work area, manage directories, and manipulate files. Then we will discuss other File

Manager operations, such as changing file attributes, launching documents and applications, and taking care of media maintenance (formatting or copying a floppy disk, for example).

Launching the
File Manager

You launch the File Manager from the Main group window in the Program Manager. To start the File Manager with a mouse, open the Main group window and double-click on the File Manager icon. To start the File Manager with the keyboard, press [Alt]W to access the Window menu, and then type the number for the Main window. Next, use the arrow keys to highlight the File Manager icon, and press [Enter] to activate it.

You can customize Windows to make the File Manager start automatically when you start Windows. To do this, drag the File Manager icon from the Main group window to the StartUp group. If you move the File Manager icon to the StartUp group, the File Manager will automatically be available as the current window the next time you start Windows.

When you are ready to exit the File Manager, either choose the Exit command from the File menu or double-click on the Control menu box.

What you'll see

After you activate the File Manager icon, you will see the File Manager application window, containing a directory window. The initial directory window displayed by the File Manager is divided in two parts, called panes. One, called the directory tree pane, lists the directories in the current drive. The other, called the directory contents pane, lists the current directory's contents—files and subdirectories. Figure 6-1 shows a maximized directory window within the File Manager application window.

At the top of each directory window, the File Manager displays disk drive icons representing the available disk drives or hard-disk volumes. (You can also have icons for network drives, RAM drives, and CD-ROM drives.) Notice that floppy-drive icons look like floppy-drive faceplates and that hard-drive icons look like hard-drive faceplates. RAM drives are given a distinctive faceplate icon, and CD-ROM drives have a specific CD-ROM icon. External floppy drives are typically given a hard-drive icon.

To the right of the disk drive icons, the directory window lists the current disk drive's letter and its name, if it has one (its volume label or network name). The title bar of the File Manager window shows the path to the current directory, along with the *.* file name pattern. The file name pattern is displayed with the directory path because you can specify a file name pattern to limit the types of files that appear in a directory contents pane. Later in this chapter, we'll show you how to use the By File Type command to accomplish this. (In a nonmaximized directory window, the directory path appears in the directory window's title bar. When you maximize a directory window, the directory path appears in the title bar of the File Manager window.)

Figure 6-1

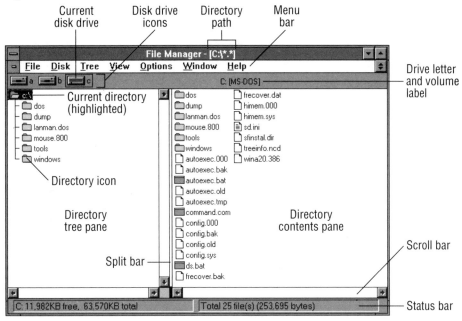

This File Manager application window displays a maximized
. directory window.

The status bar at the bottom of the File Manager application window displays two types of information. To the left, you see drive-specific information: the letter of the current drive, the amount of storage space still available on that drive, and the total storage capacity of the drive. To the right, you see directory-specific information: the total number of files in the current directory and the total size of all those files. This information can be valuable as you work with files. For example, you can use the information in the status bar to determine whether the selected files will fit into the available space on a disk.

Using the directory window

As we mentioned, the directory window displays all the directories on the current drive and all the available disk drives. To display the directory tree for a particular drive, you simply click on that drive's icon. To access the drive icons with your keyboard, press [F6] or [Tab] until the selection frame appears around the currently selected disk drive icon. Then use the arrow keys to position the frame around the drive you want to view. Next, press [Spacebar] to select the icon. Or press [Ctrl] and the key for the drive letter at the same time—for example, press [Ctrl]A to activate drive A. As another alternative, you can choose the Select Drive command on the Disk menu. In the Select Drive dialog box, choose the drive you want in the Drives list box and then choose OK.

The directory tree pane is an interactive work area that presents the directories as icons. Each miniature file folder icon in the tree pane represents an individual directory or subdirectory. The name of each directory appears next to the icon's graphic instead of appearing below the graphic as it does in the Program Manager's icons.

In the tree pane, all the file folder icons at the same level are arranged in alphabetical order for easy access. When you click on a directory icon, the File Manager will display in the adjacent contents pane the files in that directory.

Displaying directories

In the contents pane, you might notice file folder icons representing subdirectories. When you see these icons in the contents pane, you can double-click on the current directory's folder icon in the tree pane to expand the tree, displaying the subdirectories at the level immediately below the current directory. If you click on a subdirectory folder icon in the tree pane, the contents of the subdirectory appear in the contents pane. You can keep double-clicking on the folder icons to expand any further branches. Double-click on a folder icon again to collapse the entire branch of the directory tree descending from that icon. To expand a directory with the keyboard, use the arrow keys to move to the directory icon, and then press + (plus sign). To expand all subdirectories of a directory at once, press * (asterisk).

The File Manager also provides shortcuts that let you expand all the directories in the entire directory tree in a single step. To expand every directory on the directory tree, including those that are more than one level below the currently displayed directories, issue the Expand All command from the Tree menu or simply press [Ctrl]* (asterisk).

Although the File Manager does not include a command to completely collapse all the expanded directory branches, you can perform this task in just two steps. First, collapse the branch at the root directory (the first directory icon at the top of the directory tree, such as C:\) by double-clicking on the directory icon or by highlighting the icon and pressing - (hyphen), and then re-expand that branch by double-clicking on the icon again or by pressing + (plus sign). After you do this, only the subdirectories immediately below the root directory appear on the directory tree. You can adapt this technique to "prune" all the branches stemming from a particular directory, showing only the branches immediately below the directory. Simply collapse the branch at the directory and then expand it again to show the immediately subordinate directories.

Turning on subdirectory signs

Instead of guessing whether a directory contains subdirectories, you can have the File Manager display small plus (+) and minus (-) signs on the directory icons to indicate that subdirectories exist. A plus sign tells you that more directory levels can be found under the directory represented by the icon. After you expand a directory, the directory icon's plus sign turns into a minus sign. Directories without a plus sign or a minus sign contain no subdirectories.

To turn on the plus and minus signs on the directory folder icons, choose the Indicate Expandable Branches command on the Tree menu. The File Manager immediately begins to show the plus and minus signs. Choose the command again to turn off the plus and minus signs. Note that with the plus and minus signs turned on, the File Manager needs more time to display the directory tree. Turning off (or leaving off) the plus and minus signs lets the File Manager complete the directory tree faster.

A directory contents pane displays all the files and subdirectories in the current directory. You can display the contents of a directory by clicking on the directory's icon or on its name or by moving the selection frame to the directory name. As an alternative keyboard technique, you can highlight a subdirectory's name in the contents pane and issue the Open command on the File menu.

Viewing directory contents

Figure 6-2 shows a directory window for the C:\WINDOWS directory, with all its files and subdirectories listed in the contents pane.

Figure 6-2

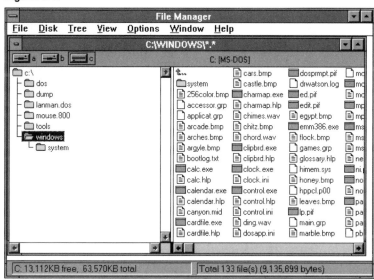

The directory contents pane lists the directory's files and subdirectories.

If a pane contains more files than it can display at one time, the File Manager will activate a scroll bar so that you will be able to view all the files by scrolling through the list. You can also resize a pane to display more files. However, some directories are so large that even if you maximize the File Manager window and the directory window, you'll still have to use the scroll bar to view the remaining files. To maximize the File Manager window or a directory window, you can either double-click on its title bar or click on its Maximize box.

Each directory window can display the directory structure of only one drive at a time and the contents of only one directory at a time. The File Manager will allow you to have windows for several drives or directories open at the same time. For example, after you launch the File Manager, you can open a window for the C:\WINDOWS directory on drive C and then double-click on the drive A icon to open a directory window for the floppy disk in drive A. When you do this, the C:\WINDOWS directory window will remain open. If you want to see the structure of the directory system and the directory contents for drive A only, click on the drive A icon only once. A single click makes the File Manager reuse the active directory window rather than open a new one. As we'll show you later in this chapter, being able to open directory windows for multiple drives is a valuable feature when you are moving and copying files and directories between drives.

When you want to see two or more directories from the same drive, you need to open another window to display the additional directory. To open another directory window for the same drive, choose the New Window command from the Window menu. Then, to see a different directory, click on the applicable directory folder icon in the tree pane. The files and subdirectories in that directory will appear in the contents pane.

If you minimize one of the directory windows, the window will become an icon at the bottom of the File Manager application window. You can move the icon anywhere on the File Manager workspace and use the icon in several of the File Manager operations that we will explain in this chapter.

Unsplitting a directory window

When you launch the File Manager, the directory window is split into a tree pane and a contents pane. You can close the split and have the window display only a directory tree or only a directory's contents.

To display only the directory tree, drag the split bar that appears between the panes (see Figure 6-1, on page 131) to the right border of the directory window. You can also choose the Tree Only command on the View menu. To display only the directory contents, drag the split bar to the left border of the directory window. You can also choose the Directory Only command on the View menu.

When the current directory window shows only one of the panes, opening another directory window with the New Window command opens a second window that also shows only that one pane. To split a directory window that shows only one pane, choose the Tree and Directory command on the View menu. The split will appear in the middle of the window.

The information displayed in the status bar depends on whether the directory window is split or unsplit and on which pane is active. If you have a split window and the tree pane is active, you see a status bar like the one shown in Figure 6-3, displaying the drive letter, the total number of bytes of free space on the drive, the total capacity of the drive in bytes, the total number of files shown in the directory pane, and the total number of bytes for those files.

Figure 6-3

You see a status bar like this one when the directory tree pane is active and the directory window is split.

If the contents pane is active (regardless of whether the window is split or unsplit), you see a status bar that resembles the one shown in Figure 6-4. This status bar displays the number of files currently selected, the number of bytes in those files, the total number of files that appear in the contents pane, and the total number of bytes contained in those files.

Figure 6-4

A status bar similar to the one shown here appears when you activate the contents pane.

If you have an unsplit directory window that shows only the directory tree and not the directory contents, you see a status bar similar to the one shown in Figure 6-5. This status bar shows the drive letter, the total number of bytes of free space on the drive, and the total capacity of the drive in bytes.

Figure 6-5

When an unsplit directory window displays only a directory tree, a status bar similar to this one appears.

You might want to provide more width for the contents pane so that you can see more of the file details. Or you might need less than half the directory window's width to display the directory tree. To adjust the split proportions, drag the split bar to a new location. Even if you choose either the Tree Only

Adjusting a
window split

command or the Directory Only command on the View menu, you can position the mouse pointer near the left window border to drag the split into the window and display two panes. When the mouse pointer is positioned on the split bar, the pointer changes to a vertical bar with two horizontal arrowheads indicating that you can move the bar to the left or the right.

To move the split with the keyboard, press [Alt]V to open the View menu, and then press *L* to choose the Split command. A thick, black vertical bar will appear in one of the panes and can be positioned horizontally with the left and right arrow keys. When you press [Enter], the File Manager will resplit the panes based on the position of the bar.

Navigating around the File Manager

If you open several directory windows in the File Manager, you'll probably want to move among them. You can do so simply by clicking on the window to which you want to move. With the keyboard, press [Alt]W to display the Window menu, and then type the number corresponding to the window you want to activate.

You also can use the keyboard to move through directory windows in the order in which you placed them on the work area. To move to the next open directory window in that order, press [Alt]- (hyphen) to access the active window's Control menu, and select the Next command from this menu. Alternatively, you can press [Ctrl][Tab] or [Ctrl][F6] to cycle among the open directory windows. The [F6] key or the [Tab] key lets you cycle within a single directory window, moving from the tree pane to the contents pane to the disk drive icons and back again to the tree pane.

You can use standard navigational techniques to move through a directory window. For example, you can click on an element to select it or use the arrow keys to move the selection frame from one icon to another within a pane. In the contents pane, press [Backspace] to display the contents of the parent (next higher) directory on the current drive.

Table 6-1 lists the accelerator key shortcuts you can use to navigate in the File Manager. Read Chapter 2 to learn about standard accelerator key techniques that apply to all applications, including the File Manager.

Rearranging the workspace

By using the Window menu's Cascade and Tile commands, you can rearrange the File Manager workspace for easier access to multiple directory windows. By default, the File Manager cascades the directory windows as you open additional ones. When the windows are stacked in a cascade pattern, you are able to see the title bars of all the windows underneath the active directory window in the workspace.

Table 6-1

Keystroke	Function
In tree panes	
[Home] or \ (backslash)	Move to root directory
[End]	Move to last directory in list
→	Move to first subdirectory of selected directory
← or [Backspace]	Move to parent directory
↑	Move to directory above
↓	Move to directory below
[Ctrl]↑	Move to directory above in same level
[Ctrl]↓	Move to directory below in same level
n	Move to next directory whose name starts with *n*
[Ctrl]*n*	Select and activate disk drive *n*
- (hyphen)	Collapse highlighted directory
+ (plus sign)	Expand highlighted directory
* (asterisk)	Expand entire branch of highlighted directory
[Ctrl]* (asterisk)	Expand all directory branches
[F6] or [Tab]	Move to contents pane
[Page Up]	Move up approximately one screen
[Page Down]	Move down approximately one screen
In contents panes	
↑	Move to file or directory above
↓	Move to file or directory below
[End]	Move to last file or directory in list
[Home]	Move to first file or directory in list or to parent directory icon
n	Move to next file or directory whose name starts with *n*
[Ctrl]/ (slash)	Select all files and subdirectories in list
[Ctrl]\ (backslash)	Deselect all files and subdirectories in list (except item enclosed by selection frame)
[F6] or [Tab]	Move to disk drive icons
[Backspace]	Move to parent directory
[Page Up]	Move up approximately one screen

(continued)

Table 6-1 *(continued)*

Keystroke	Function
[Page Down]	Move down approximately one screen
[Shift][F8]	Begin or end out-of-sequence selection
[Spacebar]	Select or deselect file or directory during out-of-sequence selection

In the File Manager

[Enter]	Open selected directory or file
[F7]	Issue Move command
[F8]	Issue Copy command
[Delete]	Issue Delete command
[Shift][F5]	Cascade all directory windows
[Shift][F4]	Tile all directory windows
[F5]	Issue Refresh command
[Ctrl][Tab] or [Ctrl][F6]	Move between directory windows
[Alt][Enter]	Display properties of highlighted item

You can use these shortcuts to navigate through the File Manager.

As you move among the directory windows, however, the active window will probably cover the title bars of other windows. If you choose the Cascade command, the File Manager will rearrange the open windows so that you can see all the title bars, as shown in Figure 6-6.

If you choose the Tile command, the File Manager will resize the directory windows and place them next to each other, as shown in Figure 6-7. When you need to use more than one directory window at a time, you'll find that tiled windows are generally easier to work with than cascaded windows. The only problem with tiling directory windows is that the next directory window opens by default as a cascaded window and covers the tiled windows already in the work area. To bring the new window in line, simply choose the Tile command again. The File Manager will tile the new window along with the others.

While you are working with directory windows, the displayed data can change as a result of your work or the activities of others. If you are working on a network, the data on network drives sometimes may not be updated automatically. You can make the File Manager update the active directory window by issuing the Refresh command on the Window menu or by pressing [F5]. One important use of the Refresh command is to display the current contents of a floppy drive. After you swap disks in a floppy drive, use this command to see the contents of the new disk instead of the contents of the previous disk.

Figure 6-6

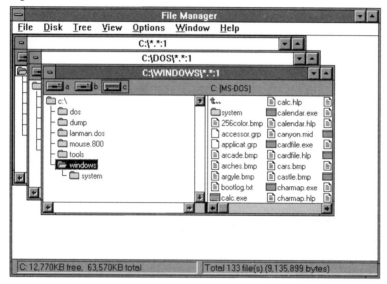

By default, the File Manager cascades windows.

Figure 6-7

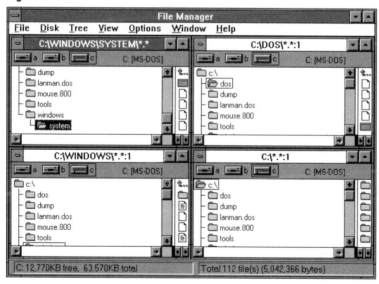

You can tile multiple directory windows with the Window menu's Tile command.

If you want to temporarily make extra room in the workspace, you can minimize any directory window into an icon. The File Manager places the icons at the bottom of the workspace. Figure 6-8 shows the File Manager with three directory windows minimized.

Figure 6-8

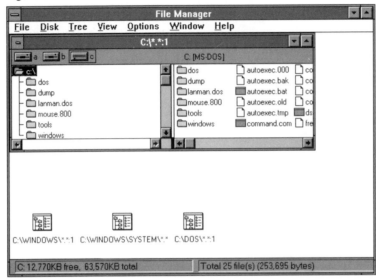

The File Manager places minimized directory windows at the bottom of the workspace.

Removing the status bar

You can remove the status bar at the bottom of the File Manager application window by issuing the Status Bar command on the Options menu. The File Manager will remove the check mark next to the command to show that it is turned off. Issuing the Status Bar command again will toggle the command on and redisplay the status bar. Although removing the status bar gives you more room to display files and directories in the work area, the information that appears on the status bar is often very useful. Note that if you have previously minimized some windows, those icons will not be repositioned when you use the Status Bar command.

Changing text in the File Manager

Some people prefer to see text on a computer screen displayed in upper-case, while others prefer lowercase. Also, many people prefer to see on-screen text displayed in a particular font size or style. By default, the File Manager lowercases all letters in directory and file names and uses an 8-point MS Sans

Serif font. To select a different font size or style or to change all the text that appears in the directory windows from lowercase to uppercase, choose the Font command on the Options menu. In the list boxes of the Font dialog box, select the font options you want to use. To change the text to uppercase, deselect the Lowercase check box. After you click on OK, the new font and case selections will affect text in all directory windows—directory names in the tree panes, and file and subdirectory names in the contents panes. These selections will remain in effect until you respecify them in the Font dialog box.

DIRECTORY FUNDAMENTALS

Now that you are familiar with the directory tree and the other elements you are likely to see in the File Manager application window, we'll turn our attention to the tasks the File Manager is designed to handle. Most of these tasks involve file management, and one of the most important concepts of file management is that of directories.

Directories allow you to create a structure for organizing your files. A well-planned directory structure can make finding files quick and easy, regardless of the size of the drive on which they are located. It's a good idea to have a directory for each application and separate directories for your data files. The data files should be organized according to the project or subject to which they pertain instead of according to the application you use to work with them. It'll be easier to remember the subject or the project than it will to remember the application in which you wrote the report or generated the data.

If the files on your hard drive are not currently organized in a directory system, don't worry. The File Manager contains all the tools you need to re-organize them. In the rest of this chapter, we'll show you how to use the File Manager to work with directories and files.

Creating directories

You can use the Create Directory command on the File menu to add new directories or subdirectories in either the tree pane or the contents pane. To create a subdirectory in the tree pane, click on the directory to which the new subdirectory will be added. Next, issue the Create Directory command to display a Create Directory dialog box like the one shown in Figure 6-9 on the following page, which displays the name of the current directory. Enter a name for the new subdirectory in the Name text box. After you select the OK button, the File Manager will add the subdirectory to the current directory unless you have specified a different path as part of the directory name in the Name text box. If you have the Indicate Expandable Branches command turned on, the File Manager will immediately add a minus sign to the current directory's icon (if it didn't have one already and if you didn't specify a different path), indicating that there is now a subdirectory one level below it.

Figure 6-9

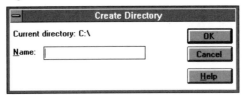

The Create Directory dialog box allows you to add a new directory or subdirectory.

To add a subdirectory in a contents pane, you also use the Create Directory command. It doesn't matter which file or directory is highlighted when you issue the command. The File Manager uses the current path (the directory whose name appears in the title bar of the current window) as the location for the new subdirectory unless you specify a different path in the Name text box.

Naming directories and files

As you work with directories and files, you need to follow certain MS-DOS rules for naming them. Many of the same rules apply to both directory and file names, but there are a few differences.

MS-DOS requires that directory and file names include no more than eight characters. You are not allowed to use spaces or any of the following symbols in a name: a period (.), a comma (,), a slash (/), a backslash (\), a vertical bar (|), brackets ([]), a semicolon (;), a colon (:), an equal sign (=), or quotation marks ("). In addition to these character restrictions, Windows reserves some names and characters to represent devices and parameters in commands: You can't use CON, AUX, COM1, COM2, COM3, COM4, LPT1, LPT2, LPT3, PRN, or NUL as a directory or file name. In addition to its one-to-eight-character base, a file name or directory name can also include an extension of up to three characters (which must be separated by a period from the base name). If you type more than eight characters in the base name of a directory or more than three characters in the extension when you enter a name in the Create Directory dialog box, Windows ignores the extra characters. If you begin a directory name with a space in the Create Directory dialog box, Windows ignores the space.

Many applications use file name extensions to recognize files they create. For example, many spreadsheet packages assign extensions that begin with the letters *WK* to all worksheet files. Other applications allow you the flexibility of using any extension you want, enabling you to identify groups of files. For example, if you use Word for Windows to write memos to five managers, you can use their initials as extensions for the memos' file names. (This system might produce the file name 8-1-91.RJO for a memo you wrote to Robert J. Ober on August 1, 1991.) This way, you can easily identify the memos for a particular manager. If you don't want to use a file name extension to group memos by manager, you can keep all the memos sent to a manager in a directory named with that manager's last name or initials.

You can use the same basic techniques to copy, move, rename, and search for both directories and files in the File Manager. You can expand an operation that you perform on one file, such as copying it, to involve several files by selecting them before you begin the operation. You can also increase the scope of an operation by performing the action on a directory that contains several files. Another method of identifying files for an operation is by selectively displaying file names in a contents pane.

To perform any of these varied operations, you must display and select the files with which you want to work. We'll begin our discussion of working with directories and files by showing you how to display and select them.

By default, in a contents pane, the File Manager lists subdirectories first and then files, sorting the names in each group in alphabetical order. The File Manager's View menu provides commands that allow you to sort the files listed in a contents pane, show different types of information about a file, and determine which types of files are included in the listing. Changing the display is useful when you are looking for a particular file or when you want to issue a command that affects a certain group of files.

Figure 6-10 shows a contents pane that displays icons for a subdirectory and numerous files. The File Manager uses icons to represent three types of files: data files, document files (application-specific data files), and launchable files.

WORKING WITH DIRECTORIES AND FILES

Controlling the display of directories and files

Figure 6-10

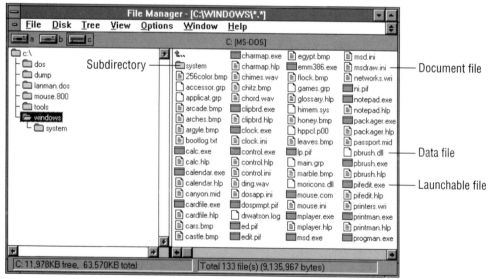

The File Manager uses icons to identify subdirectories and various types of files in the contents pane.

The icon that looks like a blank page with one corner turned down represents a data file. If the File Manager knows from the file's extension which application created the file, the file will have a document icon that looks like a ruled page with one corner turned down. Launchable files include program files (identified by the extension .COM or .EXE), batch files (.BAT), and Windows' own program information files (.PIF). Launchable files have icons that look like a rectangle with a stripe across its top, which gives the icon the appearance of a window with a title bar.

Displaying more file information

The File Manager can display more information about a file than you usually see listed in a directory contents pane. By default, the File Manager displays only the file name and an icon, but it can also display a file's size, the modification date (the date you last saved the file), the modification time (the time you last saved the file), and the file's attributes (read-only or archive). (Hidden files and system files are displayed in the contents pane only if you issue the By File Type command from the View menu and then select the Show Hidden/System Files check box in the By File Type dialog box. The icons for hidden and system files contain a red exclamation point. We'll explain more about all of the file attributes later in this chapter.)

If you want to display all the available file information, issue the All File Details command on the View menu. After you issue this command, the File Manager will alter the contents pane so that it lists only one file per line, with additional information appearing after each file name, as shown in Figure 6-11. After you issue the All File Details command, the check mark next to the Name command on the View menu will move to the All File Details command. When all the file details are displayed, you might want to either unsplit the directory window to show only the directory contents or move the split bar to make the contents pane wider.

If you want to see only some of the information about your files, you can use the Partial Details command on the View menu to choose certain parts of the information. When you issue the Partial Details command, the dialog box shown in Figure 6-12 will appear. You can use the standard mouse or keyboard techniques to choose any combination of settings. After you select your desired settings and choose OK, the File Manager will immediately redraw the contents pane to display the selected information. The File Manager will still list the files one line at a time, even if you select only one of the information options. After you use the Partial Details command, a check mark will remain beside it on the View menu until you issue the Name command or the All File Details command to change the file display again.

Figure 6-11

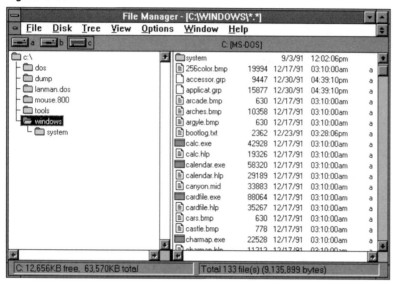

This directory contents pane displays all the available information for files, including size, modification date and time, and attributes.

Figure 6-12

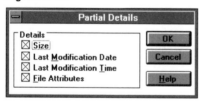

You can choose from these options to display all or some of the file details.

Although the File Manager by default lists file names in alphabetical order, you can also sort files by their type (extension), size, or modification date (date you last saved the file). You can group the files according to their extensions by issuing the Sort by Type command on the View menu. The File Manager will immediately group the files alphabetically, first by extension and then by file name within the extension group.

If you want to see the files in a directory sorted by size, with the largest files at the top of the list, select the Sort by Size command. To view the files in chronological order, with the most recently modified files first, select the Sort by Date command. (A list of subdirectories, sorted by date, will precede the list of

Sorting files

files sorted by date.) Even if you sort by size or date, you won't be able to see file sizes or modification dates in the contents pane unless you use the All File Details command or the Partial Details command to display this information.

Excluding files　　　　If you have so many files in a directory that it's hard to find the ones you want, you can tell the File Manager to filter out the files you don't need to see. To do this, issue the By File Type command on the View menu. In the By File Type dialog box, shown in Figure 6-13, you can use a combination of wildcards and file type options to select the files that you want the File Manager to list in the contents pane.

Figure 6-13

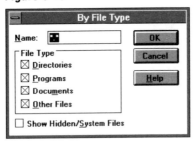

You can tell the File Manager which files to list by using a combination of wildcards for file names and a selection of file type options.

In this dialog box, you can use wildcards in the Name text box to specify which file names to include in the list. The File Manager uses ? (a question mark) to represent individual characters and * (an asterisk) to represent any series of characters. For example, if you want to see only the files that have a .WKS extension, you would type *.WKS in the Name text box. If you want to see files that have the extension .WKS, .WK1, or .WK2, you could use the wildcard pattern *.WK? or *.WK*.

To look for files that don't have a common extension or similar file names but that share other traits, you can use the options in the File Type group box to limit the scope of the listed files, restricting the display to directories, programs, documents, or other types of files. For example, to look for a Word for Windows document file that was misplaced in another directory, select only the Documents check box to view all the files with document icons. You can select more than one File Type check box to display several types of files.

You can force the File Manager to display hidden or system files (files that don't normally appear in a directory window) by selecting the Show Hidden/System Files check box. Applications sometimes hide files to prevent misuse or deletion of important information.

The display changes you make by choosing commands on the View menu affect only the active window and any new directory windows. This way, you can open several directory windows and see different types of files in each one.

Before you can issue a command from the File menu, you need to select the directory or file upon which you want the command to act. You can select directories one at a time in either the tree pane or the contents pane. You can select files only in the contents pane. In a contents pane, it is possible to select more than one file or directory at the same time.

Selecting directories and files

To select a file or directory with the mouse, you simply click on it. With the keyboard, you can use the direction keys ([Home], [End], [Page Up], [Page Down], ↑, ↓, ←, →) to highlight a file or directory.

In a contents pane, you can select a series of neighboring files and directories, or you can select them out of sequence. To select consecutive items, click on the first item in the series, hold down [Shift], and then click on the last item. The two files you clicked on and all the files between them will be highlighted. To make the same kind of selection with the keyboard, use the arrow keys to highlight the first item and then hold down the [Shift] key while you use the arrow keys to move the selection frame to the last item.

To select items that aren't adjacent, click on the first item and then hold down [Ctrl] and click on each additional item. To select non-neighboring items with the keyboard, first press [Shift][F8] to tell the File Manager you're going to select items out of sequence. A selection frame will then appear around the selected item. Use the arrow keys to move the selection frame, and press [Spacebar] to select files and directories. If you select the wrong item, move the selection frame back to that item and press [Spacebar] again to deselect it. You can continue to use [Spacebar] to select items until you press [Shift][F8] again to let the File Manager know that you have finished selecting.

If you want to select several blocks of neighboring files within a contents pane, use the [Shift]-and-click technique described above to select your first block of items. Then, select the first item in the next group by using the [Ctrl]-and-click technique. Next, [Ctrl][Shift]-and-click on the last item in that group to select it and all the files and directories between it and the first item in the second group. You can then repeat the [Ctrl]-and-click and [Ctrl][Shift]-and-click techniques to select additional groups of neighboring items.

With the keyboard, you can select the first group in the normal manner (by holding down [Shift] while you move around with the arrow keys). To select the next group, press [Shift][F8], and then move the selection frame to the first item in that group and press [Spacebar] to select it. Next, hold down [Shift] while using the arrow keys to select the remaining items in the second group. Then use the arrow keys alone to move to the first item in the third group, press [Spacebar] to select it, and use [Shift] and the arrow keys to select the rest of the items in the third group. When you have finished selecting, press [Shift][F8] again to turn off the selection frame.

To select all files and subdirectories in a contents pane, you can press [Ctrl]/ or use the Select Files command on the File menu. In the Select Files dialog box, be sure that the default file name *.* appears in the File(s) text box, and then click on Select. To deselect all the files and subdirectories in the contents pane, press [Ctrl]\ or issue the Select Files command. In the Select Files dialog box, click on Deselect (with the default *.* displayed in the text box). To deselect only one item from a group of selected files and directories, press [Ctrl] and click on the item. Keyboard users must press [Shift][F8], move the selection frame to an item, and press [Spacebar] to deselect it. Remember to press [Shift][F8] again to return to normal operations.

You can reduce the effort and frustration of selecting files that are scattered throughout a contents pane simply by issuing the Select Files command and typing a file name pattern for only the files you want to select. For example, if you want to perform an operation on all the Paintbrush (.PCX) files in the current directory, you can use the Select Files command to select all .PCX files in the contents pane. In the Select Files dialog box, type *.PCX* in the File(s) text box and click on the Select button. Then close the dialog box and issue the command that performs the desired operation. Each time you use the Select Files command, files matching the file name pattern you type are either added to (with the Select button) or deselected from (with the Deselect button) the current selection of files. This way, you can add or deselect files without starting from scratch each time.

Deleting directories and files

Now that we've talked about displaying and selecting directories and files, we can discuss the various operations available in the File Manager. We'll start by showing you how to delete directories and files.

If you don't need to use a directory or file anymore, you can delete it with the Delete command on the File menu or with the [Delete] key. To delete an item or group of items in a contents pane, first select the item and then either issue the Delete command or press [Delete]. After you do this, a Delete dialog box, like the one shown in Figure 6-14, will appear. The Delete text box in this dialog box will display the names of the items you selected for deletion, with a space separating the listed names. If you change your mind about deleting one (or more) of these items, you can remove its name from the Delete text box at this point either by highlighting the name and pressing [Delete] or [Backspace] or by using other standard editing techniques. You can also type additional item names in the text box. (Although you must remember to leave a space between the names, pressing [Spacebar] while all the names in the text box are highlighted will delete them all from the text box. Instead, use the right arrow key to move the cursor at the end of the text box one space to the right, and then type the additional name.) To delete the listed items, select the OK button. Or select Cancel to leave the Delete dialog box without deleting any items.

Figure 6-14

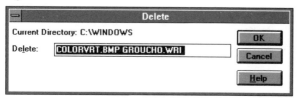

The Delete dialog box displays the current directory and the list of items you have selected for deletion.

If you choose the OK button, the File Manager will present one or more dialog boxes like the one shown in Figure 6-15, asking you to verify the deletion of each individual item. If you select Yes in one of these dialog boxes, the File Manager will delete the item named in the dialog box and will continue through the list of selected items, deleting each in turn after asking you for confirmation. If you choose Yes to All, the File Manager will delete all the selected items without asking you to verify each deletion. If you choose No, the File Manager will not delete the listed item but will continue the deletion process for the remaining items, prompting you to confirm each deletion. If you select the Cancel button at any time, the File Manager will not delete the current item and will abort the process of deleting the remaining selected items.

Figure 6-15

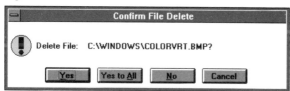

The File Manager displays a confirmation dialog box for each item you have selected for deletion.

To delete the contents of an entire directory, you can also select that directory in the tree pane. (By the way, the File Manager will not allow you to delete a root directory because doing so would make your disk unreadable.) When you issue the Delete command, a Delete dialog box like the one shown previously in Figure 6-14 will appear, but only the directory's name will appear in the Delete text box.

For example, if you select in drive C the C:\DATA subdirectory on the directory tree and press [Delete], the Delete dialog box will show C:\DATA as the current directory and will list the entry C:\DATA in the Delete text box. If you click on the OK button, the first dialog box you see will ask you to verify your intention to delete the subdirectory tree. Then, the File Manager will present a series of dialog boxes like the one shown in Figure 6-15 asking you to verify the deletion of each item in that subdirectory tree. If you choose Yes or No in this dialog box, the File Manager either deletes or does not delete the item and continues with the verification and deletion process. If you choose Yes to All, the File Manager deletes all items in the subdirectory and the subdirectory itself, and you see no more dialog boxes except those for hidden, system, or read-only files. For a hidden file, a system file, or a read-only file, a dialog box always appears, asking you to verify that you want to delete the file.

The File Manager works its way from the lowest level of files and subdirectories under the selected directory to the selected directory itself. This progression forces you to delete the contents of a directory before giving you the chance to delete the directory itself. If you have used the No option in a Confirm File Delete or Confirm Directory Delete dialog box to cancel the deletion of a file or subdirectory under the selected directory, the File Manager will not delete the selected directory during this operation. Instead, the File Manager will display a message dialog box like the one shown in Figure 6-16. To avoid this type of impasse, you need to move the files or subdirectories you want to keep to another directory before you select the parent directory for deletion. We'll show you how to move files and directories in the next section of this chapter.

Figure 6-16

If you try to delete a directory that is not completely empty,
the File Manager displays this message dialog box.

A word of caution: The File Manager provides several opportunities for you to back out of deleting the files and subdirectories under a selected directory, but it does not supply an "undo" feature that you can use to reverse the process. Once you delete a directory, that directory and all its files and subdirectories cannot be retrieved by the File Manager.

Just as you can use multiple selection techniques to select several files for deletion, you can select several directories for deletion. You can also select files and directories for deletion at the same time. The names of all the files and directories you select will appear in the Delete text box of the Delete dialog box, and the File Manager will prompt you to verify every file and subdirectory explicitly and implicitly included in the deletion.

The many confirmation prompts displayed by the File Manager can become annoying if you are well aware of the consequences of your deletion. That's why the File Manager dialog box contains the Yes to All button. Later in this chapter, we will show you another way to control and limit the number of confirmation prompts.

The File Manager makes it easy to move directories and files within a drive volume or between drives, whether you use a mouse or the keyboard.

Moving directories and files

Moving files around on a drive is especially easy. Before you move a file or directory, you must first decide where (that is, to which directory) you want to move it. Next, you need to make sure that the destination directory is represented somewhere on the File Manager workspace. The destination directory can appear as an icon on a directory tree, as an icon in a contents pane, as an open contents pane, or as an icon representing a minimized directory window. The next step is to select the item or items you want to move.

Moving items around on a drive

You can select a single directory on the directory tree or make a single or multiple selection of files and/or subdirectories in a contents pane. After you select the item(s), press and hold down the mouse button anywhere in the highlighted selection area to grab the selected item or items. When you grab the selection, the mouse pointer will change appearance to indicate that you are moving a selection. If the selection contains a single directory or file, the mouse pointer will change to include a data file icon. If the selection includes multiple files or directories, the mouse pointer will change to include an icon that looks like three stacked data file icons. If you try to drag the selection icon into an area where the File Manager can't move the selection, the mouse pointer will change into a prevent pointer (a slashed circle). The mouse pointer changes similarly when you select and drag items for copying.

After you grab the selection, drag it to the destination directory's folder icon or contents pane and release the mouse button. (If you release the mouse button before you drag the selected directories and files from their current location, only the file or directory under the pointer will be selected. So be sure to keep the mouse button held down to grab all the selected files.) To place the selected material, release the mouse button when the selection icon is over the contents pane of the destination directory or on top of any icon representing the destination. After you release the mouse button, the dialog box shown in Figure 6-17 will appear, asking you to verify your intention to move the selection. If you select Yes, the File Manager will move your selection. If you select No, the File Manager will not move your selection.

Figure 6-17

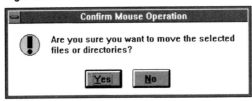

The File Manager displays this dialog box before moving a file or directory.

When you place selected items in the contents pane of the destination directory, be careful not to release the selection on top of a directory icon in the pane. If you place the icon on top of a directory icon, the File Manager will move the selected items to the subdirectory represented by the icon, instead of to the directory displayed in the pane, after asking you to confirm the move. To place the selected items in the contents pane, you must position the mouse pointer away from any directory icons in the pane before you release the mouse button.

Keep in mind that when you move a directory to another directory, the File Manager actually places the directory you are moving within the destination directory. It does not merely move the files from the original directory into the destination directory. If you want to move all the files in one directory to another directory, you need to select all the files in the contents pane and then move them to the destination directory.

At the same time, you should remember that when you move a directory, you move all its files and subdirectories. If you want to relocate specific files or subdirectories separately from the directory, you need to select and move them first.

Moving between drives

To move files and directories from one drive to another, you must also use the [Alt] key, an extra step not required when you move a selection from one location to another on the same drive. Again, you need to be sure that the item(s) you want to move are available in a tree pane or in an open contents pane and that the destination directory is accessible somewhere on the workspace. (That is, you may need to open a directory window for the destination drive.) After you select the material you are going to move, press and hold down the [Alt] key as you drag the selection. When the selection icon is positioned over the destination contents pane or directory icon, release the mouse button before you release the [Alt] key. The File Manager will display a message dialog box. Click on Yes in the dialog box, and the File Manager will complete the move.

If you want to move a selection to the active directory of a drive, you can do so by dragging the selection to one of the disk drive icons at the top of the directory window. For example, let's assume that you had been working in the \MEMO directory on the C drive and are now working with files on drive B. If you select a file and press [Alt] while you drag the selection icon to the C drive icon, Windows will move the file from the current directory on drive B to the \MEMO directory on drive C because that is the active directory on the C drive. You can also make a directory the active directory on a drive by simply highlighting that directory before switching to another drive in the directory window.

If you want to move a selection on a drive or between drives with the keyboard, you need to use the Move command on the File menu. After selecting the item(s) you want to move, press [Alt]F to access the File menu and press *M* to issue the Move command (or simply press [F7]). Next, the File Manager will display a dialog box like the one shown in Figure 6-18. The Move dialog box lists the name of every selected item (directories and files) in the From text box and prompts you for a destination path in the To text box. You should type the name of the directory to which you want to move the selected item(s) in the To text box. For example, to move selected items to the C:\DATA directory, you would type *C:\DATA*. After you enter the destination, select the OK button, and the File Manager will complete the move. If the destination directory does not exist, the File Manager will open a dialog box that asks whether you want to create the directory.

Moving with the keyboard

Figure 6-18

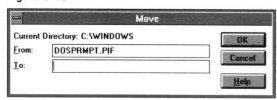

The Move dialog box prompts you for a destination path.

**Copying
directories
and files**

Within a single drive, you'll often want to simply move items around; between drives, however, you're more likely to copy items. In this section, we will show you how to copy items between drives and how to copy items on the same drive.

Copying
between drives

To copy files or directories between drives, simply select the items you want to copy in either a tree pane or a contents pane, press and hold down the mouse button in the selection area to grab the items, and drag the selection to the disk drive icon or the contents pane of the drive to which you want to copy the items. Notice that the selection icon now contains a plus sign (+) to indicate that you are copying rather than moving the selected items. The File Manager will present the dialog box shown in Figure 6-19, asking for confirmation that you want to proceed with copying.

Figure 6-19

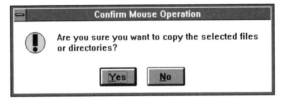

*Before copying your
selection, the File Manager
asks you for confirmation.*

As you can see, this process requires the same steps as those involved in moving selected items between different locations on the same drive. When you simply drag a selection to a new directory, the File Manager moves the selected items if the source and destination directories are on the same drive, but it copies the items if the source and destination directories are on different drives. This automatic decision by the File Manager makes it easy to use the moving and copying features in the situations in which you are most likely to want them.

Copying on
the same drive

If you want to copy files or directories from one location to another on the same drive, press and hold down the [Ctrl] key after you grab the selection, and then drag the selection icon to the destination directory. Release first the mouse button and then the [Ctrl] key to complete the copy. Before completing the copy, the File Manager will display the dialog box shown in Figure 6-19.

Copying with
the keyboard

Keyboard users can use the Copy command on the File menu or can press [F8] to copy directories or files. To copy an item or group of items, first select the items in a tree pane or in a contents pane. Next, press [Alt]F to access the File menu and press *C* to issue the Copy command (or simply press [F8]). At this point, a Copy dialog box like the one shown in Figure 6-20 will appear. The File Manager inserts the names of all selected directories and files in the From text box. You have to enter the path of the destination directory in the To text box.

When you're ready to finalize the copy, choose the OK button. As an alternative, you can copy a link to the file to Clipboard by choosing the Copy to Clipboard option in the Copy dialog box. Later, you can paste the link from Clipboard into another file without having to run the application that created the file you are copying. (This is a fairly advanced feature; see Chapters 9 and 14 for details on linking and embedding.)

Figure 6-20

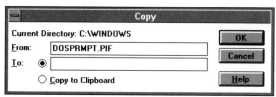

The Copy dialog box displays the source, and you specify the destination.

Changing the name of a moved or copied file

Both the Move command and the Copy command have a handy feature that you will probably take advantage of from time to time: When you use these commands to move or copy a file, you can also change the name of the file in the process. To assign a new name as you move or copy, select the file you want to move or copy, and then issue the appropriate command from the File menu. When the File Manager displays the dialog box, only the name of the selected file will appear in the From text box. You type the new directory and file name in the To text box. To have the File Manager place the file in the current directory, do not specify a directory path in the To text box.

For example, suppose you want to copy a file named REPORT.DOC and name the copy REPORT.BAK. First, select the REPORT.DOC file and issue the Copy command. When you see the Copy dialog box, type *REPORT.BAK* in the To text box and select the OK button.

You can type a unique new file name in the To text box only if you have selected a single file for copying or moving. Because every file in a directory requires a unique name, you can't specify one name for multiple files. However, you can copy or move multiple files by giving them all the same extension (and using the wildcard * for the file name) or by giving them all the same file name (and using * for the extension). On the other hand, if you copy the files one at a time, you can change their names, and they can stay in the same directory. If you attempt to enter unique new names for multiple files, the File Manager will display a message box with a red stop sign and will abort the copy.

Copying an application to a Program Manager icon

The File Manager provides a quick and easy method of creating application icons you can use in the Program Manager. If you copy a launchable file to the Program Manager, the icon for the file will become an application icon. Normally, adding an application icon to a Program Manager group window requires using a few dialog boxes and setting several options.

To use the File Manager to add an application icon to the Program Manager, first resize the File Manager application window so that part of the Program Manager is visible on the desktop. (See Chapter 2 for information about resizing windows.) Next, select the application file and drag it to one of the Program Manager group windows. As soon as you release the mouse button, Windows will place a new application icon in the Program Manager, using the file name (without the extension) as the icon's title. Once the icon appears in the Program Manager group window, you can choose the Properties command from the Program Manager's File menu to adjust the properties as necessary. You can drag multiple icons from the File Manager to the Program Manager group icon or window at the same time. You can drag to a Program Manager group any file that is a program file or is associated with a program file—this includes all .EXE, .COM, .PIF, and .BAT files as well as all document files that you have associated with a particular program through the Associate dialog box in the File Manager (which we'll discuss later in this chapter).

Renaming directories and files

If you reorganize your hard disk and want to change a directory name or the names of files to reflect the new structure, you can use the Rename command on the File menu. To rename a directory, simply select it in a contents pane or in a tree pane, and choose the Rename command. The File Manager will display a Rename dialog box like the one shown in Figure 6-21, listing the old directory name in the From text box. All you have to do is enter the new name in the To text box and select the OK button.

Figure 6-21

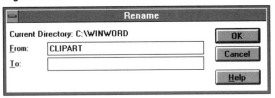

With the Rename command, you can change the name of a directory or file.

When you enter the new directory name, you shouldn't include any of the directory path that precedes the name of the selected directory. For example, to change the name of the directory C:\DATA\DOCS to C:\DATA\DOCUMENT, you would type only the name *DOCUMENT* in the To text box. After you enter the new directory name and select the OK button, the File Manager will immediately change the name of the directory you selected wherever it appears in any directory window.

To rename a file, select it and issue the Rename command. Again, the File Manager will present a Rename dialog box, this time listing the name of the file you selected in the From text box. It's up to you to enter the new file name in the To text box. As with directories, you shouldn't include the directory path before the file name you enter in the To text box.

Two warnings: First, don't rename any of the Windows program files. If you do, Windows may not work properly, if at all. This advice applies equally to application program files. Second, if you rename a file by giving it the same name as an existing file, the File Manager will replace the existing file, but only after you get a chance to confirm the change in the File Manager's Confirm File Replace dialog box.

You can use the Rename command to assign file extensions to several files by selecting the files before you issue the Rename command. When the Rename dialog box appears, it will list the names of all the selected files in the From text box. In the To text box, you should type an asterisk followed by a period and the extension you want to assign to the files. For example, to change a group of batch files that have the extension .BAT to backup files with the extension .BAK, select all the batch files and issue the Rename command. In the Rename dialog box, type *.BAK in the To text box, and select the OK button.

Assigning extensions to several files

Changing the extension of a file can affect much more than just the file's name. Because both MS-DOS and Windows recognize a launchable file by its extension, changing the extension of a program file or a batch file alters the very nature of the file. When you change a file's extension from .BAT to .BAK, you change the file from an executable MS-DOS batch file to a simple text file. As a result, the File Manager will change the file's icon from that of a launchable file to that of a data file.

After you've added several directories and files to your hard disk, you may at times have trouble finding the directory or file you need. If you know the name of that elusive directory or file, you can use the Search command on the File menu to find it. To locate a file or directory, issue the Search command to display the Search dialog box, shown in Figure 6-22 on the following page. All you have to do is type the name of the item you want to find in the Search For text box. In the Start From text box, type the name of the highest-level directory in which the File Manager should start to search. The File Manager by default inserts the current directory in the Start From text box. Also by default, the File Manager will search through the current directory and all of its subdirectories on the current drive.

Searching for directories and files

To search an entire drive, issue the Search command, and enter the name of the directory or file in the Search For text box. Then type the drive letter for the root directory in the Start From text box (for example, C:\), and leave the Search All Subdirectories check box turned on in the Search dialog box. To search only the current directory, toggle off this check box and accept the default that appears in the Start From text box. Begin the search by choosing OK.

Figure 6-22

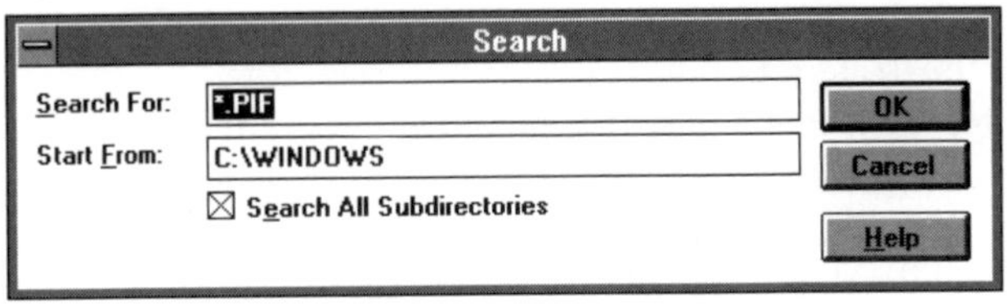

The Search dialog box lets you specify the scope of your search.

The File Manager displays all the matches to your search text as icons in a Search Results window. Each icon has the full path listed next to it. You can use the icons in a Search Results window as you would those in a directory window. You can open, delete, and rename any of the items listed in this window. (If you rename an item, you must type the full path name in the To text box in the Rename dialog box. You can't rename the item to a different directory or drive.) You can also copy or move the files listed in the Search Results window, but you can't copy or move directories into this window. (Note that deleting, copying, renaming, or moving items in the Search Results window results in a corresponding change in the contents pane but not in the Search Results window itself.) You can minimize or maximize the Search Results window just as you would any other directory window. The File Manager lists the Search Results window on the Window menu so that keyboard users can access it. When you've finished with the window, double-click on its Control menu or press [Ctrl][F4] to close it.

If you don't remember what you named the directory or file you are trying to locate, you can use wildcards to replace the forgotten parts of the item's name. For instance, if you know that the directory name started with an *S*, you could enter *S** in the Search For text box. The asterisk is a wildcard for any number (and any type) of characters. You can also use question marks to represent individual characters in your search text. If you want to look for all directories and files with a five-letter name beginning with *N*, for example, enter the search text *N????* in the Search For text box.

If you are looking for a file with an extension, you need to include the extension in your search text, using either characters or wildcards in the extension. For example, to locate every batch file on your hard drive, enter the search text **.BAT* in the Search For text box, type the root directory drive letter with a colon and a backslash (for example, *C:*) in the Start From text box, and be sure that the Search All Subdirectories check box is turned on. If you want to find every file with the name WINDOWS, regardless of the files' extensions, use the search text *WINDOWS.**.

The File Manager can nag you to death if you let it. The File Manager's usual routine is to ask for verification of a command by presenting a dialog box in which you select or verify options that affect the command. Windows adds another layer of verification by having the File Manager present confirmation dialog boxes. This can be an important safeguard because you're manipulating the underlying foundation of your disk storage—directories and files. You not only must say what you want the File Manager to do but also must mean what you say. Thus, if you didn't mean to issue an instruction, Windows will give you yet another chance to avoid a possibly dangerous action. But if you think you can manage, on your own, to avoid a serious mistake, you can turn off this extra warning message.

To change the confirmation message system, issue the Confirmation command on the Options menu to display the Confirmation dialog box shown in Figure 6-23. By default, all the check boxes are selected. Simply click on a check box to toggle it off. If you're using the keyboard, you'll use the arrow keys to move the selection frame and then press [Spacebar] to toggle a check box. Or press [Alt] and the underlined letter in the check box label. Table 6-2 lists the options in these check boxes and the functions they confirm.

Controlling messages sent by the File Manager

Figure 6-23

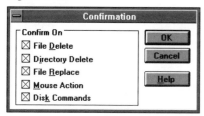

The Confirmation dialog box allows you to choose which functions will have an added layer of confirmation dialog boxes.

Table 6-2

Option	Function
File Delete	Delete files
Directory Delete	Delete directories
File Replace	Copy, rename, or move files that replace other files with the same name
Mouse Action	Drag files or directories to copy or move them
Disk Commands	Format, label, or copy a floppy disk

Each option controls confirmation dialog boxes for a certain function.

Once you're familiar with the File Manager, you can speed up operations by disabling the confirmation messages before you undertake a large project like deleting a directory with many files. If you don't turn off the File Delete and Directory Delete options, the File Manager can force you to click on OK for each directory and file deleted. If you are sure that you want to delete those directories and files, you may want to skip this confirmation and get on with your work. After you've finished, it's a good idea to turn the confirmation back on to help prevent unintentional deletions in the future.

If you don't feel comfortable turning off confirmation completely, or if you want to see a list of the files and directories the File Manager will be deleting or copying before it begins, leave the confirmations turned on and select the Yes to All button in the first message box you see. Regardless of the confirmation settings, the File Manager always asks you to verify that you want to delete or replace hidden, system, or read-only files.

Printing files

The File Manager lets you use the Print command on the File menu to print any file that is associated with an application. (We'll explain the process of associating files later in this chapter.) This command is useful when you want a hard copy of a file whose application is not running. Rather than starting the application, loading the file, and choosing the application's Print command, you can use the File Manager's Print command.

To print a file, select it and then issue the Print command. The File Manager will display a Print dialog box like the one shown in Figure 6-24, with the file name highlighted in the Print text box. When you click on OK, the Print Manager icon will appear on the desktop as the File Manager sends the file to the printer. The file is printed just as if you had printed it from its application.

As an alternative, if you have the Print Manager icon on your desktop, you can drag a file icon or a selection of file icons from the File Manager to the Print Manager icon. Windows prints the files as if you had printed them from their applications.

Figure 6-24

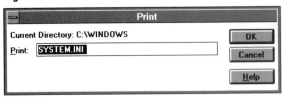

The File Manager displays a Print dialog box like this one when you issue the Print command.

The File Manager's repertoire of functions goes beyond the basics such as copying and renaming files. The File Manager also provides tools for changing file attributes, launching a document, and launching an application. You can even use the File Manager to perform media maintenance chores on disks and hard drives, such as formatting (floppy disks only), copying, and labeling.

OTHER FEATURES

File attributes are notes that MS-DOS makes about a file to indicate the limitations on what a user can do with that file. The four attributes are read-only, archive, hidden, and system. The File Manager allows you to change a file's flag, or the attribute assigned to the file, with the Properties command on the File menu. In addition, the File Manager lets you view a file's attributes with the All File Details command on the View menu. When you issue that command, you can see all the file attributes for each file in the directory contents pane. (You can also use the Partial Details command on the View menu and select the File Attributes check box in the Partial Details dialog box to see the file attributes in the contents pane.)

Changing file attributes

A read-only flag means that no one can make any changes to the file. You can't write any more information to it; you can only look at it.

An archive flag means that changes have been made to a file. The MS-DOS BACKUP command toggles this flag off after backing up a file. That way, you can back up only the files that have been changed instead of all the files on your hard drive.

A hidden file will not appear in a normal directory listing. A file might be hidden by MS-DOS, by applications, or by users as a form of copy protection for a file they don't want anyone to change or copy. Since you can't see the file in a directory, you can't manipulate it. However, you can instruct the File Manager to reveal hidden files by selecting the Show Hidden/System Files option with the By File Type command on the View menu.

A system attribute marks MS-DOS system files such as the IO.SYS and the MSDOS.SYS files in the root directory of your boot drive. These files are also hidden from view (so that you can't delete or modify them unintentionally) until you tell the File Manager to display them with the By File Type command on the View menu.

If, for example, you have a file that you want to share with other users but that should not be changed, you can flag the file as read-only by using the Properties command on the File menu. The Properties dialog box provides a check box for each type of file attribute. To flag a file as read-only, simply click on that check box and then click on OK. Notice that you can have any combination or all four flags selected for a file. You can click on the check box again to remove an attribute.

If you have selected only one file when you issue the Properties command, you will see a dialog box similar to the one shown in Figure 6-25, which lists information about the file as well as its directory and current attributes. You can change the file attributes by using the check boxes in the Attributes section of this dialog box.

Figure 6-25

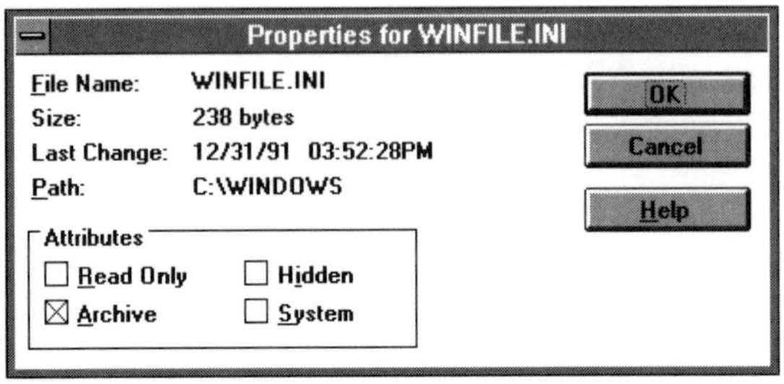

Properties for WINFILE.INI		
File Name:	WINFILE.INI	**OK**
Size:	238 bytes	**Cancel**
Last Change:	12/31/91 03:52:28PM	
Path:	C:\WINDOWS	**Help**

Attributes
☐ Read Only   ☐ Hidden
☒ Archive   ☐ System

The Properties dialog box for a single file shows the file's details, directory, and current attributes and allows you to change the attributes.

If you have selected multiple files when you choose the Properties command, you will see a dialog box like the one shown in Figure 6-26, which simply lists the number of selected files, the combined size of the files, and the file attributes. An X in one of the check boxes indicates that all the selected files have been assigned that attribute; if a check box is empty, that attribute has not been assigned to any of the selected files. If a check box is colored gray, the attribute has been assigned to at least one (but not all) of the selected files. This dialog box allows you to change the attributes for all of the selected files at once (but not for individual files).

Figure 6-26

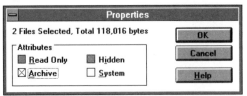

The Properties dialog box for multiple files lets you choose file attributes for all the selected files at once.

When you assign a hidden or system attribute to a file, the file's icon in the contents pane changes to a data file icon containing an exclamation point, as shown in Figure 6-27, regardless of the file's original icon.

Figure 6-27

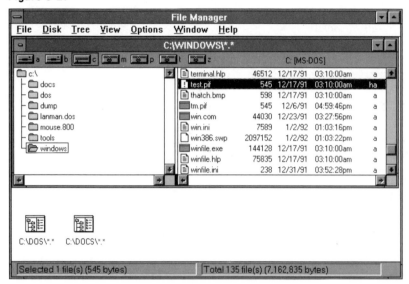

A hidden file or a system file contains an exclamation point in its icon.

Launching a document

Earlier, we explained how to create a launchable application icon for a document in the Program Manager. You can also launch an application's document from the File Manager. You can think of an icon that launches an application and immediately opens a specific file as a launchable document icon. The document's parent application determines the icon's graphic; the document's name is the icon's title. All you have to do is supply the File Manager with the file name extension and the name of the document's parent application or the type of file by issuing the Associate command on the File menu. After the file name extension is associated with an application or file type, you can simply double-click on the file's icon, and the File Manager will open the application with the specified document displayed in the application's work area.

Associating a file with an application

Many Windows applications automatically set up the association link for all documents you create with the application, as long as you use the default file name extension. You'll need to use the Associate command when the File Manager displays a message telling you that no application is associated with the file. You can also use this command to change the association of an extension from one application to another. The Associate command lets you associate any file name extension with an application. You can use it to associate all files that have the .DOC file name extension with a particular word processor, or you can associate various file name extensions with one program or file type.

To associate an extension with an application, issue the Associate command. If, for example, you have selected a file with the .INI extension, such as SYSTEM.INI, the Associate dialog box shown in Figure 6-28 will appear.

Figure 6-28

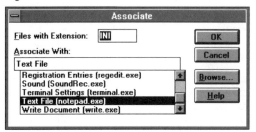

The Associate dialog box lets you associate a file name extension with a particular application by assigning either a file type or a program name.

The extension of the selected file appears in the Files with Extension text box, but you can also type a file name extension in the text box. In the Associate With section of the dialog box, either select a file type from the list box or type the program's file name and extension (including the drive and path if needed) in the Associate With text box. It is usually easier to choose a file type because program file names are often difficult to associate with the program name that you know. (For example, the File Manager's program file name is WINFILE.EXE.) Windows compiles the list of file types from applications that "register" themselves with Windows when you install them. If an application has not been programmed to register with Windows, then you must provide the program name in the text box.

If you aren't sure of the program's file name, click on the Browse button. In the Browse dialog box, shown in Figure 6-29, select the program file name from the File Name list box. If necessary, use the Directories list box to change to the directory that contains the program file. After you select the program file name, click on OK to return to the Associate dialog box. The file name you selected in the Browse dialog box will be inserted in the Associate With text box. Now click on OK. The file's icon will change into a document icon (a ruled page).

When you associate a file name extension with a specific application or file type, remember that you are associating all the files bearing that extension with the application or file type. For example, if you associate a Write memo named MEMO.WRI with Word for Windows, all your files that have the .WRI extension will be associated with Word for Windows instead of with Write.

If you later want to unassociate an extension, select a file with that file name extension and reissue the Associate command. Then select (None) in the Associate With list box, and click on OK. The File Manager will convert the icons for all files with that extension back into generic file icons (blank pages).

Figure 6-29

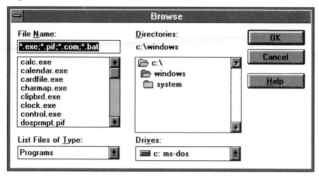

The Browse dialog box lets you browse through your directories to find the applicable program file name.

Dragging a file icon

Another way to launch a document along with its parent application is to drag the document's file icon on top of an application file icon. For example, if you want to work with a monthly report created in Microsoft Excel, you can simply drag the MONTHLY.XLS file icon on top of the EXCEL.EXE program file icon (if both icons are displayed in contents panes). The File Manager will open Microsoft Excel's application window and immediately open your monthly report. When you exit the application, Windows will return to the File Manager.

Launching an application

You can launch any file that has a launchable file icon (a rectangle with a stripe) by double-clicking on the file's name or icon. The File Manager will immediately open either an MS-DOS process or a window, depending on the application and the Windows mode you are running. If you launch a Windows application such as Calculator (CALC.EXE) from the File Manager, the Calculator window will appear on the desktop just as it does when you launch its icon from the Program Manager. To launch a file with the keyboard, select the file and issue the Open command on the File menu or simply press [Enter].

If you're going to launch applications from the File Manager, it's handy to automatically minimize the File Manager into an icon when an application starts. To do this, issue the Minimize on Use command from the Options menu. This setting stays on until you issue the command again.

It's much more elegant to use the File Manager than it is to try to launch MS-DOS commands by double-clicking on files in the MS-DOS directory. If you're familiar with MS-DOS and would rather double-click on an MS-DOS command than use the File Manager's commands, you should be aware that it will take longer to issue the same command in MS-DOS. When you issue an MS-DOS command, the File Manager has to start a full-screen process before the command can work. Also, after the command is completed, Windows returns you immediately to the File Manager. If the command simply displays information, as the MEM (memory) command does, you may not have time to read all the information.

You can double-click on COMMAND.COM to have the File Manager provide an MS-DOS prompt. If you must launch an MS-DOS command, you should go to the Program Manager and start an MS-DOS session with the MS-DOS Prompt application. A word of warning: You should never run another DOS utility from the File Manager because the DOS utility could severely damage Windows. For example, if you tried to launch PC Tools to compress your computer's hard drive from the File Manager, the DOS utility could alter the files on your hard drive. As a result, Windows might no longer run on your machine.

You can also use the Run command to start an application from the File Manager. First, open a window for the directory in which the application is located and select the associated file or executable file you want to run. (Executable files have the file name extension .EXE, .COM, .BAT, or .PIF.) Next, issue the Run command on the File menu. In the Command Line text box of the Run dialog box, the File Manager automatically inserts the name of the selected file. Now you can enter any parameters (such as a document file to open) in the Command Line text box. If you prefer, you can select the Run Minimized check box to run the application in the background on your desktop. After you click on OK, the File Manager will launch the application.

Media maintenance

The File Manager provides simple, accurate methods for formatting and copying floppy disks and for labeling floppy disks and hard drives. You can even use the File Manager to modify a disk so that you can boot your computer with it (by making it a system disk).

Formatting

Before you can store data on any type of magnetic media, you will need to format the media. A disk can't hold any information until the surfaces are mapped out so that the data has a defined place to be stored. Formatting a disk is also a good way to erase all the information on a disk so that you can reuse the disk. You can reformat a disk if parts of the media become damaged. Reformatting a disk remaps the bad spots so that the computer knows not to use them.

To format a disk, place the disk in a floppy drive and issue the Format Disk command on the Disk menu. In the Format Disk dialog box, shown in Figure 6-30, you must indicate which floppy drive the disk is in. For example, if you want to format the disk in drive A, select Drive A: in the Disk In drop-down list box. The File Manager can usually discern the highest capacity of the disk drive you are using. The Capacity drop-down list box shows the drive capacity noted by the File Manager. If you want to format the disk to a different capacity, select that capacity from the drop-down list box. For example, if you have a 1.2 MB disk drive, but the colleague to whom you want to pass a file has a 360 KB disk drive, select 360 KB from the drop-down list box to format a low-density disk at that capacity.

Figure 6-30

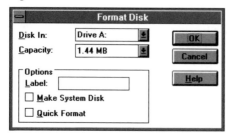

The Format Disk dialog box allows you to specify which drive and capacity to use.

Before you click on OK, you can type a label for the disk in the Label text box in the Options section. A label, which is optional, can contain as many as eleven characters and can include spaces (which count as characters). You can also instruct the File Manager to copy the boot information immediately after formatting the disk by selecting the Make System Disk check box. The Quick Format check box directs the File Manager to format only the file allocation table (FAT) and the root directory but not to check the disk for bad areas. The Quick Format option works only for previously formatted disks.

Now click on OK. Next, the File Manager warns you that formatting will erase all the information on the disk and prompts you for confirmation with the confirmation dialog box shown in Figure 6-31.

Figure 6-31

This confirmation dialog box asks you to verify that you want to erase all the data on the floppy disk.

If you're not using Quick Format, the File Manager tells you its progress in formatting the disk by displaying the percentage of formatting completed in the Formatting Disk dialog box. If you need to, you can click on Cancel in this dialog box to stop formatting the disk. When the File Manager finishes formatting the disk, it displays a Format Complete dialog box, like the one shown in Figure 6-32 on the following page, which asks whether you want to format another disk. If you click on Yes, the File Manager returns to the Format Disk dialog box. After you insert the new disk and click on OK, the File Manager formats this second disk just as it formatted the first one. If you want to format the second disk differently (for example, with a different capacity or without the boot information), make the appropriate changes in the Format Disk dialog box and then click on OK. When you have formatted all the disks you need, click on No in the Format Complete dialog box. When you click on No, the File Manager returns you to the regular workspace.

Figure 6-32

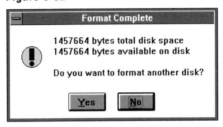

The Format Complete dialog box lets you immediately format another disk.

Making a system disk

You can also create a system disk with the Make System Disk command on the Disk menu. You may need a disk to boot your computer (or to load MS-DOS into memory so that you get an MS-DOS prompt). A system disk is useful in emergencies, such as when the hard drive fails to boot by itself. You can use the Make System Disk command to copy the system files and COMMAND.COM to boot your computer.

To make a system disk, issue the Make System Disk command on the Disk menu. If you have two floppy drives, you can specify which one you want to use by selecting it in the Make System Disk dialog box. Next, the File Manager will display a message dialog box informing you that it is copying the system files. This dialog box contains a Cancel button so that you can stop the process at any point. When the copy is complete, the File Manager will return you to the regular workspace.

You can use any empty formatted disk for a system disk. The disk must be empty because the File Manager needs to put the system files at the very beginning of the disk. If there is any data on the disk, the data will cover the area targeted for the system files. If you try to copy the files anyway, the File Manager will display the message *Cannot add system files to this disk.*

Copying disks

When you want to make working copies of application disks or copy a data disk, you can use the Copy Disk command on the Disk menu. The destination disk doesn't even need to be formatted, as it would if you used a regular Copy command. However, the Copy Disk command works only if the two disks are the same capacity—both 1.44 MB (3.5"), for instance. The File Manager will format the destination disk as it copies the information onto it. Watch out: If there's data on the destination disk, it will all be erased. This command will also give the destination disk the same label as the source disk.

To copy a disk, issue the Copy Disk command on the Disk menu. The File Manager will ask you to specify the source and the destination disks in a Copy Disk dialog box. Simply click on the appropriate drop-down arrow to display a list of available disk drives. Select the source and destination drives, and then click on OK.

Next, the File Manager will warn you with a message dialog box that it will erase all the files on the destination disk before copying any files. (It actually reformats the destination disk.) When you click on Yes to continue, the File Manager will display a Copy Disk dialog box that asks you to insert the source disk. After you insert the disk and click on OK, the File Manager will begin copying the data into your computer's memory. The File Manager will keep you informed of its progress by presenting another dialog box. Once the File Manager copies a chunk of data and prepares to write it to your destination disk, it will display a dialog box prompting you for the destination disk. After you insert the destination disk, click on OK to begin the transfer. When the File Manager has finished writing, it might repeat the sequence of copying the information from the source disk into memory and then transferring it to the destination disk until it copies all of the source disk. (This depends on how much free memory your computer has.)

Even if you have only one floppy drive, you can still copy disks. The File Manager will prompt you when it's time to insert the next disk. If you have two drives, you can use only one to complete the copy by specifying the same drive as both the source drive and the destination drive. You might need to use this technique if your computer has two drives of different capacities installed, such as 1.2 MB (5.25") and 1.44 MB (3.5").

If you specified a drive for the destination disk that is different from the drive you specified for the source disk, the File Manager will not repeatedly prompt you for disks. It will ask you for the source disk once and then ask you for the destination disk once. The copying process will also be quicker since you don't have to keep inserting disks.

If you really need to copy two kinds of disks, you can force the File Manager to copy them anyway. First, format the destination disk to erase any data. You'll need to add a label to it manually (with the Label Disk command on the Disk menu) if you want one. Next, click on the icon for the drive that contains the source disk. This action will display a directory icon for your source disk in the tree pane. Now drag the directory icon over the destination disk icon. If the Mouse Action confirmation check box is turned on, the File Manager will display a message dialog box asking if you really want to copy all the files. When you click on Yes, the File Manager will copy all files on the source disk to the destination disk. This way, it doesn't matter if the source disk is 1.44 MB (3.5") and the destination disk is 1.2 MB (5.25"), or vice versa, so long as the destination disk can hold all the files from the source disk.

In this chapter

Print Manager 7

*H*ow often have you had to wait for your applications to finish printing so that you could get on with your work? When you're battling a deadline as you insert last-minute revisions and reprint portions of a report or presentation, waiting for one file to print before you can open the next file for editing can give new meaning to the saying "hurry up and wait."

THE PRINT MANAGER

The Print Manager—Windows' built-in print spooler—lets you get back to work fast after you send a file to the printer. No longer must you wait for your document or file to finish printing before you can begin editing the next file. Instead of your application sending information directly to the printer, the Print Manager steps in to divert the information to your hard disk. (Sending the print job to a disk is normally much faster than sending the same job to the printer, especially if you are printing a long text document.) Then, operating in the background while you go on with other work, the Print Manager directs the print files from your disk to the printer. Although this adds a step that actually slows printing an individual file, it lets you get more work done by minimizing the time your application is tied up sending information to the printer.

Because the Print Manager can hold multiple print jobs on disk and send them to the printer in sequence, you can send the Print Manager another print job even before the first file is finished printing. The Print Manager maintains a "print queue"—a list of files waiting to be printed—for each of the printers installed on your system and lets you delete and rearrange items in the queue to control your printing.

Using the Print Manager is optional. You can deactivate it either when you install Windows or later, using Control Panel. To activate or deactivate the Print Manager, choose Control Panel from the Main group window in the Program Manager. Double-click on the Printers icon to open the Printers dialog box shown in Figure 7-1. Select the Use Print Manager check box in the lower-left corner of the dialog box to activate the Print Manager. Deselect it to disable the Print Manager. Once you tell Windows to use the Print Manager, it sends all print jobs from Windows-based applications to the Print Manager automatically.

Figure 7-1

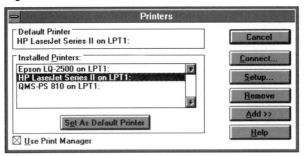

Select the Use Print Manager check box to activate the Print Manager as an automatic feature of Windows.

Printing from Windows applications

Because the Print Manager is a built-in feature of Windows, you don't have to do anything special to use it to manage your printing. You simply use the normal printing procedure in your Windows-based application. (Usually, you choose the Print command from the application's File menu.) The application will create a print file and send it to the Print Manager instead of to the printer. Then, the Print Manager will forward the file from its print queue on your hard disk to your printer and free you to work in other applications.

The Print Manager doesn't modify the print file it receives from your application, so the availability of features such as fonts and formatting depends on the originating application, not on the Print Manager. Some applications use the full range of fonts and printer effects, while others use only a default typeface. Some preview the printed output with surprising accuracy; others do not. To avoid unpleasant surprises, you'll need to be familiar with the printing characteristics of your applications.

Starting the Print Manager

Normally, the Print Manager operates entirely in the background. Windows automatically starts the Print Manager when your application sends something to the printer and closes the Print Manager when the last print job in its print queue goes to the printer. The Print Manager runs minimized as an icon on your desktop when it is queuing print jobs. If you need to view or manipulate the print queue, you can open the Print Manager application window simply by double-clicking on its icon or by using the Task Manager to switch to the Print Manager from your current application. If you need to open the Print Manager when it isn't already on your desktop, double-click on the Print Manager icon in the Main group window of the Program Manager.

If the Print Manager is operating normally as an icon on your desktop, it will close automatically when the last print job in its queue goes to the printer. If the Print Manager window is open, or if you restore or maximize the Print Manager as it is running, it won't automatically close—even if the window is inactive or minimized to an icon again. To exit the Print Manager when it's running in an open window, choose the Exit command from the View menu.

Exiting the Print Manager

Your non-Windows applications cannot use the Print Manager. Whether they operate in a window or as full-screen applications, each of these applications will use its own procedures to send data directly to the printer. Each non-Windows application will need its own printer drivers and configuration for your printer and will demand exclusive access to the printer when it prints. Because DOS-based applications were designed as stand-alone operations rather than as part of a multitasking environment, they typically have no provision for sharing resources such as printers. If you use Windows' standard mode, there is no problem because all background operations—including the Print Manager— are suspended when you run an MS-DOS session. In 386 enhanced mode, Windows can exercise some control over contention for shared resources. Chapter 3 explains how to use the various settings for 386 enhanced mode.

Printing from non-Windows applications

The Print Manager adds to Windows' "network awareness" by intelligently sensing print jobs destined for a network printer and handling them differently from files you send to a local printer. Since most networks have their own print spoolers, sending a print job through the Print Manager would be redundant. Instead, your network print jobs normally go directly to the network; they aren't added to the Print Manager's queue, and the Print Manager icon doesn't appear while the file is queued or printing on the network. The Print Manager includes several features to help you manage your network printing. (We'll discuss network printing, along with other network operations, in more detail in the next chapter.)

Printing with a network

When you open the Print Manager, you will see a window like the one shown in Figure 7-2 on the following page. Below the usual menu bar, you'll see the Pause, Resume, and Delete buttons and a message box, which gives a slightly more detailed summary of the highlighted item's status. The rest of the work area in the Print Manager window is devoted to print queues for each of the printers installed on your system. If you are connected to a network, you

EXAMINING THE PRINT QUEUE

may also see a queue for the files you've sent to the network. The detail that the Print Manager can display about your network print jobs depends on the network software, as we'll explain in the next chapter.

Figure 7-2

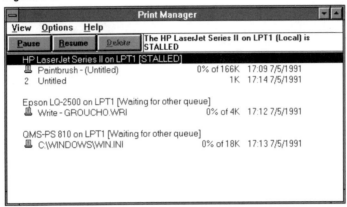

The Print Manager window includes information on each printer and each file in the print queues waiting to be printed.

Printer information lines

The first line (highlighted in Figure 7-2) is the printer information line for the first printer. Here you'll find the name of the printer, the port the printer is connected to, and its current status. An icon will appear at the beginning of the line if the printer is printing. The message box below the menu bar gives more information on the selected printer—in this case, the LaserJet printer. In the middle of the window, you can see other printer information lines for an Epson and a QMS printer. The notation *[Waiting for other queue]* indicates that the Print Manager is waiting for access to a busy port.

File information lines

Below the printer information lines are file information lines for each file in the print queue. The file information lines start with either the "printing" icon or a number showing each file's position in the queue. Beside the number (or icon) is the title of the print job—typically, the name of the originating application and the file name. Next the Print Manager lists the size of each file and shows the portion of the file that it has sent to the printer. The last entry on each file information line is the time and date the Print Manager received the file from your application. If you select a file information line by clicking anywhere on the line, additional information about that file will appear in the message box.

The file information line normally includes the date and time the file was sent to the Print Manager and the file's size. You can suppress either or both of these portions of the information line. When you select the View menu, you'll notice check marks beside the Time/Date Sent and the Print File Size commands, indicating that these options are active. To turn off either portion of the file information line, choose the corresponding command. Both the check mark beside the command and the information in the Print Manager window will disappear. To reinstate the display, choose the command again.

Time/Date and Print File Size displays

Although the Print Manager normally operates in the background and typically needs very little interaction with you, it occasionally needs to display a message, such as a notice that the printer is out of paper or jammed. You can choose the way you want the Print Manager to handle messages—that is, how persistent it should be in interrupting you when it needs your attention.

Print Manager messages

You can choose one of three alert commands on the Options menu—Alert Always, Flash if Inactive, or Ignore if Inactive—to control how the Print Manager will display messages. These commands control how the Print Manager will alert you when it is an inactive window or an icon. Of course, messages always appear immediately when the Print Manager is the active window. A check mark indicates which message alert mode is active.

If you choose Alert Always, the Print Manager will immediately display a message box over the foreground application when it encounters any situation that needs your attention. The default message display mode is Flash if Inactive. In this mode, you will hear a beep, and the Print Manager icon (or the title bar of the inactive Print Manager window) will flash to let you know that the Print Manager is waiting with a message. When you restore the Print Manager from an icon (or make it the active window), you'll see the message and be able to respond. If you don't want to be bothered and are willing to have your printing stalled without notice, choose Ignore if Inactive. This mode ignores messages unless the Print Manager is the active window.

The command you select will remain in effect until you change it. Regardless of the command you choose, you will still see system messages, such as a notice that the printer is off-line.

The Print Manager normally sends print files to the printer in the same sequence it received them from your applications. But if you want to rearrange the printing sequence, the Print Manager allows you to manipulate the print queue and manage your printing tasks. You can change the order of the items in the print queue and cancel the printing of individual print files. You can also suspend printing temporarily and change the printing speed.

CONTROLLING PRINTING

**Rearranging
the queue**

Changing the order of the items in the print queue is easy. In the Print Manager window, you simply select the file you want to move by clicking anywhere on its file information line and then dragging it into the new position. To perform the same operation with the keyboard, first use the arrow keys to move the selection frame to the correct file information line, and then press and hold down the [Ctrl] key while you reposition the file with the arrow keys. Release the [Ctrl] key when the file reaches its new position.

You can rearrange files in the queues only for local printers, and, for obvious reasons, you can't move the file that is currently printing. Although the Print Manager can show the status of some network print queues, you can't manipulate those queues with the Print Manager. You'll need to use the network printer control facilities for that.

**Pause/Resume
printing**

One of the Print Manager's handier features is its ability to temporarily suspend printing. Whether you need to interrupt printing to change a ribbon or cartridge, to add paper, or just to quiet a noisy printer while you take a phone call, you'll appreciate this capability. To suspend printing, select the printer you want to interrupt by clicking on its information line and then click on the Pause button. With the keyboard, use the arrow keys to move the selection frame to the printer information line and then press [Alt]P. This information line will change to show that printing is paused.

To restart a paused printer, select the correct printer information line and then click on the Resume button or, with the keyboard, press [Alt]R. Sometimes when the printer develops a problem—for example, it runs out of paper—you'll see the notation *[STALLED]* at the end of a printer information line. After you correct the problem, you'll need to use the Resume button to restart printing.

Another way the Pause command can be very useful is that it allows you to do your printing in "batches." Perhaps you share a printer with someone, or perhaps you just don't like the distraction of the printer chattering or whirring while you work. You can use the Pause command to hold your print jobs in the Print Manager's queue and defer printing to a later time. The trick is to pause the printer before sending any print jobs to the Print Manager. If you haven't started printing, the Print Manager won't be available as an icon on your desktop. Open the Print Manager by choosing it from the Main group window in the Program Manager. Select the printer you will be using, click on Pause, and then minimize the Print Manager. Now you can issue the Print command or its equivalent as usual, but instead of going to the printer, your file will remain in the Print Manager's queue. When you decide to print the batch of files, just open the Print Manager and select Resume.

You don't have to waste paper or time printing a file that you decide you don't need. You can simply delete the file from the print queue if it hasn't started printing. To delete a file from the queue, select the file by clicking anywhere on its information line, and then click on the Delete button or press [Alt]D. The Print Manager will open a dialog box like the one shown in Figure 7-3, asking you to confirm the action. Click on OK to remove the file from the queue, or click on Cancel to leave the file in the queue to be printed.

Deleting a file from the queue

Figure 7-3

The Print Manager asks for confirmation when you delete a print file from the print queue.

You can delete all the files in the queue by choosing Exit from the View menu and confirming the action by clicking on OK in the dialog box. This action will remove all the print files from the print queue and close the Print Manager.

The Print Manager allows you to delete the file that is currently printing, thus halting in midstream what could be a long print job. However, if you do delete a currently printing file, you may need to reset the printer. If the printer information line reads *[STALLED]*, simply clicking on the Resume button may solve the problem. But, depending on your printer, you may also need to manually reset the printer (turn it off, and then turn it back on) or clear the printer (take the printer off-line, press Form Feed, and then put the printer back on-line).

You can control how fast the Print Manager sends data to your computer's printer port with three commands—Low Priority, Medium Priority, and High Priority—on the Options menu. By changing the priority Windows will give printing activity relative to your foreground application's activities, you can exercise control over how fast both operations will run. A check mark appears beside the command that is active. (Medium Priority is the default.) To change the priority printing will receive, choose one of the other Priority commands from the Options menu.

Adjusting the printing speed

Low Priority assigns more of the computer's resources to your foreground applications, causing them to run faster and causing printing to be slower. Medium Priority gives approximately equal time to the Print Manager and to the foreground applications. High Priority gives the Print Manager more computer resources, which maximizes printing speed at the expense of performance in the foreground applications. Choose the priority setting that meets your needs. The printing priority will remain in effect until you change it.

**PRINTING
TO A FILE**

Occasionally, you may want to send your application's printer output to a file instead of to the printer. You might need to merge a file into another document, delay printing a document for several hours or even days, or print it at another location.

Before you can print to a file, you must modify your WIN.INI file to give Windows the information it needs. Begin by opening Notepad. (Double-click on its icon in the Accessories group window of the Program Manager.) Then choose the Open command from Notepad's File menu. In the File Name text box of the Open dialog box, type *WIN.INI* and click on OK.

Scroll through the WIN.INI file until you see the [Ports] section heading, and read the lines of instructions there. Position the cursor at the end of the EPT:= line, press [Enter] to start a new line, and type a file name, a file name extension such as .PRN, and an equal sign (=): *PRNTFILE.PRN=*, for example. Next, from Notepad's File menu, choose the Save command to save your changes and the Exit command to leave Notepad. Finally, quit and restart Windows.

You need to change the WIN.INI file only once. If you want to change the file name, however, you'll need to repeat the procedure using the new file name.

After you have modified the WIN.INI file, you need to set up the new .PRN file in place of a printer port by following these steps:

- Open Control Panel and double-click on the Printers icon to open the Printers dialog box.

- From the Installed Printers list box, choose the printer you expect to use to eventually print the file.

- Click on the Connect button to open the Connect dialog box. In the Ports list box, select the file name you inserted in your WIN.INI file.

- Click on OK in the Connect dialog box and on the Close button in the Printers dialog box to install the settings, and then close Control Panel.

- Now, any time you want to direct your printed output to a file, you can open your application and choose the Print Setup command from the File menu. From the Specific Printer drop-down list box in the Print Setup dialog box, select the printer you just configured with a file name as the port. Click on OK, and then choose the Print command. The file is saved in the Windows subdirectory by default. Be aware that each time you print to this file, you lose the file's previous contents.

The file to which you are printing will include all the codes required to format your output for the designated printer. Trying to print this file on another printer or by using the MS-DOS PRINT command may have unexpected results.

The simplest way to actually print this file when you're ready to do so is by using the MS-DOS COPY command. For example, if the file name you provided in the WIN.INI file was PRNTFILE.PRN, and the target printer is on LPT1, you can start an MS-DOS session (by double-clicking on the MS-DOS Prompt icon) and type the command *COPY C:\WINDOWS\PRNTFILE.PRN LPT1:* to direct the file to the printer. The output will be the same as if you had directed the file to the printer from within Windows. (Be sure to type *EXIT* to end the MS-DOS session.)

If you are using a PostScript printer and want to create an Encapsulated PostScript (EPS) file, you do not need to modify the WIN.INI file or associate a file name with a printer through the Connect dialog box. Instead, you'll need to follow these steps:

- Open Control Panel and double-click on the Printers icon to open the Printers dialog box.

- Choose the PostScript printer from the Installed Printers list box.

- Click on Setup to open the configuration dialog box for the PostScript printer you selected. In that dialog box, click on Options to display the Options dialog box.

- In the Options dialog box, select the Encapsulated PostScript File radio button. With the cursor positioned in the Name text box, enter the file name (including the drive letter and path, if needed) for your EPS file.

- Close the series of dialog boxes by clicking on the appropriate button in each one (OK or Close). Now you can print to a file by opening your application and choosing the Print Setup command from the File menu. Select the printer you just configured, choose OK in the Print Setup dialog box, and then choose the Print command as usual. Note that each time you print to this file, the file's previous contents are lost.

Your EPS file can now be imported into any application that accepts EPS files as input—for example, Ventura Publisher or Aldus PageMaker. (EPS files cannot be copied to a PostScript printer with the MS-DOS COPY command.)

In this chapter

Networking 8

*H*ow will a network affect your work with Windows? On a network, you'll be able to use network resources such as printers and modems and multiple hard drives. While the network gives you access to more resources, it actually saves your company's resources by eliminating the costly duplication of equipment and software. In fact, the computer industry provides application licensing and devices designed expressly for networks.

Fortunately, Windows facilitates your use of these resources with features in Control Panel, the File Manager, the Print Manager, and Windows Setup. In this chapter, we'll introduce you to the concept of networking and then take you on a tour of Windows' networking functions. We'll discuss using a Windows application with a network and using an application that's installed on a server with Windows. Finally, we'll show you how to communicate with other users on your network. If you are already familiar with the basic concepts of a network, you can skip the first section of this chapter and go directly to the next section, where we discuss how Windows works with the network.

NETWORK NUTS AND BOLTS

Your computer provides a wide range of capabilities that you can implement by attaching devices. For example, your computer is capable of addressing (or routing information to) drives A through E (and even through Z if, for example, you insert the line LASTDRIVE=Z in your CONFIG.SYS file). The computer can also use printer ports LPT1, LPT2, and LPT3 as well as serial ports COM1, COM2, COM3, and COM4.

Even though it is possible to attach many devices to your computer, usually only a few devices are installed. A typical computer uses drives A and B for floppy disks and drive C for a hard disk and commonly has a printer attached to the LPT1 printer port. In addition to all the basics (two floppy drives, a hard drive, and a printer), a typical computer still has the capacity to address drives D through Z, two more printers, and four serial devices.

Instead of outfitting each computer with all the devices it can use and might need, you—and other users—can share resources and information through a network. When you access a network, you usually access a computer called a server. The server has a hard drive that is divided into sections called directories, which have unique network path names. The server also has printers and modems attached to its printer and serial ports. The resources of the server are shared by the users of the network.

But how do you gain access to the network resources? How do you connect your computer (called a workstation on the network) to a printer, hard drive, and modem that are connected to a server that may be in a different part of the building—all through a single network cable? You do it by establishing links—or associations—between some of the unused device addresses (drive IDs, printer ports, or serial ports) of your computer and the server's devices. The network software and hardware will then be able to intercept requests destined for one of these addresses and redirect them to the network device linked to that address. For example, you could link your computer's drive ID F to a directory called \EXCEL on the server's hard drive to access Microsoft Excel from the network. You could also link drive ID G to the server's directory called \WORD to access Word for Windows and link drive ID H to the directory \XWS on the server's hard drive to access Crosstalk for Windows. Once you make these links, you can use drive F to run Microsoft Excel, drive G to run Word for Windows, and drive H to run Crosstalk for Windows from the network.

In addition to linking your computer's drive IDs to the directories on the server's hard drive, you can link your printer ports to the server's printers. For example, you could link your LPT2 printer port to the server's printer. You also could link your LPT3 port to the server's color printer and your COM2 port to the server's modem.

Your resources would grow from a computer with two floppy drives, a hard drive, a dot matrix printer, and your own applications to a system with all of these elements plus the resources of the network. The network resources in this example include the addition of the Microsoft Excel, Word for Windows, and Crosstalk applications, as well as two added printers and a modem.

To use all these resources, you must abide by the network's rules. These rules include permission from the server to use network applications and devices. We'll explain later how you obtain permission. As you would expect, the software on a network must be specifically licensed for multiple users, just as you must license your personal software.

Before you can expand your computer's capabilities with the resources of a network, you must learn how to use the network with Windows. We'll introduce you to network resources and point out the rules governing user access.

Many of the capabilities of a network depend on the capabilities of its server, which provides the resources that everyone on the network can use. All network users granted permission will have access to the server's devices. (We'll use Microsoft's LAN Manager network software for our examples.) In the network dialog boxes, Windows will list resources from which you may choose. We'll show you how to browse through these various lists.

Introducing the server

You also should be aware that there can be more than one server on your network. In fact, LAN Manager sets up special names for groups of servers, which are called domains. (Think of a domain as a server neighborhood.)

Servers not only share but also protect their resources. Since all the server's resources are potentially available to all users, the server must impose order on the chaos created by many workstations scrambling for resources. The server acts as a traffic cop to regulate the process of connecting to resources.

The server can provide access to its resources in two ways: through either user-level or share-level access. User-level access assigns rights and restrictions to individual users. Users who can access the server have rights to all its applications and devices. Share-level access is more restrictive, requiring specific rights to each directory and device individually. Users with rights to network resources, from either user-level or share-level access, have a password that allows them to connect to a server or to individual directories and devices.

Sharing resources

After you gain access to a directory on the server's hard drive, the server imposes another level of protection on the files in that directory. The server provides this protection by issuing privileges that define the extent to which a user can manipulate a file in a specific directory. (Files include data, program, command, and batch files.)

Restricting access to files

These privileges allow users access to each directory in varying degrees. Privileges are similar to file attributes (read-only, hidden, system, and archive, which we discussed in Chapter 6), but they are much more extensive. These privileges limit access to all the files in a directory on the server's hard drive. Some types of networks can even assign unique privileges to specific files in the directory. Networks commonly use privileges such as read-only, create, delete, write, and open.

For example, when a server shares a network version of Microsoft Excel, the server can protect the application's program files by assigning a read-only privilege to the Excel directory. Read-only means that you can launch Microsoft Excel but can't save any data files on the server's hard drive. You would need to save your data files on another disk.

Restricting access to printers

The server also restricts access to printers. Each time a user asks for access to a printer, the server verifies that the user has access privileges for that printer. For example, a printer that is dedicated to printing invoices on six-part invoice stock could be accessed only by the accounting department that issues the invoices. This restriction would prevent other users from printing memos on the accounting department's invoice printer.

Connecting to applications

In order to access the applications installed on the server's hard drive, you need to create a link between your computer and the server. You can create this link by associating a drive ID on your computer with a directory on the server's hard drive (such as \EXCEL). You can use any letter from A to Z for the link as long as your computer isn't currently using the letter for one of its own drives.

It's important to consistently connect network resources to the same drive IDs. For example, if you set up an application icon for a network version of Microsoft Excel and define the command line as G:\EXCEL\EXCEL, you'll need to be sure to always link drive G to the server's Excel directory in order to launch Microsoft Excel properly. After all, the Program Manager won't know to look anywhere else. We'll show you how to connect to directories on the server's hard drive later in this chapter.

Connecting to devices

In general, more than one user can access a network device—such as a printer, modem, or CD-ROM (a drive that stores large amounts of read-only data)—at one time because the server can juggle everyone's requests to use it. If the server is juggling the requests of other users as well as your requests, it will assess the various user needs and access privileges and assign you a turn for a percentage of the time. Don't worry—this juggling happens transparently in milliseconds, so there will be only a minor decrease in response speed.

Connecting to a printer

To print on a network printer, you must tell Windows which printer on the server you want to use and which printer port on your computer will be linked to it. Via Control Panel, Windows provides a list of printers for which you have installed printer drivers. The printer drivers should match printers available on the network. (If you do not have a printer driver for a network printer, you'll need to install the printer driver before you can use that printer.) Once you choose a network printer, you can specify which port on your computer will represent the port on the server. In this way, you link your computer's port—LPT1, for example—to the server's LPT1 port and form a logical connection. Thereafter, anything you print through LPT1 is actually sent to the network printer. We'll show you later how to connect to network printers.

When you send a file to a network printer, the file becomes part of a line at the server along with other files, awaiting its turn to be printed. This waiting line, called a network print queue, is the server's way of sharing the printer. While your file is in the network print queue, your computer is free for other work—that is, you don't need to wait for the file to print before you continue working in any of your applications.

Connecting to a modem

Connecting to a modem is different from connecting to a printer. In general, only one user can connect to a modem at a time. (You can't queue modem communication.) The next user who requests a connection to a modem will either connect to another available modem on the server or receive a message such as *Device not available*. When you connect to a modem, you use a serial port like COM2 to form the link between your computer and the modem.

Connecting to a CD-ROM

CD-ROMs are another type of device you can access on the network. To connect to a CD-ROM, you again use the technique of linking an unused drive ID to the device. However, when you access a CD-ROM, you will notice that the CD-ROM's response speed will slow noticeably as more users try to access its data simultaneously.

The network administrator

In our explanations so far, the server seems to magically assign user access rights and privileges. It's not magic, however, but hard work by the network administrator, who must define these rights and privileges. The network administrator installs and sets up the network for you and others to use. When the network administrator sets up the server, he or she divides the hard drive into directories, giving each a unique name (such as \SERVER or \ACCOUNT1). Next, the network administrator installs applications, sets up all the printers, and defines who is allowed to use which directories and applications. Finally, the network administrator assigns passwords to each user of the server or to the server's directories and devices.

The network administrator is also the network problem solver. If you see a message dialog box regarding a network error, you need to inform the network administrator so that he or she can fix the problem. For example, with several printers serving the needs of many users, you may accidentally send your letter to a printer set up for envelopes. A message dialog box will alert you to the problem, and you can notify the network administrator if you need help.

If your needs for network resources change and you want to gain access to another application or printer, you should contact your network administrator to change your access privileges.

Windows as a network liaison

Windows acts as a liaison between your computer and the network. You never have to leave Windows' friendly graphical user interface to use networking functions. The Windows Setup program sets the stage for networking by allowing you to install network drivers on your computer. The File Manager connects to network drives with its Connect Net Drive or Network Connections command. Control Panel allows you to perform network operations such as logging onto the network and sending messages over the network. The Print Manager lets you connect to network printers and observe the network print queues. We'll talk about all of these operations later in this chapter

EXPLORING NETWORKS

Since you have access to so many additional resources, working on a network can be confusing. We'll start by guiding you through some basic network operations such as accessing the network, using an application on your computer while working with data on the server, printing to a network printer, and logging off the network.

In the following examples, we'll use Microsoft's LAN Manager 2.0 network software, installed on an 80386-based PC server. An HP LaserJet IIP printer will provide network printing services. The illustrations in our examples show LAN Manager dialog boxes and windows. Although other brands of networks have unique dialog boxes pertinent to their software, the basic operations are similar.

Installing network capabilities from your computer

Before using Windows on a network, you must specify the type of network to which you're connecting. (You'll need to do this only once.) After you start your Windows session, you can install network capabilities for Windows by using Windows Setup. However, before you run Windows Setup, the network administrator must install the software and hardware that connects your computer to the network.

To start Windows Setup, double-click on its icon in the Main group window in the Program Manager. Next, issue the Change System Settings command on the Options menu in the Windows Setup window shown in Figure 8-1. To select the network type in the Change System Settings dialog box shown in Figure 8-2, click on the Network list box's drop-down arrow to display the list of networks. To choose a network, select the appropriate network name and click on OK. Windows then prompts you for a disk that contains the Windows network files for your type of network. Insert the appropriate disk in the drive, and click on OK or press [Enter] to copy the files onto your hard drive.

After Windows copies the files and modifies the SYSTEM.INI file, it presents a message dialog box asking if you want to restart Windows or return to MS-DOS. You will need to restart Windows in order to use the new network options.

Figure 8-1

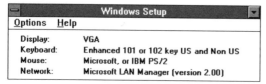

*The Windows Setup window displays your
currently installed hardware.*

Figure 8-2

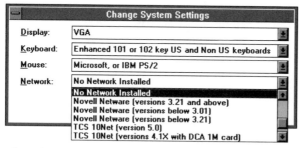

*The Change System Settings dialog box lets you
change installation options, including network type.*

Before you can use the server's resources, you must log onto the network. Logging on is a network user's way of getting the server's attention by establishing a software connection between the user's computer and the server. Logging on involves telling the server who you are by supplying your user name and a password (if required). You'll need to ask your network administrator for a user name and password.

To log onto the network, double-click on the Control Panel icon in the Main group window of the Program Manager. Next, activate the Network icon on Control Panel to display the Networks-LAN Manager window shown in Figure 8-3 on the next page. Before you log on, Control Panel will enter the message *not currently logged on* where your user name usually appears.

Now issue the Logon command on the Account menu to display a Logon dialog box like the one shown in Figure 8-4 on the next page, and enter your user name in the Username text box. (This text box isn't case-sensitive; you can use either uppercase or lowercase characters.) By default, Control Panel enters the network's generic user name in the text box. For LAN Manager, the default user name is USER.

**Logging onto
the network**

Figure 8-3

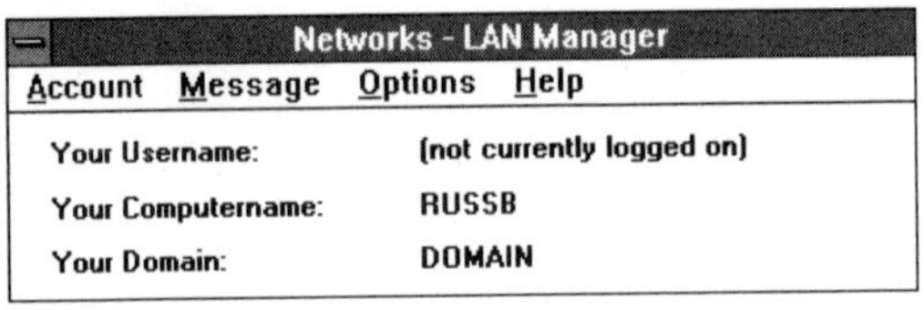

Networks - LAN Manager	
Account Message Options Help	
Your Username:	(not currently logged on)
Your Computername:	RUSSB
Your Domain:	DOMAIN

The Networks-LAN Manager window displays your user name, computer network name, and network neighborhood or domain.

Figure 8-4

Logon	
Username:	USER	Logon
Password:		Cancel
	Help

The Logon dialog box displays your user name and requests a password.

If your network requires passwords, you must enter your password in the Password text box before the network will let you log on. After you enter the password, click on the Logon button to connect to the server. When you are logged onto the network, Control Panel will automatically display your user name in the Networks-LAN Manager window.

If your network software includes a Help feature, as LAN Manager does, you can click on the Help button in the Logon dialog box to find out about logging onto the network. If you decide not to log on, simply click on the Cancel button in this dialog box to return to the Networks-LAN Manager window.

Connecting to a network path

One of the main benefits of a network is that it allows users to share data. With the File Manager, you can link an unused drive ID to a network drive. For example, if your department uses the \PAYROLL directory on a server called ACCOUNTING to share common data, you could connect the directory to an available drive ID on your computer, such as E. This would let you access the \PAYROLL directory from your own applications.

Begin by double-clicking on the File Manager icon, and then choose the Network Connections command from the File Manager's Disk menu. (Depending on the network you use, you might see two commands—Connect Net Drive and Net Disconnect—instead of the Network Connections command. In the rest of our discussion, we'll assume that you are using the single Network Connections command.)

In the Network Connections dialog box, shown in Figure 8-5, select an unused drive ID from the Drive drop-down list box (drive E in our example). Then type the network path to the directory in the Network Path text box. The network path consists of two backslash characters (\\), the network name of the server, a backslash, and the name of the directory to which you want to connect. (The network path for our example is \\ACCOUNTING\PAYROLL.)

Figure 8-5

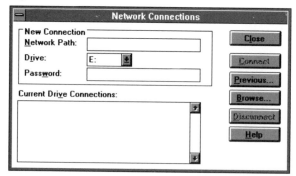

*The Network Connections
dialog box prompts you
for a drive ID to associate
with a network path.*

Figure 8-6

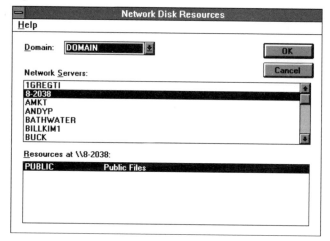

*The Network Disk
Resources dialog
box lists the avail-
able paths on the
server's hard drive.*

If you don't know the network path of the directory, click on Browse (if your network supports this function). The Network Disk Resources dialog box, shown in Figure 8-6, will appear, with a list of available servers in the Network Servers list box. When you select a server, all the directories available on that server are displayed in the Resources list box. Choose the directory you want, and click on OK to close the dialog box. The network path for the selected directory will now appear in the Network Connections dialog box.

The File Manager maintains a list of the connections you've previously established between drive IDs and network drives. The next time you want to use the same connection, you can simply click on the Previous button in the Network Connections dialog box to make a choice from a list of previous connections instead of typing in the path or browsing through all the available servers.

When you're ready to connect to the network drive, click on the Connect button in the Network Connections dialog box. The File Manager will add a drive icon to your directory window and label it with the drive ID you chose. In Figure 8-7, notice that these drive icons are different from the icons of other drives.

Under LAN Manager 2.0, if you connect to a directory on the server for which you don't have access privileges, you won't be able to open files. When you open a directory window for that directory in the File Manager, you'll get a message stating that the directory contains no files. Actually, the files are there, but you are not allowed to see them. You will need to connect to a different directory for which you have access privileges or ask your network administrator to change your access privileges.

If you connect to a read-only network drive to run an application stored there, you won't be able to store your data files on that drive. You can share a document, such as a newsletter, with anyone else on the network by saving the file on another network drive.

Figure 8-7

The File Manager adds a special network drive icon when you connect to a network path.

Saving a file to a network drive

If you create a report with Write and want to save it on a network drive, such as drive E, you would follow a procedure similar to the steps you follow for saving a file on your computer's hard drive. Simply issue the Save As command from Write's File menu, and then choose the drive ID from the Drives drop-down list box in the Save As dialog box, shown in Figure 8-8. Now enter the file name in the File Name text box and click on OK. Write will save the file on the network drive. When you save the file, it typically receives access privileges similar to those of other files in the same directory. In other words, if you save your file to your department's directory, for which only your department has access privileges, no other departments will be able to use that file.

The process that is used for assigning access privileges to files depends on which network you're using. You should check with your network administrator about how your network assigns access privileges to new files.

Figure 8-8

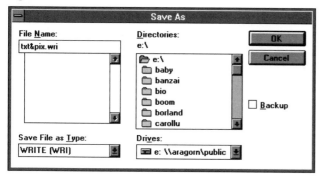

In this dialog box, the Drives drop-down list box lists any network drive IDs to which you are connected.

Disconnecting from a network drive

When you use the File Manager to establish network connections, those connections will remain effective even if you exit Windows. The next time you start Windows, the network connections are set up automatically. When you decide that you want to disconnect a network drive ID, you should also use the File Manager. Of course, if you do something drastic like log off the network, all your network drive connections and links to other network resources, like printers, will be terminated. The safe way to disconnect from a network drive is to issue the Network Connections command on the Disk menu in the File Manager. When the File Manager displays the Network Connections dialog box, shown in Figure 8-9, you'll need to choose the network drive you want to disconnect in the Current Drive Connections list box. Then click on Disconnect to complete the disconnection. Now that drive ID is available to be reassigned.

Figure 8-9

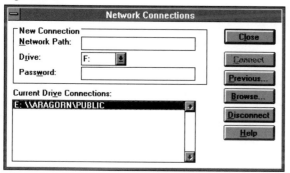

The Network Connections dialog box lets you disconnect a drive ID from a network drive.

Connecting to a network printer

Before you can print with a network printer, you must connect to it. To connect to a network printer, activate the Printers icon on Control Panel, and click on Connect in the Printers dialog box. Assuming that you are connected to the network (logged on), the Network button in the Connect dialog box will be available, as you can see in Figure 8-10. Click on Network to start the process of connecting to the network printer.

Figure 8-10

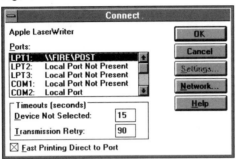

The Connect dialog box lets you begin setting up a connection to a network printer.

In the Printers-Network Connections dialog box shown in Figure 8-11, you can type in the network path and the password. If you need a list of network printers to which you can connect, click on Browse to display the Network Printers dialog box shown in Figure 8-12, which lists all servers. Just click on the server you want to use in the Network Servers list box. (If there is only one server, it will be automatically selected.) The servers in the list are grouped by domain. If your network has more than one domain, be sure to select the domain with the server you need. (Since multiple domains and servers can be confusing, you should get a list of domains from your network administrator to use for reference.)

Figure 8-11

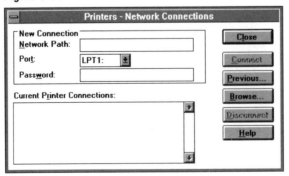

In the Printers-Network Connections dialog box, you specify the network path and the port that will be associated with the network printer.

Figure 8-12

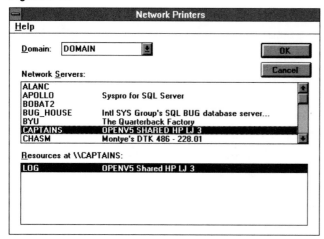

The Network Printers dialog box lists the available domains and their servers, with the active server's printers displayed below.

After you select a server, its network printers will be listed in the Resources list box at the bottom of the Network Printers dialog box. Select a printer from the list and click on OK. Control Panel will insert the selected printer's network path in the Printers-Network Connections dialog box. Next, you need to inform Control Panel which port (for example, LPT1) you want to associate with the network printer by selecting one from the Port drop-down list box.

Before you can connect to a printer that has password protection, you need to enter its password in the Password text box in the Printers-Network Connections dialog box. Finally, click on the Connect button to finish connecting to the network printer. After the printer is connected, it will be listed in the Current Printer Connections list box in the Printers-Network Connections dialog box. These connections are active and displayed until you log off the network.

When you've connected to the network printer, click on the appropriate buttons (OK or Close) to close the series of dialog boxes. After you close the Printers dialog box, you'll be able to use all your new settings.

If you want to disconnect from a network printer, click on its name in the Current Printer Connections list box in the Printers-Network Connections dialog box, and then click on the Disconnect button. If you quit Windows while you still have a network printer connected, Windows will automatically reconnect to that printer (prompting for a password if necessary) the next time you start Windows.

Normally, Windows bypasses the Print Manager to speed up printing on the network. However, you can still use the Print Manager to view the status of your file in a network print queue, as we'll explain in a moment.

**Printing from
an application**

Once you connect to a network printer, you can print your files on it. We'll use a report created in Write as an example. To print your document on the network printer, you use the same process you would use with a printer connected to your computer. First, set up your page layout, and then set up the printer with the Print Setup command on Write's File menu. In the Print Setup dialog box, choose the network printer and click on OK. Now issue the Print command on the File menu. Instead of printing the document on the printer that is connected to your computer, Windows will send the file to the network printer.

**Viewing the
network queue with
the Print Manager**

As we explained, Windows by default bypasses the Print Manager for network printing. When you bypass the Print Manager, you won't have access to its special features—allowing you to pause a printer while it's printing a file, for example—and you won't ordinarily have the same capabilities with a network printer. You can, however, tell Windows to use the Print Manager with network printers. To do this, activate the Print Manager by double-clicking on its icon in the Program Manager's Main group window. Then choose the Network Settings command from the Print Manager's Options menu. In the Network Options dialog box, shown in Figure 8-13, deselect the Print Net Jobs Direct check box, click on OK, and then close the Print Manager. You'll now be able to use all the Print Manager's commands with the network printer (if your network supports the commands).

Figure 8-13

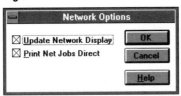

*In the Network Options dialog
box, you can choose to work with
the Print Manager or to bypass it.*

Now, when you print a file, it will go to the Print Manager first and then to the network's print queue. You can look at the print queue to check on the printing progress of your file by choosing the Selected Net Queue command on the Print Manager's View menu. The Print Manager will display a dialog box like the one that is shown in Figure 8-14, which displays the name of the selected printer in the title bar and lists all the print jobs currently waiting in line.

If you want to look at a print queue for another printer or even for another server's printer to which you're not currently connected (for example, if you have an old job waiting to print), issue the Other Net Queue command on the View menu to display the Other Net Queue dialog box shown in Figure 8-15. After you enter the network path in the Network Queue text box, the Print Manager will display the queued jobs for that printer. You can find a printer's network path by using Control Panel's Printers icon. In the Printers dialog box, click on Connect, and then click on Network in the Connect dialog box. When you click on Browse in the Printers-Network Connections dialog box, you will see a list of all the servers on the network. Select the name of a server to see a list of all printers connected to that server.

Figure 8-14

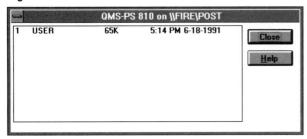

The Selected Net Queue command displays all the files waiting to be printed on the network printer to which you're connected.

Figure 8-15

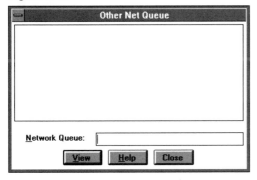

The Other Net Queue dialog box lists print jobs from another network printer.

If you try to look at a network queue with either the Selected Net Queue or the Other Net Queue command but Windows doesn't find the printer (even when you know the name is correct), the printer is either off-line or turned off.

When you've finished using the network and want to disconnect from it entirely, you can log off the network. Double-click on Control Panel's Network icon, and then choose the Logoff command on the Account menu. Logging off will disconnect your computer from any network drives. If you are still connected to any network drives when you try to log off, Control Panel will prompt you for verification with a message dialog box like the one shown in Figure 8-16 on the following page. After you click on Yes, Control Panel will finish logging you off the network.

Logging off the network

Figure 8-16

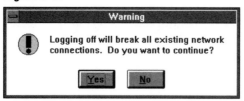

*Control Panel warns you that you'll disconnect any
existing network connections when you log off the network.*

**SENDING
MESSAGES**

Control Panel's Network application includes a function that allows you to
send a message to anyone on the network who is also running Windows. To
send a message, select the Send command on the Message menu from Control
Panel's Network application window. In the Send dialog box for LAN Manager,
first enter in the To text box the user name of the person to whom you're sending
the message. You don't have to supply your own user name; the network will
identify you and supply that information automatically. Next, type your message
in the Message text box. When you've finished typing, click on Send to transmit
the message across the network to the recipient's computer.

You can receive a message at any time with LAN Manager because it installs
a message application called WinPopup. By default, whenever you start Windows on a computer that is running LAN Manager, Windows loads WinPopup
and minimizes it to an icon on the desktop to handle the background message
functions. When a message arrives, the icon will blink and your computer will
beep to indicate that you have a message. You'll also see a WinPopup dialog box
like the one shown in Figure 8-17, telling you that you have a message. When you
click on OK, the message will appear in a WinPopup application window similar
to the one shown in Figure 8-18. After you've read the message, minimize the
window or choose Cancel to delete the message and make room for the next one.

Figure 8-17

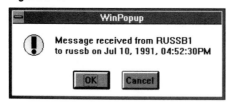

*When a message from the network arrives,
Windows notifies you with a message dialog box.*

Figure 8-18

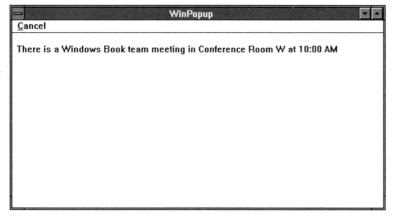

The message appears in a WinPopup application window.

Now you're ready to work with the full network capabilities of Windows. Some of these additional capabilities include installing Windows so that all your data files are automatically stored on your computer's hard drive and all Windows program files are on a network drive, changing your password, starting applications on the server's hard drive from the File Manager, and starting applications on the server's hard drive that were launched in the previous Windows session.

USING NETWORK FEATURES

Instead of installing Windows on your computer, you can use the server's copy and keep only the personal files that customize Windows. You can install Windows without disks by using the server as the source for any requests for a disk. (However, the network administrator must copy all the files to the server before you can install Windows on your computer.)

To install Windows from the server, first log onto the network from the MS-DOS prompt, and then type *SETUP /N* to install only the files necessary to run the network version of Windows with your computer. Windows will verify the hardware you're using and the applications you want to add. With this type of installation, any defaults you change with Control Panel, such as screen colors or printers, will be kept separate from other network users' preferences in separate files on either your computer or the server.

Installing Windows from the server

If your network administrator requires that you change your password periodically (to maintain security), you can use Control Panel's Network icon to enter a new password. After you open Control Panel and activate the Network icon, issue the Change Password command on the Account menu to display the Change Password dialog box. LAN Manager displays your user name by default.

Changing your password

To change a password, first enter your domain in the Change Password At text box. (Other networks will ask for different information, such as a server name.) Next, enter your current password in the Old Password text box, and then enter the replacement password in the New Password text box. As you type, Control Panel will display asterisks (*) instead of characters to maintain password security. At this point, the dialog box will look like the one shown in Figure 8-19. After all the entries are correct (and you've noted your new password), click on OK to make the change. LAN Manager will ask you to confirm the new password by entering it into a dialog box one more time.

If you forget your password, you'll need to contact your network administrator to have your password reset.

Figure 8-19

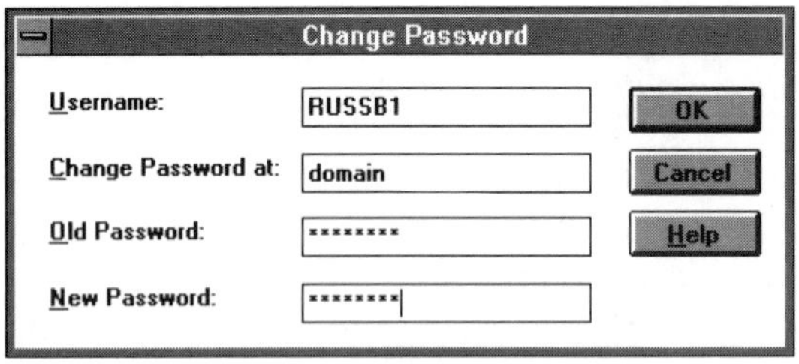

The Change Password dialog box displays your current user name and allows you to enter a new password.

The File Manager as a launching pad

The easiest way to launch network applications is from the File Manager. Connect to the network drive via the Network Connections command on the Disk menu, and then open a directory window for that drive. Now all you have to do is double-click on the program file for your application. When you exit the application, Windows will return you to the File Manager.

For example, if you want to run a version of Microsoft Excel that's stored on a server, you can issue the Network Connections command from the Disk menu to display the Network Connections dialog box. Choose an unused drive ID by clicking on the Drive list box's drop-down arrow and then clicking on a letter. Next, either enter the network path for Microsoft Excel in the Network Path text box or click on Browse and select a server and a directory from the Network Disk Resources dialog box. After you click on OK, the File Manager will enter the network path for you in the Network Connections dialog box. If you need a password, enter it in the Password text box. (If you don't specify a password when you should, you won't be able to connect to the network drive at all.) Finally, click on Connect to establish the network connection, and then close the Network Connections dialog box.

After the network drive icon appears in a File Manager window, click on it to display the files and directories on that drive. To launch Microsoft Excel, scroll through the list of files until you find EXCEL.EXE, and then double-click on that file. Windows will add an application window to the desktop (on top of the File Manager window) for this application.

If you're running Windows in 386 enhanced mode, all the settings in the 386 Enhanced dialog box on Control Panel will apply to the network applications as well as to the applications stored on your computer's hard drive. When you run a network application, the server will load the application's program files into your computer's memory. Therefore, your computer's CPU will do all the work, even when you run a network application.

The previous session as a launching pad

Starting Windows reconnects any network connections that you left set up when you quit Windows. After the first time you connect to a network server, you can let Windows make the connections for you. Then, by putting an icon for a network application in the StartUp group window of the Program Manager, the application will be launched automatically when you start Windows.

To make this work, connect to the server that contains the application—for example, \\SERVER\EXCEL. Open the File Manager, and activate the network drive that contains the application. Drag the application's icon to the StartUp group window in the Program Manager. You can then select the application's icon and choose the Properties command from the Program Manager's File menu to add parameters to the Command Line text box. The network application is now set up to run automatically every time you start Windows, as long as you quit Windows without breaking the network connection. If you log off the network, you will have to manually reconnect to the network before you can continue to use the network application.

When Windows can't find your network

If your computer can't access the network (for example, because the server is down, your network cable is unattached, or the network software on your computer is damaged), Windows will display a message dialog box warning you that you can't access the network. If the problem can't be fixed right away, you might want to disable the warning so that it won't continue reappearing every time you restart Windows. To do this, select the Disable Warning When Network Not Running check box in the message dialog box, and click on OK. After you disable the warning and correct the problem, you'll notice a change on the Options menu in Control Panel's Networks-LAN Manager window. By default, the Enable Initial Warning Message command is selected, but when you disable the message dialog box, you automatically toggle on the Disable Initial Warning Message command. After you correct the network problem, you'll need to select the Enable Initial Warning Message command so that Windows will warn you the next time it finds a problem when it's establishing network connections.

Section 2
Using Program Manager Applications

In this chapter

Introducing Applications 9

Without applications, your computer would be a useless piece of hardware. For most people, applications are the lifeblood of their computers. In the same way that compact discs allow you to use your CD player, applications unleash the power of your computer. In essence, an application is simply a program that allows you to accomplish a task with your computer.

You've probably already worked with at least one application. If you use a word processor, you may work with an application such as Microsoft Word or WordPerfect. If you use a spreadsheet, you may use an application such as Lotus 1-2-3 or Microsoft Excel. Windows comes with a number of applications. In fact, all the icons you see in Figure 9-1 start applications. In this section of the book, we'll discuss some of Windows' applications, including Write, Paintbrush, Terminal, Recorder, Notepad, Calendar, Cardfile, Calculator, Clock, Object Packager, Media Player, Sound Recorder, Minesweeper, and Solitaire. In this chapter, however, we'll focus on acquainting you with applications in general.

Figure 9-1

Each icon in the Accessories group window opens an application.

All Windows applications have a few things in common. Windows applications start the same way; and, after you open them, you'll see they share similar commands on the menu bar. Furthermore, most of these applications use a data exchange utility called Clipboard to share information. (Even non-Windows applications have a few of these characteristics when you start them from Windows.) Some Windows applications can also exchange information by using technology known as Object Linking and Embedding. In this chapter, we'll identify the common characteristics of Windows applications and explain how those elements operate. After you master some basic techniques, you'll be able to apply them to virtually all the applications that you work with in Windows.

First, we'll show you how to launch an application and issue commands that open files, edit text, save files, define page layout, and print files. Next, we'll work on such advanced features as copying data within a document or between applications. We'll also show you how to use Character Map, a new Windows accessory that lets you insert special characters into any Windows application. Then, we'll move on to explore the options that change the work area in a window. Finally, we'll discuss running non-Windows applications and explain how you can share data between Windows and non-Windows applications with Windows' data exchange capabilities.

LAUNCHING APPLICATIONS

The first step in using any application is to start or launch it. The most common place to start an application is from the Program Manager. Simply double-click on the application icon in one of the Program Manager's group windows to tell Windows to open the application window.

Launching applications without icons

If the application you want to start isn't represented by an icon, you can launch it with the Run command on the Program Manager's File menu. As we showed you in Chapter 5, you need to provide the application's path and program name so that Windows knows which application to start. One advantage of starting an application with the Run command is that you can instruct Windows to open a specific document or graphics file immediately after starting the application. For example, if you use a Write document template for all your memos, you can instruct Windows to start Write and immediately open the memo file. But using the Run command involves a dialog box and adds an extra step or two, so you'll probably want to use this method only for applications that you start infrequently. Besides, if you always open the same document every time you start an application, you can add the file name to the Command Line text box in the Program Item Properties dialog box in the Program Manager. We'll discuss how to do this later in this chapter.

You can use the File Manager to locate a program file and launch the application. As we explained in Chapter 6, you can use the Run command from the File Manager's File menu to launch the highlighted file. As a shortcut, you can simply double-click on the file or select the file name and press the [Enter] key. If the file is an executable file (that is, one with a .EXE, .COM, .BAT, or .PIF file name extension) or a data file that is properly associated with an application, Windows will run the application and will either open a window for it or start it in an MS-DOS session.

You also can use the Open command on the File Manager's File menu to launch a DOS-based application. This command launches the highlighted file, places an MS-DOS Prompt icon at the bottom of the desktop, and converts the screen from a graphical interface into a black screen containing an MS-DOS prompt. This MS-DOS interface is called a full-screen window because Windows is still running while you see the MS-DOS prompt. In standard mode, a running non-Windows application prohibits your interaction with all other applications. (This barrier is overcome when you run Windows in 386 enhanced mode.)

If you want to launch a non-Windows application from the MS-DOS prompt, double-click on the MS-DOS Prompt icon in the Main group window of the Program Manager. MS-DOS Prompt lets you run an application in an MS-DOS session without exiting Windows. Windows starts a full-screen window for the MS-DOS prompt. At that point, you can use MS-DOS commands to run your application. When you want to return to Windows, simply type *EXIT* at the MS-DOS prompt and press [Enter], which terminates the MS-DOS session and returns you to Windows.

If you frequently use the Run command to start an application and open a document simultaneously, you'll want to create an icon in the Program Manager that accomplishes this task for you. For example, if you use a memo template document frequently, you can create an icon that both launches the application and opens the template file. You can use the New command on the Program Manager's File menu to add a new icon to one of the group windows in the Program Manager, as we discussed in Chapter 5. Choose the Program Item radio button in the New Program Object dialog box. Then, in the Program Item Properties dialog box (shown in Figure 9-2 on the following page), enter the path and the startup command you use to launch the application in the Command Line text box, and append the appropriate file name to that command. You can also enter a title for the icon in the Description text box; we titled ours *Memos*. (If you don't enter a title in this text box, Windows will use the file name of the application or the document as the icon title.) When you click on OK, the new document icon will appear in the active group window of the Program Manager.

Launching applications from the File Manager

Launching non-Windows applications

Creating document icons

Figure 9-2

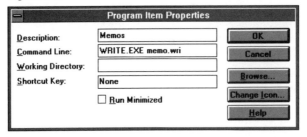

You can add a new icon that starts an application and opens the document you specify.

ISSUING COMMANDS

Issuing commands in a Windows application is as easy as pulling down a menu and selecting a command name. In addition, commands that perform the same function have consistent command names throughout the various Windows applications. Windows has even unified the keyboard equivalents that issue commands in the various applications. (Refer to Chapter 2 for specific information about how to issue commands, use keyboard shortcuts, and enter text in dialog boxes.)

Opening files

When Windows opens an application window, the application's work area will contain an empty new file by default (unless you have previously specified otherwise, as we did in Figure 9-2). If you want to work on an existing file, you will need to use the Open command on the application's File menu. The Open dialog box displays a list of existing files. For example, after you start Write and issue the Open command, you'll see a list of files like the one shown in Figure 9-3. All of Write's file names have a .WRI extension. (Each application uses a unique file name extension so that it can identify its own files. Also, a specific file name extension makes it possible for an application to list only its own files in the Open dialog box.) To open a file, you can either click on an item in the File Name list box or type the complete file name with its extension in the File Name text box. When you click on OK, Write will open the file.

Figure 9-3

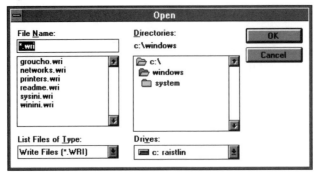

This Open dialog box lists files you can open in Write.

If you saved your file without an extension and you don't remember what you named it, all is not lost. Although you can't type the name in the File Name text box, you can direct Windows to display in the File Name list box all the files in the current directory. To list all the files, select All Files (*.*) in the List Files of Type drop-down list box, or type *.* in the File Name text box and press [Enter]. (The asterisks are wildcards that represent all files with any name and any extension.) Now Windows will display all the files in the current directory, which is noted above the Directories list box, so that you can find the file you want.

If you don't find the file you want to open in the current directory, you can use the Directories list box to move to another directory to find the file. After you change the directory by double-clicking on a directory name, Windows will display the files it finds in the current directory. The directories are listed by name. For example, in Write's Open dialog box, shown in Figure 9-3, the subdirectory SYSTEM appears in the Directories list box.

You can also move to another disk drive to find a file. The Drives drop-down list box lists the floppy drives (A and B, for example) and the various hard drives (C through F, for example). When you click on the letter of a drive, Windows will display the files in the current directory on that drive.

To open a new file, you'll use the New command on the File menu. When you issue the New command, Windows will display a window for the new file. For applications that can have only one document open at a time, Windows will close the current file and place an empty new file in the work area.

In all Windows applications, you must select text before you can edit it. Chapters 2 and 10 provide details about selecting and editing text; here, we'll review a few basics.

The most frequently used editing command is the Undo command. Undo is context-sensitive, meaning that its name changes depending on the context of your last action. For example, if you change all the characters in your document to italic and then want to undo the change, the Undo command becomes Undo Formatting. The name change tells you which action Undo can reverse—in this case, formatting. If an application can't undo your last action, the Undo command is dimmed. Note that Undo's versatility has two limitations—you may undo only your last action, and some actions are irreversible.

Selecting text works much the same way throughout the applications, including selecting text in text boxes. To select text, position the mouse pointer on the character or location where you want the selection to start, and then drag to the last character or ending position of your selection and release the mouse button. The selected characters will be highlighted.

Listing all the files

Using the Directories and Drives list boxes

Opening a new file

Editing

Using Undo

Selecting text with the mouse

Deleting text

You can use either the [Delete] or the [Backspace] key to delete characters in a document or in a text box. The [Delete] key deletes the character to the right of the cursor. The [Backspace] key deletes the character to the left of the cursor. If you want to replace the text in a text box, you can either delete the characters one at a time or highlight all the text and then press [Delete] to delete all the characters at once. If you highlight the text and then begin typing, your new text will immediately replace the old.

Saving files

Windows provides several ways to save a file. You can select either the Save or the Save As command from an application's File menu. The first time you save an untitled file (whether you select Save or Save As), you'll see the Save As dialog box shown in Figure 9-4. Once you have assigned a name to a file, however, you can bypass this dialog box by issuing the Save command to save the file, along with any changes you've made, under its original name.

Figure 9-4

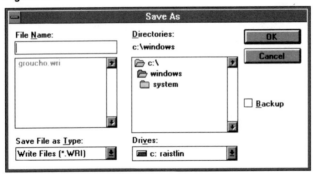

The Save As dialog box prompts you for a file name for the document.

The first thing you need to tell Windows is where you want to store the file, using the Drives and Directories list boxes. Then you must provide Windows with a name for the file. If you don't give the file name an extension, the application will add one for you. The application adds an extension that associates the file with the application. For example, Notepad adds a .TXT extension, and Write adds a .WRI extension. The default file name extension appears in the Save File as Type drop-down list box. Remember that you can have up to eight characters in a file name (not including the extension). After you have entered the file name, click on OK to save the file.

Later, if you want to save the file under a different name, you can use the Save As command to enter another file name. You'll want to use this technique if you work with templates. For example, if you use a memo in Write as a template, you won't want to overwrite the file every time you create a new memo. You can save the altered memo with a new file name and leave your original template intact.

If you want to delete a file that has been saved, you must use the File Manager, discussed in Chapter 6.

You'll probably want to print the documents you create in Windows applications. In most applications, this multistep process includes setting up your page layout, setting up your printer, and issuing the Print command.

Printing

If an application doesn't have its own unique commands for letting you adjust the page margins (as Write does), its File menu will offer a Page Setup command that lets you specify margin settings as well as create headers and footers. When you choose the Page Setup command, a Page Setup dialog box like the one shown in Figure 9-5 appears. This dialog box has a text box for the header and one for the footer. The Margins section has four text boxes to set the left, right, top, and bottom margins.

Setting up page layout

Figure 9-5

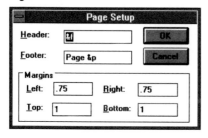

The Page Setup dialog box sets headers, footers, and margins.

Windows formats the text in a document to conform to the margins specified in the Page Setup dialog box. By default, the top and bottom margins are 1" and the left and right margins are .75". To change a margin setting, simply highlight the old margin setting and type the new setting. Windows will accept any whole or decimal number for a margin. If you type a fraction in the form *3/4*, Windows will warn you with a message dialog box that it can't use that number; you'll need to substitute the decimal value .75".

As you set your margins, keep the limitations of your printer in mind. If you set the document's left and right margins to .25", but your printer's default minimum margin is .5", your printed text will be truncated on both the left and the right margins.

You tell Windows what text you want to use for headers and footers in the Header and Footer text boxes of the Page Setup dialog box. The header and footer will always appear .75" from the top and bottom edges of the page, so be careful not to set your top or bottom margin to less than .75" if you use headers and footers. Otherwise, your document text will overlap the header or footer.

To enter text for a header or footer, click in the Header or Footer text box. A cursor will appear, and you can begin typing. If there is text in the text box already, highlight it and then begin typing. That way, the new text will replace the old text.

Windows will help you create and format your header and footer text. If you're using Windows' built-in applications, you can use special codes made up of an & (ampersand) and a letter to insert header or footer text or change its alignment. Table 9-1 lists the codes for header and footer entries. To enter a code for a header or footer, click in the Header or Footer text box and type a code. For example, if you want to print a page number on the bottom of each page and you want the word *Page* to appear next to the number, type *Page &p* in the Footer text box.

Table 9-1

Code	Function
&c	Center the header or footer
&d	Print the system date
&f	Print the active file name
&l	Left-align the header or footer
&p	Print the page numbers
&r	Right-align the header or footer
&t	Print the system time

You can use these codes to tell Windows to supply header and footer information and to format headers and footers.

Setting up your printer

Since Windows allows you to install more than one printer (as we discussed in Chapter 3), you need to choose the printer you're going to use. When you issue the Print Setup command from the File menu, the application will display a Print Setup dialog box like the one shown in Figure 9-6. If you don't want to use the default printer, click on the Specific Printer radio button, select the printer you want to use from the Specific Printer drop-down list box, and then choose OK to close the dialog box.

You can change default printer settings, such as page orientation (portrait or landscape). If, for example, you want to print a spreadsheet that has a landscape orientation, click on the Landscape radio button. After you've made the change, click on OK to return to your document.

Figure 9-6

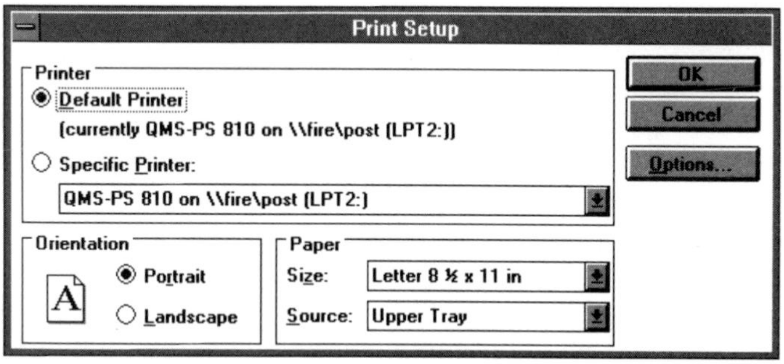

The Print Setup dialog box lists the installed printers.

To send a document to the printer, simply select the Print command on the File menu. The application will display a dialog box showing that the file is being sent to the printer. If the printer is not a network printer, and if you selected the Use Print Manager option in the Printers dialog box when the printer was installed, the Print Manager icon will appear on the desktop. At this point, you can resume working with your application while the Print Manager handles the printing of the file in the background. When the entire file has been sent to the printer, the Print Manager icon will disappear from the desktop. If something goes wrong while you're printing (for example, the printer runs out of paper), the Print Manager will alert you to the problem by displaying a warning dialog box. After you resolve the problem, you'll need to access the Print Manager to resume printing. Chapter 7 explains how to resume printing and provides other details about how to work with the Print Manager.

Issuing the Print command

It's always better to exit an application with the Exit command on the File menu than to use the Close command on the Control menu. The Close command will remove the application from the desktop, but it might not clear the application from your computer's memory or, in some cases, save the file.

Exiting applications

Windows makes it easy for you to share data between applications. With Clipboard, you can cut or copy data from one application and paste it into another. If you want to establish a dynamic link between two applications, you can do so by using Microsoft Object Linking and Embedding (OLE) or Windows' dynamic data exchange (DDE) facility. OLE and DDE allow Windows applications that support OLE or a similar DDE implementation to update data in one application with data that has been changed in another application. Windows Paintbrush, Write, Cardfile, Object Packager, Media Player, Sound Recorder,

SHARING DATA

Microsoft Excel version 3.0, and Microsoft Word for Windows version 2.0 support OLE. Word for Windows versions 1.0 and 1.1 and earlier versions of Microsoft Excel support a similar implementation of DDE.

Using Clipboard

Clipboard is a storage area for information that has been copied or cut from any Windows application. The information in Clipboard—which can be text, a Paintbrush graphic, or even a screen capture—can be retrieved by most Windows applications. For text and graphics, you'll need to use the Cut, Copy, and Paste commands on the Edit menu. For screen captures, you'll use the [Print Screen] and [Alt][Print Screen] keys. You can also use the Copy command on the File menu in the File Manager to copy a link to the file to Clipboard, as we discussed in Chapter 6. All the information-passing between applications occurs invisibly. Unlike the Print Manager icon, the Clipboard Viewer icon does not appear on the desktop when Clipboard is in use. However, you can double-click on the Clipboard Viewer icon in the Program Manager to open Clipboard and view the data in its memory.

Clipboard can hold only one item at a time. For example, if you copy text to Clipboard without pasting the text somewhere and then cut or copy different text or a graphic, Clipboard will replace the original text with the new text or graphic. You will have to copy the original text again before you can paste it. Windows imposes no specific limits on the length of text you may move or copy to Clipboard in one operation.

Moving text and graphics

Moving text and graphics within an application is a common use of Clipboard. To move text, highlight it and then issue the Cut command on the Edit menu. Now position the cursor in the place you want to move the text, and choose the Paste command. Windows will insert the text at the cursor position. For more information about moving text, see Chapter 10.

Moving graphics is similar to moving text. First, select the graphic and then choose the Cut command. Next, position the cursor in the new location and choose the Paste command. Windows will insert the graphic at the cursor position. Moving graphics can be more complicated in Paintbrush than in other applications because you have more options. Chapter 11 provides details about moving graphics in Paintbrush.

Copying text and graphics

You'll probably want to copy text nearly as often as you want to move it. Unlike cutting text, copying text leaves the selected text in its original location. Copying also provides an easy way to repeat a phrase, such as a product or company name, throughout a document. To copy text, highlight it and then choose the Copy command on the Edit menu. Whenever you want to insert the copied text, just issue the Paste command. You can continue to paste that text as many times and in as many locations as you like until you replace it in Clipboard with something else by using the Copy or Cut command again.

Windows lets you share data between applications or documents by activating the appropriate application and opening the destination document (the document to which you'll add data) before you issue the Paste command. For example, you might want to copy a company's name and address from your Cardfile address file and use it in a business letter in Write. To begin the transfer, you need to first open Cardfile, highlight the data on the card, and then issue the Copy command. Next, return to the Program Manager (remember that you can minimize or resize Cardfile's application window so that you can use the Program Manager window) and start Write. When Write's application window appears, open the business letter and issue the Paste command to insert the address at the cursor position.

Sharing text and graphics between applications

Windows can copy the current screen or active window to Clipboard. This capability is handy for creating presentations about software or about the data that the software displays. To capture the entire desktop, press the [Print Screen] key. To capture only the active window, press [Alt][Print Screen]. Now you can paste the captured screen as a graphic into another application, like Paintbrush, so that you can print it. (You might even want to edit the screen in Paintbrush before you print it.)

Capturing screens

If, for example, you need to teach your co-workers how to calculate the budget using Microsoft Excel, you could illustrate each step with a figure. The figure would include the active Excel window and a caption. To create the figure, you need to arrange the spreadsheet the way you want it, and then press [Alt][Print Screen] to capture the active window to Clipboard. Next, you can use Paintbrush to paste the screen from Clipboard into a file and then print or modify the screen. Remember, each time you capture a screen, the new screen replaces the one in Clipboard. So be sure to paste each screen or save it from Clipboard to a file before you capture the next screen.

You can open the Clipboard Viewer icon in the Main group window in the Program Manager to view the data in Clipboard or change some of the default settings. Figure 9-7 on the following page shows the Clipboard Viewer window after we copied some data—in this case, a combination of graphics and text that can serve as letterhead. By default, the Clipboard Viewer work area always displays scroll bars.

Working in the Clipboard Viewer window

Figure 9-7

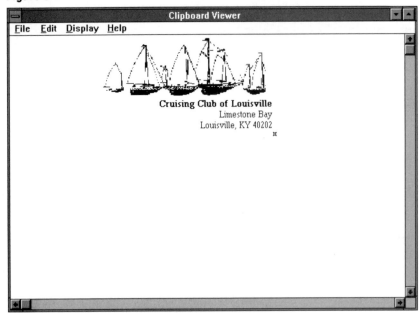

The Clipboard Viewer window displays the data in Clipboard.

Choosing a data format

Clipboard Viewer's Display menu lets you choose a format for displayed data. By default, the Display menu uses the Auto command, which automatically selects a data format that best fits the data and the application that will receive the pasted information. The other commands that appear on the menu offer the available data formats. Not every application can accept every format. You'll need to choose a different format only if the Auto command cannot or does not properly paste the Clipboard contents. For example, if you are pasting text from a Write text file for a foreign language, you might need to choose the OEM (Original Equipment Manufacturer) Text format from the Display menu. However, if two applications aren't compatible because they don't use the same kind of data files, such as Word for Windows and Micropro's WordStar, then you'll need to specify Auto loading, which will use the ASCII text format to establish a common meeting ground.

Clearing the work area

If you want to delete the data in Clipboard's memory to make that memory available for your applications, you need to open the Clipboard Viewer window and either use the Delete command on the Edit menu or press the [Delete] key. Clipboard Viewer will display a confirmation dialog box, asking you to verify that you want to clear the contents of Clipboard. Clicking on OK in this dialog box will clear the work area and Clipboard's memory.

If you want to save the data in Clipboard before you clear the work area, you can issue the Save As command on the File menu. The Save As dialog box, shown in Figure 9-8, will appear, with the file name extension .CLP displayed in the File Name text box and in the Save File as Type drop-down list box. Clipboard will save your file with a default .CLP extension if you don't specify another file name extension. Note that you can save Clipboard data to another application by pasting the data into the application's work area and then issuing that application's Save command.

Saving the data in a Clipboard file

Figure 9-8

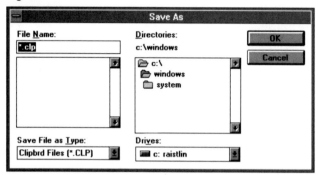

Clipboard Viewer's Save As dialog box displays the default file name extension.

If you have a favorite graphic or a commonly used address, you can copy it to Clipboard from its originating application and save it as a Clipboard file. That way, you can use Clipboard Viewer's Open command when you want to reopen the file and place the data back into Clipboard. Then you'll be ready to paste it into an application's document. To open a Clipboard file, choose the Open command from the File menu to display the Open dialog box. You can use this dialog box as you do any of the Open dialog boxes for other applications. Simply click on a file name from the File Name list box, and then click on OK to open the file and place the data in Clipboard Viewer's work area and in Clipboard's memory.

Opening Clipboard files

To exit the Clipboard Viewer window, choose the Exit command from the File menu. Clipboard Viewer will not display a warning dialog box prompting you to save your changes; it will simply close the application window. There-fore, if you want to save the displayed data in a file, make sure that you issue the Save As command before exiting Clipboard.

Exiting the Clipboard Viewer window

OLE (Object Linking and Embedding) offers you a way to include different types of information in one document. For example, you can include a spread-sheet and a chart in a report produced with a word processor. An OLE receiving

Using OLE

application lets you paste another file or part of a file from an OLE source application into a receiving file. Some applications are both OLE sources and OLE receivers (for example, Windows Write). Other applications are OLE receivers only (for example, Windows Cardfile). And still other applications are OLE sources only (for example, Windows Paintbrush and Object Packager).

The pasted information can be embedded or linked. Embedded information is stored in the receiving file. Linked information is stored in a source file; the receiving file for linked information stores only information about the source file and the application that created the source file. For both types of pasted information, you edit the source information in the original application (for example, a picture in Paintbrush).

OLE functions are easy to use. Each application that supports OLE contains menu commands for creating, inserting, and updating linked and embedded information. Most often, these commands are found on the Edit menu. The Copy and the Paste commands on the Edit menu have special OLE modifications. The Paste command inserts embedded information. In addition, the Edit menu contains a Paste Link command (for inserting linked information) and a Paste Special command for choosing between linking and embedding information or simply inserting the information as a bit map without connections to the original application. The Edit menu can also contain a Links (or Link) command for changing the type of link updating—from automatic to manual, for example.

OLE receiving applications usually provide an Insert Object command. In the dialog box for this command, you can select the type of information you want to insert. Windows then starts the appropriate source application. After you create the information in the source application, you first select the Update command from that application's File menu and then select the Exit & Return command from the File menu. This command name changes to include the name of the file in the receiving application; if you have not yet saved that file, the command name is Exit & Return to (Untitled). This command returns you to the source application and lets you see the information in your receiving file.

Windows also provides a related desktop accessory called Object Packager. With Object Packager, you can insert into an OLE receiving application an icon that represents a link to the source information. For details about Object Packager, see Chapter 14.

Inserting an OLE object

If you have text or a graphic that you want to insert into another document created with the same or another application, you use the standard Cut or Copy command on the Edit menu of the source application to place the text or graphic in Clipboard. The text or graphic from an OLE source application is an OLE object. If the application into which you paste the contents of Clipboard is an OLE receiving application, the pasted text or graphic will be an OLE object. If the application is not an OLE receiving application, then the pasted text or graphic will simply be a normally pasted piece of text or graphic without any sort of connection to the source.

To insert an OLE object into an OLE receiving application, choose the Paste, Paste Link, or Paste Special command on the Edit menu. The Paste command inserts an embedded object. The Paste Link command inserts a linked object. In the Links dialog box, accessed by choosing the Links command from the Edit menu, you can also choose whether the linked object should be updated automatically or manually. If you want the linked object to be updated each time the object changes in the source file, click on the Automatic radio button in the Update section of the dialog box. If you want the linked object to change only when you ask for an update, click on the Manual radio button in the Update section. The Paste Special dialog box displays a description of the Clipboard contents and lists the available data types. Windows usually selects the appropriate data type, but you can insert a different data type by selecting it. (The Picture type means that the data is not an OLE object but is simply a bit map with no connection to its source application.) Choose the Paste button to insert an embedded object or the Paste Link button (if available) to insert a linked object.

Changing linked object updating

If you decide later that you want to change the type of updating for a linked object, choose the Links command on the Edit menu. In the Links dialog box, select the link you want to edit, click on the radio button for the type of updating you want, and then click on OK to change the updating.

Updating a linked object

If you have chosen manual updating for a linked object, you can update the object by choosing the Links command on the Edit menu and clicking on the Update Now button in the Links dialog box.

Modifying an OLE object

To modify an OLE object, you can either double-click on the object or choose the object from the Edit menu. The object will appear in a source application window. At this point, you can change the object by using any of the tools available in the source application. When you have finished making the modifications, you can save them and then exit the source application to return to the receiving application.

Saving changes to OLE objects

After you make changes to an OLE object, you might want to save the changes in a file separate from the receiving file. When the object is embedded or linked, the Update command replaces the Save command on the File menu. Choosing the Update command sends the changes to the receiving file. Use the Save As command to save the object in a file with a different name. The source application will first ask if you want to update the object in the receiving file. After you save an object to a source application file, the File menu returns to its usual list of commands.

Creating an object from a receiving application

If you are working on a document and want to include an OLE object that has not yet been created, you can sometimes create the new object from within certain receiving applications. Choose the Insert Object command on the Edit menu (if the receiving application provides it). The Insert Object dialog box lists all the types of objects you can insert as embedded or linked objects. Select the type of object you want to insert and click on OK. The source application for the selected type of object starts running. You can create the object and then choose the Exit command from the File menu to return to the receiving application. The source application asks whether you want to update the receiving file. Choose Yes to see the object inserted at the cursor position.

Using DDE

Until OLE becomes widespread, you might still be able to take advantage of Windows' ability to perform dynamic data exchange (DDE). To illustrate how DDE works, let's suppose you create a summary report in Word for Windows that garners information from a Microsoft Excel spreadsheet. You need to copy all the pertinent information from the spreadsheet into your Word document. Without DDE, you would have to either print the spreadsheet and type in the information or copy and paste the data into your Word document with Edit commands. If some of the data in your report changes, you would have to recalculate and print the spreadsheet again and then copy and paste the correct information into your summary document in Word. Wouldn't it be nice to eliminate some of these steps and still ensure the accuracy of your report?

Let's repeat our scenario using DDE. Suppose that you complete all your statistics in Microsoft Excel and are creating a summary report in Word for Windows. You can link data in the spreadsheet to the Word report. That way, any time the data in the spreadsheet changes, Windows will update the numbers that appear in the Word report with the new values. In other words, the DDE acts as a conduit for the updating process.

To use DDE, you tell an application to retrieve data from another application with commands unique to each application. You need to supply the name of the source application (the application that will supply the information) and the name of that application's data file. Windows supplies the format of the data involved. Like Clipboard, DDE transfers data in various display formats. As you might expect, individual applications provide their own techniques for making DDE requests.

When the request has been answered and the source data appears in the requesting application, a DDE link has been established. A hot link tells the source application to automatically update the data in the receiving application as soon as linked data changes. A warm link updates data only when the receiving application (or the user) approves the transfer. (By the way, a cold link is simply unchanging data—the kind of data that is pasted with Clipboard.)

As with OLE, the best feature of DDE is that the source application does all the hard work in the background while you write your report. For example, if you are downloading stock reports from a bulletin board service with Crosstalk (the source application) to a Microsoft Excel spreadsheet (the receiving application) that calculates trends and charts the data, Excel can continuously update the chart (with a hot link) as it receives new information. In turn, the chart is part of a Word for Windows summary report linked to Excel. Therefore, as the stock information changes in Crosstalk, Crosstalk updates Excel and Excel updates Word for Windows. The report will be not only accurate but also timely.

Character Map is a simple Windows accessory that you can use from within any Windows application to insert special characters. In addition to the characters that appear on the keyboard, Windows can also display and print a wide variety of foreign-language characters and other symbols. In the past, the process of inserting special characters was both awkward and inconvenient: You had to look up the character's numeric code in a character chart, turn on the [Num Lock] key, hold down the [Alt] key, and then type the number corresponding to the character you wanted to insert. Now, with Character Map, you can see a display of available characters in various fonts, select a character, copy it to Clipboard, and then paste it into your application.

USING CHARACTER MAP

To start Character Map, double-click on its icon in the Accessories group window in the Program Manager. Windows will display the Character Map window, shown in Figure 9-9.

Figure 9-9

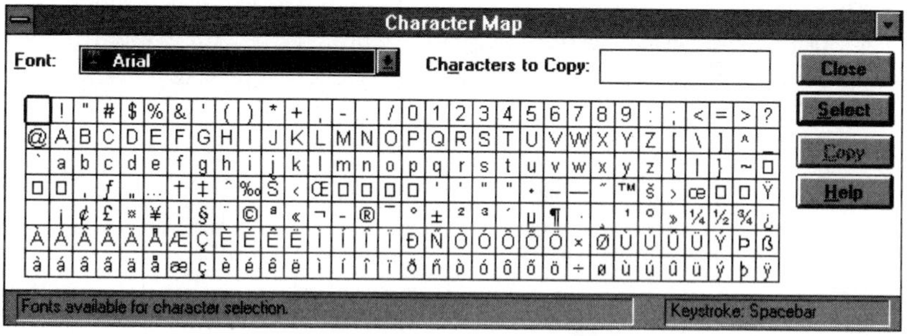

![Character Map window]

The Character Map window displays all the available characters for each installed font.

From the Font drop-down list box in the Character Map window, select the font containing the character you want to insert. To take a close look at the character, position the pointer on the character and hold down the mouse button. Character Map will give you an enlarged view of the character, as shown in Figure 9-10. This enlargement feature helps you ensure that you are selecting the correct character before you copy and paste it.

Figure 9-10

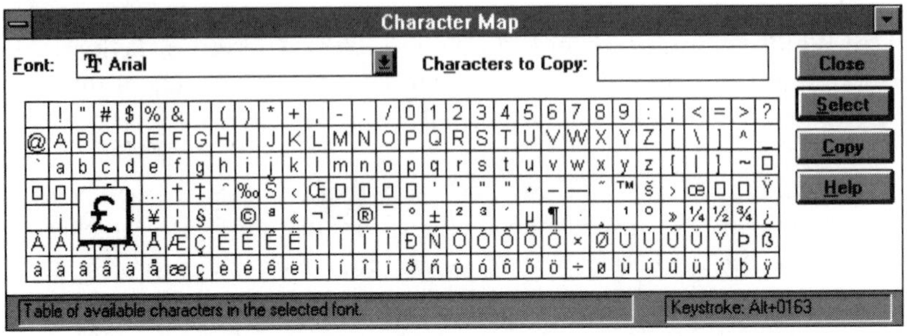

You can point to a character and hold down the mouse button to see an enlargement.

You can use two additional methods to see an enlarged character. If one of the characters in the Character Map window also appears on the keyboard, Character Map will enlarge the character when you press the key. (This can be a convenient way to compare the appearance of a character in various fonts.) Or, if you turn on the [Num Lock] key, hold down the [Alt] key, and type a character's numeric code on the numeric keypad, Character Map will enlarge the character corresponding to the character code you typed.

When you've selected the character you want to insert in your application, double-click on it. When you double-click on a character, it will appear in the Characters to Copy text box. (If you accidentally double-click on a character you don't want, simply highlight it in the text box and press the [Delete] key.) Click on the Copy button to put a copy of the character in Clipboard. You can then paste the character into your application.

If you want to insert several characters from the Character Map window at one time, double-click on each one in the order in which you want the characters to appear in your application. The characters will appear in that order in the Characters to Copy text box, as shown in Figure 9-11. Then click on the Copy button to send copies of the characters to Clipboard. You can paste the characters into your application all at the same time.

To close the Character Map window, double-click on the Control menu box or choose the Close command from the Control menu.

Figure 9-11

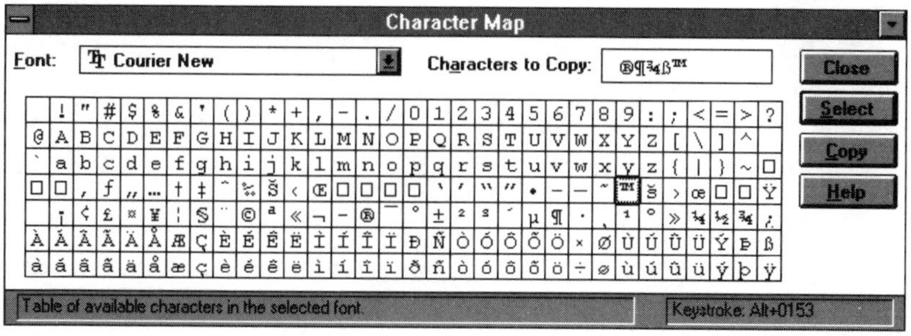

Double-click on characters to add them to the Characters to Copy text box.

As you use the various Windows applications, you'll notice that several menu bars have a View menu. The View menu doesn't work with files or the data in the work area as the other menus do; instead, it affects the work area itself. In Calculator, for example, the View menu lets you switch between two calculators, standard and scientific. The View menu has different commands for different applications but performs the same function in all of them—changing the work area. Of course, some applications, such as Notepad, will not have a View menu since their work areas cannot be changed.

ALTERING THE WORK AREA

If you're fortunate, all the applications that you use with Windows will be designed to work in Windows. Realistically, however, you'll probably need to use at least one non-Windows application to get your job done. Windows allows you to run non-Windows applications and, in some cases, even lets you share data between non-Windows and Windows applications via Clipboard.

USING NON-WINDOWS APPLICATIONS

You can launch a non-Windows application with the MS-DOS Prompt icon in the Main group window in the Program Manager, as we showed you earlier in this chapter. You can also use the Run command from either the Program Manager or the File Manager. The File Manager provides two additional ways to open a non-Windows application: You can issue the Open command or simply double-click on the application's name to launch the application.

The best way to use a non-Windows application with Windows is to manually set the memory and other program options in a PIF (program information file). Windows automatically checks for a PIF when it starts a non-Windows application. If Windows doesn't find one, it uses its default PIF. You can read more about PIFs and their settings in Chapter 17.

If you run Windows in standard mode, non-Windows applications will run full-screen and will suspend the running of all other applications. However, you can switch to any other application by using the Task Manager. To access the

Task Manager while running a full-screen, non-Windows application, simply press [Ctrl][Esc]. Windows will minimize the application into an icon and then display the Task List dialog box. After you double-click on the name of the window you'd like to switch to, Windows will activate that window and the application in it. When Windows displays the desktop, the non-Windows application will appear as a minimized MS-DOS application icon. While an icon, the non-Windows application is on hold or paused. You can return to the non-Windows application by double-clicking on its icon.

In Windows' 386 enhanced mode, you can run non-Windows applications in a window concurrently with Windows applications. To do this consistently, you should choose the Windowed radio button in the Display Usage section of the PIF Editor. (See Chapter 17 for details.) Then you must start the application by launching its PIF rather than its program file. The non-Windows application will even continue running while minimized into an icon.

If you haven't set up a PIF for your non-Windows application (and you are running Windows in 386 enhanced mode), you can use the Settings command on the Control menu of the application's MS-DOS Prompt icon. First, start the non-Windows application, and then press [Ctrl][Esc] or [Alt][Tab] to minimize the application into an MS-DOS Prompt icon and switch back to Windows. (If you press [Ctrl][Esc], you'll need to click on Cancel in the Task List dialog box.) Next, click on the application's MS-DOS Prompt icon to display its Control menu, as shown in Figure 9-12.

Figure 9-12

When you click on the application's MS-DOS Prompt icon, this Control menu is displayed.

When you choose the Settings command from the Control menu, the MS-DOS Prompt dialog box, shown in Figure 9-13, will appear. Click on the Window radio button in the Display Options section of the dialog box, and then click on OK. Now double-click on the application's MS-DOS Prompt icon. Your non-Windows application will reappear on the screen—but now it will be running in a window, as shown in Figure 9-14.

Figure 9-13

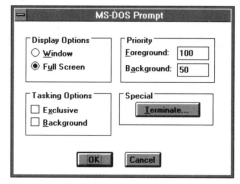

The MS-DOS Prompt dialog box lets you choose to run a non-Windows application in a window.

Figure 9-14

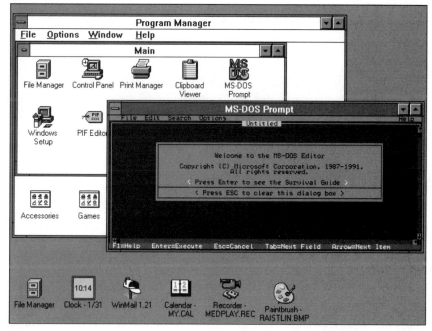

Your non-Windows application appears in an MS-DOS Prompt window.

If the text in the window of your application appears too large or too small, choose Fonts from the Control menu to display the Font Selection dialog box, shown in Figure 9-15 on the next page. When you click on one of the font sizes, the Window Preview display box shows a window of a different size, and the Selected Font display box presents a sample of text in the selected size.

Figure 9-15

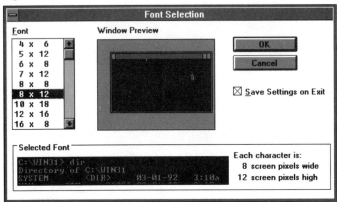

*In the Font Selection dialog box, you can choose a new font
size and preview the window size and font display.*

When you have selected the font size you want, click on OK to apply the
setting to the current MS-DOS Prompt window in which the non-Windows
application is running. If you want to save this font setting for the next time you
run an MS-DOS session in a window, be sure that the Save Settings on Exit check
box in the Font Selection dialog box is turned on before you click on OK. To
discard the setting when you exit the MS-DOS session, turn off this check box.

**Using the 386
enhanced mode
Edit commands**

If you want to transfer information from a non-Windows application to
another application (either Windows or non-Windows), you can use the 386
enhanced mode Edit commands. You'll find these commands on the Control
menu of a non-Windows application window only if you are running 386 enhanced mode. When you click on the Control menu, you'll see a menu like the
one shown earlier in Figure 9-12. To copy data to Clipboard, choose the Edit
cascading menu to display the 386 enhanced mode Edit commands shown in
Figure 9-16. Note that you can't copy graphics to non-Windows applications—
just text. The Mark command allows you to select information to be copied to
Clipboard. (After you choose the Mark command, you can select text with the
arrow keys or—if you have a Microsoft mouse and the Microsoft mouse driver—
with the mouse.) The Copy command, of course, copies the selected information. The Paste command inserts the contents of Clipboard into the application
at the cursor position. The Scroll command moves the application work area so
that you can copy the next screenful of information.

Figure 9-16

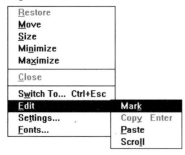

You can copy text from non-Windows applications to Clipboard using commands on the 386 enhanced mode Edit menu.

If you're running Windows in standard mode, press [Alt][Spacebar] to see if the non-Windows application supports the Control menu. If the Control menu doesn't appear, the editing commands are not available. You can access the Task Manager even if you can't open a Control menu.

When you're working with a full-screen, non-Windows application, you can copy only the entire screen to Clipboard. You can't select information; it's all or nothing. You can press [Print Screen] to copy the current screen to Clipboard.

Even though you can place information in Clipboard, you may not always be able to paste it into another application. The destination application must be able to accept the data in the original format.

In this chapter

Using Write **10**

What would you do without a word processor? Fortunately, Windows has a built-in word processor, called Write. In this chapter, we'll describe the basic operation and features of Write, discuss formatting and editing, and show you how to add graphics to your Write documents. At the end of the chapter, we'll demonstrate how Write handles files and printing.

Write is an application that will let you create, edit, print, and save documents. Write can also import text and graphics from other applications, and you can save Write documents in a form that other applications understand.

WRITE

Starting Write

To start Write, just double-click on the Write icon in the Accessories group window within the Program Manager. Windows will bring up an application window for Write, complete with a menu bar and the other controls associated with an application. Write's application window has a work area for your document. Unlike other, more powerful Windows-based applications, such as Word for Windows or Microsoft Excel, Write cannot use multiple document windows. When you open a second Write document, Write automatically closes the first one instead of displaying them both in separate document windows. You can, however, create the effect of having multiple documents open on your desktop. When you want to work with another document as well as the one already on the desktop, you can return to the Program Manager and start Write again. In the additional Write window, you can open the new document. At that point, you'll have two copies of the Write application on the desktop—each with a different document.

The Write application window

The Write application window shown in Figure 10-1 appears when you start Write. It has all the basic elements of any application window: a title bar, a Control menu box, Minimize and Maximize boxes, a menu bar, horizontal and vertical scroll bars, and a size-adjustable frame. In addition, Write features a page status bar that is displayed at the bottom of the window to the left of the horizontal scroll bar. This status bar indicates the page in which the cursor currently appears. The work area is the major part of the window and contains the end-of-file marker, the cursor, and the page-break marker. The icon that appears next to the cursor in Figure 10-1 is the end-of-file marker, which automatically appears at the end of your text. The page-break marker, which looks like a right-pointing chevron, will appear in the work area when you issue the Repaginate command. Later, when we talk about pagination, we will show you how to insert page breaks in your document.

Figure 10-1

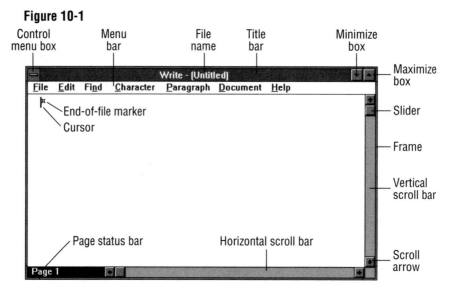

The Write application window has all the standard window elements plus a page status bar.

The ruler

The ruler is one of the features Write provides to make your work easier. To display the ruler, choose the Ruler On command from the Document menu. Figure 10-2 shows how the ruler will appear on the screen. Since the Ruler On command works like a toggle switch, the command name will change to Ruler Off after you display the ruler.

Figure 10-2

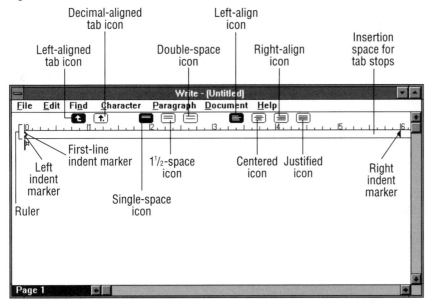

You can add a ruler to the window by choosing the Ruler On command on the Document menu.

As you can see in Figure 10-2, the ruler contains nine icons organized into three functional groups: tab icons, spacing icons, and alignment icons. We'll show you how to use these icons to format paragraphs later in this chapter.

The ruler's scale displays inches or centimeters, depending on the setting you choose with the Page Layout command on the Document menu. By default, the ruler display is set for inches. Figure 10-3 on the next page shows a metric version of the ruler. Below the scale on both versions of the ruler is an open line where you can place the tab and indent markers. The tab markers look just like the graphics that appear on the tab icons. The first-line indent marker is a dot, initially embedded in the left indent marker; it controls the indent of the first line of a paragraph. The opposing triangles under the ruler are the left and right indent markers.

It's a good idea to turn on the ruler whenever you use Write. The only time you might not want to use the ruler is when you need more space to display your document. For instance, if you are working on a table or trying to place a large graphic, you may need more of the work area.

Figure 10-3

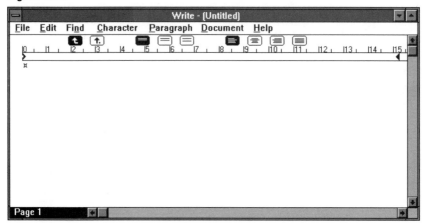

This is a metric version (in centimeters) of the ruler.

WRITE BASICS

In order to create a document with Write, you need to master a few basic skills. Specifically, you need to know how to enter text, navigate through your document, select text, and edit your work. After you learn these basics, you'll be ready to learn about formatting.

Entering text

As you type, Write enters the text into your untitled document. Write displays the text as it will appear on a printed page. This ability is commonly referred to as WYSIWYG (What You See Is What You Get).

Entering text in Write is actually easier than typing text on a typewriter. A special facility called Word Wrap lets you type a constant stream of characters without having to use carriage returns at the end of each line. If you are new to word processing, you may be tempted to press the [Enter] key as you approach the end of a line of text in order to move to the next line. Not to worry—if there isn't enough room on the current line for the word you are typing, Write will move that word to the beginning of the next line automatically.

In fact, the only time you need to press the [Enter] key as you enter text in Write is when you want to start a new paragraph. You can unnecessarily complicate your editing and formatting by placing carriage returns at the end of each line. For example, if you decide later to insert or delete text or change margins, you'll have to edit each line manually to reset your line breaks. If you let Word Wrap handle the line breaks for you, you can change the content, format, and layout of your document, and Write will automatically reflow the text.

The text you enter in a document will appear at the cursor (a blinking vertical line). If you want to enter text in another part of your document, you need to move the cursor. To do this, move the pointer (which looks like an

I-beam) to the new location and click. The cursor will then move to that spot. At that point, you can begin entering more text.

Navigating

As you polish the documents you create in Write, you'll need to move the cursor to edit the text. In Table 10-1, you'll find a description of keyboard shortcuts you can use to move the cursor quickly through the text of your document. For example, to move the cursor to the top of the document, press [Ctrl][Home]. Holding down any of the key combinations listed in Table 10-1 (continuous selection) will repeat the function until you release the key(s). For example, if you want to advance the cursor a word at a time continuously until you reach the correct word, simply hold down the [Ctrl]➔ keys. Note that you must first choose the Repaginate command from the File menu to add page breaks to your document before you can use the [Goto][Page Up] and [Goto] [Page Down] shortcuts. (The [Goto] key is the number 5 key on your keyboard's numeric keypad.)

Table 10-1

Keystroke	Movement	Keystroke	Movement
↑	Up one line	[Goto]↓	Next paragraph
↓	Down one line	[Goto]↑	Previous paragraph
→	Right one character	[Goto][Page Up]	Previous numbered page
←	Left one character		
[Ctrl]→	Right one word	[Goto][Page Down]	Next numbered page
[Ctrl]←	Left one word		
[Home]	To beginning of line	[Ctrl][Page Up]	To top of current window
[End]	To end of line		
[Page Up]	Up one window	[Ctrl][Page Down]	To bottom of current window
[Page Down]	Down one window		
[Goto]→	Next sentence	[Ctrl][Home]	To beginning of document
[Goto]←	Previous sentence	[Ctrl][End]	To end of document

These key combinations provide shortcuts for navigating in your document.

In addition to using key combinations to move through your document, you can also use the Go To Page command on the Find menu or the accelerator key [F4] to move to a different page. But before selecting the Go To Page command or using the accelerator key, you must use the Repaginate command on the File menu to paginate your document. And, after you add text to your document, you must issue the Repaginate command again to update the page numbering. After all the pages have numbers, the Go To Page command will then be able to access the page you specify. Remember, you need to reissue the Repaginate command only when you add new text that will change the page numbers. (We'll show you how to use the Repaginate command later in this chapter.) When you select the Go To Page command on the Find menu (or press [F4]), the Go To dialog box shown in Figure 10-4 will appear. To specify the page you want to move to, just type the page number in the text box and click on OK. Write will then move the cursor to the top of that page. However, if you haven't initially paginated the document, any page number you enter in the Go To dialog box will return you to the beginning of the document.

Figure 10-4

To move to another page, enter the page number in the Go To dialog box and click on OK.

Selecting text

You can manipulate or edit large parts of your document while leaving the rest alone. To do this, select only the text you want to edit or format. To select text, just drag the I-beam pointer over the text you want. As you select the text, Write will highlight it (display it in inverse video). You can highlight only one block of text at a time. As soon as you click somewhere else inside the work-space, Write will remove the highlight from the selected text.

To highlight an entire line, move the pointer to the selection bar (the far left side of the work area) until it changes to a standard arrow pointer. (The arrow will point to the right rather than the left.) If you click once, you will highlight the line next to the pointer. If you press the mouse button and drag downward, you will highlight multiple lines of text. If you double-click in the selection bar, you will highlight the entire paragraph. If you hold down the [Ctrl] key and click once in the selection bar, you will select the entire document.

Of course, if you need to select a large block of text and not the entire document, you might find it tiresome to drag through line after line of text. Another technique for selecting text uses the [Shift] key. For example, suppose you want to highlight all the text in Figure 10-5 beginning with the words *Wind brushed* in line 5 of the first paragraph and ending with *seat compartments* in line 8 of the second paragraph. Begin by clicking just to the left of the word *Wind,* and then hold down the [Shift] key and click just to the right of the period that follows the word *compartments.* Figure 10-6 shows the results.

If you prefer using only the keyboard, you can refer to Table 10-2 on page 234 for the appropriate keystrokes to select text in your document. These keystrokes are also good shortcuts for large-block selections. For example, the combination [Ctrl][Shift][Home] selects all the text from the cursor to the beginning of the document.

Figure 10-5

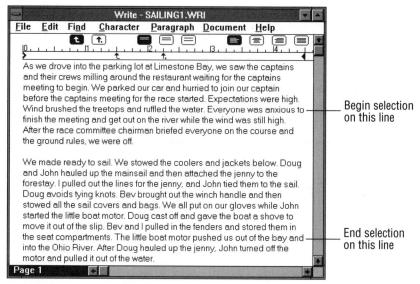

You can use your mouse and the [Shift] key to select a block of text in a document.

Figure 10-6

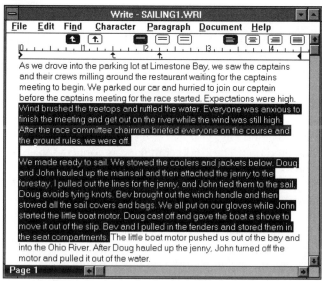

This is the same document with the text selected.

Table 10-2

Keystroke	Selection
[Shift]←, [Shift]→	One character to the left or right. If the character is already selected, moving over it again will cancel the selection.
[Shift]↑ , [Shift]↓	One line of text up or down. [Shift]↓ selects the current line and then subsequent lines when you repeat the keystroke. If the line is already selected, moving over it again will cancel the selection.
[Ctrl][Shift]←	Previous word.
[Ctrl][Shift]→	Next word.
[Shift][Home]	Text to the beginning of the line.
[Shift][End]	Text to the end of the line.
[Shift][Page Up]	Text up one window. Typing this keystroke to cross back over a selection will cancel the selection.
[Shift][Page Down]	Text down one window. Typing this keystroke to cross back over a selection will cancel the selection.
[Ctrl][Shift][Home]	Text to the beginning of the document.
[Ctrl][Shift][End]	Text to the end of the document.

You can use these key combinations to select text.

Basic editing techniques

You can replace or remove one character or a selected block of text at a time. To replace text, first highlight the old text and then begin typing to replace it with new text. The [Backspace] and [Delete] keys remove text. The [Backspace] key removes text to the left of the cursor. The [Delete] key removes text to the right of the cursor. If you press [Backspace] or [Delete] while text is highlighted, Write will delete all the highlighted text.

If you delete something accidentally, you can use the Undo command on the Edit menu to recover deleted text. The Undo command is context-sensitive. For example, when you press the [Backspace] key to delete a word, the command becomes Undo Editing. When you press [Enter] for a paragraph, the Undo command changes to Undo Typing. If the command is simply Undo, then the last command or action will be reversed. The accelerator keys that you use to undo an action are [Ctrl]Z or [Alt][Backspace].

Table 10-3 summarizes the basic editing keys. They include the [Backspace] and [Delete] keys and the accelerator keys for the Edit menu commands.

Table 10-3

Keystroke	Function
[Backspace]	Delete a character to the left of the cursor or delete selected text
[Delete]	Delete a character to the right of the cursor or delete selected text
[Ctrl]Z or [Alt][Backspace]	Undo the previous editing command or function
[Ctrl]X or [Shift][Delete]	Delete, or cut, selected text and place it in Clipboard
[Ctrl]C or [Ctrl][Insert]	Copy selected text to Clipboard
[Ctrl]V or [Shift][Insert]	Insert, or paste, text from Clipboard into a document at the cursor

You can use these key combinations to edit your document.

FORMATTING

You can enliven and clarify your text with Write's formatting capabilities. For instance, you can enhance your document by centering and boldfacing a title at the beginning of an article or italicizing a book title in a report. You can format characters, paragraphs, or an entire document. In this section, we'll show you how to change character styles, fonts, and point sizes and how to add optional hyphens. Then we'll teach you how to set paragraph alignment, spacing, indents, and tabs. Finally, we'll discuss page formatting, which includes margin settings, pagination, and the use of headers and footers.

Character formatting

You can choose a character format before you begin typing, or you can apply a new choice of format to highlighted text. Characters can be formatted for style, font, and point size. The default for Write is a Regular style in an Arial 10-point font (not italic or boldface).

Using character styles

Character styles can add emphasis to your text. For example, you can use the italic style for a book title. You can make a character bold, italic, underlined, superscripted, subscripted, or any combination of these styles. Figure 10-7 on the following page shows a sample of each style. A style is linked to a paragraph or a character. Write's Character menu will display check marks beside the active styles of selected text. To turn off a style, open the Character menu and then select the style again to toggle off the check mark.

Figure 10-7

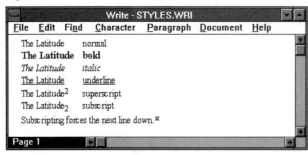

Write provides these character styles.

If you want to start typing text in a new style of type, make your choices on the Character menu and resume typing. The new text you enter will be in the new style and will continue in that style until you change it with the Character menu again. You can change the style of a selected block of text by highlighting the text and choosing the style from the Character menu. Only the text in the highlighted block will change.

You can turn off all the styles in the selected text by choosing Regular on the Character menu. This option is especially helpful if more than one style is active at a time (bold italic, for example). You can simply select Regular to cancel all special formatting instructions.

Accelerator keys are available for the Regular, Bold, Italic, and Underline commands on the Character menu. To select Regular, press [F5]. To select Bold, Italic, or Underline, press [Ctrl]B, [Ctrl]I, or [Ctrl]U, respectively. You can also choose an italic, bold, or bold italic style by using the Fonts command on the Character menu. This command displays the Font dialog box, in which you can choose one of these styles from the Font Style list box. Click on OK in this dialog box to apply the style to new or selected text.

When you use the Superscript or Subscript command in single-spaced lines, Write has to make room between lines for the superscripted or subscripted characters. Write accommodates this by adjusting the space (or leading) between the line that contains the superscripted or subscripted character and the line above or below.

Using fonts

In addition to styles, the Fonts command on the Character menu lets you choose the fonts you want to use. For example, you might be able to choose from these fonts: Courier, Arial, LinePrinter, Modern, Roman, Script, Times New Roman, Courier New, and Symbol. Figure 10-8 provides a sample of each of these fonts.

Figure 10-8

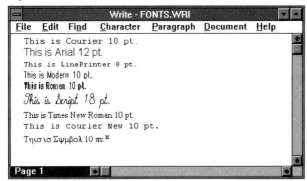

The HP LaserJet setup provides nine fonts.

You use the same technique to apply a font that you use to apply a style. You can select a font for new text or change a block of text to a selected font, and you can even have multiple fonts on a page. You can switch fonts any time by selecting a new font in the Font dialog box and resuming typing. The text you type from that point on will reflect your new font choice. If you want to change existing text to a new font, highlight the text and choose a new font from the dialog box.

Sometimes your printer will have more available fonts than Write does. If you choose a font for your printer that Write doesn't have, Write will substitute a screen font that will approximate the printer font you chose. Write will use the same spacing for the screen text as the printer will use for its output. That way, you'll have a better idea of how the page will look and how to set your tabs and spacing to achieve the desired formatting.

You can change the point size of a font in one of three ways. First, you can use the Reduce Font and the Enlarge Font commands on the Character menu. After you select the text you want to size, you can use these commands to adjust the point size by 2 points. (If the screen font doesn't change, the printer doesn't support that point size.) If you have used the Reduce Font and Enlarge Font commands repeatedly and don't remember the final point size, you can check the highlighted text by using the Fonts command to bring up the Font dialog box and checking the current size in the Size text box, as shown in Figure 10-9 on the following page.

The second way to change the point size of your text is to use the Size list box in the Font dialog box. To do this, highlight the text and choose the Fonts command on the Character menu. Click on the font you want to use, and then select the desired point size in the Size list box. The Size text box will change to match your selection.

Changing the font point size

Figure 10-9

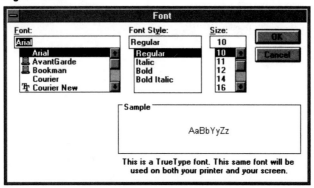

In the Font dialog box, you can choose a font, a style, and a point size and see a sample.

Finally, you can change the point size by entering the size in the Size text box in the Font dialog box. Again, highlight your text and choose the Fonts command on the Character menu. Click on the font you want to use, and then click on the Size text box and type in the new size. Remember, if you select a printer font instead of a TrueType font, the size must match one that is listed in the Size list box, or else the printer can't print it.

Using optional hyphens

As you type, Write will wrap the text to fit the margins so that you don't have to keep pressing [Enter]. Sometimes Write will have to wrap a long word that doesn't quite fit in the rest of the space on a line. When the word moves to the next line, it can leave a large empty space on the line above. If you want to reduce the white space or smooth a jagged right margin, you can insert an optional hyphen in a word. An optional hyphen will show up only if the word needs to be wrapped to the next line. If the word appears anywhere else in the line, the hyphen doesn't show up. To insert an optional hyphen in a word, position the pointer in the word where the hyphen should appear, and click to move the cursor there. Then, to add the hyphen, press [Ctrl][Shift]- (hyphen).

Of course, you can also use a regular hyphen. If your line ends abruptly, you can fill it with part of a word from the following line. Just insert a hyphen between syllables as you do when typing. Write will move the letters before the hyphen to the previous line, if they fit. If they don't fit, then they won't move until you reposition the hyphen so that fewer letters move to the previous line. Figure 10-10 shows a paragraph with regular hyphens. Be careful when you use regular hyphens; these hyphens may show up in the middle of a line if you edit the document and change the spacing.

Figure 10-10

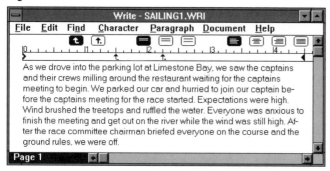

Some of the lines in this document end with regular hyphens.

Paragraph formatting creates the overall look or design of your document. You can set the alignment of the text, the line spacing, and the paragraph indents. Alignment and spacing are linked to paragraph markers, which Write inserts when you press [Enter]. Paragraph markers don't have visible characters, but they do take up a space. You can highlight and edit them like any other characters. They appear at the end of a paragraph or the beginning of a blank line. In Figure 10-11, we highlighted two paragraph markers.

Paragraph formatting

Figure 10-11

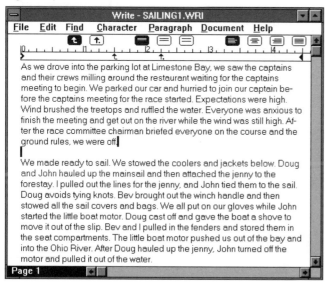

Two paragraph markers are highlighted in this document.

If you place your cursor anywhere in a paragraph and change the alignment or spacing, the entire paragraph will change. You can change more than one paragraph at a time if you highlight all the necessary paragraphs. If you hold down [Ctrl] and click once in the selection bar to select the entire document, you can even change the paragraph formatting for the whole document.

You can use a paragraph marker to format paragraphs repeatedly. Since all the alignment and spacing settings are linked to the paragraph marker, copying the marker will copy the settings, too. First, highlight the paragraph marker, and copy it to Clipboard with the Copy command on the Edit menu. Next, highlight the paragraph marker you want to replace, and choose the Paste command to replace it with the copied marker. Write will then reformat the paragraph with the new settings. You can use this method to repeat formats in a document.

The Paragraph menu controls alignment, spacing, and indents. You can reset any of these formats to their defaults by using the Normal command on this menu. When you highlight a paragraph and select the Normal command, the paragraph will be left-aligned, single-spaced, and not indented.

Setting alignment

Now that you know how paragraph markers work, let's look at how to set paragraph alignment. You can instruct Write to left-align, right-align, justify, or center your text.

To set alignment, you can use either the alignment icons on the ruler or the Paragraph menu commands. If you use the icons, just click anywhere in the paragraph, and then click on the appropriate icon to change the paragraph's alignment. For example, in Figure 10-12, we clicked on a paragraph and then clicked on the centered icon to center all the lines. Write centers only the paragraph that contains the cursor (unless you select text from more than one paragraph).

Figure 10-12

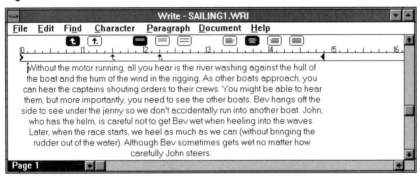

We used the centered icon to center this paragraph.

Instead of using the alignment icons, you can use commands on the Paragraph menu to change the alignment. To do this, select a paragraph as you did before, but this time select one of the alignment commands on the Paragraph menu. A check mark will appear next to the name of the command you choose. You can check only one alignment command at a time. (A check mark also will appear next to the appropriate command on the Paragraph menu when you use the icons on the ruler.)

Defining the space between lines is similar to setting the alignment, since you can set the spacing with a ruler icon or from a menu. You can choose single-spaced, 1½-spaced, or double-spaced lines. Again, the only paragraphs affected by your choices are the ones selected. To use an icon to change line spacing, select the necessary paragraphs and click on a spacing icon. Write's default is single spacing. You can format a new paragraph with different line spacing by pressing [Enter] and then clicking on one of the spacing icons. You can also choose a spacing command from the Paragraph menu to redefine the space between lines. After each formatting choice, a check mark will appear next to the name of the active command.

Spacing options

In addition to changing the space between the lines of a paragraph, you can change indents from the menu or the ruler. Commonly, the first line of a paragraph is indented five spaces. Instead of typing five spaces at the beginning of each paragraph, you can tell Write to automatically indent the line that follows a paragraph marker. To set the indent, use the Indents command on the Paragraph menu. The Indents dialog box, shown in Figure 10-13, provides three text boxes in which you can enter a left indent, first-line indent, or right indent. The Left Indent text box controls how far text is indented from the left margin for all the lines of the paragraph. The First Line text box sets the left indent for the first line only. The Right Indent text box controls how far text is indented from the right margin for all the lines. To indent the first line half an inch, type .5 in the First Line text box, and click on OK to continue. Figure 10-14 on the next page shows a paragraph with a first-line indent setting of .5". Note that the first-line indent marker (the dot) has been moved to the midpoint between 0 and 1 on the ruler.

Setting indents

Figure 10-13

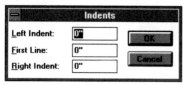

You can enter indent values in the Indents dialog box.

Figure 10-14

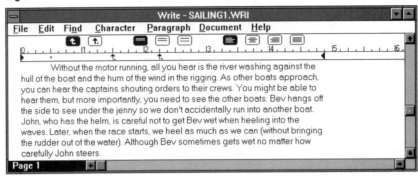

This paragraph has a first-line indent setting of .5".

If you want to create new indents for an entire paragraph, you can use the Left Indent or Right Indent text box. Figure 10-15 shows a paragraph with both the left indent and the right indent set at .5". These settings will establish indents on both sides of the paragraph, which is a useful format if you need to accent a paragraph or distinguish between speech and narrative.

Figure 10-15

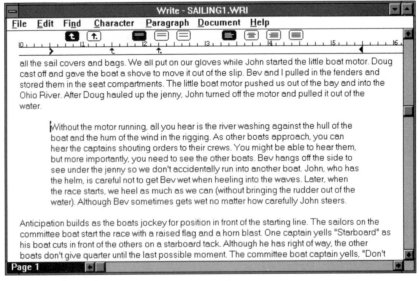

Left and right indents set this paragraph apart.

You can use a combination of indent settings to create hanging indents. In a paragraph with a hanging indent, the first line extends farther to the left than the following body of text does. To create a hanging indent, click on the paragraph that you want to indent, and then choose the Indents command on the Paragraph menu. Next, set the Left Indent text box to .5" and the First Line text box to −.5". This indents the body of the paragraph .5" and leaves the first line at the original left margin. (The first-line indent is measured as an offset from the left indent rather than from the left margin.) Figure 10-16 shows a paragraph with a hanging indent.

Creating hanging indents

Figure 10-16

First-line indent

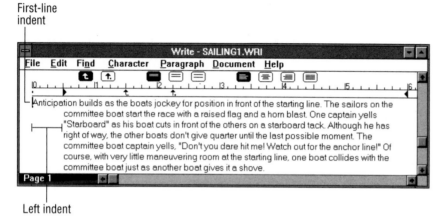

Left indent

You can create a hanging indent like this one with the Indents command or with the ruler.

Using the ruler to set indents is faster than using the Indents dialog box. The text will change as you move the indent marker, so you will see the results sooner, too. To change the indents, just drag the indent marker on the ruler. The first-line indent marker is a dot that is embedded in the left indent marker. You can drag the dot off the marker to create a first-line indent or a hanging indent, depending on the direction you drag the marker. As with other paragraph settings, the changes you make with the ruler will be reflected in the Indents dialog box.

Creating indents with the ruler

Tabs are invisible markers that you can set at any point along the ruler. You can use tabs to line up text to form columns and create tables. When you press the [Tab] key, the cursor will advance to the next tab marker on the current line of the document. By default, Write sets left-aligned tabs every half inch. When you set a new tab, Write deletes any default tabs to the left of the new tab. A

Working with tabs

word of caution: Tab settings apply to the whole document. If you create tables in a document and change the tab settings for one of the tables, Write will change the tab settings for the other tables as well. To modify the default tab settings, you can use either the ruler or the Tabs command on the Document menu to set new tabs.

Write offers two kinds of tabs: left-aligned and decimal-aligned. The left-aligned tab formats text to the right of the cursor. The decimal-aligned tab will let you add text to the left of the cursor until you type a period, and then it will add text to the right of the period. To use a decimal-aligned tab, press [Tab], enter the first part of the number, type a period, and then enter the rest of the number. This tab is handy for lining up columns of numbers in a table, as shown in Figure 10-17; the decimal points of all the numbers in the column will be aligned for easy reading.

Figure 10-17

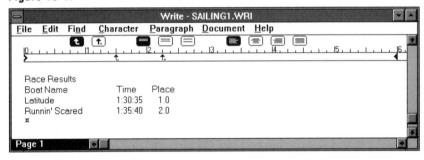

This table has both left-aligned and decimal-aligned tabs.

Setting tabs with the ruler

To set tabs with the ruler, simply select the left-aligned tab icon or the decimal-aligned tab icon, and click on the ruler at the position where you want to place the tab. The new tabs you set will replace any half-inch default tabs to the left of the rightmost tab marker. You can move the tab markers on the ruler by dragging them. To delete a tab, just drag the tab marker below the ruler. If you move or delete a tab, the text attached to that specific tab marker will change to match the new settings. If the rightmost tab is deleted or moved to the left, Write will restore default tabs at half-inch intervals in the remainder of the line.

Setting tabs with a command

To set tabs with a command, select the Tabs command on the Document menu. As you can see in Figure 10-18, the Tabs dialog box provides 12 text boxes to enter tab positions (in inches, unless you've chosen metric measurement in the Page Layout dialog box). By default, all of the text boxes are empty. The Decimal check boxes below the Positions text boxes indicate with an X that a position will use a decimal-aligned tab. Before you start entering position numbers, you need to determine where you're going to place the tabs. The Tabs dialog box will help you by displaying the location of any tabs you have set previously with the ruler, thereby providing you with a frame of reference. You can change the tab settings or add more, and you can enter the tab positions in any order. Write automatically sorts them in numeric order. After you have added the new tab positions, click on OK to return to the document and apply the new tab settings. Although you can be more precise by using the Tabs dialog box, it's easier to set tabs with the ruler because you can see the text change to match the tab settings.

Figure 10-18

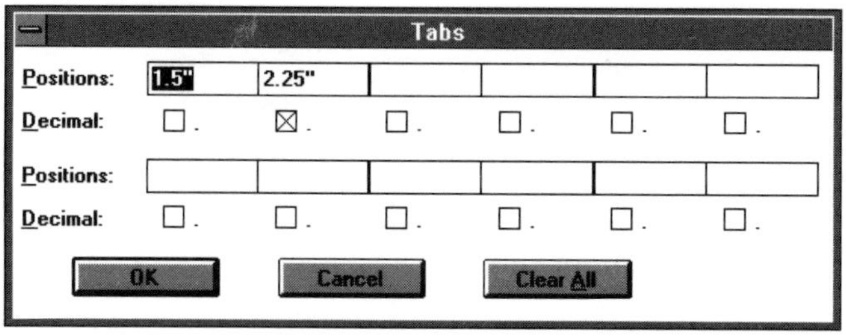

You can enter tab positions in any of the 12 text boxes in the Tabs dialog box.

To delete a tab using the Document menu, first open the Tabs dialog box with the Tabs command. Next, highlight the tab position you want to remove, and then press [Delete]. Write will delete the value and remove the tab position. If you want to delete all the tab positions, click on the Clear All button. After you have cleared all the tabs, Write will restore the default half-inch tabs. If you select Cancel, Write will change nothing and will return you to the document.

Page formatting

Page format includes margins, page numbers, page breaks, and headers and footers. You'll use the Page Layout, Header, and Footer commands on Write's Document menu as well as the Repaginate command on the File menu to format your pages.

Setting margins and page numbers

The Page Layout command on the Document menu provides a dialog box in which you can set the margins and the page numbers. The Page Layout dialog box, shown in Figure 10-19 on the following page, contains text boxes for left, right, top, and bottom margins. By default, Write sets the top and bottom margins to 1" and the left and right margins to 1.25". If you insert page numbers in a header or footer, Write prints page numbers in your document, beginning with the page number displayed in the Start Page Numbers At text box. The page number in the page status bar also reflects the starting page number you type.

Figure 10-19

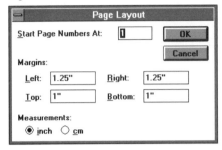

The Page Layout dialog box sets the margins and the beginning page number.

Setting page breaks

Write doesn't set page breaks until you tell it to. Before you print your document, you should tell Write to set the page breaks, by using either the keyboard or the Repaginate command on the File menu. You can use the accelerator keys [Ctrl][Enter] to insert manual page breaks. Simply position the cursor at the desired spot and press [Ctrl][Enter]. Write will then insert a dotted line above the cursor, representing the manual page break.

The Repaginate command provides an easier way to set page breaks. When you choose this command, a Repaginate Document dialog box appears, as shown in Figure 10-20. You can choose to automatically set all the page breaks, or you can ask to confirm each one individually. To begin automatically repaginating, click on OK without selecting the check box. When Write is repaginating the document, a dialog box with a *Repaginating document* message will appear. If you want to stop the repaginating, click on Cancel.

Figure 10-20

The Repaginate Document dialog box has a Confirm Page Breaks check box.

If you choose the Confirm Page Breaks option, Write will ask you to verify each page break. After Write finds a line on which to insert a page break, it will highlight the line and prompt you for verification with the Repaginating Document dialog box shown in Figure 10-21. You can change the page break by clicking on the Up and Down buttons, which move the highlight to another line. Click on the Confirm button when the page break is where you want it, and Write will continue to the next page. Write marks the new page break with a dotted line to remind you that it is now a manual rather than an automatic page break (which is designated by double chevrons). The automatic page-break marker in the selection bar will move to the line below the manual page break. Figure 10-22 shows an example of a manual page break. If you don't want to complete the process of repaginating, you can click on Cancel in the Repaginating Document dialog box.

Figure 10-21

The Repaginating Document dialog box allows you to move the page break or confirm its placement.

Figure 10-22

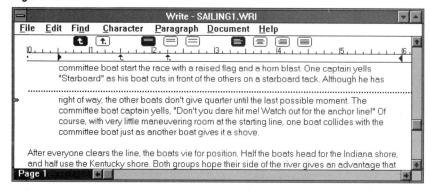

When you move a page break, Write places a dotted line in your document to show the new placement.

After working with a document, you may be dissatisfied with some of your manually set page breaks. When this happens, you can delete a manual page break by highlighting the dotted line and then pressing [Delete] or [Backspace].

If you repaginate with confirmation after you have manually placed a few page breaks, Write will display the dialog box shown in Figure 10-23, asking if you want to keep each break. You can keep the page break, remove it, or cancel the operation with this version of the Repaginating Document dialog box.

Figure 10-23

You'll see this version of the Repaginating Document dialog box when you need to repaginate and confirm existing manually set page breaks.

Creating headers and footers

You can annotate the top and bottom of every page of your document with headers and footers. A header is a line of text or numbers Write will print at the top of every page. A footer will be printed at the bottom of every page. Both headers and footers will appear in the margin space you specified with the Page Layout command. By default, they will be left-aligned and .75" from the top and bottom of the page, but you can specify a custom setting.

When you choose the Header command on the Document menu, a blank document window, like the one shown in Figure 10-24, will appear along with the Page Header dialog box. The title HEADER will be displayed in the title bar. At this point, the document window is active, and the dialog box is inactive. Click in the document window or the dialog box to move between them. With the keyboard, press [Alt][F6] to move between the two.

To create the header, type the text you want for the header in the document window. Note that you can use the commands on the menu bar to format the text any way you like. You can even have more than one line in your header; you can use as many lines as will fit in the margins. After you enter the text, you can insert a dynamic page number (a code that Write automatically changes to match the page you're printing) by using the Insert Page # button in the Page Header dialog box. If you do this, Write will print only the page number. If you want the word *Page* to precede the number, you need to type it into the header and then choose the Insert Page # button. The resulting code will look like this: *Page (page)*. Figure 10-25 shows a sample header.

Figure 10-24

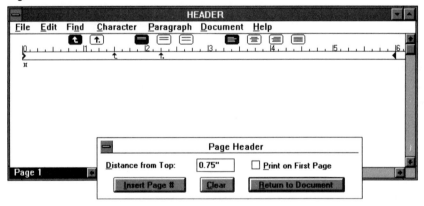

The Header command brings up a blank document window and a Page Header dialog box.

Figure 10-25

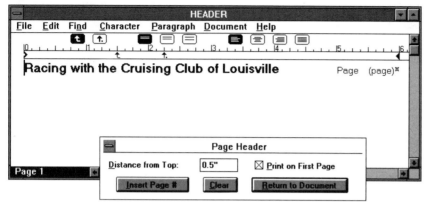

*In this sample header, the page number is changed automatically
as the document prints.*

The Page Header dialog box allows you to customize your header. Normally, the page numbers and other header information begin on the second page. However, if you want to print the header on the first page, you can select the Print on First Page check box.

By default, Write starts inserting the header .75" from the top of the document. You should note that nothing prevents a header that is larger than the header space from printing on top of the text in the document. You can make more room for the header by starting it closer to the top of the page. For instance, to add .25" to the header, change the Distance from Top value to .5" in the Page Header dialog box, as we did in Figure 10-25.

After you enter text in the header, Windows will print it on the pages of the document. If you don't want to print the header anymore, you must delete all the text and codes from the header window. Instead of doing this manually, you can simply click on the Clear button in the Page Header dialog box. When you are satisfied with the header text, click on the Return to Document button to resume working on your document.

Footers work the same way as headers. When you choose the Footer command on the Document menu, Write will display a blank document window labeled FOOTER, along with a Page Footer dialog box, as shown in Figure 10-26 on the following page. In the Footer document window and its dialog box, you can enter text, insert a dynamic page number, decide if the footer goes on the first page, and then enter a measurement in the Distance from Bottom text box. If you don't want a footer after all, you can use the Clear button. To return to the original document work area, just click on the Return to Document button.

Figure 10-26

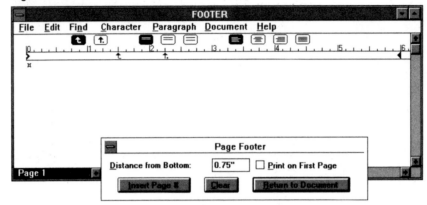

To create a footer, issue the Footer command on the Document menu.

EDITING

After you have written a document, you're ready to polish it. We've already explained some basic editing techniques, such as deleting text, selecting text, and moving around the document. Now we're going to show you how to copy text, how to move it, and how to find and change words in your document.

Copying and moving text

Commands on the Edit menu let you copy and move text. With these commands, you can remove text from one area and add it to another. You can also duplicate the text and move a copy to another area. Before you use any of these commands, however, you need to select the text you intend to change.

If you want to move selected text to another part of your document, use the Cut command. The Cut command will delete the selected text and place it in Clipboard. Then, move the cursor to the place you want the text to appear. Choose the Paste command, and Write will add your text to the left of the cursor.

If you want to reuse some text in another part of your document, you can use the Copy command to duplicate it. The Copy command will store a copy of the selected text in Clipboard. When you choose the Paste command, Write will add the text to your document at the position of the cursor.

Finding and replacing text

Using a combination of two commands from the Find menu, Find and Replace, you can systematically search your document and change every occurrence of specified text. For instance, you can use this technique to correct spelling, to add an address, or to make a name change. If you're trying to find a specific topic that you want to edit, you can search for a key word in your document to move quickly to that part of the document.

To locate a specific string of text, you use the Find command. When you choose the Find command on the Find menu, the dialog box shown in Figure 10-27 will appear. The Find dialog box displays a text box for the search text and two check boxes to qualify the search. When you enter search text, Write will look for every occurrence of that series of characters, starting from the current location of the cursor. For example, if you enter *cat*, Write will stop at *Cat, catch, catacomb,* and so forth. If you want to look only for the word *cat*, you need to check the Match Whole Word Only check box. If the word you're looking for is capitalized, you need to enter the search text with a capital letter and check the Match Case box. After you have specified the search text, click on the Find Next button to start the search. If Write can't find a match, it will display the message *Text not found.*

Using the Find command

Figure 10-27

The Find dialog box lets you enter search text in a text box.

When Write finds a match, it will stop on the first characters that match your search text and highlight those letters. (Be sure that the Find dialog box is not "hiding" the portion of the screen in which the highlighted letters appear. If necessary, you can drag the dialog box's title bar to move it out of the way.) When you see the highlighted letters, you can click in the document and make changes without closing the Find dialog box; it simply becomes inactive. To continue searching, click on the Find Next button in the dialog box. The Find dialog box will become active, and Write will move to the next match. After Write finds the last match, it will present a *Find complete* message. If you don't want to search for other words, click on Cancel or choose the Close command from the Control menu to return to the document.

One very helpful feature of Write's Find command is its ability to use the question mark character (?) as a wildcard. You can use ? in place of any single character in your search text. For example, if you type *ba?e* as your search text, Write will highlight occurrences of *bale, base, bane, bake,* and any other words that begin with *ba* followed by a single character and an *e.*

Using wildcards in searches

Wildcards come in handy for a variety of situations. For example, suppose you are working on a document in which you have not been consistent in spelling the name *Petersen.* In some cases, you have spelled *Peterson* with an *o,* and in other cases, you've spelled *Petersen* with an *e.* You can find all occurrences of the name by using the Find command and entering *Peters?n* as your search text. We'll show you an easy way to change some of the occurrences so that the spelling will be consistent throughout the document when we discuss the Replace command.

Since Write considers a question mark in your search text to be a wildcard, you may be wondering how you can search for a literal question mark in a document. Fortunately, there is a way to do this. Just enter ^? (a caret followed by a question mark) as your search text. This tells Write that instead of using the question mark as a wildcard, you want to find all occurrences of a literal question mark. You can also combine ^? with other characters in the search text. For example, suppose that you want to find all occurrences of the question *Is this correct?* in your document. You can do this by entering *Is this correct ^?* or perhaps just *correct^?* as your search text.

When you use the question mark as a wildcard character, you need to select the Match Whole Word Only check box in the Find dialog box because otherwise Write will treat spaces and punctuation as characters. This means that Write will find character patterns that cover part of two adjacent words. For example, suppose that you entered *s?on?* as the search text without selecting the Match Whole Word Only check box. In that case, Write would find *stone, others on,* and *sailors on.*

Finding special characters

Another useful feature of Write's Find command is its ability to search for special characters such as spaces, tabs, paragraph markers, or manual page breaks. To find a special character, you must insert a caret (^) followed by a specific character in your search text, as shown in Table 10-4.

Table 10-4

Search Text	Special Characters Located
^w	Spaces and/or tabs
^t	Tabs
^p	Paragraph markers
^d	Manual page breaks

These codes search for special characters with the Find command.

When you're searching for a word that needs to be edited, you can use the Replace command to find and automatically change all occurrences of that word in your document. When you choose the Replace command on the Find menu, you'll see a Replace dialog box like the one shown in Figure 10-28. This command can help you correct spelling errors. For example, instead of finding all the occurrences of *Peterson* and then manually changing each one to read *Petersen*, you could use the Replace command to have Write correct all of them for you. To do this, first enter the misspelled version in the Find What text box. Then enter the correct spelling in the Replace With text box. For example, you would type *Peterson* in the Find What text box and *Petersen* in the Replace With text box. Then you would choose the Match Whole Word Only and the Match Case check boxes.

Using the Replace command

Figure 10-28

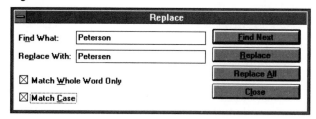

The Replace dialog box lets you find and replace text.

Now, by using the buttons in the Replace dialog box, you need to determine how Write will search for and replace your text. The Find Next button will find and highlight the characters matching the search text. The Replace button will change only the highlighted text from a search. The Replace All button will replace all of the matching search text throughout the document. If you select part of your document and then choose the Replace command or return to the Replace dialog box, the Replace All button will convert to Replace Selection. The Replace Selection button will change all the matches in the selected part of the document. When you've finished replacing text, click on the Close button to close the dialog box.

In both the Find What and Replace With text boxes, you can use most of the wildcards and special codes you used with the Find command, although you cannot use ^w in the Replace With text box.

You won't always need to make global changes; instead, you might need to vary your modifications for each match. If you want Write to simply find text without changing it or displaying dialog boxes, use the Repeat Last Find command on the Find menu. (The accelerator key is [F3].) After you set up the search with the Find or the Replace command and find at least one instance using the dialog box, you can close the dialog box and press [F3] to continue searching in your document. Write will highlight the next match every time you press [F3].

Repeating the last search

ADDING GRAPHICS   In addition to working with text, Write can also work with graphics. Write lets you place graphics from other applications, such as Paintbrush, into your document. If you can copy the graphic into Clipboard, you can import it into Write. (You'll learn how to copy graphics in Paintbrush in Chapter 11.) Once the graphic is in your document, Write can format, move, and size it. Write is an OLE receiving application. If you import a graphic from an OLE source application, such as Paintbrush, you can also modify the graphic from within Write. Keep in mind that your graphic may look distorted when you bring it into Write because the graphic's resolution is based on your printer's capabilities. If your printer has a higher resolution than your screen, the graphic won't look as sharp on your screen as it will when it's printed. For example, a typical VGA screen's 72 dpi (dots per inch) resolution is less sharp than a 300 dpi printout from a laser printer.

Importing a graphic   After you select and copy a graphic with Paintbrush or another graphics program, start Write so that you can place the graphic. Remember, you can have both applications on the desktop; just click on the Write application window instead of exiting the first application. When your document is on the screen, move your cursor to the place where you want to insert the graphic. Now use the Paste command (or the Paste Link or Paste Special command, if available) on the Edit menu to place the graphic. Figure 10-29 shows a graphic we added to our sailing document. Write will treat the graphic as a paragraph, which means that you can't wrap text around your graphic. As a result, text can appear only above and below the graphic.

Figure 10-29

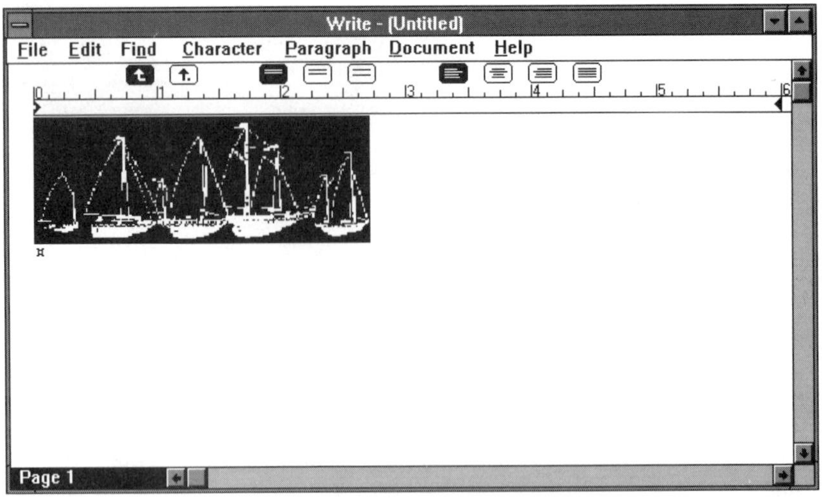

You can copy graphics from other applications and paste them into Write.

If you want to edit a graphic that you have imported into Write from an OLE source application such as Paintbrush, double-click on the graphic. Write (the OLE receiving application) will ask Paintbrush to identify the graphic and place it in a Paintbrush window. Now you can change the graphic using any of the Paintbrush tools described in Chapter 11. After you have made the changes, you can save them and then close the Paintbrush window to return to Write.

Modifying an OLE graphic

After you modify an OLE graphic, you might want to save the changes in a file separate from the receiving file. When the graphic is an embedded object, the Update command replaces the Save command on the File menu. Update sends the changes to the receiving file. Use the Save As command to save the graphic in a file with a different name. The source application first asks if you want to update the object in the receiving file. After you save the object in a source application file, the File menu returns to its usual list of commands.

Saving changes to an OLE graphic

Once you've placed a graphic in your document, you can format its alignment just as you format text, using the menu commands or the ruler icons. First, you need to select the graphic by clicking on it. The graphic will change to inverse video to show it has been selected. Next, choose one of the alignment commands on the Paragraph menu or click on an alignment icon. Write will format your graphic according to your selection. For example, we centered the sailboats graphic shown in Figure 10-30.

Formatting a graphic

Figure 10-30

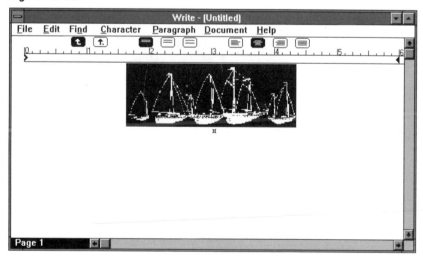

We centered the sailboats graphic by selecting the graphic and then choosing the Centered command on the Paragraph menu.

Moving a graphic

Besides aligning a graphic in the standard ways, you can move it to a unique alignment on the same line or to another part of the document. To align the graphic, select it and then choose the Move Picture command on the Edit menu. Write changes the pointer into a set of nested boxes (a box within a box). When you move the pointer away from the graphic, you'll see a gray frame that represents the size of the graphic. Click to place the graphic at the new location. Then, click again on a different line in the document to deselect the graphic. Your pointer will reassume its normal shape and function.

The Move Picture command moves the graphic to a new position on the same line. You can use the Cut and Paste commands to move the graphic to a location elsewhere in your document. To do this, first select the graphic, and then choose the Cut command on the Edit menu to store it in Clipboard. Next, move the cursor to the graphic's destination, and select the Paste command to retrieve and place the graphic back into the document at the position of the cursor.

**Duplicating
a graphic**

You can duplicate a graphic with the Copy and Paste commands. First, click on the graphic to highlight it in your document. Next, choose the Copy command on the Edit menu. Position your cursor on the line where you want the graphic inserted. Choose Paste from the Edit menu to place the graphic on that line. You can continue to paste the graphic until you issue another Cut or Copy command. As a shortcut, you can highlight the graphic, move the cursor to the desired line, and hold down the [Alt] key while you click the mouse button. This technique is useful because you don't have to copy the graphic to Clipboard and can therefore leave existing text or another graphic in Clipboard.

Although you can duplicate the graphic, you can add only one graphic to a line in your document. If you want a line filled with graphics, then you need to create the original graphic so that it's large enough to fill the line. For example, you could create multiple graphics in Paintbrush and then copy them as a group into Clipboard before pasting them into Write.

Sizing a graphic

If you want to produce a smaller or larger version of the original graphic, you can use the Size Picture command on the Edit menu. First, click on the graphic to select it, and choose the Size Picture command. When you do, the pointer will change into nested boxes. As you drag the nested box pointer, a gray frame appears as a guideline for changing both the horizontal and vertical dimensions of the graphic. To see how these dimensions change as you move the frame, look at the status bar at the bottom of the work area. The status bar changes to display the X and Y coordinates of the pointer. The X represents the horizontal position, and the Y represents the vertical position. To keep the graphic proportional and avoid distortion, drag the pointer in a diagonal direction from the lower-right corner, keeping the coordinates equal.

Now that you can format text and graphics, you can combine them to create letterheads. Once you save a file, you can use it as a template for memos and letters. Let's examine the procedure by creating a letterhead file for the Cruising Club of Louisville. We'll use the sailboats graphic you saw earlier.

Creating letterheads

- First, create the graphic in Paintbrush, and copy it to Clipboard.

- Next, start Write, and use the default new document to begin creating the letterhead.

- To position the graphic at the top of the document, place the cursor on the first line of the document, and issue the Paste command. You want to establish a link because this document will become a template. With a link, future changes to the graphic will be updated automatically both in the template and in any new memo or letter you write.

- Now add the name and address in 10-point type. To make the name bold, highlight it and issue the Bold command on the Character menu.

- Finally, highlight both the graphic and the text, and then click on the left-align icon to create the final version of the letterhead, as shown in Figure 10-31.

Figure 10-31

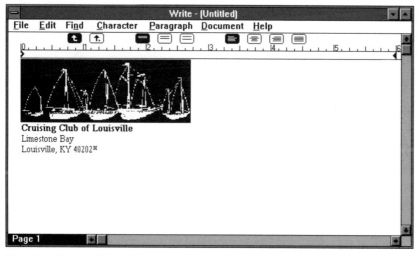

The logo for our letterhead combines text and graphics formatting techniques.

Once you've placed your text and graphic, it's relatively easy to reformat them as a unit. You'll need to experiment to achieve the effect you want. For example, we didn't like the way our letterhead looked, so we selected the text and the graphic and aligned them with the Right command on the Paragraph menu. You can see the effect of this change in Figure 10-32.

Figure 10-32

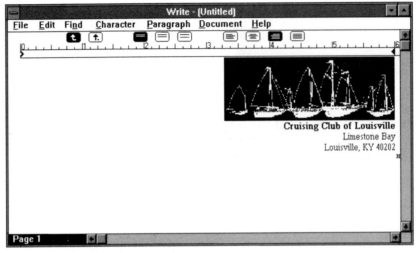

We reformatted the letterhead to right-align our logo.

When your letterhead looks the way you want it, save it under a name that will identify it as your template. To use the letterhead file as a template, just open it, add your text, and then save your letter under a different name. It's crucial that you save your letter file under a new name each time so that you don't replace the original letterhead file. This way, you can continue to use the letterhead file as a template for all your correspondence. (Another way to ensure that you don't mistakenly change or replace your letterhead file is to assign it a read-only file attribute. In the File Manager, select the letterhead file, and then choose the Properties command from the File menu. In the Properties dialog box, select the Read Only check box and click on OK. For more details on file attributes, see Chapter 6.)

FILE HANDLING

After you've finished working with a document, you need to save your work. Write provides options that let you either save the file as a Write document or save it to be used with another word processing application. After you save your work, you're ready to create a new document or work on an existing one. The File menu commands let you accomplish all these tasks.

To save your work, use the Save or the Save As command on the File menu. The first time you save a file with the Save command, Write will ask you for a file name. The next time you save the file with the same command, Write will automatically save the file by replacing the old one. If you don't want to replace the old file, you can use the Save As command to create a separate copy of the old file with a new file name.

Saving your work

The Save As command allows you to save a file in other formats. The Save As dialog box, shown in Figure 10-33, contains a drop-down list box of available file formats (the Save File as Type list box). The Text (.TXT) format will save your file as an ASCII text file. You can use text files to export Write documents into another application, such as WordPerfect or WordStar, which will then convert the text file into its own file format. The Word for DOS (.DOC) format will let you save the Write file so that Microsoft Word can open the file without converting it. (Note that this is a Microsoft Word format, not a Word for Windows format. If you try to use Word for Windows to process a Write document saved in .DOC format, Word for Windows will display a Convert File From dialog box with Microsoft Word highlighted, allowing you to convert from Microsoft Word format to Word for Windows format.) A word of warning: Do not use any format other than Write (.WRI) if you have graphics in your document, because Windows will remove the graphics during the conversion.

Exporting files

Figure 10-33

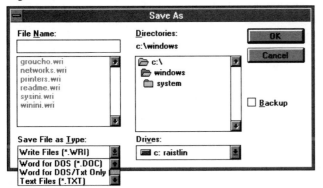

Write's Save As dialog box lets you specify other file formats.

Turning on the Backup check box in the Save As dialog box creates backup copies automatically. When you save a file with the Save As command and the Backup option, Write will back up your file whenever you save it again with either the Save or the Save As command. When Write makes a backup, it saves the file with the chosen extension and saves a copy with a .BKP extension in your current

Backing up your work

directory. (If you saved your file with a .DOC extension, in Word format, the extension for the backup will be .BAK.) The first part of the file name is the same so that you can match originals with backups.

Starting a new file

To create a new document, either start one when you first bring up Write or use the New command on the File menu. Write calls the new document Untitled until you save and name it. If you start a new document before saving the current one, Write will present a dialog box like the one shown in Figure 10-34, asking whether you want to save the changes. After you close this dialog box, Write will replace the current document with an untitled one.

Figure 10-34

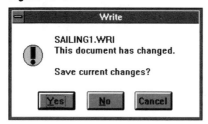

Write asks whether you want to save your changes before starting a new document.

Opening an existing file

To open an existing file, use the Open command on the File menu. When you issue this command, Write will display the Open dialog box, shown in Figure 10-35. All the Write files in the current directory are listed in the File Name list box. Notice that all the files Write creates use the .WRI extension. (To see a list of other types of files, choose a different type from the List Files of Type drop-down list box.) You can either click on a file name in the File Name list or type the name in the File Name text box. You can choose another directory or drive if your file is at a location other than the current directory or drive. Click on OK, and Write will open your file and display it in the work area.

Figure 10-35

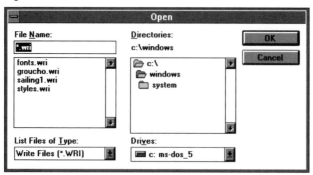

The Open dialog box lets you locate and open Write files.

After you've written the document and then formatted, edited, and perhaps added a few graphics to it, you're almost ready to print it. Before you print the document, however, it's always a good idea to save the file so that you won't lose any work. To get ready to print, you need to select a printer and set printing options. For a more detailed examination of printing basics, see Chapter 3.

PRINTING YOUR DOCUMENT

Before you can print a document, you need to choose the printer you're going to use from the list of installed printers. If you have not chosen a printer already, select the Print Setup command from the File menu to display the Print Setup dialog box, shown in Figure 10-36. Write displays the default printer. To choose another printer, select the Specific Printer radio button, and then choose one of the installed printers in the Specific Printer drop-down list box. You can also change printing features such as page orientation, paper size, or paper source. Click on OK when you've finished setting these options.

Preparing to print

Figure 10-36

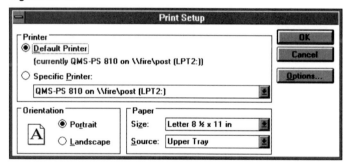

The Print Setup dialog box displays the default printer.

After you select a printer and specify the appropriate settings, you're ready to print the document. First, choose the Print command from the File menu. Write will then present a Print dialog box like the one shown in Figure 10-37 on the following page. The name of the printer you selected will appear at the top of the dialog box. Enter the number of copies in the Copies text box, and then specify which pages to print in the Print Range section. You can choose the All button to print the entire document, the Selection button to print selected (highlighted) text only, or the Pages button to print a specific range of pages. If you choose Pages, you will need to enter page numbers in the From and To text boxes to specify the starting and ending page numbers.

Using the Print command

You can also set several other options in the Print dialog box. First, if you prefer to get a rough draft quickly instead of printing at the highest resolution, you can choose a lower resolution from the Print Quality drop-down list box (for example, 75 dpi instead of 300 dpi). When you print at a lower resolution,

graphics may appear as empty boxes on some printers. Second, if you don't
have a printer connected, you can send the printed version of the document to a
file instead. Then you can print that file at a later time or print it from a computer
that is connected to a printer. To send the printed version to a file, turn on the
Print to File check box. (For details about printing to a file, see Chapter 7.)
Finally, if you need collated copies of your document and your printer has a
collator, be sure that the Collate Copies check box is turned on. (This check box
is selected by default, but it causes no problems for printers without collators.)

Figure 10-37

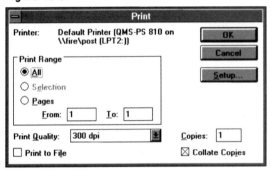

*The Print dialog box lets
you select the number of
copies, the portion of the
document to be printed,
and the print quality.*

When you have set all the necessary options in the Print dialog box, click on
OK. Write will display a dialog box with a message telling you that your
document is printing. If you have not selected the Print to File option, Write will
send the file to the Print Manager (or to the printer directly if the Print Manager
is inactive). You can cancel sending the file by clicking on the Cancel button in
the Write message box. If the icon area of your display is uncovered and the Print
Manager is active, you'll see the Print Manager icon on the desktop. After the file
is sent to the Print Manager, the Write message box will disappear. The Print
Manager, in turn, will send the file to the printer.

If your printer isn't connected, the Print Manager will send a message informing you that it can't send anything to the port. Click on OK in the message
dialog box, and the Print Manager will pause printing until you resolve the
problem. After the printer is connected, you need to tell the Print Manager to
resume printing by double-clicking on the Print Manager icon and clicking on
the Resume button in the Print Manager window. When you minimize the Print
Manager, Windows will return you to your document. You can read more about
the Print Manager in Chapter 7.

After you've finished working with Write, you can exit the application and return to the Program Manager by issuing the Exit command on the File menu. If you didn't save your document before you selected the Exit command, Write will present a message asking if you want to save it. If you click on Yes, Write will save your file. Click on No, and Write will not save your changes. If you click on Cancel, Write will return you to the current document.

EXITING WRITE

In this chapter

Using Paintbrush **11**

*P*roducing a memo, report, or newsletter with correctly spelled words and printing it with attractive fonts isn't enough in today's communication-saturated world. To capture attention, the printed page needs a dash of flash. Windows has the answer: Paintbrush, its graphics application.

Paintbrush helps you create graphics for many types of documents, such as greeting cards, newsletters, and memos with letterheads. In this chapter, we'll show you how to use Paintbrush's tools to create both simple and complex drawings and how to edit and print your drawings.

PAINTBRUSH

As an OLE source application, Paintbrush can supply graphics to other applications such as Write and Cardfile. After a graphic is pasted into an OLE receiving application, you can modify the graphic "in place." OLE calls on Paintbrush to provide tools that allow you to modify the graphic, although the embedded graphic remains in the receiving application's file. A linked graphic is kept in a Paintbrush file but appears in the receiving application's file.

We created the poster in Figure 11-1 on the next page to demonstrate the capabilities of the Paintbrush tools. At the end of this chapter, we'll show you how we made the poster. You'll see many of the elements in the poster as you learn about Paintbrush.

As you read this chapter, note that Paintbrush uses both mouse buttons, the left as the primary button and the right for special functions. We strongly recommend that you use a mouse with Paintbrush—it's faster, easier, and a lot more fun. However, if you must use the keyboard, you can press [Insert] instead of clicking the left mouse button and [Delete] instead of clicking the right mouse button. Press [F9][Insert] for a left button double-click and [F9][Delete] for a right button double-click.

Figure 11-1

This poster presents a variety of images you can create with Paintbrush.

Starting Paintbrush

To start Paintbrush, double-click on the Paintbrush icon in the Accessories group window of the Program Manager. The Paintbrush application window will appear, as shown in Figure 11-2.

Paintbrush provides a wide assortment of tools and functions. On the left of the application window, you'll see all the "tools" in a vertical stack known as the Toolbox. Below the Toolbox is the Linesize box, which contains a series of increasingly thick lines. To the right of the Linesize box, you'll find the Selected Colors box, which displays the foreground and background colors. Next to the Selected Colors box is a set of colors called the Palette. The middle of the window is your work area. By default, Paintbrush adds horizontal and vertical scroll bars to the window so that you can move to all parts of the work area.

GETTING YOUR SUPPLIES

Before you begin drawing a graphic, you'll want to determine the size of your image and the color scheme. The Image Attributes command on the Options menu lets you do this. In the Image Attributes dialog box shown in Figure 11-3, you choose a unit of measurement and specify a width and height for your work area. (The default size of the work area depends on the specific graphics card used in your computer.) In the Units section, you can choose to measure your work area in inches, centimeters, or pels. (Pels, or pixels, are the "dots" from which an image is created.)

Figure 11-2

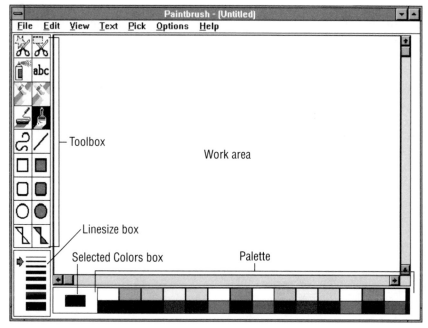

The Paintbrush window includes a Toolbox, Linesize box, Selected Colors box, Palette, and work area.

Figure 11-3

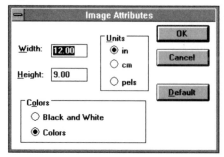

The Image Attributes dialog box lets you choose the size of your work area, the colors, and the unit of measurement.

In the Colors section, you can choose either the Black and White or the Colors radio button to define your Palette. By default, Paintbrush initially sets up a color Palette. You can also create a custom Palette, which we'll discuss later in this chapter. When you've made all your selections, click on OK in the Image Attributes dialog box. Paintbrush will then set up a new work area, after giving you a chance to save the contents of the previous work area.

MOVING AROUND YOUR DRAWING

When you specify large dimensions for a drawing, you'll need to scroll through the work area as you create and edit the drawing. Paintbrush provides some keyboard shortcuts for moving around your drawing. Although you can use the scroll bars, the accelerator keys listed in Table 11-1 are faster; when you use accelerator keys, Paintbrush doesn't need to repaint the screen for each line, as it does when you click on a scroll arrow. For example, if you finish drawing shoelaces on the tennis shoes of a tall basketball player and then want to start sketching the player's eyes, you can simply press [Home] to move to the top of your drawing instead of scrolling through the whole drawing.

Table 11-1

Keystroke	Function
[Home]	Move to top
[End]	Move to bottom
[Page Up]	Move up one screen
[Page Down]	Move down one screen
[Shift]↑	Move up one line
[Shift]↓	Move down one line
[Shift][Home]	Move to left edge
[Shift][End]	Move to right edge
[Shift][Page Up]	Move left one screen
[Shift][Page Down]	Move right one screen
[Shift]←	Move left one space
[Shift]→	Move right one space

You can use these keyboard shortcuts to move around your work area.

DRAWING BASICS

To create your masterpiece with Paintbrush, you'll need to know what tools are available, how to control them, and how to use the Palette. The following sections will explain how to use the graphics tools, the Text tool, and the editing tools and how to manipulate the elements you create with the tools.

Tool overview

Table 11-2 lists all the tools in the Toolbox, their icons, and the tool-specific pointer you see when you select each one. To use a tool, click on it, and move the pointer into the work area, where it will assume its tool-specific shape. Clicking will activate the tool for the duration of the click; holding down the mouse button will continuously activate the tool. Dragging the tool moves the pointer while keeping the tool active. Some tools perform advanced functions when you select them and use a key such as [Ctrl] or [Shift] in combination with the mouse button. We'll show you these special functions when we talk about these tools.

Table 11-2

Tool Name	Tool Icon	Tool Pointer	Tool Name	Tool Icon	Tool Pointer
Scissors			Pick		
Airbrush			Text	 abc	
Color Eraser			Eraser		
Paint Roller			Brush		
Curve			Line		
Box			Filled Box		
Rounded Box			Filled Rounded Box		
Circle/Ellipse			Filled Circle/Ellipse		
Polygon			Filled Polygon		

You can use all these tools from the Toolbox to create drawings.

Dealing with color

You'll probably use the Palette as much as you'll use the Toolbox. The Palette, located at the bottom of the screen, provides a choice of 28 colors. With the Palette, you tell Paintbrush which colors you want to use for foreground and background colors. The center box in the Selected Colors box contains the foreground color, and the surrounding box contains the background color. When you click with the left mouse button on a color in the Palette, you choose the foreground color; when you click with the right mouse button on a color, you choose the background color. As you draw, Paintbrush uses the foreground color for the lines you draw and for filled shapes and borders your images with the background color. (The size of the border depends on the line size you've selected.) For instance, if you draw boxes with the Filled Box tool, the boxes will be the foreground color, framed in the background color. If your background color is white, like the work area background, the border shows up only when one filled box crosses another, as shown in Figure 11-4.

However, if you don't want lines to show up around the boxes, you can eliminate the distinction between the background and the foreground. To make the background color match the foreground, click with the right mouse button on the foreground color. The Selected Colors box changes to match your choice. Figure 11-5 shows overlapping filled boxes without borders.

Figure 11-4

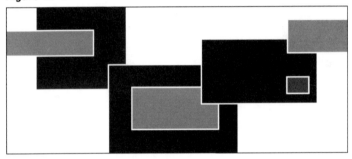

Because our background color is white, these overlapping filled boxes have white borders.

Figure 11-5

These overlapping filled boxes don't have borders because the background and foreground colors match.

If you are going to print your graphic and don't have a color printer, you might want to use the black-and-white Palette. If you want to plot your graphic or send the image to a color printer, you'll want to use a color Palette. (Remember that you set up your Palette when you choose the Black and White radio button or the Colors radio button in the Image Attributes dialog box.) The techniques described here apply to both the color and the black-and-white Palettes.

Some of the colors on the Palette work in a unique way with the Paint Roller tool. These colors (marked with X's in Figure 11-6) are actually dithered colors (a mixture of two colors). When you paint an area with a dithered color, you can't repaint it again with the Paint Roller tool. Later, we'll show you how you can use the Color Eraser tool to replace the dithered color.

Figure 11-6

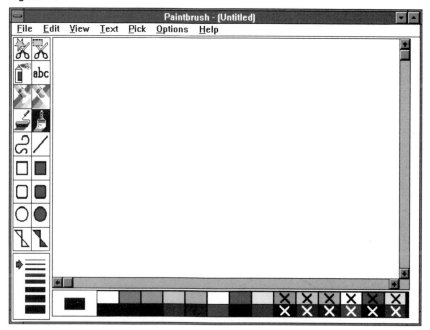

We marked the dithered colors in this default Palette with X's.

With the Linesize box, you can vary the thickness of the lines you draw. The Linesize box doesn't simply affect line width; it affects other graphics tools, too. The thicker the line, the larger the area the tool affects. For example, the width of the Brush pointer will widen as you increase the size of the line. Figure 11-7 on the next page shows the changes in the Brush pointer as you choose thicker lines in the Linesize box. Linesize affects all the tools except the Text tool, the Paint Roller tool, and the Scissors and Pick tools.

Selecting a line size

Figure 11-7

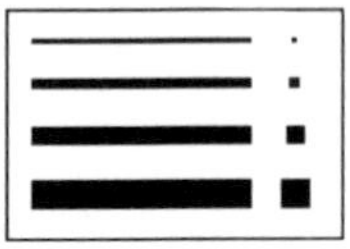

The Brush pointer on the right gets thicker as you choose wider lines.

If you're using the Line tool and a single mouse click to draw a dot, you'll notice that the dot changes as the line size changes. (The finest line doesn't form a dot with a single click unless you move the mouse slightly.) Paintbrush uses a unique shape to create each of the available line thicknesses in the Linesize box. Figure 11-8 illustrates the different widths and shapes. The wider the line, the more nearly round the ends. In fact, when you draw the widest line, the ends of the line will be round. Later, when we show you how to use the Eraser tool, you can see how to square off the ends of the line.

Figure 11-8

The shape of the dot changes as you choose various line sizes.

A TOUR OF TOOLS

Paintbrush's Toolbox has a wide assortment of tools: graphics tools, a Text tool, and editing tools. The graphics tools include the Line, Box, Filled Box, Rounded Box, Filled Rounded Box, Circle/Ellipse, Filled Circle/Ellipse, Polygon, Filled Polygon, Curve, Brush, Airbrush, and Paint Roller tools. The editing tools include the Eraser, Color Eraser, Scissors, and Pick tools.

A look at graphics tools

The graphics tools can create a variety of shapes and patterns, such as lines, squares, circles, polygons, and curves. You also can create freehand shapes with the Brush or Airbrush tool. If you want to change a large area to a new color, you can use the Paint Roller tool. When you draw one line or shape on top of another, the line or shape on top determines the color of that area. The colors won't mix; the one on top just covers up the others.

You can draw horizontal, vertical, and diagonal lines as well as small shapes (such as tiny square dots) with the Line tool. To draw a line, first choose the Line tool, position the pointer in the work area where you want to start the line, and press the mouse button to anchor the line. Then drag the pointer to stretch the line to its destination point. When you stretch the line, a guideline will appear, to show where the line will go. When you release the mouse button to finish the line, the guideline will change into a line with the color and thickness you selected.

Paintbrush is very careful to do exactly what you tell it. However, the result might not always be what you want. If you want a horizontal or vertical line but release the mouse button one bit off a perfectly straight line, you will end up with a jagged line. To avoid mishaps, hold down the [Shift] key while you drag the guideline. Using the [Shift] key tells Paintbrush to allow only perfectly horizontal, vertical, or diagonal lines. Paintbrush assumes a 45-degree angle for its diagonal lines.

You also can use a combination of lines to create free-form polygons. After you draw one line, leave the Line tool in the same place and then start drawing again in a different direction. All you have to do to start another line is drag the guideline to the next spot.

In addition, you can use the Line tool to create small shapes, such as a square dot. If you click once without dragging the mouse, you will create the shortest possible line—a dot.

For example, you can create a flower using the Line tool. Figure 11-9 on the next page illustrates the steps you might follow to draw a dandelion.

- To begin, choose the Image Attributes command from the Options menu to open the Image Attributes dialog box. Select a black-and-white Palette and, if you like, set up a new page size. Click on OK to close the dialog box and display a new work area.

- After choosing a dark gray from the Palette, select the Line tool, hold down the [Shift] key, and draw a vertical line for the stem, as shown in Step 1.

- Next, add a series of light gray, thin diagonal lines for dandelion fluff, as shown in Step 2. Don't use the [Shift] key here because you need a variety of diagonal lines instead of just 45-degree lines.

- Finally, put leaves on the stem of the flower by creating dark gray, jagged-edged polygons. Use a fine, dark gray line to add seeds to the dandelion by clicking to create small shapes, as shown in Step 3.

Figure 11-9

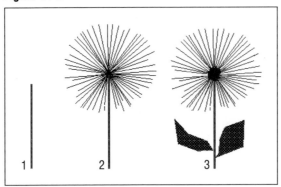

You can use the Line tool to create this dandelion.

Using the Box tools

Paintbrush's Box tools let you create rectangles, perfectly proportioned boxes, and lines. The Box tool uses the foreground color for its frame, leaving the interior of the box empty or unfilled. When you use the Filled Box tool, however, its frame is the background color, and the interior is the foreground color. (Note that the background color in the Selected Colors box is, by default, the color of your work area.)

To draw a box, choose your foreground color and line width, and then select the tool (Box or Filled Box). Position the pointer where you want to start your box (the pointer becomes a crosshair). Press the mouse button, and box guidelines will appear. Continue holding down the mouse button and drag the guidelines until they are the size and shape you want. Then release the mouse button. The guidelines will turn into a final graphic with the line width and color you selected.

In addition to rectangles and boxes, you can draw lines with the Box tools. If you create a rectangle with very little height or a rectangle with very little width and then release the mouse button, the final shape will be a line. This technique is useful when you want to quickly draw a line without changing to a different Paintbrush tool.

When you draw nested boxes with the Filled Box tool, you might end up with white frames like the ones you saw in Figure 11-4. To avoid odd-colored frames, choose the same colors for foreground and background when you are drawing layers of filled boxes. If you want the frame around a filled box to be a different color for contrast, you can choose a different background color with the right mouse button and then draw the box.

Windows in Color

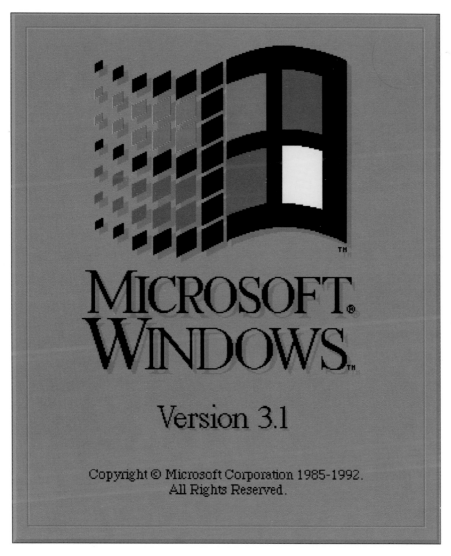

Microsoft Windows 3.1 provides a colorful working environment. The following illustrations display some of its color settings and some of the vivid effects you can create.

The Main group window of the Program Manager contains the Control Panel icon. With Control Panel, you can change window colors and graphics effects.

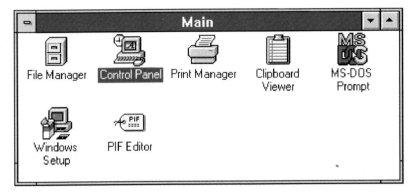

The Control Panel window displays the Color icon and the Desktop icon. These tools allow you to set specific color and design options that affect the appearance of all the application windows.

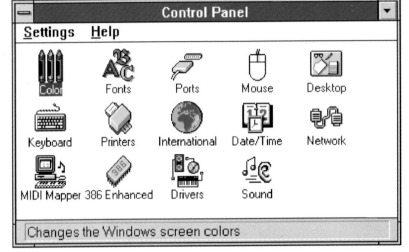

The Accessories group window of the Program Manager contains multicolored icons for many of Windows' built-in applications. Paintbrush is a color drawing application.

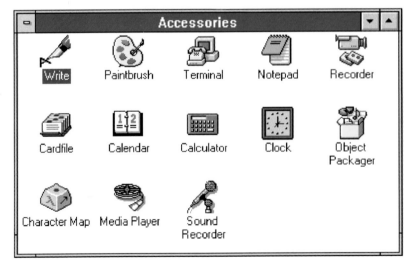

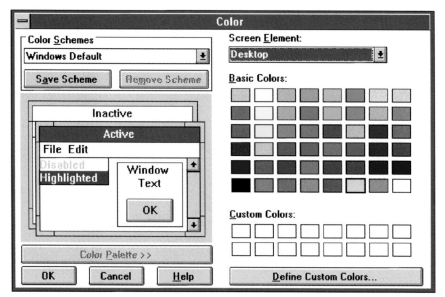

In the expanded Color dialog box, the Basic Colors and Custom Colors palettes let you change a built-in color scheme or even create an entirely new color scheme.

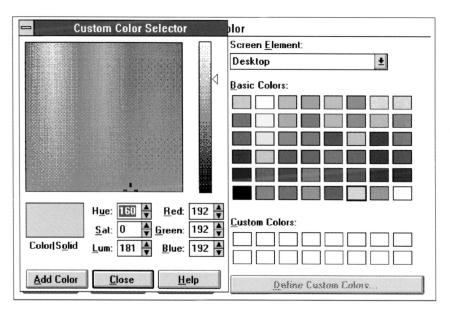

With the Custom Color Selector, you can define your own custom colors, which you can then apply to various screen elements.

In the Color dialog box, you can preview a color scheme for your screen. Here are eight of Windows' built-in color schemes.

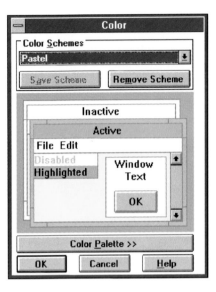

Pastel

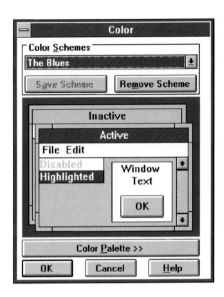

The Blues

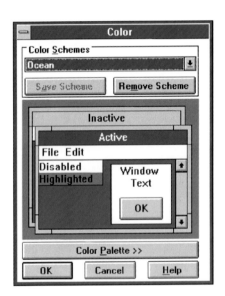

Ocean

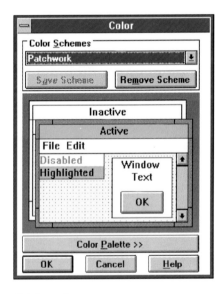

Patchwork

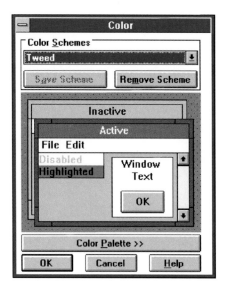

Tweed

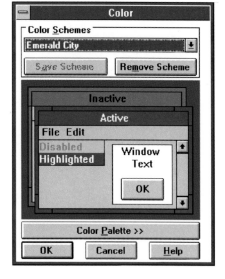

Emerald City

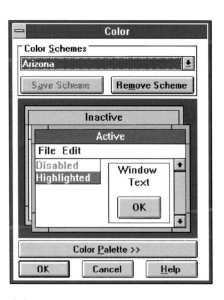

Arizona

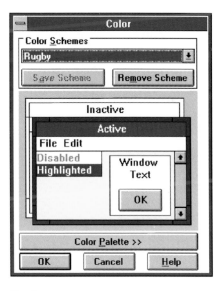

Rugby

In the Desktop dialog box, you can choose wallpaper, a decorative background for your screen. You can display any of the various wallpaper styles as a centered tile on your computer desktop or as a background that completely covers the desktop.

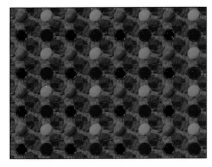

256 Color

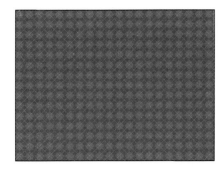

Argyle

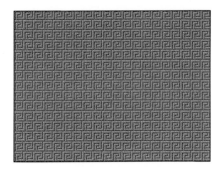

Egypt

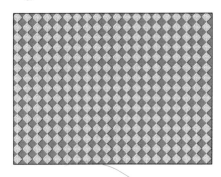

Arcade

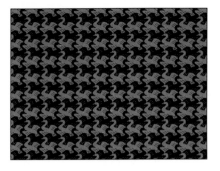

Flock

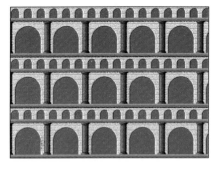

Arches

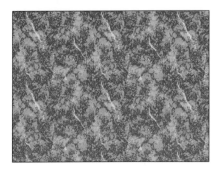

Marble

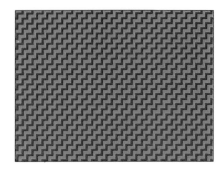

Zigzag

*With Windows'
Paintbrush
application, you
can create a variety
of colorful images.
Try creating your
own artwork and
displaying it as
custom wallpaper.*

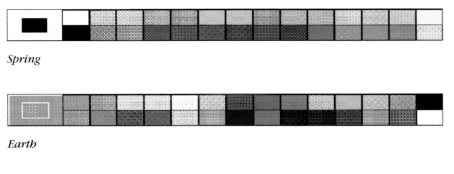

*You can alter the
colors of the
Paintbrush Palette.
You can also create,
save, and reuse
custom Paintbrush
Palettes for
particular jobs.*

Spring

Earth

Blue Seas

Default

The Select Card Back dialog box lets you choose your favorite deck of playing cards when you play Solitaire.

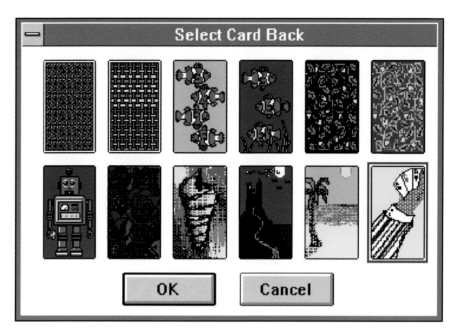

By choosing color settings, adding desktop designs, and customizing colors, you can enhance the visual appeal of all your Windows applications.

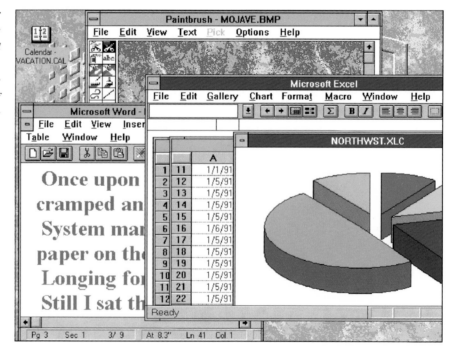

You can use the Box and Line tools to draw a cube. As you can see in Figure 11-10, it takes just a couple of steps to complete the graphic.

- With the Box tool, draw a small box. Then draw a larger box on top of the first one, but offset, to the lower right, as shown in Step 1.

- With the Line tool, draw connecting lines between the corresponding corners of the boxes, as shown in Step 2.

Figure 11-10

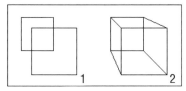

With only the Box and Line tools, you can draw a cube.

Both the Rounded Box and the Filled Rounded Box tools form boxes with rounded corners. When you drag the tool pointer for these tools, the guidelines form a box with rounded corners. When you release the mouse button, the final box reflects your choice of line size and color. Figure 11-11 shows the three steps involved in drawing an electronic piano keyboard.

Using the Rounded Box tools

- First, choose white for the foreground and black for the background, and then draw the full-length white key with the Filled Rounded Box tool, as shown in Step 1.

- For Step 2, draw another white key with the Filled Rounded Box tool and add a black key on top of the two white keys. (Remember to change the foreground color to black before drawing the black keys.) Keep adding more keys (black and white) to form an electronic piano keyboard.

- Finally, add a frame (a black unfilled rounded box), and use gray lines to add shading around the keys and the frame.

Figure 11-11

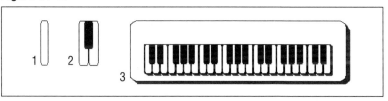

We created a keyboard with the Rounded Box, Filled Rounded Box, and Line tools.

**Using the Circle/
Ellipse tools**

With the Circle/Ellipse and the Filled Circle/Ellipse tools, you can create filled and unfilled ellipses, circles, and ovals of various sizes. As you did with the other tools, first select the line width and color. Next, select one of the Circle/Ellipse tools and move the crosshair pointer to the work area. To start drawing your circle, hold down the mouse button to anchor the guidelines and then drag them to form the circle. If you want to draw a perfect circle instead of an ellipse, hold down the [Shift] key while you drag the guidelines to the size you want. Figure 11-12 shows the shapes you can create with the Circle/Ellipse tool. As with the Box tools, if you use the Circle tools to draw a circle with very little height, the result will be a horizontal line; drawing a circle with very little width produces a vertical line.

Figure 11-12

*The Circle/Ellipse tool can create
an evolving series of circular shapes.*

You can use a combination of the tools we have discussed so far to draw a glass cookie jar. Figure 11-13 on the next page shows the series of steps.

- Use unfilled ellipses for the base and top of the jar, as shown in Step 1.

- Add lines to connect the ellipses, as we did in Step 2.

- To create a cookie, first draw an unfilled ellipse. Next, add chocolate chips by drawing small filled ellipses or filled boxes inside the cookie. If you like cream-filled cookies better, draw black filled ellipses on either side of a white rounded box. As you can see in Step 3, we put both chocolate chip cookies and cream-filled cookies in our cookie jar.

- To put a cover on the jar, use the Circle/Ellipse tool to create overlapping ellipses for the different diameters of the lid. You'll learn how to erase overlapping lines with the Eraser tool later in this chapter, to make your lid look like the one in Step 4.

Figure 11-13

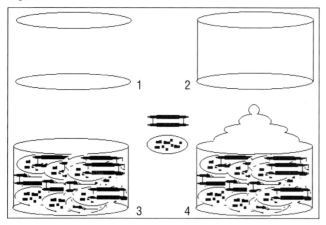

You can draw a cookie jar using the Circle/Ellipse,
Rounded Box, Filled Box, and Line tools.

Using the
Polygon tools

The Polygon and Filled Polygon tools are different from the tools we've used so far because they don't have predetermined shapes. Instead, the Polygon tools let you continue putting sides on a graphic until you close it with the last line. You can draw lines, triangles, trapezoids, parallelograms, and so forth.

To draw a polygon, select the Polygon tool (or the Filled Polygon tool) and move the crosshair pointer into the work area. Drag to form the starting line, and then release the mouse button. When you click in another part of the work area, Paintbrush will add a line connecting the two points. You could also click to start a new line and then drag the end of the line to its new location. The graphic won't be complete until you connect to your starting point to close the shape. To close the shape, you can either click on the first point again or double-click to have Paintbrush automatically add the final line and complete the shape. Double-clicking is easier than trying to hit the first point exactly. After the shape is closed, the lines become the width and color you selected earlier. If you were using the Filled Polygon tool, Paintbrush will fill enclosed areas with the selected fore-ground color, beginning with the areas adjacent to the starting line.

You can use the Polygon tool and a double-clicking technique as a quick way to draw a triangle. After you draw the base line, move the pointer into position for the third point of the triangle, and double-click to connect to both ends of the starting line, forming the triangle.

To create a perfectly straight horizontal, vertical, or 45-degree diagonal line, hold down the [Shift] key while you drag the guideline.

You can use the Filled Polygon tool with the Box tool to draw a wood plank. Follow the steps shown in Figure 11-14 to create the plank.

- Using the Image Attributes dialog box, set up a 4" by 6" work area, and choose a color Palette.

- When the new work area is set up, select a thin line size, and choose the Box tool. Now draw a rectangle for the basic shape of a wood plank, as shown in Step 1.

- Form the wood grain inside the rectangle with the Filled Polygon tool by creating narrow and long multi-edged shapes, as shown in Step 2. Now you have a wood plank that you can use to "build" complex shapes. We will use the wood plank again later in this chapter.

Figure 11-14

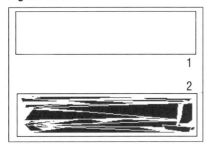

By filling a rectangle with a series of long and narrow varied polygons, you can draw a wood plank.

Using the Curve tool

The Curve tool is like the Line tool, with a twist. After you draw the line, you can pull on either side of it to form a curve. The final curve will reflect the foreground color and line width you chose. The Curve tool can draw curved lines, double-curved lines, and other complex shapes.

To draw a curved line, select the Curve tool and move the crosshair pointer into the work area. Drag the guideline to the length you want, and then release the mouse button. Next, drag the pointer to either side of the line. Notice that the guideline bulges and curves in the direction you drag the pointer. You are creating a mid-point that pulls the line into a curve, anchored at the two end points. Each line you create with the Curve tool can have two mid-points. Release the mouse button to place the first mid-point, and then drag again in a different direction to create a compound curve. After you release the button the second time, the curve will be finished. If you don't want a double curve, you can click on the ending point of the line to finish the curve.

The Curve tool can create other complex graphic shapes besides the double curve. You can flex the curved line into a loop by double-clicking to start the line and then dragging the guideline to the length you want. A double-click puts the starting and ending points of the guideline in the same place. After you set the line length, you can drag to form a narrow loop. To do so, drag the guideline to one side to pull open the loop. After you release the mouse button, the shape of the graphic will be final.

Figure 11-15 shows a variety of curves you can create with the Curve tool. The first curve is a line pulled up with the pointer. The second is a line pulled down. The third and fourth are pulled right and left, respectively. The fifth is pulled down and slightly to the left. The sixth is a loop created by a closed curve.

Figure 11-15

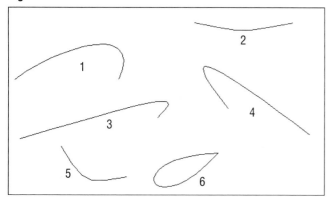

You can use the Curve tool to create a variety of curved lines.

You can use curved lines with some of the other tools we've talked about so far to create a balloon. Figure 11-16 on the next page shows the three steps involved in drawing the balloon.

- Using the Filled Circle/Ellipse tool, draw a filled circle for a guideline, as shown in Step 1.

- Use the Curve tool to draw sloping sides on the balloon, as shown in Step 2.

- With the Filled Box and Line tools, add the basket for the balloon, as we did in Step 3.

Figure 11-16

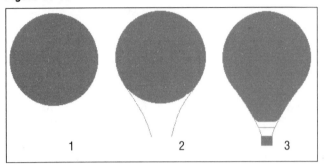

You can use the Paintbrush tools we've discussed to draw a balloon.

Using the
Brush tool

The Brush tool lets you draw freehand with six kinds of brushes. With the Linesize box, you can choose the size of the brush. You can also choose a brush shape with the Brush Shapes command. The Brush tool paints with the foreground color.

To draw freehand, select the Brush tool and move the pointer into the work area. Notice that the pointer changes into a small square—the default brush shape. If you drag the Brush tool, a line will trail behind the pointer. This is a final line and not a guideline. The Brush tool lets you draw lines, curves, and shapes. By clicking once, you can draw a dot that is the same shape as the brush.

You can change the brush shape with the Brush Shapes command on the Options menu. You can also double-click on the Brush tool for a shortcut to the Brush Shapes dialog box. The Brush Shapes dialog box, shown in Figure 11-17, displays a box around the shape you are currently using. You can change the brush from a square into a circle, a horizontal line, a vertical line, a diagonal right line, or a diagonal left line by clicking on one of the brush shapes and then clicking on OK. The pointer changes to match your choice. The brush shapes apply only to the Brush tool.

Figure 11-17

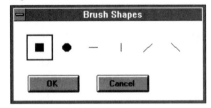

The Brush Shapes dialog box lets you choose from six brush shapes.

You can use the Brush tool to create calligraphy like that shown in Figure 11-18. If you want to create more than one letter, it's a good idea to draw some guidelines before you start writing. We used the [Shift] key as we drew our guidelines so that they would be perfectly straight. If you draw a guideline with a color that isn't used in the rest of the drawing, you'll be able to erase only that color with the Color Eraser tool, which we'll discuss later.

Figure 11-18

You can use the diagonal brush shape for calligraphy.

Here's a trick you'll want to try with the [Shift] key: Hold down the [Shift] key as you draw a line. The Brush tool will draw a straight line. As long as you hold down both the [Shift] key and the mouse button, the Brush tool extends the line, no matter how far away from the line you move the mouse pointer. You will be able to move in only one direction (horizontal or vertical) while you press the [Shift] key. This key keeps your line from changing directions.

The Airbrush tool is similar to the Brush tool because it creates free-form shapes. The Airbrush tool simulates a burst of spray paint, creating a circular pattern of dots. The color on the drawing increases in density as your dragging speed decreases (just like spray paint). You also can use the Airbrush tool to add shading to your drawing for a three-dimensional effect.

Using the Airbrush tool

Select the Airbrush tool and move the crosshair pointer into the work area. Drag the crosshair to begin coloring. If you keep going over an area with the Airbrush tool, the color will become more intense (more like a solid color). When you move the pointer slowly, the area also looks more like a solid color. If you select the Airbrush tool, hold down the [Shift] key, and drag the pointer, you'll produce a perfectly horizontal or vertical line. Using the [Shift] key also will let you go back over your line to extend it in either direction. If you click the button once, the Airbrush tool will create a shape that is the lightest density; you won't be able to make it any darker by clicking on it again. To make the line darker, you need to drag the pointer.

Since you can see through the shape you're drawing (because the background isn't completely covered), you can draw on top of another color and simulate mixing the two colors. The Airbrush tool uses the foreground color. If you move the pointer quickly to get a lighter density of dots, you'll get a better mix of colors.

You can use the Airbrush tool to create clouds by airbrushing the darker background color with white. In Figure 11-19, we drew clouds to form a backdrop for our balloon drawing. We made the centers of the clouds opaque by moving the Airbrush tool slowly and going over the area several times. The transparent look of the edges is created by moving the Airbrush tool quickly, leaving a thinner pattern of white dots over the blue of the background.

Figure 11-19

You can use the Airbrush tool to create clouds.

Using the Paint Roller tool

The Paint Roller tool, like a real paint roller, covers a wide area with color. In fact, this tool will continue filling in color until it reaches the boundaries of a graphic or framed area. If the frame isn't perfect (for example, if you leave a small opening), the color could spread into another area or even into the entire drawing. Never fear: Choosing the Undo command on the Edit menu will remove all the color the Paint Roller tool dumped into your drawing.

To use the Paint Roller tool, select it from the Toolbox and move the pointer into the work area. When you do, the pointer looks like a paint roller. Select the foreground color you want to use, move the pointer to the area that needs the new color, and click. The area will change to your selected color.

You can also change line colors with the Paint Roller tool, but you must be very careful. Remember, the active area of the Paint Roller pointer is the point formed by the paint dripping from the roller. In order to change the color of a line, you must position the pointer's active area precisely on top of the line. When you do, the pointer (at the tip) will change to another color (the pointer changes to contrasting colors as you move it over different colors) to let you know that the pointer is in the correct place. Then, you can click to change the line's color. (Remember that you can't repaint a dithered color with the Paint Roller tool.)

A word of warning: If you use the Undo command to remove a color, this command will remove everything you have done with the Paint Roller tool since you last selected it. Therefore, it's a good idea to reselect the Paint Roller tool for each area or color you're painting. Also, if you mistakenly change a line to the same color as the fill of the shape and then try to change the line back to its original color with the Undo command, the fill will change, too. Unfortunately, Paintbrush assumes that everything of one color (the frame and the filled area) is one shape and replaces it all.

In the case of complex graphics with overlapping lines, a fill might not work in some detailed areas when the Paint Roller's active area is not fine enough to fit. You will need to use the Zoom In command from the View menu to color in particularly small areas. We'll talk about the Zoom In and Zoom Out commands later in this chapter.

For example, to fill in the background of the *Kentucky!* calligraphy we created in Figure 11-18, first choose the Paint Roller tool and then a color for a new background. Click on the work area outside the letters so that the Paint Roller tool will fill it in. In Figure 11-20, notice the isolated white pixels in the letters that didn't fill in.

Figure 11-20

The Paint Roller tool filled in the background but missed the areas that are blocked off.

**A look at the
Text tool**

abc

Paintbrush provides the Text tool to give you the power to add text to your graphics. However, the text you add is actually a graphic itself. In other words, each text character isn't a specifically coded character (ASCII code) that you'd find in a word processor like Write. Each letter Paintbrush adds to your drawing is a bit map that looks like a letter. Since each letter is a miniature drawing, you can't edit Paintbrush text as you would regular text. In this section, we'll show you how to choose colors, fonts, sizes, and styles for Paintbrush text.

Using the Text tool

The Text tool is very easy to use. To add text to your drawing, select the tool and move the I-beam pointer into the work area. Click to position the cursor where you want Paintbrush to add the text. The cursor will assume the height of the text and will move to the right as you type. (A word of caution: The text will overwrite any graphics already in your drawing.) Because Paintbrush won't wrap the letters when you reach the right side of the drawing's work area, you will have to press [Enter] to move the cursor to the next line. The cursor will return to the same horizontal position where you first started your text.

You can continue to change your text (active text) until you make it final by doing one of the following: choosing another tool, clicking somewhere else on the drawing, or scrolling the drawing. You can use the [Backspace] key to delete any mistakes. To save time and avoid frustration, you should create your text in small sections. You'll need to make all necessary changes in a section before going on to the next one.

The Text tool uses the foreground color, which can be any color you choose, including dithered colors. The background color in the Selected Colors box is not used by the Text tool.

**Setting the font
and point size**

To set the font for your text, choose the Fonts command on Paintbrush's Text menu, which produces the Font dialog box, shown in Figure 11-21. In the Font list box, Paintbrush lists all installed Windows fonts. Paintbrush will add or subtract fonts on the list to match the capabilities of your printer. If you don't have a printer installed, Paintbrush will use the fonts your monitor supports.

Paintbrush allows you to use multiple fonts in your drawing. In order to use a new font, you need to select it from the list box and click on OK before you click to start your text. You can change fonts while you are entering text. Just select a different font, and any text you've already typed will change to that font. However, after you finalize the text (for example, by choosing another tool), you can't change the font in which it appears.

You can also vary the size of your text. The Size list box in the Font dialog box shows all the point sizes of the current font. The number in the Size text box indicates the size the Text tool is currently using.

You can change the point size the same way you change the font. It's a good idea to decide on all the fonts and point sizes you will use before you begin typing, because you can't change them after you've finalized your text. To choose a point size, select the size from the list box and click on OK. When the dialog box closes, Paintbrush will automatically resize your active text. You can continue to change the point size for your text until you finalize it by clicking somewhere else on the drawing or clicking on another tool.

Notice that the Sample section of the Font dialog box displays sample letters in the currently selected font, style, and point size so that you can view what you've chosen before you click on OK to close the dialog box.

Figure 11-21

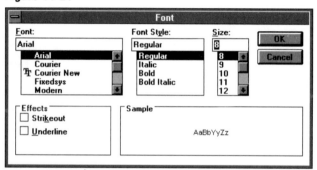

The Font dialog box lets you choose the font, style, and point size of Paintbrush text and displays sample letters.

Besides changing the size and font, you can change the style of your text by using any of several methods. In the Font dialog box, you can set a bold, italic, bold italic, or regular (normal) style by selecting it in the Font Style list box at the same time you choose the font and point size. The Effects section of the dialog box offers two additional options for text of any style: Strikeout and Underline. Selecting the Strikeout check box places a single horizontal line (a strikeout, or strikethrough) through the letters and spaces of the active text. Choosing the Underline check box underlines your text.

You can also change the text style by using the other commands on the Text menu. As you can see in Figure 11-22 on the next page, the Text menu is divided into several sections. The first section contains the Regular command, which cancels any styles you've assigned to your text. The next section's commands are Bold, Italic, and Underline. When you select one of these style commands, a check mark appears next to it to show that it's active. (You can choose more than one of these style commands at a time.) Selecting a command again toggles it off. The third section contains the Outline and Shadow commands. Unlike the

Enhancing your text

previous section, in which you can choose more than one style command at a time, only one of these choices can be active. When you use the Outline or Shadow command, the outline or shadow color is the background color. (If the background color is the same as the background where the text appears, you won't see the shadow or outline effect.)

Figure 11-23 shows a sample of each of these styles. Paintbrush also provides some keyboard shortcuts for changing the style of your text. You can press [Ctrl]B for bold, [Ctrl]I for italic, or [Ctrl]U for underlined text.

Figure 11-22

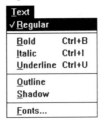

The Text menu allows you to apply styles to text.

Figure 11-23

Here are samples of the styles you can use for text.

A look at editing tools

Now that you know how to add text and graphics to your drawing, let's see how you can use the editing tools to edit the various elements of your drawing. Paintbrush provides four editing tools: the Eraser, Color Eraser, Pick, and Scissors tools. The [Delete] and [Backspace] keys also can remove elements from your drawing.

Using the Eraser and Color Eraser tools

With the Eraser and the Color Eraser tools, you can remove or change colors in your drawing. The Eraser tool changes colors to the background color, while the Color Eraser tool erases colors selectively. The pointer for the Eraser tool is a box; the Color Eraser pointer is a crosshair centered on a box. The box determines the area that is erased. You can change the size of the box with the Linesize box; the finer the line, the smaller the box.

When you move the Eraser tool over an area, anything the pointer covers will change to the background color. If you change the background color, the Eraser tool will change the color of anything it encounters to match the new background color. For example, you can use the Eraser tool to clean up any stray lines in your drawing. Remember the wood plank you drew with the Filled Polygon and Box tools? As you can see in Figure 11-24, the Eraser tool can be used to remove any part of the wood grain that overflowed the boundaries of the wood plank.

Figure 11-24

You can use the Eraser tool to clean up the stray lines in this drawing.

If you want to be a bit more selective, use the Color Eraser tool. It erases only colors that match the selected foreground color. The Color Eraser tool changes any pixels of the foreground color it encounters into the selected background color, offering a convenient way to change only part of your drawing.

You can drag the Eraser tools to remove colors or just click the button once to remove one box of color. Since the Eraser tools move in a free-form pattern in the same way that the Brush tool does, you can use the [Shift] key to move the Eraser tools in a perfectly straight horizontal or vertical line (to help you square off the rounded ends of a line, for example). Just as you can extend either end of a line with the Brush tool using the [Shift] key, you can extend color changes in the same manner with the Eraser tools.

For example, you can erase the calligraphy guidelines from Figure 11-18 (on page 281) with the Color Eraser tool because the guidelines are a different color than the calligraphy. To do this, choose the guideline color for the foreground and white for the background. Now you can erase the guidelines without removing the calligraphy.

You can also color parts of a complex drawing with the Color Eraser tool. If you want to change one color on a part of the drawing, like the black in the drawing shown in Figure 11-25 on the following page, just change the foreground color to black and the background to a new color (light blue). Now move the Color Eraser tool over the area to be changed. The Color Eraser tool changes only the black and leaves the other colors alone.

Figure 11-25

The Color Eraser tool changes only one color and leaves the other colors alone. Here we changed black to light blue.

You can use the Color Eraser tool to make global changes to your drawing. Suppose you want to change everything that is blue on your drawing to purple, but the background and many small items are blue. Using the Paint Roller tool or erasing with the Color Eraser tool to make a change would involve a great deal of work. However, you can take a shortcut with the Color Eraser tool to change the colors. First make the foreground of the Selected Colors box blue and the background purple, and then double-click on the Color Eraser tool. All the blue in your drawing will change to purple.

Using the Scissors and Pick tools

The Scissors and Pick tools are often both called the pick tools because you can use the Pick menu commands only after you select something with these tools. The tools use a dotted line as a guideline to show you what area is selected. After you select a part of your drawing, you can move it, use the Pick or Edit menu commands, or even "sweep" the image to form a series of duplicates. (We'll talk about sweeping later in this chapter.)

Use the Pick tool to select a rectangular area around a graphic. First select the Pick tool from the Toolbox and move the crosshair pointer into the work area. Hold down the mouse button to anchor the guidelines in one corner, and drag to form a box that encloses the graphic you want to select. If you make a mistake, you can click in another spot to remove the guidelines.

If the area you want to select has an irregular shape, you should use the Scissors tool. Select this tool from the Toolbox and move the crosshair pointer to the area you want to select. Then press the mouse button and drag the guideline around the area. To finish selecting, connect the guideline to the starting point. If you release the mouse button before you arrive at the starting point, Paintbrush will connect the starting and ending points with a straight line.

You can use the editing features of Paintbrush to improve on the basic design of your drawing. You can rearrange graphics or even duplicate them. Paintbrush gives you artistic license to manipulate your drawing without starting over. In this section, we'll show you how to make changes, via Clipboard and Edit menu commands, with advanced functions of the pick tools and the Pick menu. You'll learn how to move graphics, change their size, flip them horizontally or vertically, invert their colors, and even tilt them.

IMPROVING ON THE BASIC DESIGN

Chapter 9 showed you the basics of moving data around in a document with the Cut, Copy, and Paste commands. You use the same commands to move graphics around in your drawing. To use the Edit menu commands, first select a graphic with the Pick or Scissors tool. Next, issue the command you need to move or copy the graphic. Cutting the selected shape will remove it from the drawing and place it in Clipboard. Copying will not remove the shape from the drawing but will place a copy in Clipboard. Pasting will add the contents of Clipboard to your drawing in the upper-left corner of the work area. When the pasted copy appears, it will already be selected so that you can easily move it to a new location. You can paste an object more than once, quickly reproducing a common element in your drawing. We used the Copy and Paste commands to facilitate drawing the electronic keyboard in Figure 11-11, for example.

Editing via Clipboard

In addition to the Edit menu commands, Paintbrush provides other ways to move and copy your graphics. You can use the Pick or Scissors tool to move, copy, or sweep a selected graphic.

Selection tool functions

To move a graphic that you selected with the Pick or Scissors tool, just move your pointer inside the guideline box and drag the graphic. If you select only part of a graphic, only that part will move. If you mistakenly omit part of the graphic from your selection, you can use the Undo command to return the graphic to its original condition if you have not performed any intervening actions. Undo works only for your last action; when you choose another tool, you can't undo an action performed by the previous tool.

Moving cutouts

When you move a graphic, you can place it in one of two ways: transparent placement or opaque placement. If you move an unfilled box using the left mouse button and place it on top of another graphic, you will see the lines of both graphics (transparent placement). If you move the graphic with the right mouse button, it will be opaque (and will include any background you selected) and will cover up the other graphic (opaque placement). (Note, however, that if the background color of the selected graphic is different from the currently selected background color, the placement will be opaque, regardless of the mouse button used.) Figure 11-26 on the next page shows two series of boxes, one using transparent placement and the other using opaque placement.

Figure 11-26

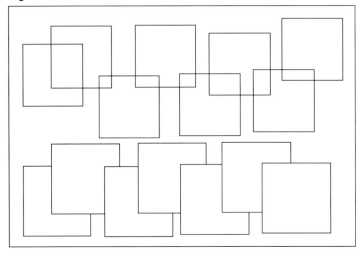

*The top series of squares uses transparent placement of graphics;
the bottom series uses opaque placement.*

**Using the pick tools
to copy a shape**

To avoid repeatedly creating the same element, you can use a shortcut to duplicate the element and place it in your drawing. Select the element with a pick tool, and then hold down the mouse button and press [Shift] to copy the element. When you drag the element, the pointer will pick up the copy. Press [Shift] again when the copy is positioned at the desired location. For example, to draw the horse stable shown in Figure 11-27, reusing the wood plank you created earlier, you need to follow these steps.

• Open the file in which you saved the wood plank. Select the wood plank with one of the pick tools, and copy it to Clipboard using the Copy command on the Edit menu.

• Open a new file by choosing the New command on the File menu.

• Paste the wood plank into your new file by choosing the Paste command on the Edit menu.

• Click on the wood plank to select it, and then press [Shift] to duplicate the plank. Drag the copy to its new location, and press [Shift] again to position it. We used both vertical and horizontal planks to build the walls and stable door shown in Figure 11-27.

• You can add such details as hinges and a handle to the door by using the Box, Circle, and Polygon tools. We also added straw with the Line tool and then copied it to spread it on the floor. We drew the horseshoe above the stall with the Curve tool and placed the transparent copy over the door.

Figure 11-27

By duplicating the wood plank, you can create a building like this stable.

Instead of cutting and pasting a graphic repeatedly to create a series, you can sweep the graphic to form a cascade of opaque or transparent images. A transparent sweep looks like Figure 11-28; an opaque sweep looks like Figure 11-29. As you can see, the lines from the underlying shapes show through in a transparent sweep, but not in an opaque sweep.

Sweeping a graphic

Figure 11-28

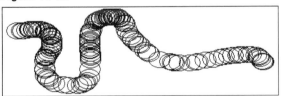

This is a transparent sweep of circles.

Figure 11-29

This is an opaque sweep of circles.

To sweep a graphic, select it with a pick tool and then hold down the [Shift] key and drag the graphic where you want to place it. To complete the sweep, release the mouse button or the [Shift] key. Use the left mouse button for a transparent graphic or the right button for an opaque one. You can change the graphic effect by altering the speed of your mouse movements.

Improvising with the Pick menu

Once you select a graphic with one of the pick tools, you can improvise on that graphic theme with the commands on the Pick menu. You can resize the graphic, flip it horizontally or vertically, tilt it, and invert its colors. You also can tell Paintbrush to remove the original graphic and replace it with the new version by using the Clear command.

Sizing selected graphics

As you know, it's much easier to draw a large graphic than a small one, but with Paintbrush, you can draw a large graphic and then make a reduced copy of it with the Shrink + Grow command on the Pick menu. When you're ready to shrink the graphic, frame it with a pick tool, and select the Shrink + Grow command. After you select the command, position the crosshair pointer at one corner of the area where you want the newly sized graphic to appear. Drag the pointer to form a guideline box representing the new size you want. You can change the proportions of the graphic by making the guideline box longer or wider. If you want the new size to have the same proportions as the original graphic, hold down the [Shift] key as you drag the guideline box. Figure 11-30 shows a series of balloons we created with the Shrink + Grow command.

Figure 11-30

The Shrink + Grow command lets you create proportional copies of balloon graphics.

When you select the Shrink + Grow command, Paintbrush adds a check mark next to the command. The command remains selected until you toggle it off, select a tool, choose the Tilt command, or reselect a graphic with one of the pick tools. Note that you must turn off the Shrink + Grow command before you can use the Flip Horizontal, Flip Vertical, or Inverse command.

You can flip a selected graphic horizontally or vertically. To flip a graphic, first select it with a pick tool, and then choose one of the flip commands from the Pick menu. You can follow the steps below to flip a graphic, as illustrated in Figure 11-31.

Flipping a graphic

- We've added arrows to the graphic in Step 1 so that you can see the original orientation of the square.

- To flip the square horizontally, first select the square with a pick tool, and then choose the Flip Horizontal command from the Pick menu. When you flip the square, it will look like Step 2.

- If you flip the original square vertically with the Flip Vertical command instead, it will look like Step 3.

If you try to flip a graphic but nothing happens, check to see whether a toggle command on the Pick menu—either Shrink + Grow or Tilt—is turned on. These commands must be inactive before you can flip the graphic. You should also suspect that one of these toggle commands is turned on if the guidelines don't remain on the screen when you try to select the graphic.

Figure 11-31

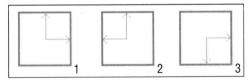

The selected graphic can be flipped either horizontally or vertically.

In addition to flipping or resizing a graphic, you also can tilt it. All you have to do to tilt a graphic is select it and then choose the Tilt command from the Pick menu. Because Tilt is a toggle command, you can keep producing tilted shapes as long as it's active. After you activate the Tilt command, move your pointer into the work area, and click to draw the guideline box and anchor one corner. Now drag the pointer to change the orientation of the box. The farther you move the pointer from the anchor point, the greater the tilt. When you release the mouse button, the graphic will orient itself to the tilt of the guideline box. Figure 11-32 on the next page shows the "Leaning Tower of Louisville," first straight and then tilted with the Tilt command.

Tilting a graphic

Figure 11-32

We created a leaning tower with the Tilt command.

Inverting a graphic

We've talked about changing the shape of a graphic; now let's talk about changing the colors with the Pick menu. The Inverse command on the Pick menu will change all the colors of a selected area to their complementary colors. (A complementary color is one that is opposite a selected color on a color wheel. For example, the complement of red is green.) You must carefully select the area you want to invert because both the foreground and background colors will be affected. If you use a pick tool to select a graphic, the frame and the interior will change color, as well as any exterior selected area. If you invert a pattern, all the dots that make up that pattern will change to their complementary colors.

Using the Clear command

The Clear command on the Pick menu works with the Tilt and Shrink + Grow commands. The Clear command helps reduce the number of duplicate graphics in your work area by clearing the original selected graphic from the work area after you create a variation by using the Tilt or the Shrink + Grow command. You need to be sure that the Clear command is toggled off if you want to leave the original graphic untouched while creating variations.

ADDING DETAIL

Instead of attempting to produce a perfect drawing on the first try, you can use the zoom commands to clean up your drawing and add fine detail. We used the zoom commands to clean up many of the graphics in this chapter. In this section, we'll also show you how to use the Cursor Position box as a ruler for your drawing. The Cursor Position box is a special dialog box that dynamically displays the coordinates (X, Y) of your mouse pointer in the work area.

Zooming in for a closer look

To view and adjust the minute details of your drawing, you can use the Zoom In command on the View menu to look at the pixels, or bits, that form images. When you choose the Zoom In command, the pointer turns into a box. Move the box pointer over the area you want to start viewing, and then click the left mouse button. As you can see in Figure 11-33, the work area becomes a grid of bits that is an enlarged view of the section of the graphic you selected with the box pointer. (In Figure 11-33, we selected a small part of the *Kentucky!* calligraphy shown in Figure 11-20.) To provide a reference point, a box in the upper-left corner of the work area displays the actual size of the part of the graphic you're viewing. By using the scroll bars, you can look at minute aspects of your graphic. Both the bit map and the display box will present a new part of your drawing when you use the scroll bars.

If you want to change any of the bits on the bit map, you must use either the Brush or the Paint Roller tool. You'll find that you can't select any of the other tools in the Toolbox or their related commands. The Brush tool will let you change one bit at a time. If you select the Brush tool and then move the pointer into the work area, you will notice that the pointer doesn't change to a brush shape but remains an arrow pointer. The Paint Roller tool's pointer, on the other hand, keeps its unique shape and functions.

With the Brush tool, you can click on a single bit to change it to the selected foreground color or drag to change bits as you move the pointer. As you change the bits in the bit map, the actual-size view changes to match your bit changes, giving you a better idea of what the drawing looks like.

Figure 11-33

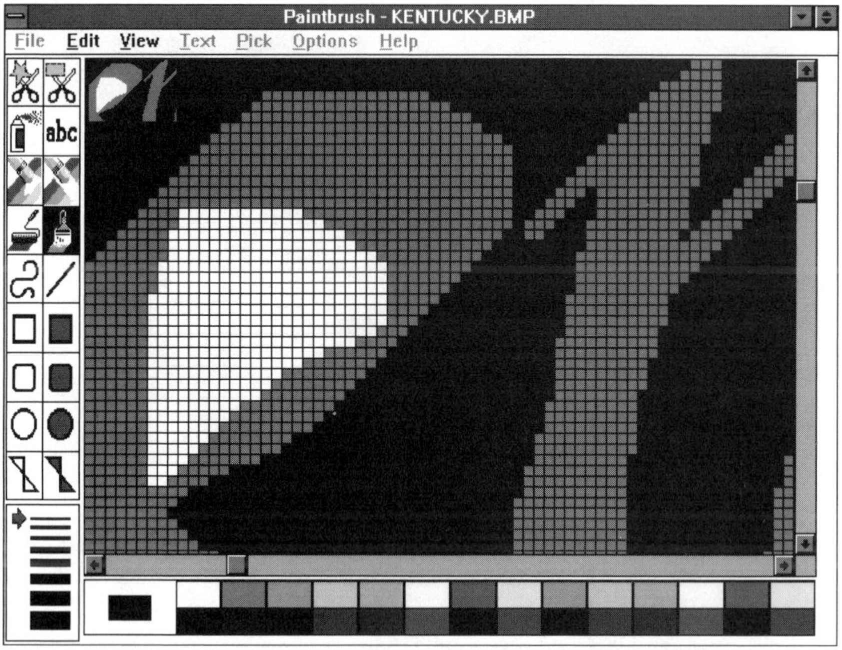

After you use the Zoom In command on the View menu, the work area turns into a bit map, with an actual-size view in the upper-left corner.

For example, if you wanted to clean up the edges on a graphic because it had gaps and you couldn't fill it with the Paint Roller tool without filling the rest of the drawing, you could zoom in to fix it. To do this, select the Zoom In command, place the box pointer over the problem area of the graphic, and click. Once the bit map appears, choose the Brush tool, and make sure the selected foreground color is the one you want. Next, move the pointer into the work area, and click on the bits that will fill in the gap.

If you have an enclosed space to fill in the repaired graphic, go ahead and choose the Paint Roller tool. As you move the Paint Roller tool onto the zoomed-in graphic, the Paint Roller pointer will appear. The Paint Roller tool can fill in only the area displayed on the screen. You'll need to scroll through the rest of the shape as you fill in all the bits with the new color.

You can see why the Zoom In command is used only for detail and not for large areas. For example, small areas like the ones in the *Kentucky!* calligraphy (Figure 11-20) need to be filled in with the Paint Roller tool and the Zoom In command. In Figure 11-33, we zoomed in on one part of the calligraphy that needed the background filled in. Figure 11-34 shows this section of the calligraphy after we filled in the background with the Paint Roller tool.

Figure 11-34

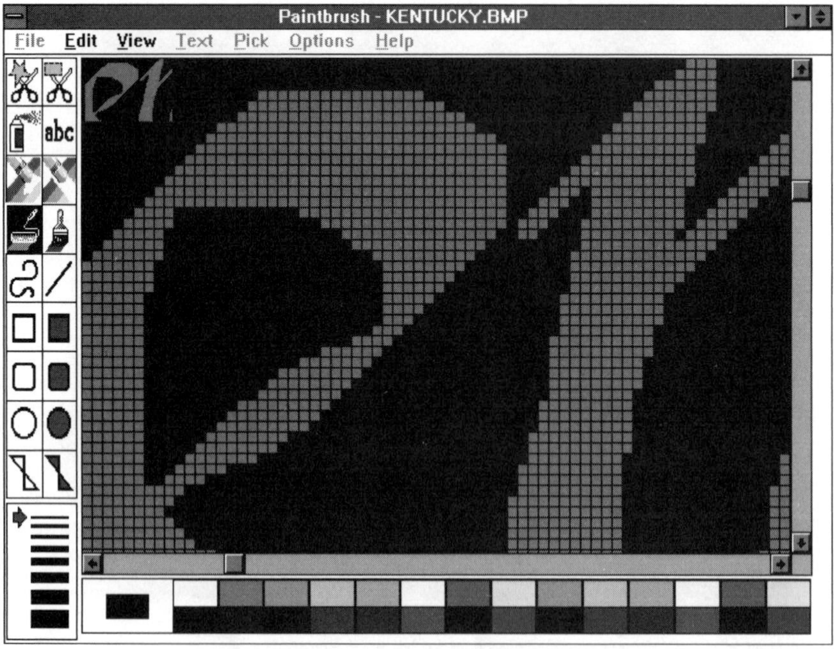

Using the Zoom In command and the Paint Roller tool, we cleaned up a part of the calligraphy that needed the background filled in.

When you have finished working with the zoomed-in graphic, choose Zoom Out on the View menu to return to your original work area. If you want to go a step further, you can choose the View Picture command on the View menu to view the entire drawing instead of just what is displayed in Paintbrush's window. When you click on this command, Paintbrush will display the entire drawing without the Toolbox, Linesize box, Palette, menus, or other screen elements. To return to the regular Paintbrush window, click anywhere on the screen. Figure 11-35 and Figure 11-36 (on the following page) show a regular view and a View Picture view of the same drawing.

Figure 11-35

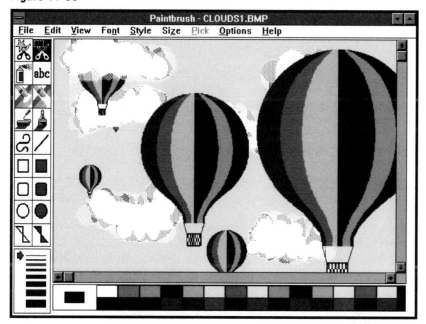

The work area displays only part of the balloons.

If you want Paintbrush to display more of your drawing so that you can manipulate it without relying heavily on the scroll bars, you can temporarily remove the Toolbox, the Linesize box, or the Palette. When you select the Tools and Linesize command on the View menu, the Toolbox and the Linesize box will disappear. If you look at the View menu again, you'll notice that the check mark next to this command is gone. If you select the command again (toggle it on), the check mark, the Toolbox, and the Linesize box will reappear.

Figure 11-36

You can use the View Picture command to display the entire picture.

The Palette command on the View menu is also a toggle command. If you toggle the check mark off the Palette command, Paintbrush will remove the Palette from the work area.

If you want to see the entire drawing and still be able to work on it, you can use the Zoom Out command with a drawing of normal size. After you issue Zoom Out, Paintbrush will redisplay the entire drawing in the boundaries of your work area, regardless of the window size. However, not all the tools are active. You can use only the Pick tool and some Edit menu commands (Cut, Copy, Paste, Copy To, and Paste From). We'll discuss those commands at the end of the chapter.

Using cursor position as a ruler

Although you can't display a ruler in the Paintbrush window, you can use the Cursor Position command on the View menu to provide a reference and add consistency and accuracy to your drawing. When you select this command, a dialog box like the one in Figure 11-37 appears on the title bar.

Figure 11-37

The Cursor Position dialog box tracks the horizontal and vertical coordinates of the pointer in your drawing.

The dialog box displays two numbers: the horizontal and vertical coordinates of the cursor position. The upper-left corner of a drawing has the coordinates 0, 0. The coordinates of the lower-right corner depend on the size of the drawing and the resolution of your display. If your initial Paintbrush window is maximized, the lower-right coordinates can be as large as 543, 369 on a standard VGA monitor. However, because you can use any dimensions you want for your drawing, the coordinates for the lower-right corner can exceed the default coordinates. If the pointer leaves the work area, the values in the dialog box will freeze at the exit point's coordinates.

Let's suppose you want to draw a stack of boxes. Instead of guessing how wide the first one is when you're trying to match the second one, you can use the Cursor Position dialog box as a reference. Just remember the starting and stopping horizontal points when you draw the first box. You can move the pointer to the exact horizontal starting point before you draw the next box so that the boxes will be the same width. If you want identical heights for the boxes, you can increment the vertical coordinates the same amount for each box. Of course, if you want identical boxes, it would be easier to select the first box with the Pick tool and then use the Copy and Paste commands.

You can close the Cursor Position dialog box by toggling off the Cursor Position command or by double-clicking on the dialog box's Control menu box.

SAVING YOUR WORK

As soon as you complete a drawing or even a major portion of it, you should save your work. You can save the file on your hard drive or on a floppy disk. To save the file, choose the Save command on the File menu. If you have not previously saved the file, a Save As dialog box, like the one shown in Figure 11-38, will appear.

Figure 11-38

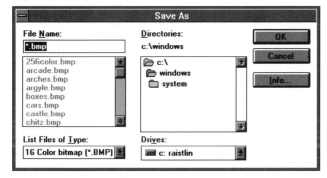

The Save As dialog box lets you save your drawing.

When you save the file, Paintbrush saves it with a .BMP or .PCX file name extension, depending on the file type. To see the available file types in the Save As dialog box, use the Save File as Type drop-down list box. After you type the file name in the File Name text box and check to be sure that the correct directory and drive are specified in the appropriate list boxes (Paintbrush uses the Windows directory by default), you can click on OK. After the file is saved, you'll notice that the Paintbrush title bar displays the new file name. From now on, Paintbrush won't ask for a file name when you use the Save command; it will update the file it already has.

If you select the Info button in the Save As dialog box, you will see a Picture Information dialog box, like the one shown in Figure 11-39. This dialog box contains information about the height, width, number of colors, and number of planes of the currently displayed picture.

Figure 11-39

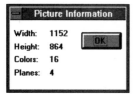

The Picture Information dialog box describes the currently displayed picture.

If you want to save a copy of your drawing in a different file, you must use the Save As command on the File menu. Then, you can enter the new file name in the Save As dialog box. Even if you don't want to save another copy under a different file name, you can still use the Save As command to save the file in a different place on your hard drive or on a floppy disk. It's a good idea to keep a backup copy on a floppy disk in case of accidents or equipment failure. In addition, it's always a good idea to save your drawing before you print. That way, if the printer causes your computer to lock up, you won't lose any of your drawing when you reboot.

PRINTING YOUR DRAWING

At some point, you'll want to print your drawing. Before you can send your drawing to the printer, you need to make sure that the page and the printer are set up correctly. Setting up a page involves setting the margins for a printout of your drawing. To set up a printer, you specify any variations in the options of an active printer (such as page orientation or paper size). When the page and printer settings are correct, issue the Print command to tell Paintbrush to print the drawing. You also can specify how much of the drawing to print. In this section, we'll explain the commands and settings you use to print your drawings. We'll also explain options for printing partial drawings or multiple copies.

Before you issue the Print command, you need to tell your printer how you want the drawing positioned on the page. The Page Setup command controls the header, footer, and margins. When you choose the Page Setup command on the File menu, the Page Setup dialog box will appear. By default, the Header and Footer text boxes are empty in Paintbrush.

Page setup

The margins are also set up in the Page Setup dialog box. The header and footer will always be .5" from the top and bottom of the page. Paintbrush won't let you change those margins.

After you have set up the page, you might want to verify that the printer is also set up the way you want it. To do this, choose Print Setup on the File menu. When the Print Setup dialog box appears, you can choose the default printer or select a specific printer from the drop-down list box. Make sure the printer that is hooked up and installed on your computer is selected and is using the right port. If it doesn't have a port or if the port is incorrect, use Control Panel to assign one. In Figure 11-40, we've chosen the default printer, an HP LaserJet Series II on LPT1. In the Print Setup dialog box, you can change the orientation, the paper size, and the paper source. See Chapters 3 and 9 for more details about printing options.

Printer setup

Figure 11-40

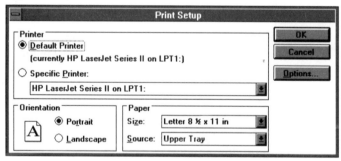

The Print Setup dialog box allows you to choose a specific printer and change the printing options.

Now that you have set up the page and the printer, you're ready to actually print a drawing. When you choose the Print command on the File menu, the Print dialog box shown in Figure 11-41 on the following page will appear. In this dialog box, you can choose the quality of the printout, the part of the drawing to print, the number of copies, and the printer resolution setting.

Using the Print command

Figure 11-41

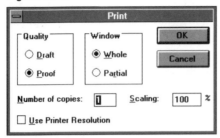

The Print dialog box appears when you use the Print command.

Setting the quality

You can control the quality of your printout by selecting the Proof or Draft setting in the Quality section (if a Quality section is provided for your printer). A high-quality printout, or a proof, uses all the features of your printer but prints more slowly than a lower-quality printout. A lower-quality printout, or a draft, prints faster but ignores the advanced features of your printer. If you have a dot matrix printer, the draft printout will be lighter than a proof, and the image will have rough edges. In a proof, the printout will be dark, and the edges of the images and text will be smooth. Drafts are good for checking your work before you print the final copy. (You can also use the View Picture command on the View menu to see the entire drawing on the screen, which should help you catch mistakes before you print.)

Choosing the number of copies

The Number of Copies text box in the Print dialog box lets you specify how many copies you want to print. Simply type a number to change the number of copies. (By default, this text box is selected when you open the Print dialog box.)

Setting the printer resolution

Another setting you may need to adjust is the printer resolution. The Use Printer Resolution check box in the Print dialog box tells the printer to use its idea of how large a pixel is instead of how large the screen thinks it is. Your screen uses larger pixels than your printer does. If you do not select this option, Paintbrush will size your image according to your specifications in the Image Attributes dialog box—the printed image should approximate the image size on your screen. If you select Use Printer Resolution, the printer will translate each screen pixel to one of the printer's native-size pixels. For example, a 300 dpi laser printer will reduce an image that fills your VGA screen to only 1.5" high.

You may need to adjust your printer resolution again if you run into memory problems. The higher the resolution, the more memory it will take to print a drawing. If your drawing is only partially printed even though you selected Whole in the Print dialog box, you might have exceeded the limits of your printer's memory. Try reducing the size of the image by using the Scaling text box. You can reduce the area within which Paintbrush prints the image, which also reduces the number of pixels to be printed and makes it easier for Paintbrush to print within your printer's memory limits.

When you use a color printer, you need to be aware that printing the drawing will consume more memory if you use a Palette with more colors or if your drawing includes scanned images. A 256-gray-level scanned image, for instance, actually has 256 colors. Refer to your color printer's manual for details about printer memory management.

Although you'll usually want to print your entire drawing, at times you may prefer to print only part of it. Paintbrush allows you to print part of a drawing by offering the Partial option in the Window section of the Print dialog box. A whole printout, of course, prints everything. A partial printout will send only a selected area to the printer.

Selecting all or part of a drawing

To select an area, choose the Partial radio button and click on OK. The entire drawing will appear in the work area, with a crosshair pointer. You can drag the pointer to form a selection box around part of the drawing. After you have outlined the part you want, release the mouse button to send the selection to the printer.

When you send a whole or partial printout to the printer, Paintbrush lets you know it's printing by displaying a Printing message dialog box. If you want to cancel the printing, just click on the Cancel button. After the dialog box appears, you'll also see the Print Manager icon on the desktop (if the icon area of the desktop isn't covered).

After the drawing is sent to the Print Manager, the Printing message dialog box will close, but the Print Manager icon will stay on the desktop until your drawing comes out of the printer. If you are having trouble or want to stop printing, double-click on the Print Manager icon. See Chapter 7 for more about using the Print Manager.

You can either start a new untitled file with the New command on the File menu or you can open an existing file. To work on a drawing you have already started, choose the Open command on the File menu. The Open dialog box, shown in Figure 11-42 on the next page, has a text box in which you enter the file name of the drawing. If the file is in another directory or on a different drive, you can use the Directories and Drives list boxes to move to that path. The available files are displayed in the File Name list box, where you can click on the file name instead of typing it in the text box. Paintbrush normally looks for .BMP extensions when listing files. If you want to look for files that have .MSP or .PCX extensions, you must choose the appropriate item from the List Files of Type drop-down list box. A .MSP file is used with versions of Microsoft Paint before Windows 3.0. A .BMP extension is used by Windows wallpaper files, and a .PCX extension is used by Paintbrush as an alternative format.

OPENING FILES

Figure 11-42

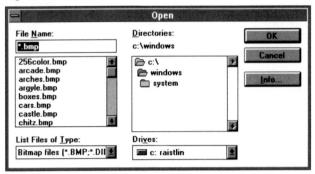

The Open dialog box lets you choose from lists of files and file types.

If you try to open a file or start a new one without saving the existing one, Paintbrush will present a message dialog box asking if you want to save the drawing. If you click on Yes, Paintbrush will update the file or ask you for a file name. If you click on No, Paintbrush will not save the file and will replace it in memory with the next file. If you click on Cancel, Paintbrush will not save the file or open another file but will return you to the current drawing.

ADVANCED PAINTBRUSH FEATURES

Now that you can create basic drawings with Paintbrush, you're ready to explore advanced Paintbrush features. In this section, we'll explain the more complex features of Paintbrush, such as converting old Microsoft Paint files, exporting files to other applications, creating custom colors, converting color Palettes, using a scanner, and making wallpaper files for the desktop.

Converting old Microsoft Paint files

So far, you've opened only other Paintbrush files. If you have Microsoft Paint files that you created with an older version of Windows, you can convert them into Paintbrush files. If the file has a .MSP extension, Paintbrush will know what kind of file it is and will automatically convert it into a Paintbrush file with a .BMP extension. All you have to do is use the Open command on the File menu and, when you enter the file name, include the .MSP extension. Paintbrush will do the rest.

Once a file has been converted into Paintbrush format, you won't be able to convert it back. To use a file with both Microsoft Paint and Paintbrush, you must copy the Microsoft Paint file and then convert the copy to Paintbrush.

Using drawings in other Windows applications

As we mentioned in the introduction, you can use the graphics you create in Paintbrush with other applications to make letterheads, greeting cards, newsletters, and so forth. If you want to use a logo you created in Paintbrush as part of your letterhead, you can do so simply by adding your address and phone number. Then, you can add the letterhead to a letter in Write by copying the letterhead to Clipboard with the Copy command on Paintbrush's Edit menu and pasting it into your document with the Paste command on Write's Edit menu. Unless your printer can print gray scales, it's best to use black and white for your image attributes if you have a black-and-white printer. If you have a color printer that Windows supports (for example, the IBM Color Printer), your letterhead can be in color. Remember that you can have both a Paintbrush window and a Write window open on the desktop to facilitate this process.

Editing drawings in other applications

If you add a Paintbrush graphic to a document created in an OLE receiving application such as Cardfile, you can edit the graphic from the receiving application. When you double-click on the graphic, it appears in a Paintbrush window. You can then change the graphic using any of the Paintbrush tools. When you finish making the changes, choose the Exit and Return To command on the File menu, and then choose Yes to update the graphic and return to the receiving application.

Saving changes to OLE drawings

After you make changes in an OLE graphic, it might be useful to save the changes in a file that is separate from the receiving file. When the graphic is an embedded object, the Update command (which will send the changes to the receiving file) replaces the Save command on the File menu. Use the Save As command on the File menu to save the object in a file with a different name. The source application will first ask if you want to update the object in the receiving file. After you save an object in a source application file, the usual list of File menu commands will reappear.

Saving graphics to a file

In addition to saving entire documents, you can save parts of your drawings in separate files so that you can reuse them for future projects. For example, if you use your company logo or slogan with most of your presentations, it would be handy to simply paste it instead of having to open a file, select the graphic, copy it, open the file in which you want to use it, and paste it in. By using the Copy To and Paste From commands on the Edit menu, you can avoid time-consuming steps.

To save a graphic to a special paste file, first use a pick tool (the Scissors or Pick tool) to select the graphic you want. Then select the Copy To command to save the selected graphic to a file. Paintbrush will present a Copy To dialog box, as shown in Figure 11-43 on the following page, asking you for a file name. Just name the file and click on OK; then, when you want to use that graphic again, select the Paste From command, and choose the file you want from the File Name list box in the Paste From dialog box, as shown in Figure 11-44 on the next page. Paintbrush will paste the graphic in the upper-left corner of the work area, as it does with other graphics you paste from Clipboard into your work area.

You also can paste a drawing from a file into the work area without using the Copy To command. Simply issue the Paste From command, and then select the file name of the drawing and click on OK. Paintbrush will insert the drawing into your work area the same way the Paste command inserts a graphic from Clipboard.

Figure 11-43

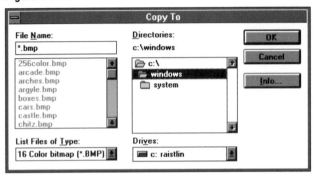

You can save a graphic to a special paste file with the Copy To command.

Figure 11-44

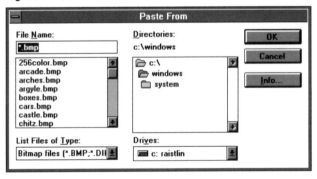

You can use the Paste From command to retrieve a graphic.

For example, we decided to save The Cobb Group's Best seal in a file so that we could use it in various drawings, as shown in Figure 11-45. You can follow the steps listed here to save and paste a reusable graphic into another drawing.

- Open the original drawing file, and select the graphic.

- Choose the Copy To command, and save the graphic file. (We called ours THEBEST.BMP.)

- Close the first file, and open the target file.

- Choose the Paste From command, and select the graphic file (for instance, THEBEST.BMP).

- Relocate the graphic (the Best seal) within the drawing.

Now whenever we want to use the Best seal, we can simply use the Paste From command. Although the process of storing the graphic in a file takes as long as using the regular Cut and Paste commands, you save time later when you need to reuse the graphic.

Figure 11-45

We saved the Best seal as a reusable graphic.

In Chapter 9, you learned how to capture the screen or active window to Clipboard by using the [Print Screen] and [Alt][Print Screen] keys. Once the image is in Clipboard, you can use the Paste command from the Edit menu to place it in the Paintbrush work area, where you can edit it. If you need to export the image, you can save it in a different file format.

Using screen capture files

**Creating custom
Palettes**

Another advanced feature of Paintbrush is its ability to customize the colors on the Palette. All you have to do is choose the Edit Colors command on the Options menu to see an Edit Colors dialog box like the one shown in Figure 11-46. Paintbrush displays the current foreground color in the display box that appears on the right of the dialog box. The three scroll bars represent the three primary colors—red, green, and blue. All possible colors can be defined by mixing the three primary colors in different proportions. You may remember that the Custom Color Selector dialog box, accessed from Control Panel's Color dialog box, also displayed red, green, and blue values, as well as hue, saturation, and luminosity indicators.

Figure 11-46

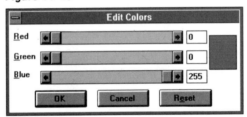

The Edit Colors dialog box lets you customize any of the Palette colors.

If you want to change the color, just drag the sliders on any of the three bars in the Edit Colors dialog box until the box on the right displays the color you want. Changing a color on the color Palette doesn't change that color in your drawing; it simply gives you a different color to work with. If all three sliders are on the left of the scroll bars, the color will be black. If they are all on the right, the color will be white. The numbers corresponding to the position of the sliders range from 0 to 255. The colors mix the way light does rather than the way paint does. That's why the primary colors are red, green, and blue (light primaries) instead of red, yellow, and blue (paint primaries). When you've finished changing the color, click on OK to put it in the Palette. After you finish using your new color, you may want to reset the sliders to restore the original color settings. Simply click on Reset in the Edit Colors dialog box to return to the original color settings. The new color will be effective until you change it or quit Paintbrush. When you start Paintbrush again, the original color Palette will return.

You can use a shortcut to see the Edit Colors dialog box. All you have to do is double-click in the color Palette on the color that you want to change. The Edit Colors dialog box will appear with that color in the display box.

After you have changed the necessary colors, you can save those changes to use again later. To save the changes, choose the Save Colors command on the Options menu. The Save Colors As dialog box, shown in Figure 11-47, will appear. All the Palettes are named with a .PAL extension. The Directories and

Drives list boxes will let you save the file anywhere on the hard drive or on a floppy disk. After you type in the new file name, click on OK to save the file.

Figure 11-47

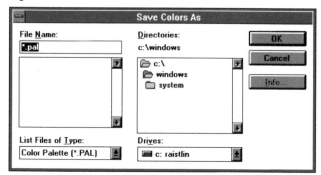

The Save Colors As dialog box saves your color changes in a .PAL file.

When you want to use the colors you saved, select the Get Colors command on the Options menu. The Get Colors dialog box, shown in Figure 11-48, displays all the available .PAL files. Click on the one you want, and choose OK to replace the current Palette with the new one.

Figure 11-48

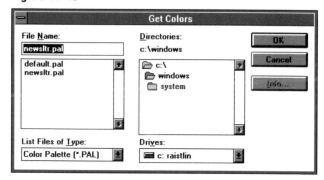

The Get Colors dialog box replaces the current Palette with the selected .PAL file's Palette.

It's a good idea to save the original palette with a file name like DEFAULT.PAL so that you can return to the original default color Palette without having to exit and restart Paintbrush.

Converting a drawing to black and white

Paintbrush can convert a graphic file from color to black and white. (The color graphic needs to be in a file created with the Copy To command or saved in a regular file.) First, you must select the Black and White radio button in the Image Attributes dialog box or simply open a black-and-white drawing. (The drawing must use a black-and-white Palette and not just the black and white colors from a color Palette.) Next, issue the Paste From command to paste the graphic file into the work area. Paintbrush will convert the graphic into black and white. All solid colors will translate to black, while dithered colors will translate into a black-and-white composite of colors that looks like gray. You can also paste a graphic from Clipboard into a black-and-white drawing to achieve the same effect.

Importing scanned images

Apart from the Paintbrush tools you can use to create images, you can use a number of popular scanners. You can scan a picture (photo, artwork, and so forth) and then add the resulting graphic to your drawing. (We used an HP ScanJet Plus with HP's Scanning Gallery software to import photographs into Paintbrush.) If your scanning software won't produce a .PCX or .BMP file for Paintbrush to read, you may need to use a conversion utility, such as Hijaak, to convert the file to a .PCX or .BMP format. Then you can open the file as you would any other Paintbrush file.

Scanners convert your photo or artwork into a graphic, possibly replacing the colors with shades of gray (gray scales). You can also set up a scanner to produce a graphic using only black and white, with no gray shades.

Resolution plays an important role in the scanning process. You need to consider three resolution variables: scanner resolution for creating the graphic, printer resolution for printing it, and screen resolution for viewing it. The scanner can vary the resolution of the graphic when it scans (digitizes) your photo. The scanner determines the graphic's inherent resolution. When you print the graphic, you can vary the graphic's resolution again by changing the resolution settings that are accessed by selecting the Printers icon on Control Panel (described in Chapter 3). For example, we scanned images at 75 dpi with the HP ScanJet Plus and HP Scanning Gallery software and then imported the images into Paintbrush for editing. The images were nearly actual size on our screen, because the VGA resolution of 640 by 480 pixels approximates 72 dpi on a standard-size monitor. We printed on an HP LaserJet, letting Paintbrush, not the printer, control the final image size.

When you save the scanned image with the scanning software, such as HP's Scanning Gallery, select a Paintbrush format (.PCX or .BMP) or a .TIFF (Tagged Image File Format) format option. If you use a format other than .PCX or .BMP, you will have to convert the file to a Paintbrush-compatible file format with a purchased file utility such as Hijaak. Once you have a .PCX or .BMP file, you can open it with Paintbrush.

You can put your company logo in your documents by scanning it and pasting it to Clipboard. You can use the Copy To command to place the logo in a reusable format. You can paste your logo into any application that accepts graphics, such as Write, Cardfile, or Word for Windows. We scanned our logo (which is shown in Figure 11-49), converted the .TIFF file to a .PCX file, and then opened it.

Figure 11-49

You can scan your logo, convert it,
and then modify it with Paintbrush.

Making wallpaper

Paintbrush lets you make your own wallpaper to customize the background for your desktop. You can make it full-screen, or you can make a smaller image that can be tiled. Simply save your drawing in a file with a .BMP extension.

When you create a drawing for wallpaper, you need to choose the correct size for your work area. If you want the wallpaper to cover the whole screen on a VGA monitor, use a pel setting of 640 (height) by 480 (width) in the Image Attributes dialog box. If you want it smaller so that you can tile it, use a setting of 320 by 240. If you don't want to tile the image, you can make it any size smaller than 640 by 480. If it's larger, part of the image will not appear on the desktop when you select it for wallpaper. You can create a small image (32 by 32) and tile it for a pattern, like the Arcade image that comes with Windows. Figure 11-50 shows the Arcade image and a resulting section of a tiled desktop.

Figure 11-50

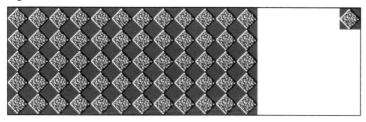

The Arcade building block is a small graphic
that you can tile to fill the desktop.

In Figure 11-51, for example, you can see a full-screen wallpaper file that we created using a scanned picture of horses and roses.

Figure 11-51

You can create wallpaper like this with scanned images.

To create your own full-screen wallpaper from one or more scanned images, you can follow the steps listed here.

- Activate the Paintbrush icon twice, and set up both work areas with default image attributes of 640 by 480 pels, and then select the Colors radio button in the Image Attributes dialog box to set up a color Palette. (One window will serve as a sketch pad and the other as the destination window for your drawing.)

- Retrieve one of the scanned image files, like our scanned rose, in the sketch pad window.

- Select the image with a pick tool, and manipulate it with the Shrink + Grow command. Flip the images horizontally or vertically to vary the orientation of some of the images. Use a pick tool to select the variations you want to use, and then use the Copy command to copy them to Clipboard.

- Click on the destination window in which you're creating the wallpaper, and choose the Paste command on the Edit menu to paste the image into the work area. Drag the image to the place you want it. Repeat the copy and paste routine as many times as it takes to include all the images in the wallpaper file.

- Add color to your wallpaper with the Color Eraser or Paint Roller tool. If you want to change only selected areas of dark gray to red, for example, use the Color Eraser tool to change only those areas. You can change all the dark gray to red by double-clicking on the Color Eraser tool. You can also use the Zoom In command to clean up any stray marks or paint that overflows from the Paint Roller tool.

Wallpaper can be more than just decorative. For instance, you can use Paintbrush to create some interesting combinations of images and stock messages—*Gone to Staff Meeting, Out to Lunch,* or *Don't Touch: Processing*—that you can put on the desktop whenever you need them.

At the beginning of this chapter, you saw a poster we created using a variety of Paintbrush's tools (Figure 11-1). Now that you've been introduced to all of Paintbrush's capabilities, we'll explain how we made the poster. We won't show each brush stroke because we've explained many of them throughout this chapter.

HOW WE MADE THE POSTER

- We used the wallpaper from Figure 11-51 as a starting point for our poster by opening its file and using the Save As command to save a duplicate of the poster called POSTER.BMP.

- We used the Paste From command on the Edit menu to add other drawings to the poster. We added the *Kentucky!* calligraphy and the balloons to the drawing and then changed the background to create a blue sky.

- We added the text *The Bluegrass State* with the Text tool.

In this chapter

Using Terminal 12

*E*lectronic mail, file transfers, mainframe communications, bulletin boards, information services—these are hallmarks of the information age. Personal computers are rapidly evolving from isolated number-crunching tools into the vital links of a worldwide information network, sharing information with other computers in the next office, the next city, or on the other side of the world.

Terminal—the communications application that comes with Windows— allows your computer to converse with remote computers and to transfer files. You can check on your stock portfolio with an information service, correspond with a colleague via electronic mail, get sales data from the corporate mainframe, or send a spreadsheet file to an associate in another city.

TERMINAL

Like the other Windows accessory applications, Terminal is somewhat limited but quite functional. It offers a scant selection of file transfer protocols and terminal emulations and does not provide scripting capability. Nevertheless, although Terminal lacks some of the features of more sophisticated applications such as Crosstalk for Windows, it may be all you need for basic communications.

Your computer will require some extra hardware to talk to the outside world. You'll need a Hayes-compatible modem, an available COM port, and access to a phone line for the computer. (You might have to bypass your office switchboard since some electronic phone systems are not compatible with data communications.) You can substitute a null modem cable for the modems and phone line if you want to connect two computers in the same room.

In this chapter, we assume that you are familiar with basic communications concepts. However, you don't need a detailed understanding of all the settings, such as baud rate, parity, and flow control. Terminal's settings must be appropriately adjusted for each host computer, so you can simply get the correct settings from the host computer's operators and match those settings in Terminal.

Starting Terminal

You'll find Terminal's icon in the Accessories group window of the Program Manager. Simply double-click on the icon to launch Terminal. Terminal is designed to communicate; all its features won't come alive until you begin a dialog with another computer. But you can explore many of the menus and settings without dialing another computer. When you get ready to leave Terminal, select Exit on the File menu.

The Terminal window

As you can see in Figure 12-1, the Terminal window has the usual menu bar across the top, above a large workspace where Terminal will display your dialog with the remote computer. This workspace will be empty until you establish a connection and begin to exchange information. Terminal's work area will be linked to your modem. It will "echo," or display on-screen, the prompts your modem receives from the remote computer and the responses you type. You can type in the work area only during a communications session; you cannot type directly into the work area as if it were a document in Write. During file transfers, a status bar will appear along the bottom edge of the work area. Terminal uses the status bar to keep you informed of its progress during the file transfer.

At the bottom of the Terminal window shown in Figure 12-1, you can see the optional function-key display. As we'll explain later, Terminal allows you to define custom functions for these on-screen buttons. Along with the function keys, Terminal will display a timer in the box in the lower-right corner that tracks the duration of your communications session.

Figure 12-1

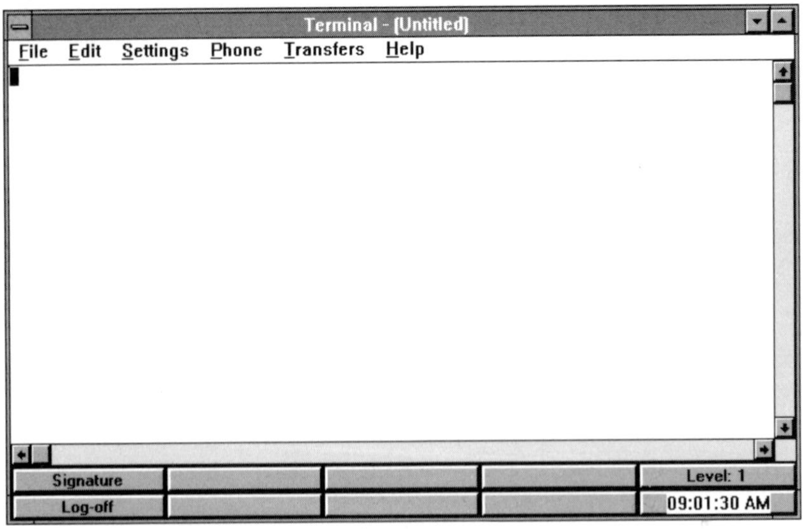

The optional function-key display and the timer are visible at the bottom of this Terminal window.

As you read this chapter, it will be helpful to remember the fundamental steps you'll go through each time you communicate with a remote, or host, computer. The details will vary greatly depending on the nature of the remote computer and your on-line activities, but the overall framework of your communications session will remain consistent.

- Establish (or verify) the hardware connections—make sure your modem, COM port, and phone line are all connected and operating properly.

- Launch Terminal.

- Adjust Terminal's settings to match the remote computer's requirements, either individually or by opening the appropriate Terminal settings file.

- Dial the remote computer using Terminal's Dial command.

- Identify yourself to the remote computer by completing the specified log-on procedure.

- Read and send messages, transfer files, and conduct your other on-line business.

- Sign off from the remote computer using the suggested log-off procedure; don't just hang up.

- Hang up the phone line with the Hangup command.

- Save the Terminal settings for this remote system in a file for future use.

- Exit Terminal.

The world of data communications is a complex one, with numerous "standards" for dealing with the many complicated issues that arise when two computers try to exchange information over telephone lines. Despite all the complications, different computers can talk to each other successfully if they both use a common set of rules.

Setting communications standards and protocols for two computers is not unlike arranging negotiations between two opposing factions. Before either party will begin discussions, you must first obtain agreement on the number and rank of the representatives from each side, the shape of the table and the seating arrangements, how meal breaks will be scheduled, even the language that will be used for the negotiations.

Fortunately, you have an advantage over the diplomats and negotiators: You won't have to guess what settings will be acceptable to both computers or find out by trial-and-error. The operators of most remote systems make the protocols and settings for their systems available to their potential users. The large information services such as CompuServe and MCI Mail supply sign-up kits. If you need to connect to your company's mainframe or network, you can probably get the correct settings with a quick phone call to the corporate computer center. You don't need to understand what all the settings do to use them—just match Terminal's settings to those of the remote system, and the computers should be able to communicate.

Once you've configured Terminal to communicate with a specific remote computer, you can save the settings in a file. The next time you communicate with that remote system, you can open the file to load the settings. In fact, you can use .TRM (Terminal) files from previous versions of Windows' Terminal.

Using the Settings menu

Some of the necessary settings, such as the phone number of the remote computer, are obvious and self-explanatory. Others, such as parity, might be harder to understand if you don't have a background in data communications. Most of Terminal's settings are "host specific"—that is, they must conform to the requirements of the remote computer. Generally, if the host system does not specify a selection for one of Terminal's options, you can assume that the default will work.

To adjust Terminal's settings to communicate with a new host, select commands on the Settings menu one by one, and review or adjust the options in the dialog boxes Terminal opens. Initially, it is probably a good idea to make sure you select every command on the Settings menu each time you set up for a new host so that you won't forget to adjust any settings. After adjusting Terminal's settings to work with your modem and a remote computer, you can save the settings in a file. Later, when you become familiar with Terminal's options, you can quickly create a Terminal settings file for a new host by using an existing settings file as a template. You can open a file for a host that uses similar settings, change only the settings that are unique to the new host (such as the phone number), and then use the Save As command on the File menu to save the new settings in a file with an appropriate name. Let's examine some of the commands on Terminal's Settings menu.

Modem Commands

The Modem Commands dialog box displays the commands that Terminal uses to instruct your modem to dial a number, hang up the phone, and so on. Although Modem Commands is near the middle of the Settings menu, it's probably the first group of settings you should check before you begin to use Terminal. Once you establish the correct modem commands for your modem, they normally remain the same for all your communications with various hosts.

Terminal comes configured to work with most Hayes-compatible modems, and the odds are good that the defaults will work without alteration. However, if you need to fine-tune the way Terminal works with your modem, you can change the commands in the Modem Commands dialog box. Be sure to consult your modem's documentation before you change any of these commands.

Select Modem Commands on the Settings menu to open the dialog box shown in Figure 12-2. The radio buttons in the Modem Defaults group box allow you to change the defaults that appear in the Commands group box. Initially, when you start Terminal, you'll see defaults for Hayes and Hayes-compatible modems. You can switch to the default commands for the other listed modems if you have one of those modems. Selecting the None radio button erases the default commands so that you can enter a custom set of commands if they are required by your modem.

In the Commands group box, the first line is the Dial command for your modem, with text boxes for a prefix and suffix. Terminal uses the Dial command to tell the modem to dial the remote computer's phone number. ATDT tells the modem to dial using touch tones. If you are connected to older, rotary pulse phone lines, you should change this setting to ATDP to tell the modem to dial with pulses rather than tones. Following the dial prefix, Terminal will send the remote computer's telephone number (which you'll enter later in the Phone Number dialog box) to the modem and then add the suffix to the end of the number to complete the dialing instruction for the modem.

Figure 12-2

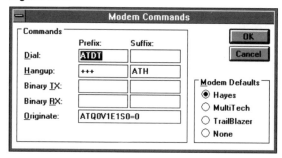

In this dialog box, you specify the commands Terminal will use to control your modem.

This prefix/data/suffix format allows considerable flexibility as you build the Dial command. For example, if you must dial 9 for an outside line on your office phone system, you could add 9 and a comma to the prefix. (The comma instructs Hayes-compatible modems to pause for two seconds.) Terminal would dial 9 for the outside line and then pause before dialing the phone number. Similarly, you could add your long-distance ID code in the Dial Suffix text box to follow the telephone number. You can also incorporate the 9 for an outside line or the long-distance code in the Phone Number dialog box; either of these techniques will work equally well.

Another useful trick is to change the prefix to ATDT*70,, to automatically disable Call Waiting. Although Call Waiting is a handy feature of modern phone service, the click or beep that alerts you to another caller on the line can disrupt a data communications session, especially during a file transfer. Dialing *70 and waiting for a second dial tone before you dial a phone number will usually disable Call Waiting for the duration of that call. (The procedure or code that disables Call Waiting may vary in some areas; you should check with your local phone company.)

Immediately below the Dial command in the Modem Commands dialog box is the Hangup command. Terminal will send the command it finds here to the modem when you select Hangup from the Phone menu. Your modem documentation might refer to this action as "disconnect," "drop carrier," or going "on-hook." Whatever the name, most modems will sever a connection when they receive the command +++ATH from the computer.

When you send a binary file, Terminal uses the settings you enter in the Binary TX Prefix and Suffix text boxes to signal the modem at the beginning and end of the transmission. The Binary RX command's Prefix and Suffix settings serve the same function when you receive a binary file. Normally, the Prefix and Suffix text boxes for these commands are empty. Check your hardware documentation to see if your modem requires the Binary TX and Binary RX commands.

The last command switches the modem into Originate mode. The default should handle most situations. Check your modem documentation if you need to make changes in this command.

Communications

The dialog box accessed by the Communications command is where you get into the real minutiae of data communications. These settings are crucial. But, as we've said before, you can simply match them to the settings used by your host. If terms such as "data bits" and "parity" seem intimidating, just think of these as the computer's grammar and punctuation rules.

When you select Communications on the Settings menu, Terminal will open a Communications dialog box like the one shown in Figure 12-3. All the settings in this dialog box must be correct before you call the remote computer.

Figure 12-3

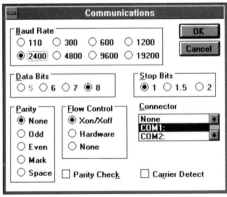

The Communications dialog box allows you to match Terminal's communications settings to those of the remote system.

"Matching the specifications from the host" sounds simple. Sometimes it is, when the specifications use the same terminology you see in Terminal's dialog box. Often, however, the remote system's operator will use a sort of shorthand to describe the correct settings: "N81 at 2400 baud" is typical. This means that the remote computer operates at no parity, 8 data bits, 1 stop bit, and at speeds up to 2400 baud. Let's use this description as an example and adjust the settings in the Communications dialog box accordingly.

Baud rate is the speed at which the modems send data back and forth. Normally, to transfer information as quickly as possible, you'll want to set Terminal to operate at the highest speed supported by both your modem and the remote computer's modem. If you have a 2400-baud modem, you would click on the 2400 radio button in the Baud Rate group box to tell Terminal to operate at that speed. If your modem operates at a maximum of 1200 baud, you would select 1200. Typically, the remote computer's modem will adjust automatically to the slower speed. (Nearly all modems can function at their rated speed or at any of the slower, standard speeds.) Occasionally, you may want to use a slower baud rate to compensate for noisy phone lines or to take advantage of lower connect-time charges on the commercial information services.

Data bits are the number of digits in the binary numbers that computers use as "words." Click on the 8 radio button in the Data Bits group box to tell Terminal to use 8-bit "data packets." Most remote computers will use either 7 data bits or 8 data bits, with 8 being the most common. If the remote computer uses fewer than 8 data bits, you will not be able to use the XModem protocol for binary file transfers.

Stop bits are like the spaces between words in a sentence. They keep the words from running together into an unintelligible string of letters. To match our example settings, click on the 1 radio button in the Stop Bits group box.

Parity is a rudimentary form of error checking the computer can use to verify the data it receives. Since parity "borrows" the eighth data bit, parity checking isn't possible when all 8 data bits are used for data. Terminal recognizes this and automatically sets parity to None when you select 8 data bits. It will also change your Data Bits setting to 7 if you select any of the radio buttons in the Parity group box except None.

The Xon/Xoff selection is the default in the Flow Control group box, and you should rarely need to change it. The Flow Control setting dictates the method Terminal will use to tell the remote computer, "Whoa, you're going too fast for me." Normally, Terminal will use "software handshaking" (Xon/Xoff) to tell the remote system to stop sending data when Terminal has all the data it can handle and to resume transmitting data when Terminal catches up. Some systems use hardware rather than software to control the flow of data, and a few remote systems use no flow control at all. Xon/Xoff flow control is not compatible with hardware flow control, so to configure Terminal to communicate with a host using hardware flow control, you would click on the Hardware radio button. You would also need to make sure that your hardware is compatible with the remote system.

To tell Terminal where to find the modem, select the communications port to which your modem is connected from the list in the Connector group box. You should note that while Terminal is running, the settings in this dialog box will supersede those you established with Control Panel for this COM port.

The Carrier Detect check box allows you to switch between two methods of detecting a successful connection to another computer (as opposed to a human voice or a fax machine). One method is built into your modem; the other is within Terminal. If all the other settings are correct and you still have trouble connecting, change this setting and try calling the host again.

The Parity Check check box enables a diagnostic tool you'll probably never need. If you select this option, Terminal will display the byte in which a parity error occurs instead of a question mark when it receives a corrupted character.

Phone Number

The Phone Number dialog box appears when you select the Phone Number command from the Settings menu. As you can see in Figure 12-4, the Dial text box, where you enter the remote computer's telephone number, is the main feature of this dialog box. Since your modem will ignore parentheses, hyphens, and spaces, you can use those characters to make the phone number easier to read. You can also enter commas (for a two-second pause) and other characters that will have a special meaning to your modem. For instance, *9, 1 (800) 555-0000* would instruct the modem to dial 9 for an outside line, pause, and then direct-dial the long-distance phone number.

The Timeout If Not Connected In option controls how long Terminal will wait for the remote computer's modem to respond. Terminal starts counting as soon as it begins dialing, so you may want to change the Timeout value to 45 or 60 seconds, especially for long-distance numbers.

Figure 12-4

In the Phone Number dialog box, you specify the number you want Terminal to dial and how long it should wait for a connection.

Two check boxes complete this dialog box. If you check Redial After Timing Out, Terminal will hang up and dial the number again if it does not successfully establish a connection within the time limit you specified in the preceding option. It will keep trying until it connects with the remote computer or until you click on the Cancel button in the dialog box Terminal displays while it is dialing. If you activate the Signal When Connected option, Terminal will beep to alert you when it establishes a connection. You'll find these two options especially helpful when you are attempting to call a computer system that is very busy. Terminal will patiently dial the number over and over while you attend to other business. Then, Terminal will beep when it finally succeeds in connecting with the remote computer.

Terminal gets its name, in part, from its ability to make your computer act like or emulate a terminal when it is communicating with a remote computer. (A terminal is a single-purpose piece of hardware whose function is to communicate with another computer system.) With the appropriate terminal emulation selected, you'll be able to use the special formatting and functions normally available on dedicated terminals. You can also control line wrap (for text that runs past the right edge of the screen), the terminal font, and other preferences.

To choose the terminal you want to emulate during communications with a remote computer, select Terminal Emulation on the Settings menu. The short list of alternatives appears in the Terminal Emulation dialog box, as shown in Figure 12-5. Select one of the emulations by clicking on its radio button and then clicking on OK to confirm the choice.

Figure 12-5

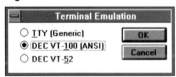

You can choose one of three terminal emulations in this dialog box.

If you select TTY (Generic), Terminal transmits only the standard alphanumeric characters and the carriage return (the [Enter] key), backspace, and tab characters to the remote computer. Use this option if you don't know what terminal the remote system supports.

Terminal can emulate either the DEC VT-100 or the DEC VT-52 terminal, two of the terminals that are most commonly used with large mainframe hosts. When you select one of these emulations, Terminal will be able to transmit the special formatting and control codes the remote system expects to receive from that terminal. If a remote system expects an ANSI terminal, use the VT-100 emulation. This should allow Terminal to respond to the ANSI codes that control screen colors and display formatting.

Terminal Preferences

You can go beyond selecting a terminal emulation to control details of the way Terminal handles the information it receives from the remote system and how it displays the information on your screen. You'll find these controls in the Terminal Preferences dialog box, shown in Figure 12-6, which you display by selecting Terminal Preferences on the Settings menu. The default settings will handle most situations, but Terminal allows you the flexibility to change the settings when needed. You can even modify many of these settings while you are on-line with a remote system.

In the Terminal Modes group box, you'll find check boxes to turn the Line Wrap, Local Echo, and Sound options on or off.

If you turn the Line Wrap check box on, Terminal will break any lines of text it receives from the host that are too long to fit on your screen and will wrap them to the next line. With Line Wrap turned off, you'll lose any information that runs beyond the edge of your screen. (If you run Terminal in a window that is less than the full width of the screen, you will not lose information that is wider than the window as long as it fits within the full screen. You can use the scroll bar to view long lines.)

Figure 12-6

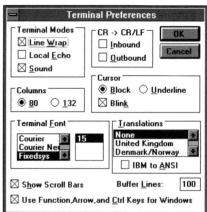

The Terminal Preferences dialog box allows you to control the way Terminal presents information on your screen.

The Local Echo option displays your keystrokes on your screen as Terminal sends them to the remote system. Oddly enough, you will normally want this option turned off. Most remote systems operate in "full duplex" mode and echo each character they receive back to your screen. Thus, if you have Local Echo turned on, each character you type might appear on your screen twice. Your screen could look something lliikkee tthhiiss! If you "see double" when you type, make sure you turn off Local Echo. If you connect to a remote system that operates at "half duplex" and doesn't echo your keystrokes, turn on Local Echo so that you can see what you type.

The last option in the Terminal Modes group box is Sound. Normally, Sound is on, but you can turn it off if you don't want the remote system to be able to make your computer beep at you.

In the Columns group box, select a radio button to tell Terminal to display information in the wide 132-column format or the standard 80 columns (80 characters per line). Normally, you would base your selection on your monitor type, but Windows can squeeze 132 columns of information onto an 80-column monitor or stretch 80 columns out to fill a 132-column monitor if you want.

Terminal can use any of the installed system fonts to display information in its work area. You can select the font you want Terminal to use from the list box in the Terminal Font group box. After you select a font, you can also specify its size. Your selection will take effect when you click on the OK button to confirm your selections in the Terminal Preferences dialog box.

The scroll bars on the Terminal window are optional. You can turn them on and off with the Show Scroll Bars check box in the lower-left corner of this dialog box. Obviously, you'll need scroll bars when you run Terminal in a small window, but they are useful even when Terminal is maximized to full-screen size. Terminal saves a certain amount of the information that scrolls off your screen in a buffer, and you can use the scroll bars to recall that information instead of requesting the remote system to retransmit it.

Terminal can automatically convert each carriage return you send or receive into a carriage return plus a line feed. (A carriage return moves the cursor to the beginning of the current line; a line feed moves it down to the next line.) Some remote systems automatically add line feeds with each carriage return; others do not. The check boxes in the CR -> CR/LF group box allow you to instruct Terminal to add line feeds to either inbound or outbound data, or both. Your selection will depend on how the remote computer handles the end of lines. If each line you receive from the host appears on top of the previous line, you need to add line feeds to incoming data. If incoming data appears double-spaced, you need to turn CR -> CR/LF translation off for incoming data. The same applies to outbound data.

The Cursor group box contains two radio buttons for controlling the appearance of the cursor, which can be displayed either as a block or as an underline. A check box lets you control whether the cursor will blink.

You can send and receive information in a foreign language by selecting a language setting from the list box in the Translations group box. Terminal will translate the information you send and receive into the International Standards Organization character set for the language you specify. Select None if you and the remote computer are both using the same language. If you are receiving extended or accented characters, turn on the IBM to ANSI check box.

The Buffer Lines text box lets you control how much space Terminal reserves to save information that scrolls off your screen. You can type a number between 25 and 400 in the Buffer Lines text box.

The last item in the Terminal Preferences dialog box is a check box labeled Use Function, Arrow, and Ctrl Keys for Windows. This check box allows you to determine whether these keys will be used to perform Windows tasks or whether they will be passed on to the remote computer and interpreted by the software running on the remote computer.

Text Transfers and Binary Transfers

One of the main reasons to establish communications with another computer is to exchange files. You can transfer spreadsheets, word processor documents, programs, or electronic mail files. You can capture incoming text in a file, and you can send a text file to the remote computer instead of laboriously typing a message. But before you transfer a file, you'll need to establish the rules that will govern the exchange. You can change these settings while you are on-line, if necessary, unless a file transfer is in progress.

Terminal can transfer two basic types of files: text or binary. Text files, also known as ASCII files, contain only the printable ASCII characters plus a few simple formatting codes, such as those for carriage returns. You normally create these files with a text editor, though most word processors can also create a text file by saving a document without any of the normal formatting information. Binary files, on the other hand, can include any character recognized by the computer. Binary files might be created by a database application, a spreadsheet, a word processor, a graphics program, or a programming language. Any file on a personal computer can be considered a binary file.

Terminal uses different rules for transferring text files and binary files. The text in text files is essentially the same as the text you type at the keyboard, and Terminal can handle it the same way. Binary files require special transfer methods that check and recheck the data as it is transmitted, to ensure there are no errors. You'll need to tell Terminal how to handle each type of file. Let's look first at transferring text files.

To specify the flow control, or pacing method, that Terminal will use to transfer text files, begin by selecting Text Transfers on the Settings menu to open the dialog box shown in Figure 12-7.

Figure 12-7

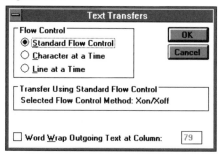

The options in the Text Transfers dialog box tell Terminal how to control the pacing of the text files you transmit.

The Flow Control group box offers three options: Standard Flow Control, Character at a Time, or Line at a Time. Standard Flow Control, the default, allows Terminal to use the flow control method (such as Xon/Xoff) that you specified in the Communications dialog box for normal text communications with the host. If you choose Character at a Time, a different group box (labeled Transfer a Character at a Time) will open in the middle of the dialog box. There, you can instruct Terminal to delay for a fixed amount of time after each character it transmits; you can specify the exact length of the delay by changing the value in the /10 Sec text box. The other option in the Transfer a Character at a Time group box is the Wait for Character Echo radio button. If you choose this option, Terminal will send one character, wait for the host to echo the character back, and then check that it is the correct character before sending the next character in the file. The Line at a Time option is similar to Character at a Time, except that Terminal transmits a line of text before pausing instead of pausing after each character. With the Transfer a Line at a Time group box, you can select a fixed amount of time to delay after each line of text or choose Wait for Prompt String. This is similar to Wait for Character Echo, except that Terminal will wait for a specific prompt from the host (usually a carriage return, which is signified by ^M) before sending the next line of text. You can specify what character or string Terminal should wait for.

You might want to use one of these slower options if you find that the remote computer's processing isn't fast enough to process all the information you transfer. You'll know when this happens because the remote computer will "drop," or lose, some of the characters or lines you send.

At the bottom of the Text Transfers dialog box, you'll find the Word Wrap Outgoing Text at Column option. If you select this option, Terminal will wrap any lines of text in your outgoing files that exceed the value you type in the text box. This is a handy way to make sure you don't exceed the maximum line length of the remote system.

When you select Binary Transfers on the Settings menu, Terminal will open the dialog box shown in Figure 12-8. From the settings in this dialog box, you can choose which of the two transfer protocols you want to use for binary file transfers. Click on the appropriate radio button to make your choice, and then click on OK to confirm it.

A transfer protocol is a set of error-checking rules the computer uses to ensure accurate reproduction of the data. To successfully transfer a binary file, both the remote computer and Terminal must use the same protocol. There are many different protocols in use in data communications today, each with its own advantages and weaknesses. Terminal includes two of the most common.

Because the XModem protocol uses all 8 data bits, it is appropriate only when communicating with a remote system that operates at 8 data bits and no parity. Kermit, on the other hand, can work with any data bit setting. It is the protocol of choice for systems that require communications settings such as 7 data bits and even parity.

Figure 12-8

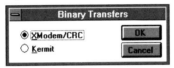

The Binary Transfers dialog box allows you to choose an error-checking protocol for transferring binary files.

Local settings

The three commands at the bottom of the Settings menu control how Terminal operates on your computer. They have no effect on communications with the remote system. All three are toggle commands that you can easily switch on or off as needed, even in the middle of a communications session with a remote computer.

Printer Echo

Choose the Printer Echo command to send your dialog with the remote computer to the printer. When you enable Printer Echo, everything that appears in Terminal's work area—all the remote system's prompts and all your keystrokes—will also go to the printer. A check mark appears beside the command when Printer Echo is active. Select the command again to turn it off. You can toggle the option on and off as often as needed to control what gets printed.

Using Printer Echo usually slows the progress of your communications session noticeably as the remote system waits for the printer to catch up before sending the next line, thus increasing the cost of an on-line session.

Show Function Keys

The display controlled by the Show Function Keys command represents Terminal's user-defined, on-screen function keys. We'll explain how to define the function keys later in this chapter. To display the function-key buttons and the timer across the bottom of the Terminal window, select Show Function Keys on the Settings menu. When the function-key display is on, the command becomes Hide Function Keys; selecting this command will remove the function-key display.

Timer Mode

The timer appears in the optional function-key display at the bottom of the Terminal window. The Show Function Keys command must be turned on to display the timer. The timer display shows either the current time, according to your system clock, or the elapsed time for the current on-line session. Showing the system time is the default. Toggle the Timer Mode command on to time your calls (by displaying elapsed time).

GOING ON-LINE

After you've adjusted all of Terminal's settings to conform to the remote system's requirements, you are ready to begin using Terminal for its intended purpose: going on-line to communicate with a remote computer. The three examples in this section will demonstrate Terminal's main features and how to use them to perform typical communications tasks.

Reading electronic mail

For our first example, let's discuss the steps you might follow to read your electronic mail on a large mainframe system. We will use the commands and procedures for MCI Mail in this example, but the basic operations for getting messages from a corporate mainframe or from a local electronic bulletin board are similar.

Dialing the host and logging on

The first step is to adjust Terminal's settings to match the host system. Once the settings are established, you can place the call to the remote computer by selecting Dial on the Phone menu. Terminal will display a dialog box like the one shown in Figure 12-9 while it dials the phone and waits for the remote computer to answer and establish the modem connection. You'll see the phone number Terminal is dialing and the number of seconds it will continue to wait for the connection. You can cancel the call by clicking on the Cancel button.

Figure 12-9

You'll see this dialog box while Terminal waits for the remote system to respond.

When Terminal makes the connection with the remote computer, the dialog box will disappear, and the word *CONNECT* will appear in Terminal's work area. This is a message from your modem informing you that it is connected to another modem. You'll often need to send a few characters from the keyboard to get the host's attention. For MCI Mail, pressing [Enter] once or twice will do the trick. When you see the MCI prompt *Please enter your user name:*, type the "user name" that identifies you to the host computer, and then press [Enter]. (MCI Mail user names are typically a first initial and last name, with no spaces or punctuation—something like *GWASHINGTON.* Other systems might use numbers or other codes to identify individual users.) After you enter your user name, MCI Mail presents the *password* prompt. Type your password at the prompt and press [Enter], but don't be surprised when you don't see the characters on the screen as you type the password. As a security precaution, MCI, like most host systems, does not display your password. Identifying yourself to the host computer with a name or ID and a password is called logging on.

Reading mail on-line

As soon as you complete the log-on procedure, MCI Mail will display its welcome messages and alert you if you have electronic mail messages waiting. Then the host system will display a prompt, such as *Command:*, and wait for instructions from you. Each system will be different, but to read messages on MCI Mail, you would first type *SCAN INBOX* and then press [Enter] to see a numbered list of the messages addressed to you. At the next *Command:* prompt, you would type *READ 2* and press [Enter] if you wanted to read message number 2. MCI Mail would then send the message to your screen, and you could read it from the monitor. If you activate the Printer Echo command on Terminal's Settings menu, everything that appears on your screen will also go to your printer, giving you a printed record of your communications session. You can toggle Printer Echo off and on to selectively control how much of your dialog with the host gets printed.

Receiving text files

Using Printer Echo is hardly the best way to get a copy of your messages; it's slow, and you can't edit or reformat the printout. Instead, you can capture the information in a text file. Later, you can view the file with Terminal's View Text File command or edit and print it with your word processor. This technique works because the data from the remote system is in the same ASCII text format as the data in a text file. Therefore, you can use Terminal's ability to send and receive text files to capture messages from the remote computer in a file.

To begin saving incoming text in a file, select Receive Text File on the Transfers menu. As you can see in Figure 12-10, the Receive Text File dialog box resembles the familiar Save As dialog box. You can use the Drives and Directories list boxes to select the drive and directory where you want to save the file, and you can type a name for the text file in the File Name text box.

Figure 12-10

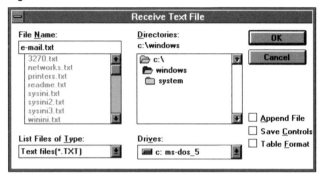

The Receive Text File dialog box includes three special handling options as well as file name specifications.

In addition to the file name specifications, the Receive Text File dialog box also contains three check boxes for special handling options. The Append File option lets you add the incoming information to an existing file. For instance, if you have a file named MESSAGE.TXT, you could add the new messages to it instead of starting a new file or replacing an existing file. The Save Controls option instructs Terminal to keep extra formatting codes that might be in the incoming file, even if they are not "pure ASCII." The Table Format option is especially useful with spreadsheet and database files. When you select this option, Terminal will translate two or more spaces in the incoming file into a tab character. You can select any combination of these options to handle a variety of file transfer needs.

When you click on OK in the Receive Text File dialog box, Terminal will begin sending all the incoming text it receives to the text file you have designated. With the text file open and recording data, you can issue MCI Mail's READ command to read your messages. You might want to instruct the host system to send your messages "nonstop" instead of pausing every few lines to allow you enough time to read the text on the screen. The text file can accept the data as fast as the host system can send it, and you'll be able to read the messages at your own pace later, after you log off.

Terminal displays the status of the file transfer in the status bar across the bottom of the work area, as shown in Figure 12-11 on the following page. The status bar includes the name of the file and the amount of data received so far. It also includes on-screen buttons to stop, pause, and (alternately) resume the file transfer. These buttons duplicate the functions of the Stop, Pause, and Resume commands on the Transfers menu.

Figure 12-11

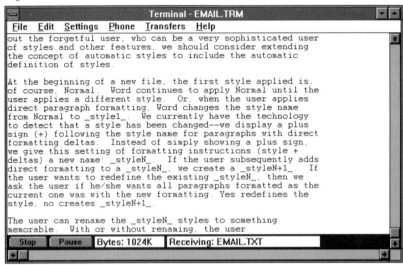

The status bar across the bottom of the Terminal work area displays the status of file transfers.

A unique capability of Terminal's text file transfers is the ability to pause and resume sending or receiving text files. You can select the Pause command on the Transfers menu or click on the Pause button in the status bar to temporarily halt a text transfer. Click on the same button again (now labeled Resume) or select Resume on the Transfers menu to continue recording incoming text in the file. Pausing a text transfer stops the recording of text in the file; it does not interrupt the communications with the host system. You can pause at the end of a message, issue a series of commands to the host without the commands or prompts appearing in the text file, and then resume recording to capture another group of messages. You can stop the text file transfer and close the text file by selecting Stop on the Transfers menu or by clicking on the Stop button on the status bar.

Logging off

After you've read or captured your messages, it's time to disconnect from the host system. Each system will have a log-off procedure that you should use to end the on-line session. For instance, to leave MCI Mail, you type *EXIT* and press [Enter] at the *Command:* prompt. After you log off the host system, select Hangup on the Phone menu to tell your modem to disconnect from the phone line. Following the proper log-off procedure is important. You need to tell the host system you are leaving so that it can make room for other users. But, perhaps more important, you want to make sure you aren't charged for extra access time. Most systems will periodically check for activity from each user who is logged on and will detect that a user has disconnected, but it may take several minutes. If you just hang up without first logging off, you may see an increase in your computer information service bill.

After you complete your first successful communications session with a remote system, you'll want to save the Terminal settings in a file. When you want to call that host again, just open the file to reinstall those settings. Select Save As on the File menu, and give the file an appropriate name in the dialog box. (MCI-MAIL might be a good choice for our example.) By default, Terminal uses the .TRM file name extension for any files you save.

Saving settings

You can use Terminal's built-in file viewer to read text files—such as the hypothetical file of electronic mail messages we created with the Receive Text File command. When you select View Text File on the Transfers menu, Terminal will open a dialog box like the one shown in Figure 12-12. As you can see, the View Text File dialog box is similar to the Open dialog box, and you use it the same way to select a file. Two check boxes in the lower-right corner allow you to control how Terminal will handle the line feeds in the file. If the text file lacks line feeds, causing each line of text to overwrite the preceding line, you should select the Append LF check box. Choose the Strip LF check box to remove superfluous line feeds if the text file appears double-spaced. Terminal's text file viewer reads the contents of the file into Terminal's buffer and displays the status bar, just as Terminal does when receiving text files. Since the buffer can hold only a limited amount of text, you will need to use the Pause and Resume buttons on the status bar to import the file in manageable chunks. The scroll bars will allow you to scroll through the portion of the file in Terminal's buffer.

Viewing text files

Figure 12-12

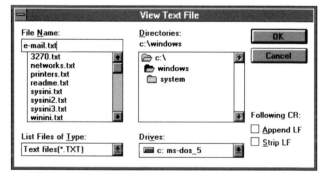

You can select a text file to view in Terminal's workspace with this View Text File dialog box.

Sending electronic mail

Most host computers that offer any electronic mail services include an on-line editor that lets you create messages. However, these editors can often be awkward, difficult to use, and slow. Using an on-line editor can get expensive if you have to pay for the connect time while you grope for the right wording for a message. Even if there is no cost involved, it's usually more pleasant and convenient to compose your message in Notepad, Write, or your favorite word processor and save it as a text file. Then you can use Terminal to send the text file instead of typing the message into the host's on-line editor.

Let's continue with the example we started earlier. Suppose that you want to send a response to one of the electronic mail messages you received. First, jot down the electronic mail address to which you want to send the message. Then compose the message in Write, and save it with the Word for DOS/Text Only option in Write's Save As dialog box.

Next, switch to the Terminal window. (We'll assume that you left Terminal running in an inactive window.) If you've changed any of the settings, you can load the correct settings for MCI Mail from the file you saved after your last session. Choose the Open command from the File menu. Then select the file MCI-MAIL.TRM in the Open dialog box, and click on OK. Terminal adjusts its settings according to the information in the file and displays the file name in the title bar at the top of the Terminal window.

Select Dial from the Phone menu, and log on to MCI Mail as described earlier. When you've successfully logged on to the host system, type the command to start creating a new message. (For MCI Mail, you would type *CREATE* and then press [Enter].) At the appropriate prompts, type the electronic mail address and subject for your message. When the host system prompts you to start entering text, you'll want to send your text file instead.

Sending text files

When you select Send Text File on the Transfers menu, Terminal opens the dialog box shown in Figure 12-13. Select the message file you created in Write, and click on OK. Terminal will immediately start sending the contents of the file. To the host system, it simply seems that you are typing very fast; it can't tell the difference between the text coming from your keyboard and the text Terminal transfers from a file. If the lines of text overlap or appear double-spaced, you'll need to stop the transfer, cancel the message, and try again by checking the Append LF or the Strip LF option in the Send Text File dialog box.

The status bar across the bottom of the Terminal work area will show the progress of the file transfer. When you send files, a small progress meter bar replaces the file's size counter. The Stop, Pause, and Resume commands are available on the Transfers menu, and the Stop, Pause, and Resume buttons are available in the status bar, just as they are when you receive text files. When Terminal reaches the end of the file, it will stop automatically.

Figure 12-13

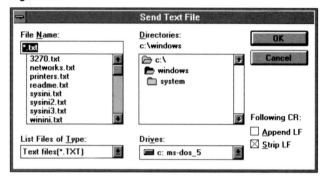

The Send Text File dialog box allows you to select a text file to transfer to the remote computer.

Usually you'll need to tell the host system that you've reached the end of the message. (MCI Mail looks for a slash [/] on a line by itself as the instruction to switch from the message editor back to command mode.) Finish sending the message by giving the host system handling instructions and by typing *YES* and pressing [Enter] at the *Send?* prompt. With the message on its way, you can log off and hang up.

Because text files contain the same kind of data as the text that Terminal sends to the remote computer, the remote computer can't tell the difference between a message you type at the keyboard and one you transfer from a text file. Terminal, in turn, can't tell whether incoming text originated from a text file, a programmed system prompt, or the keyboard. All of it can go into a text file and onto your screen simultaneously.

Binary files are a little different. Both Terminal and the remote computer treat each binary file as a discrete entity and do not attempt to display the file's contents. Both systems must use a matching file transfer protocol to ensure that the data is transferred accurately. Typically, a host computer will have several protocols available for file transfers. You'll need to select either XModem or Kermit from the available choices and then make sure you instruct Terminal to use the same protocol. Each remote system will have its own procedures you will need to follow to prepare for a file transfer using a specific protocol.

Once the remote system is set to receive a binary file, you can select Send Binary File on the Transfers menu. In the Send Binary File dialog box, shown in Figure 12-14 on the next page, you can select the file to send. When you click on OK, Terminal and the remote computer will begin transferring data, carefully checking for errors and retransmitting any questionable sections of the file. You won't see the data scroll by in the Terminal work area as you do in text file transfers, but the status bar will show the progress of the transfer.

Sending the message and logging off

Working with binary files

Binary file transfers

Figure 12-14

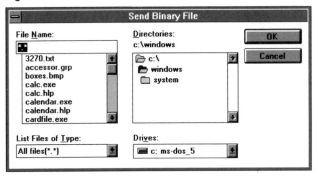

The Send Binary File dialog box lets you choose a binary file to transmit to the remote system.

The process of receiving a binary file is nearly the same as the process of sending one. First, use the remote system's own procedures to instruct it to send a specific file using one of the protocols supported by Terminal. Make sure that Terminal is set to use the same protocol. Then select Receive Binary File on the Transfers menu, and supply a file name in the Receive Binary File dialog box, shown in Figure 12-15. When you click on the OK button in the dialog box, the computers will begin transferring the file.

Figure 12-15

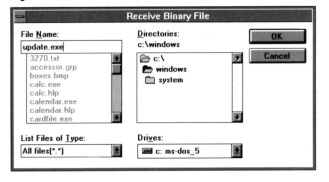

You can supply a file name and location for the incoming file in the Receive Binary File dialog box.

The status bar at the bottom of the work area, shown in Figure 12-16, lets you check the progress of the file transfer. Notice that the Pause button is missing because that option is not available during binary file transfers. You can stop the file transfer by clicking on the Stop button in the status bar or by selecting the Stop command on the Transfers menu. However, you will not be able to resume the transfer. The Retries box at the right end of the status bar shows how many times the file transfer protocol has detected errors and re-transmitted corrupted sections of the file.

Figure 12-16

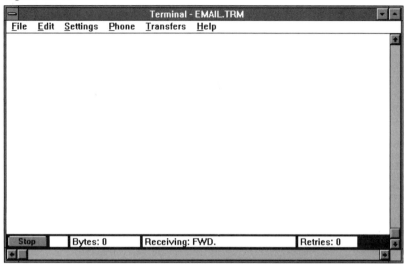

The status bar adds a Retries box to track errors during a binary file transfer. Binary file transfers won't display text on the screen.

Using Clipboard with Terminal

Because Terminal's work area is a little different from the work areas of other Windows applications such as Write, Notepad, and Paintbrush, Clipboard acts a little differently as well. You can copy text from the Terminal work area to Clipboard, but you cannot cut text from the work area. To copy text from the Terminal work area, drag the pointer across the text you want to copy to Clipboard, and then select the Copy command on the Edit menu. If you want to highlight all the text in Terminal's buffer, choose the Select All command on the Edit menu. Then you can switch to another application and use that application's Paste command to paste from Clipboard in the normal manner. In Terminal, however, when you choose the Paste command on the Edit menu, Terminal transmits the contents of Clipboard to the remote system.

Once you understand how Clipboard works with Terminal, you can use it to your advantage. For example, you can copy a message from Terminal's work area to Clipboard and then paste the message from Clipboard into Write or Notepad, where you can edit, print, or save the message in a file. If you reverse the procedure, you can use Clipboard to send a message you composed in Notepad or Write to a remote computer, without having to first save it as a text file and then select the Send Text File command.

The Send command on the Edit menu has the same effect as copying text to Clipboard and then selecting Paste to send it to the remote computer; it simply condenses the action into a single step. (Press [Ctrl][Shift][Insert] as a shortcut for this command.) You can select the Clear Buffer command on the Edit menu to clear out the work area and Terminal's buffer.

Using function keys

Terminal lets you define as many as 32 special function keys that will type frequently used phrases and commands for you. Terminal saves the function-key definitions along with other settings when you save a Terminal file, so you can have a custom set of function keys for each remote computer you contact.

During a communications session, you can click on an on-screen function-key button, and Terminal will type the text string or command you defined for that function key and will send it to the remote system. You can also use the function keys in the active level from the keyboard by pressing the [Alt] and [Ctrl] keys along with one of the function keys (for example, [Ctrl][Alt][F1]).

Defining
function keys

Figure 12-17 shows the Function Keys dialog box, where you can define four sets, or "levels," of eight function keys each—a total of 32 programmable keys. For each function key, you can define a key name and a command up to 27 characters long. The commands can contain the standard alphanumeric characters, plus control codes, and special codes to program a delay, to dial or hang up the modem, and to send a break code. Select Function Keys on the Settings menu to open the dialog box.

Figure 12-17

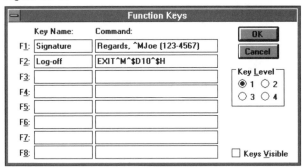

You can define up to 32 custom commands in the Function Keys dialog box.

To begin defining keys, type a descriptive name in the Key Name text box beside the function key you want to define. As you can see in Figure 12-18, this key name will appear on the label of the corresponding button in the function-key display at the bottom of the Terminal window. In the Command text box, type the string of characters and control codes you want Terminal to send to the remote system when you use this function key.

Figure 12-18

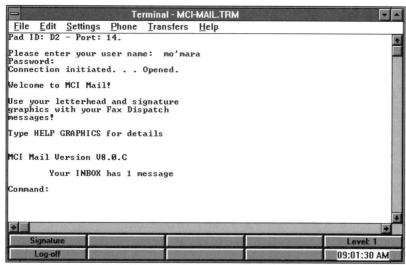

The function-key display at the bottom of the Terminal window
makes your function-key commands instantly available.

You can define and use a command without giving it a key name. Simply enter the command in the Function Keys dialog box and leave the accompanying Key Name text box empty. No key name will appear for that function key in the function-key display, but if you click on the blank function-key button, the "hidden" command will be sent to the remote system.

The four radio buttons in the Key Level group box of the Function Keys dialog box let you switch between the four sets of eight function keys. When you click on the radio button for one of the key levels, the Key Name and Command text boxes in the dialog box will display the definitions for the function keys of that level. As you use Terminal, one set of eight function keys will be available at a time. Terminal will show the names of the active set of function-key commands in the function-key display. To use function keys from different levels, click on the Level button above the timer box in the function-key display to switch to the next level of function-key commands. To change to a different function-key level from the keyboard, choose the Function Keys command from the Settings menu. In the Function Keys dialog box, press [Alt]L to move to the Key Level radio buttons, use the arrow keys to select the radio button for the new level, and then press [Enter].

The Keys Visible check box in the lower-right corner of the Function Keys dialog box controls whether Terminal will show the function-key display at the bottom of the Terminal window automatically. Activating this option is like selecting the Show Function Keys command each time you open the file containing these function-key definitions. You can always switch the function-key display on or off by selecting the Hide/Show Function Keys command on the Settings menu. Once defined, the function keys are available from the keyboard even if the function-key display is hidden. However, you'll probably want the keys to be visible, especially if you define keys on more than one level.

Most of your function-key definitions will probably be text strings you use frequently, such as your company name or a signature line for messages like this: *Regards, Joe (123-4567)*. But they may also include control codes (such as the commonly used codes listed in Table 12-1) that signal carriage returns or instruct Terminal to delay for a few seconds before proceeding.

Table 12-1

Code	Function
^A through ^Z	Control code A through control code Z
^G	Bell
^H	Backspace
^J	Line feed
^M	Carriage return
^$D00	Delay for "00" seconds, and then continue
^$C	Same as the Dial command on the Phone menu
^$H	Same as the Hangup command on the Phone menu
^$L*n*	Change to level *n* function-key set
^$B	Break

These are the control codes you're most likely to need in your function-key definitions.

The following example is a function-key definition that would automate the log-on sequence for MCI Mail we described earlier:

^M^$D05user^M^$D02secret^M

^M	Sends a carriage return (like pressing [Enter])—to get the remote system's attention
^$D05	Instructs Terminal to pause for five seconds to allow time for the host system to respond with the prompt for the user name
user	Types the text *user*—just as if you typed it at the keyboard

^M	Sends a carriage return
^$D02	Waits for two seconds
secret	Types *secret*
^M	Sends a carriage return

Please note: Computer security principles and common sense dictate that you should *never* include your password in an automatic log-on sequence. You shouldn't even store it on disk in an unencrypted form. We do *not* recommend including your password in a function-key definition! We chose a log-on as an example because it illustrates our points and because the sequence is familiar to most readers. But automating the sequence of commands to read your electronic mail messages would be a better use for Terminal's function keys.

Do as we say—not as we do!

You can take advantage of Windows' multitasking capability with Terminal. For instance, suppose you need to transfer a large file to another computer. You could run Terminal, log on to a remote computer, and start a binary file transfer. Once the file transfer starts, you can minimize Terminal to an icon on your desktop and run your spreadsheet, word processor, or other Windows application. As long as no other application conflicts with Terminal's use of the COM port, Terminal will continue the file transfer in the background while you attend to other business. When Terminal completes the file transfer, it will alert you by sounding a beep, and the Terminal icon will blink. Then you can simply restore Terminal to a working-size window to complete the communications session.

Background operation

In this chapter

Using Recorder 13

Windows' Recorder will record keystrokes and mouse movements and play them back at the touch of a key. With Recorder, you can automate simple, repetitive tasks or produce training demonstrations that can run continuously. Recorder will operate in the Windows environment, in any of the standard Windows accessories, and in most Windows-based applications.

RECORDER

Recording is exactly what this accessory does—it records keystrokes and mouse movements. The recorded sequence of keystrokes and mouse movements is called a macro. But don't confuse this with the kind of macros you can create with the macro commands in an application such as Microsoft Excel. Recorder is not a programming, script, or batch language. You can't pause for input, use variables, or add logic structures. You don't write and edit macros with Recorder; you simply record and run them.

Recorder may not offer all the power of a rich macro language, but it is exceptionally easy to learn and use. Recorder allows you to create your own shortcut keys for many of your routine tasks and, consequently, to make your computer more responsive to your personal needs and working style.

To automate a procedure in Windows, you instruct Recorder to watch as you perform the task. It records each keystroke and mouse selection and even records the time between the actions. Just as a video recorder can play back a tape, Recorder can play back the recorded actions to repeat the task. You simply select the macro's name from a list or press a special shortcut key to tell Recorder which macro you want to play. Recorder will play back the macro, reproducing your original actions—typing a line of text, for example, or starting another application and automatically loading a file.

Recorder allows you considerable flexibility to tailor the way you record and play back your macros. You can create macros that will work in any Windows application or macros that will work only in the application for which you recorded them. You can record mouse positions anywhere on the screen or track mouse movement relative to the active window. For demonstrations, you can play back macros at the same pace they were recorded, or you can put Recorder into "fast forward" and send the computer commands at high speed. You can save your macros in a file and, by loading separate Recorder files, have a unique set of macros available for each type of work you do or for each person using the computer.

Starting Recorder

To start Recorder from Windows' Program Manager, select the Accessories group window and double-click on the Recorder icon. After you create a set of macros and save them in a Recorder macro file, you may want to modify Recorder's startup command so that the macro file is loaded automatically each time you start Recorder. (See Chapter 5 for information on starting an application with a specific file open.) Normally, you will start Recorder, load the file of macros you plan to use, and then immediately minimize Recorder to an icon on your desktop. Recorder's macros will be available at the touch of a shortcut key, and you will need to restore Recorder to the active window only to load another macro file or record a new macro.

A TEXT MACRO

The best way to learn about Windows' Recorder is to use it. In the next few sections, we'll demonstrate the principal features of Recorder, and then we'll explain Recorder's other options.

In the first example, we'll create a simple text macro that will type your name in Write with a keystroke. This is the simplest of macros, but it's the sort of macro you might use dozens of times a day.

Preliminaries

Begin the process by starting Recorder and minimizing it to an icon on your desktop. You must run the Recorder application before you can create or use any macros.

Before you start recording a macro, you will need to configure your desktop and the application in which you'll use the macro so that everything is ready for the activity you want to record. In this case, the only applications you'll need are Recorder (which should already be on your desktop) and Write. Start Write by selecting the Accessories group window in the Program Manager and double-clicking on the Write icon. Write will open a new, untitled document with a cursor blinking on the first line. For now, resist the temptation to maximize the Write window, since you'll want easy access to the Recorder icon that appears on your desktop.

With your desktop ready and the application open, you're ready to start recording the macro. Activate Recorder by double-clicking on its icon, and then select Record from the Macro menu. The Record Macro dialog box will appear, as shown in Figure 13-1.

In the Record Macro dialog box, you can control most of the recording and playback options for your macro. The default settings will be suitable for most situations, including this example. Recorder requires you to fill in either a name or a shortcut key for your macro. In the Record Macro Name text box, you can give the macro a descriptive name up to 40 characters long. For this example, type *My Name.*

Even when it is inactive or minimized, Recorder monitors the keyboard. If it detects a keystroke that matches one of the keys (or key combinations) defined in the current set of macros, Recorder steps in to execute the macro. By using shortcut keys, you can use your macros from within any Windows application while Recorder is running in a window or as a minimized icon.

We'll assign the [Ctrl]N key combination as the shortcut key for this macro. Click on the text box in the Shortcut Key group box, and type the letter *N.* Make sure that the Ctrl check box is selected and that the Shift and Alt check boxes are not. Once the macro is recorded, you'll be able to run it by pressing [Ctrl]N.

You must give each macro either a name or a shortcut key so that Recorder can identify the macro—it is not necessary to do both. However, we recommend that you name all your macros, even the ones you execute with shortcut keys. As your list of macros grows, you'll find the names helpful, if not essential.

Figure 13-1

The Record Macro dialog box allows you to specify a shortcut key and other options for your macro.

The rest of the Record Macro dialog box can retain the default settings. (We'll explore the other options in a moment.) To start recording the macro, click on the Start button. Recorder will minimize itself automatically and return you to Write. Notice that the Recorder icon will blink to indicate that it is recording.

Next, type your name the way you will want to insert it in your Write documents. Recorder will record each key you press and each mouse selection you make. If you mistype and use the [Backspace] key to make a correction, Recorder will register that as well.

Saving the macro

Once you finish performing the action you want to automate—in this case, typing your name—you need to tell Recorder to stop recording. Click on the blinking Recorder icon. Recorder will then open a dialog box that allows you to save the macro, resume recording, or cancel recording. As Figure 13-2 shows, the Save Macro radio button will be selected by default. When you click on the OK button or press [Enter], the macro will be stored in Recorder's memory (though not yet saved on disk), and the Recorder icon will stop blinking to indicate that it is no longer in record mode.

Figure 13-2

When you stop recording, this dialog box allows you to save the macro, resume recording, or cancel recording.

Testing the macro

It's always a good idea to test a new macro to make sure it was recorded properly. (Besides, you want to see your first macro work, don't you?) After saving the macro, Windows will return you to your Write document. Start a new paragraph, and type some miscellaneous text to simulate creating a typical document. When you want to insert your name, press [Ctrl]N. Recorder will execute the macro you recorded, playing back all the keystrokes as if you were typing them—except much faster. Using the macros you create with Recorder is just that easy.

Now, double-click on the Recorder icon to bring up the Recorder application window. As you can see in Figure 13-3, Recorder's work area now lists *ctrl+N* and *My Name*. Creating this kind of simple macro with Recorder is so fast and easy that you'll find yourself recording macros "on the fly" to avoid typing repetitive phrases in a letter or report.

Figure 13-3

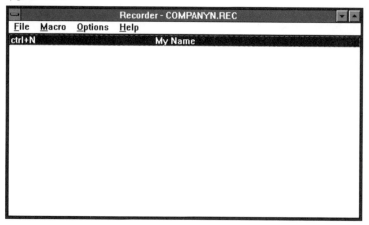

The Recorder window displays a list of the macros currently at your disposal.

A COMMAND MACRO

With Recorder, you can create macros that issue commands as well as macros that play back text. In fact, command macros will often be more useful than macros that produce a line or two of text from a single keystroke.

The problem with mouse selections

To issue commands in most Windows applications, you normally use the mouse to make selections from menus. After all, that is one of the key features of a graphical interface. However, selecting menu items with a mouse can create problems in a macro.

Recorder registers mouse selections as position coordinates that are either relative to the full screen or relative to the active window. When you click the mouse button, Recorder remembers the position of the mouse, but not what is under the pointer. If you move or resize a window for which you've recorded a macro that involves mouse movements or mouse clicks, the effects of running the macro can be unpredictable. A mouse click you recorded in a macro may now occur on a different menu selection or fall completely outside the active window.

When you record macros, it's wise to avoid using the mouse. Instead, use keyboard equivalents to issue commands whenever possible. (We'll use that technique in this example.) Windows provides keyboard equivalents for essentially everything you would normally do with the mouse. It is even possible (though awkward) to use Windows without using the mouse at all. You may want to review Chapter 2 for information on the keyboard techniques used in making menu selections and accessing such Windows features as the Control menu and the Task Manager.

Fortunately, to record a macro, you'll need to perform a task with the keyboard only once. After that, Recorder will handle the playback, and you won't need to remember the keyboard or mouse selections.

Setting up the application

To develop an example of a macro that issues commands, we will add formatting attributes to a line of text in Write, attributes that will make the line of text look like a title. Obviously, Recorder must be running on your desktop, either minimized or in an inactive window, and Write should be in the active window. Just to make things interesting, maximize the Write window or move it so that it obscures the Recorder icon or window on your desktop. Type a short line of text into a new document in Write, and then highlight it by dragging the pointer across the line.

This will be the starting point for the macro—with the line of text already highlighted. The macro automates the process of adding formatting attributes to any text you might select. Since you might use the macro to format text anywhere in a document, selecting the text is *not* part of the macro.

Normally, you will want to make a "test run" through the procedure you intend to automate before you start recording the macro. That way, you can make notes of the steps and commands you'll want in the macro and the keyboard alternative for each mouse selection. After the test run, you should carefully return all settings to the starting configuration. In this case, however, you can skip the test run and simply follow the instructions below.

Using the Task Manager to activate Recorder

After you configure your desktop and the application, it's time to activate Recorder, name the new macro, assign a shortcut key, and start recording the procedure. Since the Write window covers the Recorder icon, you can't activate Recorder by double-clicking on the icon as you did in the previous example. Instead, use Windows' Task Manager to activate Recorder. Press [Ctrl][Esc] to open the Task List dialog box, shown in Figure 13-4, and use the mouse or the arrow keys to highlight Recorder. Then click on the Switch To button to open the Recorder window. You can use this technique to access Recorder (or any running application) when the icon or inactive window is obscured by other windows. Refer to Chapter 2 for more information on the Task Manager and the Task List dialog box. You'll find many uses for this handy tool as you work with Recorder macros.

Recording the macro

Once Recorder's window appears, select Record from the Macro menu, just as you did in the previous example. When the Record Macro dialog box appears, type *Title Style* in the Record Macro Name text box.

Figure 13-4

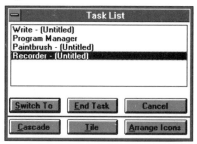

Windows' Task Manager lets you switch to any running application—even if the icon or inactive window is obscured.

To specify one of the standard alphanumeric keys as a shortcut key, you simply click on the text box in the Shortcut Key group box and type the key you want to use, as you did in the last example. However, to specify one of the non-alphanumeric keys, you must choose the key from the Shortcut Key drop-down list box in the Record Macro dialog box. To use [Ctrl][F2] as the shortcut key for this macro, for example, be sure that the Ctrl check box is selected in the Shortcut Key group box and that the Shift and Alt check boxes are not. Then open the Shortcut Key drop-down list box, scroll through the list until F2 is visible, and click on it. Recorder will place F2 in the text box as the shortcut key. As you can see by scrolling through the drop-down list box shown in Figure 13-5, you can use the arrow keys, [Tab], and most of the other keys on your keyboard as shortcut keys.

Specifying
shortcut keys

Figure 13-5

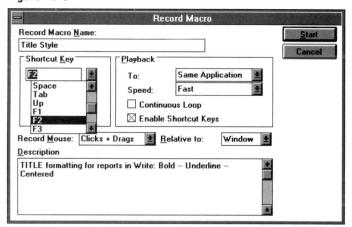

You can use non-alphanumeric keys from the drop-down list box as shortcut keys for your macros.

Using the
Description
text box

At the bottom of the Record Macro dialog box, you'll find the Description text box. You can click on this large text box and type several lines of text to describe your macro and its actions. (Avoid pressing [Enter] as you type your description; the [Enter] key can activate the Start button, which could begin recording before you're ready. Instead, let Recorder wrap your text for you.) As your macro collection grows and you share macros with other Windows users, you'll find these descriptions very useful for documenting your macros.

When you finish selecting the macro recording options in the Record Macro dialog box, click on the Start button to minimize Recorder and start recording the macro.

Using the keyboard

In your Write document, the line of text should be highlighted, ready to receive formatting commands. To record the procedure, first press [Alt]P to pull down the Paragraph menu. (Remember that you're using keyboard equivalents rather than selecting commands with the mouse.) Press *C* to select Centered from the menu and center the highlighted text on the page. Next, press [Alt]C to pull down the Character menu, and select Bold by pressing *B*. Finally, press [Alt]C again to access the Character menu, and then press *U* to select Underline.

Saving the macro

After you complete the actions you want in the macro, press [Ctrl][Break] to stop recording. When you are recording a macro, pressing [Ctrl][Break] has the same effect as clicking on the Recorder icon. The Recorder dialog box shown in Figure 13-2 (page 346) appears, giving you the choice of saving the macro, resuming recording, or canceling what you've recorded. In this case, the Resume Recording radio button is selected by default. Instead of accepting the default, click on the Save Macro radio button, and then click on OK. Instead of using [Ctrl][Break], you could also stop recording by selecting Recorder from the Task Manager. But if you use this method, you'll sacrifice speed, because Recorder will add these steps at the end of the macro.

Using the macro

To use this macro in Write, you must first highlight an appropriate line of text. In this case, you'll probably need to type a new, short line of text to serve as a candidate for a title. Drag the pointer across the text to highlight the entire line, and then press [Ctrl][F2]. Recorder will recognize the shortcut key for the macro you just recorded and will repeat the procedure on the new text.

**Saving the
macro file**

The macros you create with Recorder exist only in your computer's memory until you save them on a disk in a Recorder file. Only the macros that appear on the list in Recorder's work area are available for you to use at any given time. You can load a set of macros by opening a Recorder file or add to the list by recording new macros. Recorder doesn't limit the number of macros in a single file, but you'll probably want to create additional files for macros you use as sets.

Recorder's File menu supplies the usual complement of file management commands that allow you to save, open, and start files. There is also a Merge command, which we'll discuss later.

To save your macros in a file, activate Recorder and select Save As from the File menu. In the familiar Save As dialog box, type a file name in the File Name text box, and select the appropriate drive and directory in which you want to save the file. When you click on OK, Recorder will save the file and (unless you included your own extension) will add the .REC extension to the file name.

AN "ANY APPLICATION" MACRO

In the preceding examples, you recorded two macros for use only in Write. The commands to format text in the Title Style macro would be inappropriate in another application. At best, there would be no equivalent menus or commands, and the application would probably sound an error beep when it received unrecognizable instructions. If another application had menus and commands that used the same keyboard equivalents, the macro would issue those commands, and the results would be unpredictable. For this reason, Recorder notes which application is active when you record a macro and by default restricts the macro to running in only that application.

You can, however, change Recorder's default and specify that a macro can run in all applications. When used carefully, the Any Application option is a very powerful feature. The following example creates a macro that will activate the File Manager from your desktop or from within any Windows application (except the Program Manager).

Of course, the first step is to set up your desktop with the applications you will use in the macro. In addition to having Recorder available on your desktop, you'll need the File Manager running as an icon or inactive window, plus any other application running in the active window.

Recording the macro

To start recording the macro, activate Recorder and select Record on the Macro menu. In the Record Macro dialog box, type *File Manager* as the macro name, and specify [Ctrl]F as the shortcut key. In the Playback group box, open the drop-down list box for the To option by clicking on the button, and select Any Application. After you make these selections, you can click on the Start button to begin recording the macro.

Next, access the Task Manager by pressing [Ctrl][Esc], and select the File Manager from the Task List. If you use the mouse to select the File Manager from the Task List, the macro will probably select the wrong application if you play it back when a different task occupies that position in the list. Instead, press *F* to jump the highlight to the first task starting with an *F*, and then press [Alt]S or [Enter] to switch to the File Manager. Since none of the other standard Windows applications begin with *F*, this technique has a much better chance of reliably selecting the File Manager each time you run the macro.

To stop recording, click on the Recorder icon, and then select the Save Macro option from the dialog box and click on OK.

Using the macro

The sole purpose of this macro is to create a fast, easy way to get to the File Manager from anywhere in the Windows environment—even in cases when the File Manager icon or window is not readily accessible. To demonstrate the macro's usefulness, activate another application, such as Write or Terminal, and maximize it to occupy the full screen. When you press [Ctrl]F, the macro will bring up the File Manager, even though you recorded it in another application.

A "DEMO" MACRO

As a final example, we'll create a macro that will show off several other Recorder features. This macro will play back continuously at the same speed it was recorded and will repeat indefinitely. Both features are well suited to training and product demonstrations. This macro is another example of one that plays back in any application, and it also illustrates how you can nest macros within other macros.

Preparing to record

As always, you need to have the appropriate tools available before you begin recording (or playing back) a macro. For this macro, you'll need Recorder, the File Manager, and Write on your desktop. (You might also want to double-click on Control Panel's Mouse icon and turn on the Mouse Trails check box in the Mouse dialog box. The Mouse Trails feature makes it easier to see the mouse pointer when the macro is being recorded or played back.) After you minimize the applications, drag each icon a few pixels on the desktop. If you manually position an icon on your desktop, it will return to that position each time you minimize it during this Windows session. If you allow Windows to position the icons, minimized applications are placed on a grid in first-come, first-serve fashion, which may shuffle their positions. If the icons change positions, your macro may select the File Manager when it is supposed to activate Write.

The other example macros described in this chapter must be available in Recorder, and Write should start with a new, untitled document.

Since this macro will play back at the same speed you record it—complete with all your pauses and hesitations—you might want to practice the sequence of actions before you record them. In this mode, recording a macro is akin to recording a performance.

To begin, activate Recorder by double-clicking on its icon, and then select Record from the Macro menu. In the Record Macro dialog box, type *Demo Macro* as the macro name, but do not assign any shortcut key.

Playback options

Now turn your attention to the Playback group box. Open the drop-down list box for the To option, and highlight the Any Application option. This will allow the macro to function in the various applications you'll use.

Using the same process, select Recorded Speed for the Speed option to have Recorder replay your actions at the same pace you use when you record them, rather than dumping the commands into the computer as fast as possible. In addition to its obvious implications for training and demonstrations, you may find this option useful when you automate procedures that require time to complete one step before starting the next. Recorder always registers the timing of your actions as you record a macro, regardless of how the Speed option is set. Later, you can switch between Fast and Recorded Speed playback modes.

To have Recorder automatically repeat the macro until you stop it, click on the Continuous Loop check box. This is another feature you can activate or deactivate after you record the macro. The Continuous Loop option is especially helpful for creating self-running product demonstrations.

The Enable Shortcut Keys check box allows you to nest other macros within this macro. You can select this check box in order to include another macro's shortcut key as part of this macro. You can disable this feature (deselect the check box) when necessary—for example, when you have created a macro that uses the same shortcut key as a command in an application and you want to issue the application's command rather than run the macro.

Mouse settings

The Record Mouse text box lets you adjust the way Recorder registers mouse movements and selections. For this example, you can use the default setting, Clicks + Drags. Recorder will capture the position of the mouse each time you press the mouse button and will track its movement during drags. The Ignore Mouse and the Everything options in the drop-down list box have Recorder either ignore the mouse completely or record all mouse movements (even when no mouse button is pressed). You'll rarely need to use these options.

The Relative To drop-down list box controls whether Recorder tracks mouse movements relative to the entire screen or to the active window. Select Screen from the drop-down list box to record mouse movements anywhere on the desktop. Generally, mouse actions relative to the active window are more reliable—especially actions within fixed-size windows, such as dialog boxes. However, we want to demonstrate Recorder's full-screen mouse-sensing capability, and this macro will create a controlled situation that minimizes the chances of an unexpectedly resized window causing problems.

When you have properly set all the options, press [Enter] or click on the Start button to begin recording the macro.

Conducting the demo

You're ready to start recording the demonstration. Recorder will register each key you press and each mouse selection you make. It will also record the speed at which you type and make selections. When you're playing the macro, the actions will be repeated at exactly the speed you recorded them.

First, activate Write by double-clicking on its icon. Type a short headline in Write, and then press [Enter] twice. Below the title, type a paragraph of miscellaneous text. The content isn't important, as long as you include your name so that you'll have a chance to demonstrate the My Name macro.

Nesting macros

At the appropriate place in the paragraph, press [Ctrl]N to insert your name. Recorder will then run the My Name macro and register the shortcut key in the macro you are recording. It won't record the contents of the nested macro. If you replace the My Name macro with a new macro using [Ctrl]N as its shortcut key, Recorder will use the new [Ctrl]N macro the next time you run this macro.

Next, use the mouse to drag the pointer across the top line of text, the one you typed as a headline or title. With the line of text highlighted, press [Ctrl][F2]. Again, Recorder will play back the Title Style macro that adds formatting to the text but will record only the shortcut key in this macro.

Your demo isn't confined to a single application. For example, you can press [Ctrl]F to activate the File Manager and then use the mouse or keyboard to browse through a couple of directories on your hard disk.

Returning to the starting configuration

Since you want this macro to repeat itself in a continuous loop, you need to return the desktop to its starting configuration before ending the macro. First, you'll need to minimize the File Manager. Next, select New from the File menu in Write, and then click on the No button in the warning dialog box to dispose of the untitled sample document you were using for this demonstration. Finally, minimize Write by clicking on the Minimize box.

Saving the macro

As soon as you return the desktop to its original state, press [Ctrl][Break] to stop recording the macro. When the dialog box shown in Figure 13-2 (page 346) appears, select the Save Macro radio button and then click on the OK button. If you want to save all the macros on disk, activate Recorder by double-clicking on its icon, and then select Save from the File menu.

Starting the macro

You've run the other macros by pressing shortcut keys, but you didn't assign a shortcut key to this macro. So how will you run it? You can select and run any of your macros from the Recorder window. This procedure is handy for less frequently used macros to which you don't assign shortcut keys or for those times you simply forget which shortcut key activates a certain macro. When you activate Recorder, you'll find Demo Macro listed in the Recorder window along with your other macros. You can execute this macro by clicking on the line containing its name and then selecting Run from the Macro menu (or by simply double-clicking on the macro name). Recorder will minimize itself into an icon and execute the macro.

Because you selected the Continuous Loop playback option, this macro won't stop. When it ends, it will return to the beginning and start over, repeating until you halt it. When you want to stop the macro, just press [Ctrl][Break], and confirm your action by clicking on OK in the dialog box that Recorder presents.

Continuously running the macro

Recorder also includes tools that allow you to manage your macro files and to control many of the macro recording and playback options.

OTHER OPTIONS

The Merge command on Recorder's File menu is similar to the Open command. When you choose Merge, you'll see the Merge dialog box shown in Figure 13-6. You can select a Recorder file from your disk and load the macros from that file into memory. The difference between the Open and the Merge commands is that Open removes all the existing macros from the list in Recorder's work area and replaces them with the macros from the file you select. Merge, on the other hand, doesn't remove the existing macros. It adds the macros from the file you select to the macros that are already active, thereby "merging" the two sets of macros. If Recorder encounters two macros with duplicate shortcut key assignments, it will alert you with a dialog box and will erase the problem shortcut key from the newly imported macro. After the merge operation, you can use the Properties command on the Macro menu to assign a new shortcut key to the problem macro.

Merging files

Figure 13-6

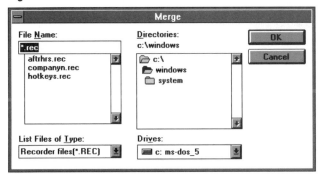

The Merge dialog box lets you select a file of macros to add to the macros already in memory.

The Delete command on the Macro menu allows you to remove a macro from the macro list in Recorder's work area. To get rid of an unneeded macro, simply highlight the macro in the list by clicking on the macro name with the mouse or by moving the highlight with the arrow keys, and then select Delete. Recorder will prompt you for confirmation that you want to delete the macro. When you click on the OK button, Recorder will erase the macro from memory. However, if the macro is in a Recorder file on disk, the disk version will not be changed until you save the altered file.

Deleting macros

Changing a macro's properties

Selecting the Properties command from the Macro menu will display the properties of the currently highlighted macro in the Macro Properties dialog box. In this dialog box, you can change nearly all the options you set when you originally recorded the macro. In fact, as Figure 13-7 shows, the Macro Properties dialog box resembles the Record Macro dialog box. The Macro Name, Shortcut Key, Playback, and Description areas are the same in both appearance and operation. The significant difference is in the mouse options. You cannot change the way Recorder sees mouse selections once they are recorded. The Macro Properties dialog box shows information about whether mouse coordinates were recorded relative to the screen or to the active window and on what type of display. This information can be essential in determining whether you will be able to share a macro with someone working on another system.

Figure 13-7

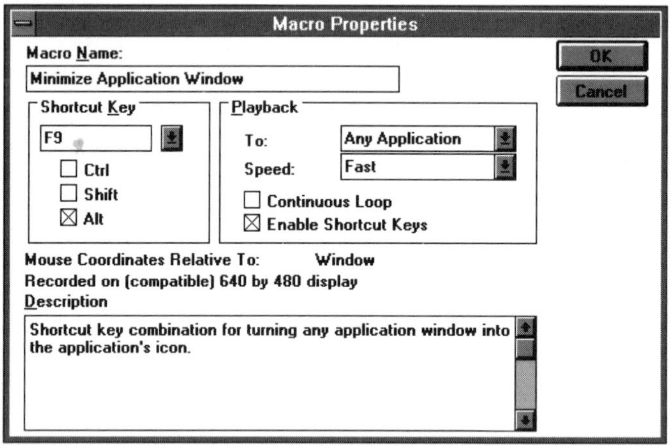

The Macro Properties dialog box allows you to change nearly all original macro settings and displays the mouse recording options used in the macro.

Temporarily disabling Recorder

Occasionally, you may want to disable Recorder temporarily without removing it from your desktop. At least, you may need to disable Recorder's reaction to shortcut keys to avoid conflict with the shortcut keys in an application. The Shortcut Keys command on the Options menu is a toggle command that will allow you to turn on and off Recorder's ability to sense shortcut keys. The default is for shortcut-key sensing to be active, as indicated by a check mark beside the command on the menu. Simply click on the command to force Recorder to ignore shortcut keys. Repeat the same action to reinstate shortcut-key sensing. While shortcut keys are disabled, you will still be able to run macros by opening the Recorder window, highlighting a macro in Recorder's list, and selecting the Run command from the Macro menu.

Normally, Recorder minimizes itself automatically when you start recording a macro, stop recording a macro, or select and run a macro from the Recorder window. If you would rather have Recorder remain on your desktop as an inactive window instead of as an icon, use the Minimize On Use command from the Options menu. This toggle command switches the feature on or off; a check mark indicates that it is active.

Minimizing Recorder

Pressing [Ctrl][Break] will normally stop recording a macro or halt execution of a running macro. You also press [Ctrl][Break] to stop a macro that you have set to play back repeatedly in a continuous loop. You can, however, create a "bullet-proof" demo that will run with no possibility of interruption from random keyboard input by disabling Control+Break Checking. You can turn off Control+Break Checking on the Options menu to tell Recorder to ignore [Ctrl][Break]. If you run a continuous loop macro with Control+Break Checking disabled, the macro will continue to repeat itself until you reboot the computer. Like Shortcut Keys and Minimize On Use, Control+Break Checking is a toggle command with a check mark to indicate when it is active.

Running an uninterruptible demo

If you find yourself changing playback settings or mouse options nearly every time you start to record a macro, you can save time by changing the defaults. Select Preferences from the Options menu to bring up the Default Preferences dialog box, shown in Figure 13-8. If you change the settings here and then click on the OK button, Recorder will use your selections instead of the original defaults in the Record Macro dialog box.

Changing defaults

Figure 13-8

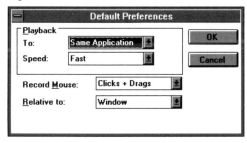

You can change the default settings that appear in the Record Macro dialog box from this Default Preferences dialog box.

With Recorder, it's easy to create macros that will help with many of your routine tasks. However, as you record and use macros, there are a few things you should keep in mind so that your macros will be reliable and trouble-free.

CARE AND FEEDING OF YOUR MACRO

**Preparing
the environment
for macros**

Pay attention to your Windows environment when you record your macros and when you use them. What applications are running? Which are minimized, and which are inactive windows? What is the size and position of each open window? If any of these factors have changed from when you recorded the macro, running the macro in the changed Windows environment might cause unpredictable results. For example, our File Manager macro discussed earlier in this chapter assumes that the File Manager is available on the desktop and that it is the only application available in the Task List dialog box whose name begins with an *F*. The macro will not have the intended effect if either assumption is not true. Macros that play back in any application and macros that use the mouse (especially relative to the full screen) are particularly vulnerable to changes in the Windows environment.

A good place for notes about a macro's environment requirements is in the Description box at the bottom of the Macro Properties dialog box.

**Selecting
shortcut keys**

When you select shortcut keys for your macros, you'll want to avoid selecting keys and key combinations that your applications need for normal operations. Obviously, you wouldn't use a standard typewriter key alone or combined with [Shift] as a shortcut key. If you did, you couldn't use that key to type text while Recorder was active. You'll also want to avoid most [Alt] letter combinations since they are used extensively to access Windows' menus. Combinations that use the [Ctrl] key are generally safer selections for shortcut keys. Also, combinations that use more than one of the "shift" keys ([Shift], [Ctrl], [Alt])—[Ctrl][Shift]S, for example—will almost never conflict with an application's predefined shortcuts.

Mousing about

Use your mouse sparingly when you record macros. Remember that Recorder registers the position of the pointer when you click the mouse button. It does not record the effect of the mouse action. The macro will have the same effect when you play it back only if the window, menu, or command you selected with the mouse is in the same position as it was when you recorded the macro. Remember also that Windows is a dynamic environment with windows that may be different sizes and in different positions each time you use a macro. Mouse movements relative to the active window are generally more reliable than movements relative to the entire screen area (especially within fixed-size windows, such as dialog boxes).

Use the keyboard equivalents instead of the mouse to issue commands and make menu selections in your macros. Windows allows you to duplicate essentially every mouse action with the keyboard. The Help information for most Windows applications offers a brief listing of the keys used specifically by that application. (Keys and their functions are also listed and summarized in the Quick Reference Cards at the end of this book.) If you must use the mouse in a macro, you may want to first maximize the window to help ensure more predictable positioning by standardizing the window size and position.

Sharing macros

Sharing your Recorder macros with other people who use Windows 3.1 is as simple as giving them a copy of the Recorder file containing your macros—provided they have the same applications and use similar settings and hardware.

If you record macros on one computer and attempt to play them back on a different computer, you may encounter problems if both systems don't use the same display adapter and keyboard. Recorder senses mouse movements relative to the screen resolution of your system. If you record a macro that includes mouse selections on one system, it will seldom work on a system that uses a different display adapter.

A similar but less severe problem occurs when you record a macro on a system with one type of keyboard and play it back on a system with a different kind of keyboard or a different Country setting. While most keystrokes may be the same on both systems, you should be alert for potential problems arising from the keyboard differences.

Using Recorder with non-Windows applications

Recorder was designed to work with Windows and Windows-based applications. If you are running Windows in standard mode, Recorder might work with some non-Windows applications. However, the reliability of your macros will be questionable, at best. We don't recommend the practice.

Macros will *not* work with non-Windows applications if you use Windows 386 enhanced mode. The same technology that allows Windows to perform multitasking and advanced memory management also insulates a DOS-based application running under Windows too thoroughly to allow Recorder to work with the application.

In this chapter

Using Desktop Accessories 14

Windows provides useful and interesting tools in its desktop applications. Notepad, Calendar, Cardfile, Calculator, and Clock are applications that will help you with schedules, appointments, phone numbers, and the countless details that must be managed to keep your office or your projects operating efficiently. Object Packager, a new OLE accessory, will help you easily assemble a document containing different kinds of data by inserting an icon that represents linked or embedded data into a document file. Media Player and Sound Recorder even provide controls for installing and playing multimedia devices and files. Because you can minimize these applications into icons on your desktop, they are available from any Windows-based application. You can find these application icons in the Accessories group window in the Program Manager, as shown in Figure 14-1. In this chapter, we'll show you how to use the desktop applications to enhance efficiency and creativity and how to exchange data between applications.

Figure 14-1

You can start these applications from the Accessories group window.

NOTEPAD

Jotting down an idea for later use is an important part of the creative process. The Notepad application will help you keep track of your ideas, great and small. You also can use Notepad to keep a phone call log, a things-to-do list, a time log, or even a diary. Notepad is a simple word processor whose built-in search functions give you easy access to your notes for a particular date, phrase, or idea. It creates an ASCII text file that has no hidden character formatting like Write's invisible paragraph markers.

To start Notepad, double-click on the Notepad icon in the Accessories group window (which you'll find in the Program Manager) to view a Notepad window, shown in Figure 14-2. As you can see, the window contains all the standard elements (Control menu box, title bar, frame, scroll bars, and so on). Besides the standard File, Edit, and Help menus, Notepad also offers a Search menu. The flashing cursor is automatically positioned in the upper-left corner of the work area. When you move the pointer into the work area from the desktop, it will change from an arrow into an I-beam.

To exit Notepad, choose the Exit command from the File menu.

Figure 14-2

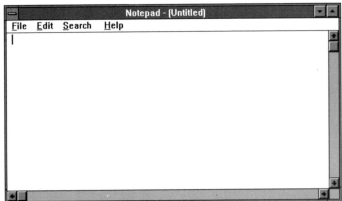

Notepad's window includes a Search menu.

Entering and editing text

Notepad starts with an untitled notepad. To make an entry in your active notepad, simply begin typing. Your text will appear to the left of the flashing cursor. If you want to open and enter text in an existing notepad, choose the Open command from the File menu, and Notepad will display the Open dialog box. As you can see in Figure 14-3, this dialog box lists all the available Notepad files in the current directory. You can either select one of the files in the File Name list box or type a file name in the File Name text box. (For more about opening files, see Chapter 9.)

Figure 14-3

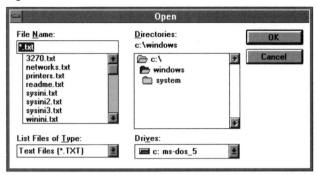

The Open dialog box displays all available Notepad files in the current directory.

Sometimes you may need to refer to information in one notepad while you're working in another. You can do this easily because Windows lets you load several copies of Notepad. If Notepad is running and you want to open another Notepad window, you will need to resize or move the first window to gain access to the Notepad application icon in the Program Manager. When you double-click on the Notepad icon again, a new, untitled Notepad window will appear, and you'll be ready to start typing additional information.

To tell Notepad where you want your lines of text to end, you can use two techniques. One way is to press [Enter] to add a carriage return manually. If you don't want to keep pressing [Enter], you can use the Word Wrap command on the Edit menu to tell Notepad to automatically wrap the lines. However, you'll still need to press [Enter] to start a new paragraph.

Applying Word Wrap

Word Wrap is a toggle command. When it is active, a check mark will appear beside it on the Edit menu. Because Word Wrap isn't active by default, you'll need to select it every time you start Notepad. You can also tell that Word Wrap is on when the horizontal scroll bar disappears. The horizontal scroll bar isn't necessary with Word Wrap since Notepad wraps the text within the left and right boundaries of the window. If you change the width of your window to accommodate other windows on the desktop, the text will conform to the new space. As you add text, the slider on the vertical scroll bar will move down.

If you make mistakes or want to change anything in your document, you will need to use Notepad's editing features. Notepad lets you insert and delete characters; cut, copy, and paste words; and insert spaces for a limited type of formatting. You can delete a character by backspacing to remove the character to the left of the cursor or by pressing [Delete] to remove the character to the right of the cursor. You can delete a series of characters by dragging the pointer over the characters to highlight them and then pressing [Backspace] or [Delete].

Making changes

You can also delete highlighted characters by choosing the Delete command from the Edit menu. The Cut command removes any highlighted text and puts it in Clipboard. The Copy command copies highlighted text and places it in Clipboard. The Paste command takes text from Clipboard and inserts it at the position of the cursor.

In addition to deleting or adding text, you can format text by using tabs or spaces. Notepad tabs are predefined as eight spaces in the 12-point Fixedsys font (about 0.5"), and you can't change or set additional tabs. We used tabs, spaces, the Word Wrap feature, and manual carriage returns to type and format the text in Figure 14-4. If you need more control over spacing, you should copy the file into Write.

Figure 14-4

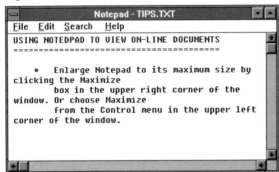

You can do simple text formatting in Notepad with tabs, spaces, Word Wrap, and manual line breaks.

Searching for words and phrases

Notepad's search functions let you look for particular characters, words, or phrases in your text. For example, if you want to copy a name and phone number but can't find them, select Find from the Search menu. In the Find dialog box, shown in Figure 14-5, enter the character, word, or phrase you want to locate in the Find What text box. If case is important, select the Match Case check box. Because punctuation makes a difference, be sure that you include any spaces, slashes, hyphens, or other punctuation in your search text.

Figure 14-5

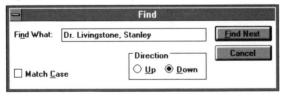

The Find dialog box helps you search for text.

Notepad will start its search from the location of the cursor. You can control the direction of the search, either forward from the cursor or backward, by selecting the Up or Down radio button. After you enter the search text and select the appropriate button, press [Enter] or click on the Find Next button. Notepad will find the text and highlight it. If it can't find the text, Notepad will present an information dialog box like the one shown in Figure 14-6, displaying the message *Cannot find* and the search text. Click on OK to return to the Find dialog box. If you want to carry out a new search, change the search text in the text box. You can quickly start the new search by using the mouse to position the cursor at the beginning of the file. Then select the Down radio button and click on Find Next in the Find dialog box.

When you have finished your search, you can either click on the Cancel button in the Find dialog box or double-click on the Control menu box to close the dialog box and return to your document.

Figure 14-6

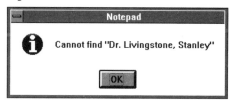

This information dialog box lets you know when Notepad can't find a match for your search text.

You can repeat a search for a string of characters (*93 East Street*) or a word (*Bruce*) by clicking on Find Next in the Find dialog box. If you have already closed the Find dialog box, you can simply select Find Next from the Search menu or press the accelerator key [F3] instead of reissuing a Find command to repeat a search. If Notepad can't find additional matches, it will notify you by presenting an information dialog box. The Find Next command is handy if you have misspelled a word the same way throughout your notepad and need to correct each occurrence.

Your notepad entries can be a valuable resource if you design them with a plan for retrieving the information they contain. For example, if you want to be able to track phone calls by time and date, you should incorporate that information into the text of the messages. To add the time and date, select the Time/Date command from the Edit menu or use the accelerator key [F5]. As you can see in Figure 14-7 on the following page, Windows inserts the time and date at the position of the cursor. (Remember, you can change the format of the time and date as well as the actual time and date through Control Panel, as we explained in Chapter 3.) Next, add the caller's name, phone number, and message. Later, you can easily copy the name and phone number into Cardfile.

Using Time/Date

Figure 14-7

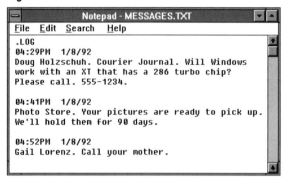

You can insert a time and date line into your notepad entry.

Another way to insert the time and date is to use an embedded .LOG command. Windows will then insert the current time and date at the end of your notepad the next time you open the document in Notepad. You can also use Notepad's time and date capability to keep a time log for a project. For instance, open a notepad, and type *.LOG* in all capital letters as the first entry on the first line of your notepad. You can insert the time you started working by pressing [F5], perhaps type the project name, and make notes about the project. You can then minimize this notepad into an icon and open the application containing your project. When you complete the work session for your project, maximize the icon, save the notepad, and then reopen it from Notepad. When you reopen this time log notepad, Notepad automatically inserts the current time and date at the end of the file. As a result, you'll have a history of your project.

Saving and printing a notepad

After you have made all the entries in your notepad, you need to save the document as a Notepad file. As we showed you in Chapter 9, you can save your file with the Save or the Save As command on the File menu. To save a new file, choose the Save As command, and enter the file name (which can be up to eight characters) in the File Name text box of the Save As dialog box, shown in Figure 14-8. Click on OK to save the file. When you save the file again, choose the Save command. Notepad won't present a dialog box and prompt you for a file name; it will simply save your file with the same name. To save the file under a different name, use the Save As command.

The file name you choose for your notepad is important. Since the file name appears on Notepad's title bar and on its minimized icon, you'll want to use a descriptive and easily recognizable name. If you don't add a file name extension, Notepad adds a .TXT extension. Figure 14-9 demonstrates the value of naming your Notepad files so that you can distinguish between multiple minimized Notepad documents.

Figure 14-8

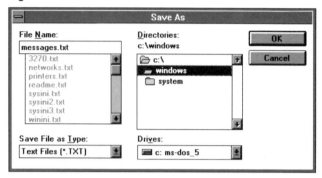

Use the Save As dialog box to save a new Notepad file.

Figure 14-9

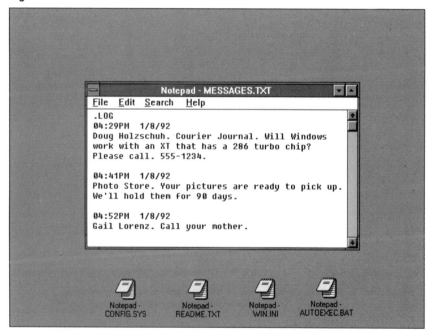

Descriptive file names are essential when more than one notepad is open.

You'll probably want to print some of your Notepad files, but before you send a file to the printer, you need to define your margins, specify any header or footer information, and choose a printer. The Page Setup command on the File menu lets you define the margins, headers, and footers, while the Print Setup command lets you set up your printer.

Setting margins, headers, and footers

To set up margins, headers, and footers, issue the Page Setup command to display the Page Setup dialog box shown in Figure 14-10. Settings for the left, right, top, and bottom margins are expressed in inches. To change a margin setting, click on the appropriate text box and then type the new measurement. The default margins are 1" for top and bottom and .75" for left and right. The header and footer are printed in the 1" top and bottom margins, respectively. You can enter codes in the header and footer that will align the header/footer or add system information. For example, if you want today's date left-aligned at the top of every page, enter *&d &l* in the Header text box. If you want the word *DATE* to appear next to the current date, type *DATE &d &l* in the Header text box. Chapter 9 provides a table listing these codes (Table 9-1). By default, Notepad prints the file name as the header and the page number as the footer.

Figure 14-10

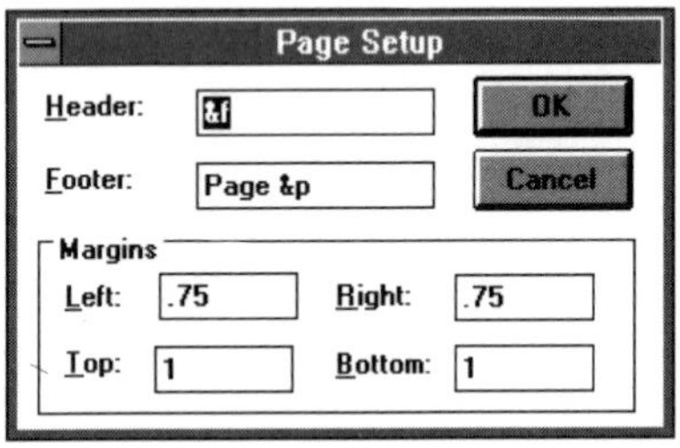

You can use the Page Setup dialog box to set the margins and header and footer text.

Setting up the printer

After the page is set up, use the Print Setup command on the File menu if you need to set any printer options before you print your document. (We cover printer settings in more detail in Chapter 3.) In the Print Setup dialog box, like the one shown in Figure 14-11, you'll see the name of the default printer. To choose another printer, select the Specific Printer radio button, and then choose one of the installed printers in the drop-down list box. If you need to modify any of the other default print settings, do so and then click on OK.

Figure 14-11

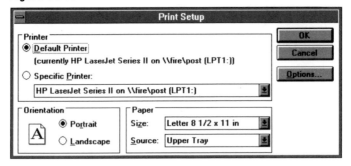

The Print Setup dialog box lets you set printing options.

Once you've established the page and printer settings, you're ready to print your file. To do this, select the Print command from the File menu. The Print Manager icon will appear at the bottom of the desktop, and a dialog box like the one shown in Figure 14-12 will tell you that Notepad is printing your text and that you can cancel the printing if you want.

Printing your file

Figure 14-12

A Notepad dialog box provides a Cancel button to let you stop printing a notepad.

Your printed document will look exactly like the document on your screen because Notepad uses only ASCII characters with no formatting codes. If you used Word Wrap, the printout will have the same appearance as the wrapped text on your screen. If you need better formatting, you'll have to copy your notepad into Write before you print it.

If you want to print a Notepad file when Notepad is not running or is not active, you can drag the Notepad file icon from the File Manager to a minimized Print Manager icon on your desktop. The Print Manager will print the Notepad file as if you had opened it in Notepad, chosen the Print command from the File menu, and then clicked on OK to accept default printing. If a .LOG command is the first line of your Notepad file, the printed document will contain a timestamp with the time and date the Print Manager printed the file.

Now that you have mastered the basics, you're ready to try some of Notepad's other features. You can use the Copy and Paste commands to move data between Notepad and other applications, such as Write and Cardfile. For example, if you want to transfer names and phone numbers from a notepad to Cardfile, just highlight the name and phone number from the Notepad document and then select Copy from the Edit menu. Notepad will copy the text to Clipboard. Next, open the Cardfile application, and then open your phone number card file and select Paste from Cardfile's Edit menu. (We'll discuss Cardfile in greater detail later in this chapter.) You'll want to size the Cardfile application window so that you can see the Notepad window, too. Both the Notepad and Cardfile applications will now be visible on the desktop. To repeat the process, just move the mouse pointer to the notepad, select a new name and phone number, and copy them. Then, you can move the mouse pointer to the Cardfile window, add a new card, and paste the information onto the card.

Using Notepad files with other applications

Although you can copy and paste text from other applications into Notepad, you can't copy and paste graphics. Notepad, which is an ASCII text editor, uses only characters that are represented by an ASCII code. Graphics are not based on ASCII codes and therefore can't be pasted into Notepad. If you need to combine text and graphics, you should use Write.

You can also use Notepad files with applications other than those running under Windows. Communications programs can send Notepad ASCII text files over a modem. You can create program files that any compiler will accept because the files will not contain formatting characters that might disrupt compiling. Notepad also can edit or create MS-DOS batch files and other MS-DOS system files, such as AUTOEXEC.BAT and CONFIG.SYS.

CALENDAR

You can use Windows' Calendar to keep a record of appointments and important events. By using Calendar and Notepad's time-logging capabilities, you can keep an accurate record of how you spend your time. Calendar's alarm will help you keep track of important appointments.

Before we explain how Calendar works, we need to introduce a couple of terms. We call Calendar's files *books*, but you need to determine the time frame for the book and your use for the book. We call one day's appointments a *page*.

Windows permits you to keep more than one calendar book. For example, an administrative assistant can keep a calendar book on the desktop for each of several managers in a company. The calendar book can be assigned a specific manager's name; remember that it is important to label files distinctively so that you can find them easily. The administrative assistant can print the day's appointments and distribute them. If the company uses a network, each manager could make changes to the calendar books on-line. Since the calendar books are shared, the administrative assistant could work with the same file so that all the changes occur in one place.

To start Calendar, double-click on the Calendar icon in the Accessories group window. An untitled calendar book, like the one shown in Figure 14-13, will appear. The Calendar window has all the standard window controls plus a few additional ones for the Calendar appointment area. The top of the window has a standard Control menu box, title bar (with file name), Minimize box, Maximize box, and menu bar. The status bar beneath the menu bar displays the time and date. The scroll arrows on the status bar let you scroll through the different appointment pages by date. Below the status bar, you see an appointment page where you can enter text at the cursor beside the 24-hour stack of time slots. You can use the vertical scroll bar to move through the different time slot entries on the page. Below the appointment page is a scratch pad, which you can use to jot down notes, lists, or reminders.

Figure 14-13

File name (calendar book)

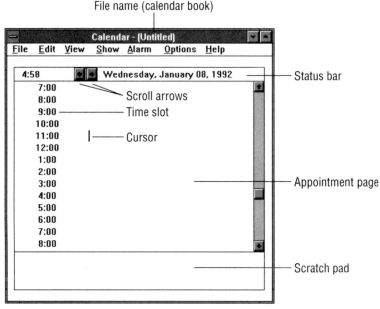

Status bar

Scroll arrows

Time slot

Cursor

Appointment page

Scratch pad

The Calendar application window features a status bar,
appointment page, and scratch pad.

If you've previously saved a calendar book and want to work on it, select
the Open command from the File menu. The Open dialog box, shown in Figure
14-14, will appear. Calendar will look for all files with the .CAL extension and
will list them in the File Name list box. If the file you're looking for isn't there,
you can use the Directories or the Drives list box to look in another directory or
drive. To open the file, click on the file name, and then click on OK.

Figure 14-14

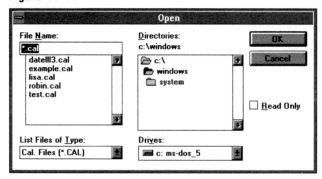

The Open dialog box
lists Calendar files.

Notice that Calendar's Open dialog box contains a Read Only check box. If you select this option, you won't be able to make changes to the file. The Read Only option prevents you from making accidental changes to your calendar book or to someone else's book.

If you are working on one calendar book but want to start a new one, you can choose New from the File menu to create an untitled calendar book. For instance, you can start a new book for each fiscal year. Calendar will ask you whether you want to save any changes you've made to the current book before it opens the new one.

When you have finished using Calendar, exit the application by choosing the Exit command from the File menu.

After you've learned to use Calendar's commands and features, you may want to speed up some of the processes by using accelerator keys. Table 14-1 lists Calendar's accelerator keys and their functions.

Table 14-1

Keystroke	Function
[F4]	Show date
[F5]	Set alarm
[F6]	Mark
[F7]	Add special time slot
[F8]	Display day view
[F9]	Display month view
[Ctrl][Page Up]	Show previous day or month
[Ctrl][Page Down]	Show next day or month

Accelerator keys can improve Calendar's performance by speeding up your access to various functions.

Using time slots

To make an entry in one of the time slots in a calendar book, click on the time slot or use the arrow keys to position the cursor. The pointer in the appointment page is an I-beam, indicating that you can enter text there. You can enter up to 80 characters in your message. If you exceed that limit, Calendar will beep, and you will see a *Text truncated* message like the one shown in Figure 14-15. If you want to return to the beginning of a long message that you have typed in one of the time slots, press the [Home] key.

As you are making entries in your calendar book, you might have an appointment at a time other than the ones listed on the page. You can easily add a new time slot or even restructure the page to add more time slots at smaller time increments.

Figure 14-15

If you exceed the 80-character limit for a time slot, you'll get a message like this one.

To add a new time slot, select Special Time from the Options menu or press [F7]. The Special Time dialog box, shown in Figure 14-16, contains a text box for your time entry. For example, you might want to add a new time slot for a 10:05 AM appointment. First enter the time, and then choose the AM radio button. Click on Insert to add the new time slot to the appointment page.

Adding a special time slot

Figure 14-16

The Special Time dialog box lets you add a time slot to your appointment page.

Calendar has a feature that will let you divide your day into time slots of hour, half-hour, or quarter-hour segments, which we'll explain in a moment. It's important to note that Calendar insists on your use of the correct time format. If you accidentally enter a semicolon for a colon or add too many numbers, Calendar will display a message dialog box telling you that you have made an incorrect entry. If you try to add a special time slot that already appears on the appointment page, Calendar will notify you that the specified time is already being used.

Later, you might want to delete the special time slot you created. To delete a special time slot, issue the Special Time command on the Options menu. Simply enter the time you want to remove in the Special Time text box, and then click on Delete. If you click on the special time slot before you open the Special Time dialog box, Calendar will insert that time slot in the Special Time text box. Note that you can't delete a regular time slot; you can delete only those time slots that you added with the Special Time command.

Deleting a time slot

If you want to restructure and reformat a page in smaller time increments, choose Day Settings from the Options menu. As you can see in Figure 14-17 on the following page, the Day Settings dialog box lets you set the appointment

Formatting time slots

page's hour format and the starting time slot. The three Interval options let you format the page in quarter-, half-, or one-hour increments. Just choose the appropriate radio button. The Hour Format's default setting is a 12-hour system that uses AM and PM notation. The 24-hour format is used for military or European time. The Starting Time text box lets you specify the first time slot on the appointment page. The default Starting Time option is 7:00 AM.

Figure 14-17

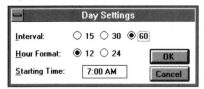

The Day Settings dialog box lets you set up time-slot
intervals and the starting time on your appointment page.

Editing an entry

To edit a time slot entry, begin by clicking on it. You can use the [Backspace] key or the [Delete] key to remove text at the cursor, or you can simply insert new text. You can make more sophisticated changes by using the Cut, Copy, Paste, and Remove commands on the Edit menu.

Cutting text

You can cut characters or blocks of text and paste them in another time slot or application. For instance, if you need to reschedule a meeting, you could cut the message from the original time slot and paste it into a new one. To do this, highlight the message and then select Cut from the Edit menu. (Remember that cutting text deletes the text from the current document and places it in Clipboard.) Then, find the new time slot, click there, and select Paste from the Edit menu. If you make a things-to-do list in Notepad (and name the file DO_LIST), you could also add the appointment to that list. After you paste the appointment in the new time slot in your calendar book, open or activate the DO_LIST notepad (it would be handy to have it already minimized on your desktop), and paste the message into the list.

Copying text

If you want to repeat a message, you can use the Copy command. For instance, if you have a weekly Wednesday staff meeting at the same place and time, you can copy the appointment to each Wednesday of the month. To do this, highlight the message and select the Copy command from the Edit menu. You can then paste the message to other Wednesdays several months in advance. Copying and pasting the information is another way to get the message to your DO_LIST notepad.

Remove, one of the more powerful commands on Calendar's Edit menu, lets you delete an entire page of appointments. Unlike the Cut command, which deletes only one entry or part of an entry and then allows you to retrieve the entry with the Paste command, Remove deletes the appointments for a set block of time. The page does not go to Clipboard. The only way to retrieve data if you remove it accidentally with the Remove command is to exit the calendar book without saving your changes and then reopen it. (This works only if you have previously saved the appointments.)

To use the Remove command, select it from the Edit menu. The Remove dialog box, shown in Figure 14-18, provides two text boxes in which you can type the time frame of the appointments you want to delete. You enter the starting date in the From text box and the ending date in the To text box. When you click on OK, Calendar will remove all the appointments between and including these dates. If you want to remove only one page of appointments, make the From and To dates the same or leave the To text box blank.

Removing a page's appointments

Figure 14-18

You can delete pages of appointments within a range of dates by using the Remove dialog box.

You also can use the scratch pad, the empty box below the appointment page, to remind yourself of important events. For example, you can use the scratch pad for compiling a short things-to-do list or for jotting down notes that can be copied or cut and then pasted into your calendar. To enter text on the scratch pad, click in the area or press [Tab], and then type or paste the text. Calendar automatically wraps the text in the scratch pad but won't scroll text to let you add more text than the displayed area will hold. To return to the time slots, click on a time slot or press [Tab].

Using the scratch pad

Another interesting Calendar feature is the alarm. By default, the alarm sound is a beep. (If you have installed a sound card, you can choose another sound.) You can set the alarm to go off at one or more of the times represented by the time slots on your appointment page. For example, you can set the alarm to alert you for your 10:05 meeting by first selecting the 10:05 time slot and then choosing the Set command on the Alarm menu. In Figure 14-19 on the following page, notice that a bell symbol appears next to the 10:05 appointment. If you select Set again, the alarm will toggle off. The Alarm menu places a check mark beside the Set command to show that it is active for the selected time slot. When you select the command again, the check mark disappears.

Setting the alarm

When the system time matches the time slot you marked, the alarm will go off, and an information dialog box will appear. In Figure 14-20, the information dialog box tells you to remember your appointment and displays the message you typed in that time slot. If Calendar is an inactive window, its title bar will flash when the alarm goes off. If Calendar is a minimized icon on the desktop, the icon will flash when the alarm goes off. You will need to click on either the flashing icon or the flashing title bar to read the message. When you click on the icon or the title bar, Calendar will display the information dialog box containing your message.

Figure 14-19

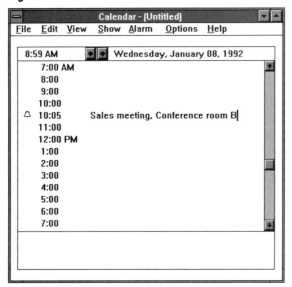

The alarm symbol appears next to the time slot of the selected entry when you choose the Set command from the Alarm menu.

Figure 14-20

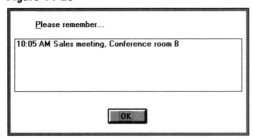

After the alarm goes off, Calendar displays your message.

With the Controls command from the Alarm menu, you can control when the alarm goes off and whether the computer will play the alarm's sound. The Alarm Controls dialog box shown in Figure 14-21 contains a text box for Early Ring. To have the alarm go off at the exact time indicated by the time slot, set Early Ring to 0. If you want a 10-minute warning before an actual appointment time, set Early Ring to 10. The Sound check box will let you toggle the alarm's sound on and off. The sound is on by default.

Controlling the alarm

Figure 14-21

The Alarm Controls dialog box lets you control how early an alarm will go off.

You can page through your calendar book quickly with the Show menu commands and the status bar. If you want to look at an appointment just a few days away, you can use the scroll arrows on the status bar. The right arrow will advance you one day at a time, while the left arrow will scroll the page to the appointments of previous days, also one full day at a time.

Moving between pages

The Next and Previous commands on the Show menu perform the same actions as the right and left scroll arrows. Alternatively, you can use the accelerator keys [Ctrl][Page Down] for Next and [Ctrl][Page Up] for Previous. If you hold the keys down, you'll scroll continuously until you release the keys.

The Date command on the Show menu will let you open the Show Date dialog box and enter the destination date, as shown in Figure 14-22. After you enter the destination date, click on OK, and Calendar will move to the day you selected. You can use hyphens or slashes to separate the date elements. For example, either 4-12-91 or 4/12/91 is acceptable. If you use any other marks as separators, a Calendar information dialog box like the one shown in Figure 14-23 on the following page will remind you of the correct format.

Figure 14-22

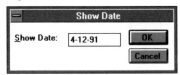

The Show Date dialog box offers a text box for entering the destination date.

After you have moved through your calendar book for a while, you may find yourself far from the starting point, the current date. Instead of entering the current date in the Show Date dialog box to return to that date's page of appointments, simply choose the Today command from the Show menu. Calendar will then display the page that matches your system date. If your system date is correct, the page will be the current date.

Figure 14-23

A Calendar information dialog box reminds you of the correct date format if you enter a date in the wrong format in the Show Date dialog box.

Viewing months and marking days

Another quick way to move between dates is to select them from a month view. If you select the Month command from the View menu or press [F9], the calendar book's dates will appear in month view, as shown in Figure 14-24. Calendar changes only the appointment area of the window. The status bar and scratch pad are unchanged. Since the scratch pad is available, you can display daily information for the highlighted date. If you double-click on a date in the month view, the appointment page for that date will appear in the window. You can then use [F9] or the Month command to move back to month view.

Figure 14-24

Calendar - (Untitled)						
File **Edit** **View** **Show** **Alarm** **Options** **Help**						
10:08 AM ◄|► Wednesday, January 08, 1992						
January 1992						
S	M	T	W	T	F	S
			1	2	3	4
5	6	7	> 8 <	9	10	11
12	13	14	15	16	17	18
19	20	21	22	23	24	25
26	27	28	29	30	31	

You can view your calendar by month.

You can move between months using the same techniques you used to move between days. In month view, the right and left scroll arrows let you page forward or backward one month at a time. The Next and Previous commands on the Show menu or the [Ctrl][Page Down] and [Ctrl][Page Up] keys will also scroll the display a month at a time.

If you want to be able to track activities by month, you can add symbols to, or mark, the days in the month view. The month view always marks the current date. For example, on the eighth day of the displayed month, the calendar entry is marked > 8 <. If you click on a date, it becomes active, or selected. You can add other marks to month view, such as X's for vacation days, boxes for birthdays, or dots for project deadlines. To mark a date, first select it by clicking on it. Calendar will then highlight the date and add a blinking cursor. Now choose the Mark command from the Options menu or press [F6] to display the Day Markings dialog box, as shown in Figure 14-25. You can mark a day with more than one symbol, checking as many symbols as are listed for any single day. If you want to track your vacation days, you can use the X to mark your vacations over the year. You could also mark birthdays, anniversaries, pay days, doctor's appointments, and so forth. The calendar in Figure 14-26 marks vacation days with X's, birthdays with boxes, and project due dates with dots. (Note that the boxes and solid dots on the calendar are actually generated by symbols 1 and 3 in the Day Markings dialog box, a set of brackets and a small open circle.)

Figure 14-25

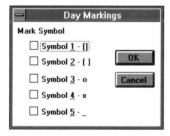

The Day Markings dialog box provides an assortment of calendar marks you can use to flag special dates.

Figure 14-26

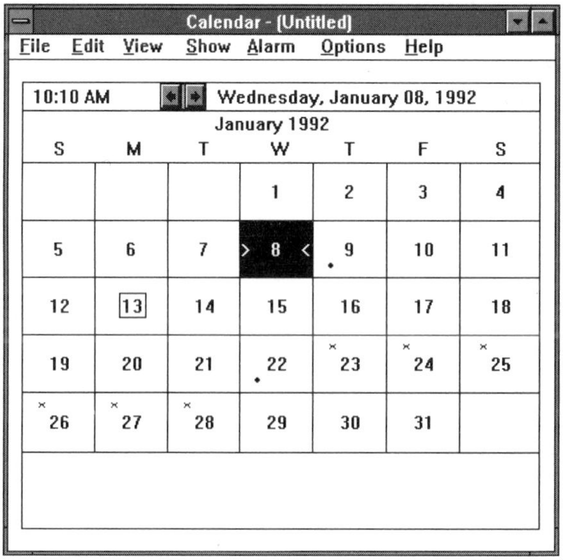

\	Calendar - (Untitled)					
File	Edit	View	Show	Alarm	Options	Help

10:10 AM		Wednesday, January 08, 1992				
			January 1992			
S	M	T	W	T	F	S
			1	2	3	4
5	6	7	> 8 <	9	10	11
12	[13]	14	15	16	17	18
19	20	21	22	× 23	× 24	× 25
× 26	× 27	× 28	29	30	31	

In this sample calendar, X's mark vacation days, boxes mark birthdays, and dots mark project due dates.

**Saving and printing
a calendar book**

It's always a good idea to save the calendar book before you print and after
you have made changes or added entries. That way, if the printer has trouble and
Calendar locks up, you won't lose the work you've completed so far. To save
your work, select Save from the File menu. If you are working on an untitled
calendar book, Calendar will prompt you for a name with the Save As dialog
box. Type a distinctive name in the File Name text box, and click on OK. Calendar uses a .CAL file name extension by default.

If you want to save a copy of an existing book, choose the Save As command
from the File menu, and enter a new file name in the Save As dialog box.
Because you are saving the book with a new file name, you will have two
otherwise identical books with different names. You can use the new one as a
template for another calendar or as a back-up copy. In general, it's a good idea
to keep all your appointments in one place to limit confusion.

You can print the appointments in your calendar book. Calendar prints only
the time slot entries and the scratch pad from the day view, not the symbols
shown in the month view. Before you print your appointment pages, you need
to set up the margins, headers, and footers. Then, you need to verify which
printer you're going to use and define its settings. After all the preparation,
you're ready to print. Let's go over page setup first.

Setting up the page

If you want to use headers and footers on your printout, choose Page Setup
from the File menu. The Page Setup dialog box has text boxes for the header and
footer codes. Along with the code, you can include text. (Refer to Chapter 9 for
a list of the codes.)

You set the left, right, top, and bottom margins in the Margins section of the
dialog box. To change a margin, click on its text box, and the cursor will appear
in the box. Delete the old number, and then type the new margin size.

**Setting printer
options**

After the page is set up satisfactorily, select the Print Setup command from
the File menu if you need to choose printer options. In the Print Setup dialog
box, you can change settings such as paper size or page orientation.

**Printing a range
of dates**

After you've specified the page setup and printer setup, you're ready to
print. When you select Print from the File menu, you'll see the Print dialog box
shown in Figure 14-27. In this dialog box, you can enter the dates of the appointment page or pages you would like to print. You can specify one page or a range
of pages by entering dates in the From and To text boxes. Remember that you
need to enter the dates with hyphens or slashes. If you fail to use the correct
punctuation, a *Dates are not valid* message will appear. If you want to print only
one day's appointments, enter the same date in each text box or leave the To
text box blank.

Figure 14-27

In this dialog box, you can enter the dates of appointment pages you want to print.

When you select OK, Calendar will call on the Print Manager to control the printer and print your pages. As an alternative, you can drag your calendar file's icon from the File Manager to a minimized Print Manager icon on your desktop. This method prints all the appointments in the calendar book. (For more about the Print Manager, see Chapter 7.)

When Calendar sends a page to the Print Manager, it sends only those time slots and scratch pads that contain messages. Figure 14-28 shows a sample printout with an appointment and a scratch pad entry.

Figure 14-28

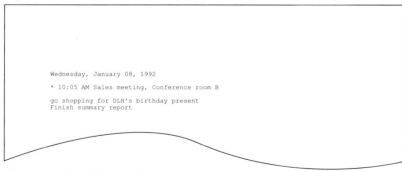

We printed a calendar book appointment page.

Cardfile is another Windows accessory application. You can think of Cardfile as a sophisticated box of index cards you can use to keep a list of names, birthdays, and phone numbers, or even a price catalog. If you keep your phone messages in a Notepad file, you can copy names and phone numbers from that file and paste them onto cards in Cardfile to create an electronic phone number file. Then, you can print your cards on perforated card stock and create a traditional card file system. You can embed or link graphics from Paintbrush or data from any OLE source application on a card. Embedded or linked graphics and text could be the basis for a product and price catalog, for example.

To start Cardfile, double-click on Cardfile's icon in the Accessories group window in the Program Manager. The Cardfile application window, shown in Figure 14-29 on the following page, will open a new, untitled file.

CARDFILE

Figure 14-29

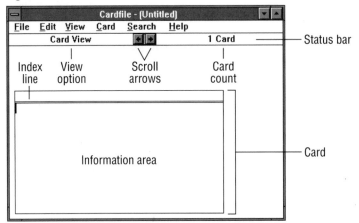

When you first open Cardfile, the application window displays a new file containing one empty card.

Cardfile's workspace displays an empty card with two places to enter information. The index line holds the word or phrase that Cardfile uses when it sorts your cards, while the information area stores all the details. You can have more than one card in the workspace, but the active card (the one you are working with) will always be in front of the others. You can maximize the Cardfile application window to display more cards in a series, or stack. The index lines are always visible in the stack of cards so that you can choose the card you want to work on.

The status bar above the workspace has three display areas: scroll arrows, the card count, and the view option. You can use the scroll arrows in the status bar to move through the stack of cards one at a time. The card count tells you how many cards are in your stack. The view option can be either card view or list view. Card view is the default setting and displays a card or stack of cards. List view displays only the index line of each card. Either the Card or the List command will be checked on your View menu to indicate the view setting.

Although you can change the size of the Cardfile window, you can't change the size of a card. Cardfile shows as much of the active card as possible within the window's size.

To exit Cardfile, choose the Exit command on the File menu. This command returns you to the Program Manager.

Cardfile uses accelerator keys, just as Notepad and Calendar do. Table 14-2 summarizes Cardfile's accelerator keys; this table can serve as a handy reference as you use this application.

Table 14-2

Keystroke	Function
[F3]	Repeat search
[F4]	Access specific card
[F5]	Set up autodial
[F6]	Add text to index line
[F7]	Add a new card

These are Cardfile's accelerator keys.

Listing the index lines

When you select the List command from Cardfile's View menu, the status bar and the workspace change. As you can see in Figure 14-30, the view option indicates list view instead of card view. The workspace displays only the index lines, in alphabetical order or in numeric order if your index lines begin with numbers. (If you have more than nine cards whose index lines begin with numbers, you should use leading zeros with the numbers 1-9 if you want to have the cards listed in correct numeric order. Because Cardfile left-aligns all index lines and sorts on the first character, you'll see a listing of 1, 10, 11, 2, for example, if leading zeros are not used.)

Figure 14-30

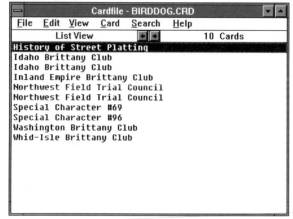

The status bar and the workspace change when you select the List command on the View menu.

If you double-click on an index line or choose the Index command from the Edit menu, the Index dialog box, shown in Figure 14-31, appears. You can then change the index line in the text box.

Figure 14-31

The Index dialog box lets you change the index line.

Adding information to a card

You can add text to two parts of a card: the index line and the information area. By default, the index line and the information area are blank. When you start a new file or open Cardfile for the first time, a blank card appears in the workspace.

To add text to the index line, choose the Index command from the Edit menu and enter the text in the Index Line text box. The index line can contain only a limited number of characters; Cardfile will warn you when you have reached the limit. Because Cardfile uses the index line to sort the cards, you should be sure to put the most important word first on the index line. Then click on OK to place the text on the card's index line.

To add text to the body, or information area, of the card, simply begin typing. Cardfile automatically wraps lines of text to fit the card, so you don't have to press [Enter] at the end of each line. To end a line early, press [Enter]. You can also use spaces or tabs to format your text. Cardfile uses an eight-space tab, which you cannot change. You'll find that it's easier to use tabs to align text than to use spaces.

Adding a card

When you add a new card with the Add command on the Card menu, Cardfile gives you a shortcut for adding text to the index line. Instead of requiring you to issue the Index command before entering the text, Cardfile immediately presents the Add dialog box, shown in Figure 14-32, so that you can enter the index line in one step. After you click on OK, Cardfile adds the card with the specified index line to the front of the stack. Now the cursor is in the information area of the new card so that you can enter the card's text.

Figure 14-32

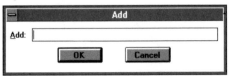

The Add dialog box prompts you to supply the text for a card's index line.

When you edit text in a card's information area, you can use the same editing commands you use in Notepad and in Calendar. You can delete characters and tabs with the [Delete] or [Backspace] key. When you want to work with more than one character, you can cut or copy text and then repeatedly paste it on any card or in any Windows application. Simply highlight the text you want to cut or copy, issue the Cut or Copy command, click on the spot where you want that text to appear, and then issue the Paste command from the Edit menu. By using the text box in the Index dialog box and the keyboard shortcuts for the Cut, Copy, and Paste commands, you can even cut text from the information area of a card and paste it into the index line of another card, and vice versa.

Editing a card

To edit the index line of a card, click on the card you want to edit and then either double-click on the index line or issue the Index command from the Edit menu. When the Index dialog box appears, the characters in the Index Line text box will be highlighted so that you can type new text or edit the existing text.

Editing the index line

From time to time, you might want to find a specific piece of text in the information area of one or more cards. For example, suppose you have a file or stack of cards that contains the names of business contacts, including several contacts at one company. If that company changes its phone number, you need to find all the cards for that company and change the number. The Find command on the Search menu lets you find text on cards in a file.

Finding text on a card

When you choose this command, the Find dialog box is displayed. In the Find dialog box, type the text you want to locate. Click on the Find Next button to find the first occurrence of the text on the card nearest the front of the stack. Cardfile ignores capitalization (unless you select the Match Case check box) and doesn't distinguish between whole words and parts of words. When you are ready to repeat the search for the same text, click on the Find Next button again. If you have closed the Find dialog box, you can choose the Find Next command from the Search menu or press [F3] to repeat the last search. If the text doesn't occur again on the front card, Cardfile jumps to the next card that contains the text. Cardfile lets you know if the text does not appear on any card. When you've finished searching, click on Cancel to close the Find dialog box.

One of the editing commands unique to Cardfile is the Restore command, a more powerful version of the Undo command. While a card is active and at the front of the stack, you have the option of using the Restore command. If you don't like any of the changes you've made to a card since you made it active, you could restore it to the condition it was in when you first brought it to the front of the stack. Once you make another card active, you can't use the Restore command to undo editing changes to the previous card.

Restoring a card

Deleting a card

If a card is no longer useful, you can delete it by moving it to the front of the stack and then choosing Delete from the Card menu. When you choose the Delete command, a message dialog box appears, asking you to verify the deletion. If you delete the wrong card, the only way you can retrieve it is to close the file without saving the changes and then reopen it. This means that all your changes from that work session are gone, too. (This method works only if you have previously saved the file.)

Adding graphics to a card

Once you've mastered the basics of Cardfile, you can move on to one of its more advanced features: adding graphics. The only limitation is that the graphic must be Clipboard-compatible or from an OLE source application so that it can be pasted onto your card. All of Windows' applications are compatible with Clipboard, and Paintbrush, Microsoft Excel version 3.0, and Microsoft Word for Windows version 2.0 are OLE source applications.

The easiest way to insert a graphic is to generate and save it in Paintbrush, select it with Paintbrush's Pick or Scissors tool, and then use the Paintbrush Edit menu to copy it to Clipboard. For example, you could create the graphic of a logo in Paintbrush, copy the image to Clipboard, and then paste it onto a card. Remember that as long as the information in Clipboard comes from an OLE source application, Windows embeds or links the information into an OLE receiving application when you use the Paste or the Paste Link command.

Before you can paste the graphic onto the card, you need to tell Cardfile that you want to use graphics with the active card. To do this, select the Picture command on the Edit menu. Now you can paste the graphic onto the card with the Paste command. Figure 14-33 shows a card after we pasted the graphic. You can move the graphic around by dragging it with the mouse or by using the direction keys on the keyboard.

Figure 14-33

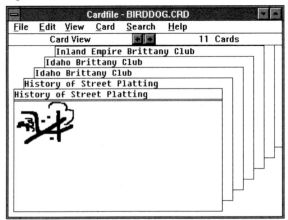

We pasted a graphic onto the active card.

The graphic you paste onto a card can be larger than the dimensions of the card. However, when you print the card, only the displayed part of the graphic will be printed. Although you can have only one graphic per card, you can overcome this limitation by selecting two graphics at once in Paintbrush and copying them both to Clipboard with the same Copy command. Both graphics can then be pasted onto a card with Cardfile's Paste command.

If the graphic you insert on a card was received from an OLE source application, such as Paintbrush or Microsoft Excel, you can edit the graphic on the card. To edit a Paintbrush OLE graphic, you can either double-click on the graphic or select the graphic and then choose the Edit Paintbrush Picture Object command from the Edit menu (for an embedded object) or the Link command from the Edit menu (for a linked object). When you choose the Edit Paintbrush Picture Object command, Windows starts Paintbrush and displays the embedded graphic in the Paintbrush window, where you can edit or modify it. When you have finished editing the graphic, choose the Update command on the File menu if you want to leave Paintbrush open and simply switch back to Cardfile. This command sends changes made in Paintbrush to Cardfile. If you want to close Paintbrush, choose the Exit & Return To command from the File menu. If you have made changes to the graphic, Paintbrush then displays a message dialog box asking if you want to update the embedded object. Choose Yes to send the changes to Cardfile, choose No to close Paintbrush without sending changes to Cardfile, or choose Cancel to abort closing Paintbrush.

Editing graphics on a card

When you want to edit a linked graphic from Paintbrush, select the graphic and use the Link command on the Edit menu instead of the Edit Paintbrush Picture Object command. In the Link dialog box, shown in Figure 14-34 on the following page, you see the name of the linked object (Paintbrush Picture) and the name of the file (MIRO.BMP, in this case) that contains the graphic. The Update section provides radio buttons for automatic and manual updating. If you select Automatic, the graphic will change in Cardfile every time the graphic changes in Paintbrush. If you select Manual, the graphic will change in Cardfile only when you click on the Update Now button in this dialog box. The Cancel Link button breaks the link to the Paintbrush file that stores the graphic. When you click on this button, the graphic becomes a picture and can no longer be edited from Cardfile.

To begin editing the linked graphic, click on the Edit button in the Link dialog box. When you click on Edit, Windows starts Paintbrush, and the graphic appears in the Paintbrush window. Now you can edit the graphic using any of Paintbrush's tools. To save changes to the linked graphic, choose the Save or the Save As command from the File menu in Paintbrush. To return to Cardfile, choose the Exit command from the File menu or simply switch to Cardfile by using the Task Manager or by clicking on the Cardfile window.

Figure 14-34

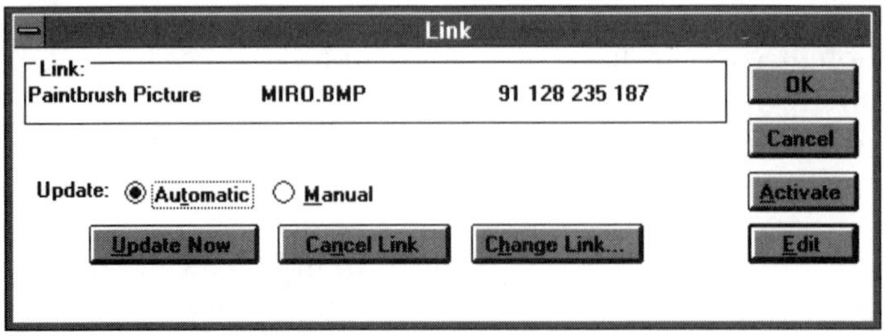

┌───┐
│ —   Link   │
│ ┌─ Link: ──────────────────────────────────┐ ┌────────┐ │
│ │ Paintbrush Picture   MIRO.BMP   91 128 235 187 │ │   OK   │ │
│   └────────┘ │
│   ┌────────┐ │
│   │ Cancel │ │
│   └────────┘ │
│ Update: ◉ Automatic ○ Manual   ┌────────┐ │
│   ┌──────────┐ ┌───────────┐ ┌───────────┐ │Activate│ │
│   │Update Now│ │Cancel Link│ │Change Link│ └────────┘ │
│   └──────────┘ └───────────┘ └───────────┘ ┌────────┐ │
│   │ Edit │ │
│   └────────┘ │
└───┘

The Link dialog box gives you a way to edit a linked graphic.

Mixing text and graphics

After you paste a graphic onto a card, you can add text to the card. Before you can add text, you need to choose the Text command on the Edit menu. As you type, you'll notice that Cardfile won't wrap the text around the graphic; instead, the text will overwrite the graphic. You'll need to use the [Enter], [Tab], and [Spacebar] keys to manually wrap the text around the graphic. After you've finished entering text, choose Picture from the Edit menu, click on the graphic, and use the mouse to position it. Figure 14-35 shows a finished card with both text and a graphic.

Figure 14-35

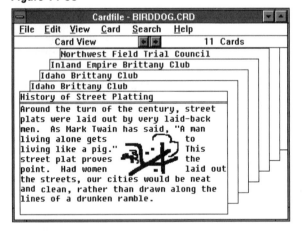

You can put both text and a graphic on the same card.

Duplicating a card

If you find that you are using the same basic card information over and over, you can save some time by duplicating the card. To do this, activate the card to bring it to the front of the stack, and then select the Duplicate command from the Card menu. Cardfile will insert a duplicate, which will become the active card, at the front of the stack. The Duplicate command will copy everything on the card, including linked or embedded objects and the index line. You'll usually want to edit the index line after creating a duplicate card.

The easiest way to move between cards in the workspace is to click on the card's index line, causing Cardfile to move that card to the front of the stack. Another way is to use the scroll arrows on the status bar. The left arrow brings the last card in the stack to the front. The right arrow brings the first card under the active card to the front. If you continue selecting a scroll arrow, you will eventually return to the top of the card stack. From the keyboard, press [Ctrl][Page Down] to move to the next card in the stack. Press [Ctrl][Page Up] to move to the last card in the stack.

You can also use the list view to move to a card. After you display the list of cards with the List command, click on an index line and then switch back to card view. The list view method of selecting the active card is especially useful with large stacks. You also can use a shortcut to move to a card: Simply press [Ctrl]n, where n is the first letter of the index line. If two or more index lines start with the same character, continue pressing [Ctrl]n until you reach the card you want. If the first character on the index line is a number, you'll need to press the number key for the first number of the index line.

If your stack of cards grows so large that you can't see all the index lines in the window, you can use the Go To command on the Search menu to help you find the card you want to see. The Go To command ignores the current front card and always brings another card to the front of a stack (unless Cardfile can't find the specified card).

To bring a card to the front, choose Go To from the Search menu or press [F4]. In the Go To dialog box, type any distinguishing text from the card's index line. (Go To ignores capitalization.) Click on OK to bring the card to the front. For example, if a card's index line contains the word *Sailing*, you could type *Sail*, *Ailing*, or *sai*, and the Go To command will find the card with *Sailing* in its index line, providing no other card has a similar combination of letters in its index line. If more than one card contains the text in its index line, Cardfile moves to the front the first card it finds (searching from the front). You can continue using the same search text to search through the remaining cards in the stack. Cardfile lets you know if no index line contains the specified text.

Cardfile offers a perk for frequent phone users: You can have your computer dial the phone for you. You need a modem that shares the phone line with your phone set. First, highlight a phone number on one of the cards in your card file. Next, select Autodial from the Card menu. In the Autodial dialog box, shown in Figure 14-36 on the following page, Cardfile inserts the phone number you selected. If you did not select a phone number, Cardfile selects the first number it finds on the card, starting with the index line. You can edit the number in the Number text box if you need to. Select the Use Prefix check box if your phone system uses a prefix, and then click on OK. The computer will dial the phone through your modem.

Moving between cards

Dialing a phone number from a card

Figure 14-36

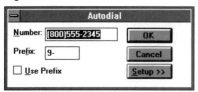

You can use the Autodial dialog box to have the computer dial the phone through a modem.

If you haven't configured your modem port from Control Panel, you can set it up from the Autodial dialog box. Click on the Setup button to expand the Autodial dialog box. The expanded dialog box, shown in Figure 14-37, has settings for the type of dialing, the port, and the baud rate. The most common settings are tone dialing using COM1 at 1200 baud. If you have a rotary dial phone, you have a pulse telephone line and need to use pulse dialing. The port and the baud rate depend on your computer hardware and modem hardware. (Check your modem manual for the baud rate.) Click on OK when you're ready to have Cardfile dial the phone.

Figure 14-37

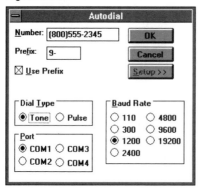

The expanded Autodial dialog box lets you establish settings for the type of dialing, the port, and the baud rate.

Merging files

If you inherit a phone number list from someone who also uses Cardfile, you can merge the cards from both files into one stack without copying each new card. To merge two files, open one of the files and choose the Merge command from the File menu. The File Merge dialog box, shown in Figure 14-38, lists all available Cardfile files. You can double-click on a file from the File Name list box to choose it and issue the Merge command. To look in other drives or directories for a file, you can use the Directories or the Drives list box.

After you select a file, Cardfile adds all the cards from the selected file to the file in memory. It automatically reindexes the stack to put the new cards in alphabetical order. Now you can save the merged stack under a new file name. This way, neither of the original files will be changed.

Figure 14-38

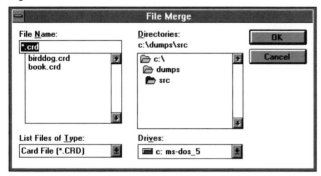

The File Merge dialog box displays available Cardfile files.

Saving and printing with Cardfile

Before you print your cards or exit Cardfile, you should always save your work. You can save your stack of cards by choosing the Save or the Save As command from the File menu, as you did with Notepad and Calendar.

Printing the cards in your stack is similar to printing a Notepad file or a Calendar appointment page. You'll need to define the page setup and the printer setup before you print, as you did in Notepad and Calendar.

When you are using card view, Cardfile offers two printing commands. The Print command prints the front, or active, card of your stack. The Print All command prints the entire stack, with several cards per page. Cardfile prints the card as you see it on your monitor, as shown in Figure 14-39, with an index line and a frame around the card. When list view is active, only the Print All command, which prints the entire list, is available.

As an alternative, you can print a file by dragging the file icon from the File Manager to the minimized Print Manager icon on the desktop.

Figure 14-39

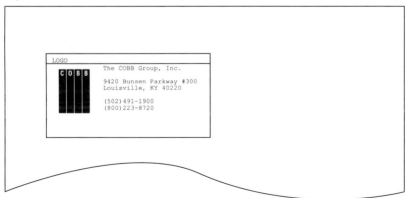

Cardfile prints a card exactly as you see it on the monitor.

CALCULATOR

Windows' Calculator is another desktop accessory that can interact with your other applications. You can't print from Calculator, but you can paste any number you generate with Calculator into another application. In this section, we'll show you how to use the standard and scientific modes of Calculator. We'll explain the functions, calculator buttons, and keyboard equivalents.

To open Calculator, you simply double-click on the Calculator icon in the Accessories group window. A Calculator window like the one shown in Figure 14-40 will appear. The Calculator window cannot be sized; it can only be minimized. Calculator initially appears in its standard mode.

Figure 14-40

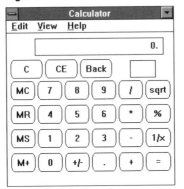

*The standard mode is the default
view when you first start Calculator.*

The two Calculator modes—standard and scientific— use the same title bar, menu bar, and number display in the Calculator window. In both modes, the keys are color-coded and grouped according to their functions, although the specific functions and related buttons differ in the two modes. Buttons framed in blue are numbers or letters that enter information into the display; buttons framed in red are mathematical or logical operators; buttons framed in pink are memory functions; and buttons framed in green are advanced mathematical functions. The display areas are black-framed boxes.

You can select the mode you want with the View menu. The Standard command displays the standard mode calculator, and the Scientific command displays the scientific mode calculator. A check mark will appear next to the selected command. Calculator will always open in the mode in which you last closed it.

The easiest way to work with Calculator is to use your keyboard's numeric keypad to enter numbers and then use your mouse to click on function keys. In order to use the numeric keypad, you must have [Num Lock] turned on.

To exit Calculator, you must close the window. There is no Exit command. Calculator doesn't need an Exit command since you don't use data files that have to be saved.

The standard mode of Calculator performs basic mathematical functions for quick calculations. For instance, you can use it when you want to determine a discount for a customer or balance your checkbook.

Standard mode

To start a calculation, enter a number by either clicking on a key or typing on the numeric keypad. For example, if you want to offer a 15% discount on a customer purchase of $495, you need to calculate a new price that is 85% of the original price. To do this, type *495*, click on * for multiplication, type *.85*, and then either click on = or press the [Enter] key on the numeric keypad. The display will then change to 420.75, which is the discounted price.

Starting a calculation

Table 14-3 lists the calculator button and its keyboard equivalent for each function in the standard mode. You can use either a period or a comma for the decimal point, depending on which format you chose in the International dialog box from Control Panel (explained in Chapter 3).

Table 14-3

Button	Keystroke	Function
+	+	Add
-	-	Subtract
*	*	Multiply
/	/	Divide
+/-	[F9]	Apply positive or negative sign
.	. or ,	Insert decimal point
%	%	Calculate percentage
=	= or [Enter]	Calculate (Equals)
1/x	R	Calculate reciprocal
Back	[Backspace] or ←	Delete last number entered
C	[Esc]	Clear current calculation
CE	[Delete]	Clear last function or displayed number
M+	[Ctrl]P	Add displayed number to value in memory
MC	[Ctrl]L	Clear memory
MR	[Ctrl]R	Recall value from memory without removing it from memory
MS	[Ctrl]M	Store displayed value in memory
sqrt	@	Take square root of displayed number

This table lists the calculator button and the keyboard equivalent for each function in Calculator's standard mode.

If you make a mistake in a calculation, you can erase just the current entry, or you can clear the entire calculation and start over. To clear only the current entry, click on the CE button. If you want to clear the entire calculation, click on the C button. If you are using the keyboard instead of a mouse, use [Delete] for CE and [Esc] for C.

Using memory functions

Calculator's memory buttons (the pink ones) let you store one number in memory. When you put a number in memory, an M will appear in the display box just under the number display, as shown in Figure 14-41. To put a number in memory, type or click on the number in the display, and then click on the MS button to store it. (All the keyboard equivalents for the memory buttons are listed in Table 14-3 on page 393.) If you want to store a number that is a result of a calculation, complete your calculation and, when the result is displayed, click on the MS button. Suppose you want to redisplay the number you stored. All you have to do is click on the MR button to recall the number from memory at any time. You can use this technique to reuse a number during a calculation. Instead of re-entering the number, just click on MR when you would normally enter the number in your calculation.

Figure 14-41

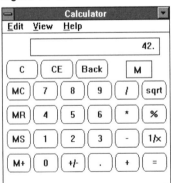

Calculator displays an M if a number is in memory.

Keeping a running total is easy when you use the M+ button. If you click on M+, the number in the display will be added to the value in memory. If you click on M+ each time you enter a number, the value in memory will be the sum of the numbers.

If you don't want the number to remain in memory, you can clear it with the MC button. After you clear the memory, notice that the M in the display box disappears. Once the value is gone, the M will be gone, too.

Using Clipboard with Calculator

You can copy a displayed number to Clipboard for use in another application. Just select Copy from the Edit menu when the number you want is in the Calculator display. For example, if you are keeping customer history cards with

Cardfile and need to record each customer's discounted purchases, you can copy and paste the purchase records to the customers' cards in Cardfile after you calculate the discounts.

You can also paste a number or an equation from another application into Calculator's display. First copy the number from the application to Clipboard. Then select Paste from Calculator's Edit menu, and Clipboard will enter the number into the Calculator display.

Calculator also accepts letters from Clipboard, which are interpreted as command shortcuts. For example, receiving the text *84:m* from Clipboard tells Calculator to store the value 84 in memory because typing *:m* is the equivalent of using [Ctrl]M. Table 14-4 lists these letter shortcuts and their related commands.

Table 14-4

Character	Command
:c	Clear memory. [Ctrl]L
:e	In decimal mode, specifies scientific notation; you can use plus and minus signs after the *e* for the exponent. In hexadecimal mode, specifies the number E.
:m	Store displayed number in memory. [Ctrl]M
:p	Add displayed number to value in memory. [Ctrl]P
:q	Clear current calculation. [Esc]
:r	Display value that is in memory without removing it from memory. [Ctrl]R
: (colon)	If used with letters, interpreted as [Ctrl] key. If the colon precedes a letter, then the colon and the letter form a control-key sequence. (For example, :P means [Ctrl]P.)
	If used with numbers, interpreted as a function key. (For example, :8 means [F8].)
\ (backslash)	Represents the Dat button [Insert].

In both standard mode and scientific mode, you can paste letters from Clipboard that Calculator will interpret as commands.

Scientific mode

To change from standard to scientific mode, select the Scientific command from the View menu. As you can see in Figure 14-42 on the following page, the Calculator window will expand to include new display areas and buttons. In scientific mode, you can still perform basic calculations, use memory functions, and work with Clipboard, just as you can in standard mode. But scientific mode provides many additional functions and lets you carry out more advanced mathematical operations.

Figure 14-42

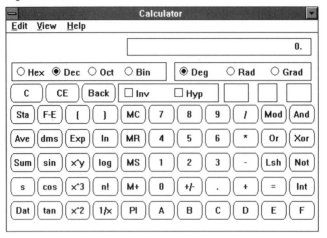

Calculator's scientific mode provides sophisticated settings and additional functions.

Let's examine Calculator in scientific mode. The title bar, menu bar, and number display do not change when you leave standard mode. Two number-system settings boxes appear below the number display. The second-level function settings (inverse and hyperbolic) are centered below the number-system section. The three status boxes to the right indicate whether statistics, memory, and parentheses options are active. Figure 14-43 shows the display boxes with sample settings.

Figure 14-43

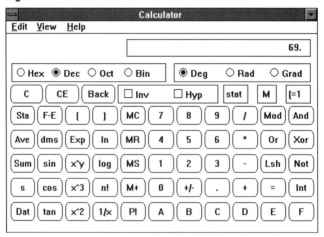

Calculator uses three status boxes to show the status of statistics, memory, and parentheses options.

When you first choose scientific mode, Calculator uses the decimal (base 10) number system as the default. The number-system settings area lets you choose to use the hexadecimal (base 16), decimal, octal (base 8), or binary (base 2) number system by selecting the Hex, Dec, Oct, or Bin radio button. Table 14-5 lists the various calculator buttons and their keyboard equivalents for the number-system functions.

Choosing a number system

Table 14-5

Button	Keystroke	Function
Bin	[F8]	Use binary number system
Dec	[F6]	Use decimal number system
Hex	[F5]	Use hexadecimal number system
Oct	[F7]	Use octal number system

This table lists the buttons, keyboard equivalents, and related number-system functions.

When you are using the default decimal system, the settings area on the right will provide choices between degree (Deg), radian (Rad), and gradient (Grad) for trigonometric calculations. When you use the hexadecimal, octal, or binary system, the radio buttons change so that you can choose Dword (full 32-bit version of the displayed number), Word (16-bit version), or Byte (8-bit version).

Calculator will convert the displayed number if you need to change number systems after you enter or calculate a number. Calculator rounds off the displayed number to an integer if you are converting from one number system to another.

Calculator also knows (and lets you know) if the number you typed fits into the selected number system. It will let you use the letter buttons to enter hexadecimal numbers, but it will not let you use them with any other number system. If you press the 9 key on your numeric keypad while you are using the binary system, Calculator won't accept the entry.

For example, if you want to convert a hexadecimal number to a binary number, you need to click on the Hex radio button to change the number system to hexadecimal. Then, for example, enter the value 300. Now click on the Bin radio button. Calculator will convert the number to binary 1100000000.

If you look on the far right side of the Calculator display, you'll see more red buttons in addition to the standard mathematical operators. These are the logical operators. The two black-framed parentheses buttons to the left of the

Using logical operators

memory buttons are also considered logical operators. You can use up to 25 nested parentheses. Table 14-6 lists the logical operator buttons, their keyboard equivalents, and their functions.

Table 14-6

Button	Keystroke	Function	Inverse Function (Inv + button) (i + key)
(	(	Start new level of calculation	None
)	)	Close level of calculation	None
And	&	Calculate bitwise AND	None
Int	;	Display numbers to the left of decimal point (integer)	Display numbers to the right of decimal point (fraction)
Lsh	<	Shift bit register left one bit	Shift bit register right one bit
Mod	%	Display modulus or remainder of x/y	None
Not	~	Calculate bitwise inverse	None
Or	¦	Calculate bitwise OR	None
Xor	∧	Calculate bitwise exclusive OR	None

The logical operators can be used with numbers or letters across number systems.

Applying statistics

Calculator has advanced statistics functions waiting inconspicuously under the Sta button. When you click on the Sta button, a Statistics Box, like the one shown in Figure 14-44, will appear. It has a large list display area, with four buttons and a population value (n=0) at the bottom. Calculator adds a scroll bar to the list display after you enter enough numbers. You can't use any of the statistics buttons in scientific mode without having the Statistics Box open. Table 14-7 summarizes the calculator buttons and keyboard equivalents for all the scientific mode statistics functions. You can move the Statistics Box to a corner of the desktop to make the rest of Calculator more accessible.

To begin a statistics calculation, you enter the numbers you are going to work with into the Statistics Box. For instance, if you were trying to find the

Figure 14-44

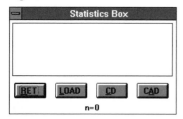

The Statistics Box is used with advanced statistics functions in Calculator's scientific mode.

Table 14-7

Button	Keystroke	Function	Inverse function (Inv + button) (i + key)
Ave	[Ctrl]A	Calculate mean or average	Calculate mean or average of squares
Dat	[Insert]	Enter displayed number into Statistics Box	None
s	[Ctrl]D	Calculate standard deviation, population=n-1	Calculate standard deviation, population=n
Sta	[Ctrl]S	Open Statistics Box	None
Sum	[Ctrl]T	Calculate sum or total	Calculate sum of squares

This table summarizes the calculator buttons and keyboard equivalents for the scientific mode statistics functions.

average of 28 test scores, you would enter all the students' scores into the Statistics Box. To enter a number, first click anywhere in Calculator's window to activate it. Next, type the number into Calculator's display with the numeric keypad, or click on the calculator keys and then click on the Dat button to enter the number into the list in the Statistics Box. After you've entered all the scores, you'll notice that the population value at the bottom of the Statistics Box has changed to match the number of scores you entered (n=28). Now, click on Ave to display the average or mean. You can then click on the s button to get the standard deviation based on the population value (n-1).

Sum is another statistical function you can use with the Statistics Box number list. After you've entered a list of numbers, click on Sum to display the total of all the numbers.

You can select the Inv (inverse) check box on the scientific mode Calculator with the statistics buttons to use variations of the statistics functions. If you select this check box and then click on the Ave button, Calculator will compute the mean using the squares of the values in the Statistics Box. If you use Inv with Sum, you will get the sum of the squares. Inv with the s button will find the standard deviation using a population of n instead of n-1. Calculator automatically toggles off the Inv check box after you click on a function button so that the rest of your calculations will work the way you planned.

The list of numbers in the Statistics Box appears in one column, with one number highlighted. Although you can click on another number to highlight it, Calculator won't let you select more than one number at a time. Click on the scroll arrows or use the arrow keys to move up and down the list.

Three of the four buttons at the bottom of the Statistics Box work with the numbers in the list. LOAD copies the highlighted number to Calculator's display, CD removes the highlighted number from the list, and CAD removes all the numbers from the list. The fourth button, RET, activates the Calculator window. You can simply click on the Calculator window to do the same thing. To return to the Statistics Box, you can click on it or click on the Sta button again. After you finish using the statistics functions, you can close the dialog box by double-clicking on the Control menu box in the Statistics Box or by choosing the Close command on the Control menu. When you reopen the Statistics Box, the display will be clear.

Other functions

The scientific mode has many more function buttons besides the statistical ones, including trigonometric functions and scientific notation. Table 14-8 lists some of the remaining scientific mode functions. Calculator's scientific mode also contains a number button for the value of pi, located below the column of memory function buttons.

If you are using the trigonometric functions, remember that a couple of check boxes will affect the sin, cos, and tan buttons and the number display. If you check Hyp, the hyperbolic of the function will be calculated. The group of three radio buttons on the right (Deg, Rad, and Grad) determine the unit of measurement (degrees, radians, or gradients). The dms button changes the number display to degree-minute-second format. All trigonometric functions must use the decimal number system.

When you use exponents or scientific notation, you must work within Calculator's limits. When you use the Exp button, for example, the exponent can be as large as 307. Numbers larger than 10^{15} are always displayed exponentially. Note that you can use exponents and scientific notation only with the decimal number system.

Table 14-8

Button	Keystroke	Function	Inverse function (Inv + button) (i + key)
sin	S	Calculate sine	Calculate arc sine
cos	O	Calculate cosine	Calculate arc cosine
tan	T	Calculate tangent	Calculate arc tangent
dms	M	Display number in degree-minute-second format	Display number in degrees
Exp	X	Enter exponent for scientific notation	None
F-E	V	Toggle scientific notation on or off	None
ln	N	Calculate natural logarithm (base e)	Calculate e raised to the xth (displayed number) power
log	L	Calculate common logarithm (base 10)	Calculate 10 raised to the xth (displayed number) power
n!	!	Calculate factorial	None
PI	P	Display pi	Display pi x 2
x^y	Y	Calculate x raised to the yth power	Calculate yth root of x
x^2	@	Calculate square	Calculate square root
x^3	#	Calculate cube	Calculate cube root
1/x	R	Calculate the reciprocal of the displayed number	None

Other scientific mode functions are listed here.

CLOCK

Windows' Clock application displays the time whether the application is open or minimized to an icon. Clock uses your computer's system time. If you change the system time with the Date/Time icon on Control Panel or with an MS-DOS command, Clock changes its displayed time, too.

To start Clock, activate the Accessories group window in the Program Manager and double-click on the Clock icon. Clock always displays the same clock face it had when you last closed it .

To exit Clock, close the Clock window by double-clicking on its Control menu box or by choosing Close from the Control menu.

Clock faces

Clock has two faces: analog and digital. Figure 14-45 shows both choices. Both faces use predefined system colors and aren't affected by the colors you set with Control Panel. The first time you use Clock, it has the analog face (with clock hands). To change the face, open the Settings menu, and choose Analog or Digital. The time and date formats on the digital face reflect the settings you chose in Control Panel.

Figure 14-45

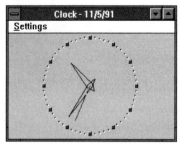 

Clock has an analog face and a digital face.

You can choose to hide the date or the seconds on either clock face by using the Date or the Seconds command on the Settings menu. The Date command controls the display of the date. When this command is toggled off, the date disappears from the title bar of the analog clock, and the digital clock displays only the time, as shown in Figure 14-46. When you choose the Date command again, the date returns to the digital clock face or to the title bar of the analog clock. When you minimize Clock, the date appears as part of the icon's title if the Date command is turned on. (Note that the digital clock face in Figure 14-46 displays "embossed" numbers, a style that is used when you maximize or enlarge the digital clock window to certain sizes.)

Figure 14-46

The date display is turned off on this digital clock face.

The Seconds command turns the display of seconds on and off. On the analog clock face, the second hand disappears; on the digital clock face, only the hours and minutes are displayed. To restore the seconds display, simply select the Seconds command again. A minimized Clock icon displays only the hour and minutes, even if the Seconds command is turned on.

When you choose the Set Font command on Clock's Settings menu, the Font dialog box shown in Figure 14-47 appears. In this dialog box, you can select one of several fonts for the digital time and date display. (The Set Font command is not available when you are using an analog clock face.) When you select a TrueType font, Windows displays a sample of the font in the Sample area of the dialog box. Choose the font that you want Clock to use to display the time and date on a digital clock face, and then click on OK.

Figure 14-47

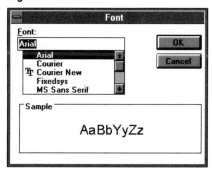

In Clock's Font dialog box, you can choose a font for the time and date display on a digital clock face.

To make the clock look more elegant and stylistically "cleaner," choose the No Title command on the Settings menu to display the clock without the title bar and the menu bar, as shown in Figure 14-48. The No Title command is a toggle command, but you can't open the Settings menu to toggle it off when the menu bar is hidden. To display the title bar and the menu bar again, double-click anywhere inside the clock face or press [Esc] to toggle the No Title command off.

Figure 14-48

A digital clock face without a title bar or menu bar.

Making Clock float

You can set up Clock so that it "floats" above all other open and active windows. Normally, Windows displays the active window on top of all other windows, with the active window covering up portions of any other windows that are displayed beneath it on the screen. But if you keep the Clock icon visible at all times, you can check the time at a glance without having to activate the Clock window and then reactive the window in which you're working.

To make the Clock window or the icon float, choose the Always on Top command from Clock's Control menu. Clock's window or icon will now float—that is, it will always be visible, no matter which window is active or how large you make a window—until you turn off the Always on Top command.

OBJECT PACKAGER

Object Packager is an OLE accessory that you can use to insert an icon into an OLE receiving application file. The icon can represent a data file (text or graphics) or a command that starts an application or a process. With Object Packager, you can create compact, compound documents. A compound document is one that contains different types of data—text, graphics, charts, and spreadsheet cells, for example. A document that imports this data by means of an Object Packager icon is compact because the icon usually takes much less space than the full-sized form of the data. Yet the data represented by the icon is readily available when you need it, in a window of its source application.

To start Object Packager, double-click on its icon in the Accessories group window of the Program Manager. The Object Packager application window, shown in Figure 14-49, will appear.

Figure 14-49

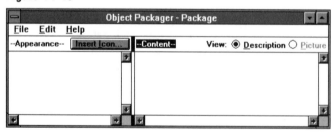

The Object Packager application window contains two document windows: Appearance and Content.

In the Object Packager window, you will see two document windows. The Appearance window displays the icon and the title associated with an Object Packager package. The Content window shows the name of the document that contains the object or a presentation of the object.

To exit Object Packager, choose the Exit command from the File menu.

Before you can place an Object Packager icon in a file, you must create a package. A package contains the icon, its contents, and the additional (but invisible) instructions needed to open the file and run the associated application.

Creating a package

To create a package, choose the Import command from the File menu to see the Import dialog box, shown in Figure 14-50. In the Import dialog box, type or select the name of the file you want to insert as an icon. For example, from your Windows directory, select the WIN.INI file. Then choose OK to create a package. If you have previously associated .INI files with Notepad, you will see an Object Packager window like the one shown in Figure 14-51.

Figure 14-50

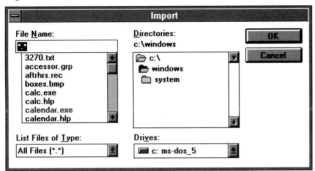

The Import dialog box shows you the files available for import—all files on all available disks.

Figure 14-51

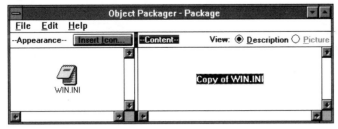

After you choose OK in the Import dialog box, you see the icon and its contents in Object Packager's windows.

If you haven't associated the selected file with any application, you will see a copy of the Object Packager icon in the Appearance window. The file must be associated with an application before you can see the associated application's icon. To associate a file type with an application, select a file (such as WIN.INI) in the File Manager. Choose the Associate command from the File Manager's File menu, and then type or select the name of the program. For WIN.INI, type or select *C:\WINDOWS\NOTEPAD.EXE*. Or use the Browse button to locate the program file.

Adding a package to another file

After you create a package, you are ready to insert the package and display its icon in another application's file. First choose the Copy Package command from Object Packager's Edit menu. Then start the receiving application and open the receiving file. Choose the Paste command from that application's Edit menu. When the icon appears, position it wherever you like.

As an example, start Cardfile by double-clicking on its icon in the Accessories group window of the Program Manager. Choose the Picture command from Cardfile's Edit menu to make the card ready to accept a picture. Then, choose the Paste command from Cardfile's Edit menu to insert the package. Your card will look something like the card shown in Figure 14-52, to which text has also been added.

Figure 14-52

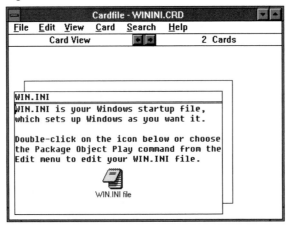

Pasting an Object Packager package onto a Cardfile card displays the icon and its title.

Running a package

After you insert a package into a file, you can view the contents or start the action associated with the package's icon. To run (or "play") the icon, double-click on the icon or choose the Package Object Play command from the Edit menu. (When you choose the Package Object command from the Edit menu, a cascaded menu appears, containing two associated commands. Choose the Play command from this cascaded menu.) For example, to play the WIN.INI icon in Cardfile, be sure that the Picture command from the Edit menu is turned on. Then double-click on the icon or choose the Package Object Play command from the Edit menu. You will see a window that resembles the one shown in Figure 14-53.

Figure 14-53

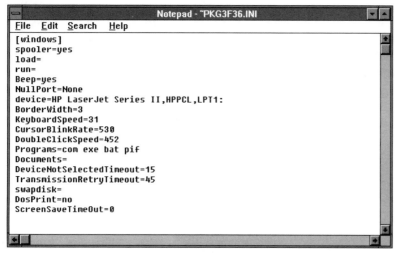

Double-clicking on the WIN.INI Object Packager icon displays the contents of WIN.INI in a Notepad window.

If you edit the linked or embedded object, be sure to use the Save As command on the source application's File menu to save the changes. Windows will ask whether you want to overwrite the existing file; choose Yes to save the changes. You can use the same setup to make editing other system files handier. For example, you could also set up a card for your AUTOEXEC.BAT file or your CONFIG.SYS file.

You can change any icon you see in Object Packager's Appearance window to any other available icon without affecting the actions of the package. To change the icon, click on the Insert Icon button at the top of the Appearance window. You'll see the Insert Icon dialog box shown in Figure 14-54.

Changing a package's icon and title

Figure 14-54

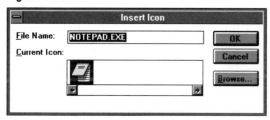

Use the Insert Icon dialog box to change the icon used by a package.

To change the icon, select a different icon from the Current Icon horizontal scroll list. If you want to use an icon that is not in the scroll list, type the full path name and file name of the application that provides the icon. For example, you could type *C:\WINDOWS\NOTEPAD.EXE.* An easier approach is to choose the Browse button and select the program name that supplies the icon you want.

Most programs supply only one icon. If you want a choice of several icons, select the PROGMAN.EXE file (for the Program Manager) or the MORICONS.DLL file, both of which supply a number of icons. After you select an icon, choose OK to see the new icon in the Appearance window.

When you use the Import command to create a package, the icon's title is the name of the imported file. In the example we used earlier, the title was *WIN.INI.* You may have noticed, however, that in Figure 14-52 the title of the icon appeared as *WIN.INI file.* To change the title of a package's icon, choose the Label command from the Edit menu. You'll see the Label dialog box, shown in Figure 14-55.

Figure 14-55

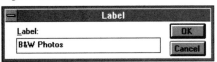

You use the Label dialog box to change the title of a package's icon.

In the Label text box, you can edit the current title, type an entirely new title, or delete the text altogether (to omit the title). Then choose OK to see the new title displayed below the icon. In Figure 14-56, you see a Paintbrush icon for a Paintbrush bit map file. The title was changed from *COLORVRT.BMP* to *B&W Photos.*

Figure 14-56

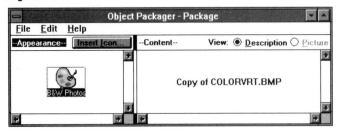

This package's icon title was changed from the file name to a descriptive title.

Creating a command package

Besides containing a data file, an Object Packager package can contain an MS-DOS command line (the same as a Run command line from the File menu of the Program Manager or the File Manager). When you double-click on the icon for a command package, Windows will run the command line. This type of package lets you create a file containing the icons for DOS-based programs so that they are readily accessible.

You can start a new package by choosing the New command from Object Packager's File menu. The Object Packager window becomes blank. Now issue the Command Line command from the Edit menu to see the dialog box shown in Figure 14-57.

Figure 14-57

In the Command Line dialog box, type the command line you want the package to run.

In the Command text box, type an MS-DOS command line. Figure 14-57 shows the command line *c:\dos\qbasic.exe c:\dos\gorilla.bas*. This command line starts the Microsoft QBasic interpreter, which comes with MS-DOS version 5, and loads the QBasic program file GORILLA.BAS. After you type the command line and choose OK, the command line appears in Object Packager's Content window. To complete the package, insert an icon by using the Insert Icon button. Using the Label command on the Edit menu, create a title, such as *Gorilla Game*, for the icon. Then copy the package with the Copy Package command on the Edit menu, move to another application (such as Cardfile), and choose the Paste command from the application's Edit menu. Remember that Cardfile must be in Picture mode (choose Picture from the Edit menu) before you can insert a package. The result appears in Figure 14-58.

Figure 14-58

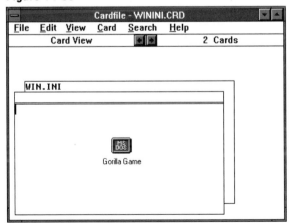

A command package icon, such as the one shown here, looks very similar to a data package icon.

MEDIA PLAYER

Media Player lets you control various kinds of media files and hardware. With this new application, you can play animation, sound, and MIDI sequencer files, and you can also control CD-ROM drives and videodisc players. Media Player is also an OLE source application; you can link or embed a MIDI sequencer file in an OLE receiving application such as Write.

When you use Media Player, you simply specify a media device, open an appropriate media file (if necessary), and then play the device. To start Media Player, double-click on its icon in the Accessories group window of the Program Manager. The Media Player window, shown in Figure 14-59, will appear.

Figure 14-59

The Media Player window provides controls for playing multimedia devices.

You can use either the mouse or the keyboard to work in the Media Player window. Table 14-9 lists the keys you'll probably find most useful.

Table 14-9

Keystroke	Function
[Tab]	Move from button to button (left to right)
[Shift][Tab]	Move from button to button (right to left)
[Spacebar]	Select a button
←	Move the playing position back when the scroll bar is selected
→	Move the playing position forward when the scroll bar is selected

You can use these keys in the Media Player window.

To quit Media Player, choose the Exit command from the File menu. Quitting Media Player ends playback of animation, MIDI sequencer files, and waveform audio. Audio compact discs and videodiscs will continue playback after you close Media Player.

Media Player supports two types of devices: simple and compound. The Device menu displays the names of the Media Control Interface (MCI) devices you installed using the Drivers icon on Control Panel. (Refer to the description of the Drivers icon in Chapter 3 for details about installing devices.)

Specifying a media device

To specify a simple device, choose the device name from the Device menu. To specify a compound device, you also choose the device name from the Device menu; names of compound devices are followed by an ellipsis. For compound devices, Media Player will then display the Open Media File dialog box. Select or type the name of the file you want to open, and then click on OK. The file name will appear in the title bar of the Media Player window, along with the playing status. The device and the file are now ready to play.

For simple devices (such as an audio compact-disc player), you don't need to specify a media file because the device will play whatever programming is loaded in the device. Compound devices (such as a sound card or a synthesizer that plays waveform audio) require you to specify a media file. You can use the Open command on Media Player's File menu to open other files for the same compound device. If you want to open a file for a different device, you must first select the device from the Device menu.

After specifying a media device and opening a file, you can use the buttons in the Media Player window, shown in Figure 14-60, to control the device.

Playing a media device

Figure 14-60

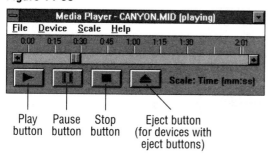

During play, the title bar indicates that the device is playing, and the slider moves along the scroll bar.

Play button   Pause button   Stop button   Eject button (for devices with eject buttons)

When you start playback, the title bar displays the word *(playing)* following the file name. For other actions, other appropriate terms will appear in the title bar: *(paused)* after you click on the Pause button, and *(stopped)* after you click on the Stop button. The scale above the scroll bar displays playing progress, showing either the track that is playing (for a multiple-track device) or the elapsed and total playing time. The Scale label beside the Eject button shows the currently selected scale. The track display is particularly useful for playing devices that use different tracks, such as audio compact-disc players.

You can change the playing position by clicking on the scroll arrows or the scroll bar or by dragging the slider to the time or track position you want. Click on the Play button to begin playback. For single-track devices and files, changing the playing position jumps forward or backward in the file you are playing. For multiple-track devices, changing the playing position on the tracks scale selects a different track.

Opening a different file

If you have already specified a compound device, you can open and play files appropriate for that device. For example, if you've specified a MIDI sequencer device, you can open and play MIDI files. But if you've specified a MIDI sequencer device and you now want to open a waveform file, you must first go back to the Device menu and select an audio device. If a simple device is open, the Open command on the File menu is not available.

To open a different file to play, be sure that you have selected the right device for that file, and then choose Open from the File menu. Select or type the name of the file you want to play, and then click on OK. Windows 3.1 includes four sound files in WAVE format (CHIMES.WAV, CHORD.WAV, DING.WAV, and TADA.WAV) and two sample MIDI files (CANYON.MID and PASSPORT.MID) in your Windows directory.

Changing the scale

You can change the scale display that appears above the scroll bar. The two scale options are Time and Tracks. The Time scale, which is shown in Figure 14-61, shows the total playing time of the file and displays time increment marks along the scroll bar. The time measurement appears next to the Scale label below the scroll bar.

Figure 14-61

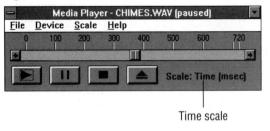

The Time scale shows the total playing time of the file and a scale for elapsed playing time.

Time scale

The Tracks scale, shown in Figure 14-62, displays the total number of tracks in the file or on the device and a mark for each track so that you can select the track you want to play. To change scales, choose the scale name (Time or Tracks) from the Scale menu. Choose the Time scale when you want to move within a track or when the device provides only one track. Choose the Tracks scale when you want to select a track to play.

Figure 14-62

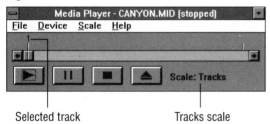

The Tracks scale shows the total number of tracks and which track you selected.

Selected track   Tracks scale

SOUND RECORDER

As we explained in Chapter 3, you can use the Sound icon on Control Panel to assign sounds to various Windows events. Windows 3.1 provides some built-in sound files, but, with Sound Recorder, you can also personalize this feature by recording your own sound files and using them with Control Panel's Sound icon. For example, you could record part of your favorite musical theme and have it play whenever you start Windows.

In addition, increasing numbers of Windows applications now allow you to use sound to create a friendlier and more interesting working environment. You can add voice annotation to include reminders and tips, or you can use music or other sounds to alert you to computer events and potential problems or simply to spice up your everyday work routine. In some applications, you can even embed a recorded sound file and use it to send a message to a colleague who receives or shares the application's file.

Like Media Player, Sound Recorder is an OLE source application. You can link or embed a WAVE sound file in an OLE receiving application such as Write.

Sound Recorder lets you play, record, and edit sound stored in the WAVE file format. Besides opening, playing, creating, recording, and saving a sound file, you can edit a sound by making it softer or louder, slowing it down or speeding it up, adding an echo, reversing the sound, deleting part of the sound, inserting another sound, and mixing in another sound.

To start Sound Recorder, double-click on its icon in the Accessories group window of the Program Manager. The Sound Recorder window, shown in Figure 14-63, will appear.

Figure 14-63

The Sound Recorder window provides controls for playing, recording, and editing WAVE sound files.

When you are working with the Sound Recorder window, you can use either the mouse or the keyboard. Table 14-10 provides a description of the most commonly used keys.

Table 14-10

Keystroke	Function
[Tab]	Move from button to button (left to right)
[Shift][Tab]	Move from button to button (right to left)
[Spacebar]	Select a button
[Page Up]	Move back 1 second when the scroll bar is selected
[Page Down]	Move forward 1 second when the scroll bar is selected
[Home]	Move to the beginning of the sound when the scroll bar is selected
[End]	Move to the end of the sound when the scroll bar is selected

To quit Sound Recorder, choose the Exit command from the File menu.

Playing a sound file

You must open sound files before you can play or edit them. To open a sound file, choose the Open command from Sound Recorder's File menu. In the Open dialog box, type or select the name of the sound file, which will have a .WAV file name extension, and then click on OK. If you have another sound file open for which you haven't saved your changes, Sound Recorder will ask whether you want to save the changes before it opens the file you've just selected. Windows opens the sound file in the Sound Recorder window and displays the name of the file in the window's title bar, as shown in Figure 14-64.

Figure 14-64

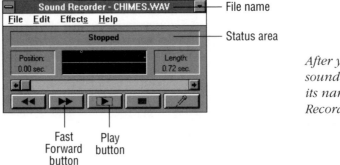

File name

Status area

After you open a sound file, you see its name in Sound Recorder's title bar.

Fast Forward button

Play button

After you open a sound file, the Play and Fast Forward buttons become active. The status area below the menu bar displays the current action of Sound Recorder. The window also displays the current play position of the sound in seconds (from the beginning of the sound) as well as the total length of the sound in seconds. The scroll bar shows you visually the percentage of the sound that has been played or recorded. You can now play or edit the sound.

To start playing a sound, click on the Play button. When a file is playing, the wave box graphically displays a representation of the sound as if it were being shown on an oscilloscope, as you can see in Figure 14-65.

Figure 14-65

Wave box

The wave box shows the "shape" of the sound as it plays.

Rewind button

Stop button

Record button

The status area tells you that the file is playing. The slider in the scroll bar moves to the right to show the progress of play, and the Position display shows the number of seconds that have elapsed. The Stop button becomes active. After the sound finishes, the Rewind button becomes active. You can "rewind" the sound by clicking on this button. If you click on the Play button with the slider at the right end of the scroll bar, Sound Recorder rewinds and then plays the sound again.

To play the sound from a position other than its beginning, click on the scroll arrows or the scroll bar or drag the slider along the scroll bar to the starting position you want, and then click on the Play button.

To stop playing, click on the Stop button. To resume playing, click on the Play button again. Sound Recorder will begin to play the sound from the stop position to the end.

To create a new sound file, choose New from the File menu. If you have another sound file open, Sound Recorder will give you a chance to save any changes to that file before it creates the new file. You can create a new sound file by recording a sound, inserting a sound file, or mixing a sound file. Or you can combine all three methods.

Creating and saving a new sound file

After you record or edit a sound file, you'll want to save the file for playing in the future. To save a new file (or to save an existing file under a different name), choose the Save As command from the File menu. In the Save As dialog box, type a file name and then click on OK. To save changes to an existing file, simply choose Save from the File menu.

Recording a sound file

You record sound through a microphone attached to your sound card. (See the sound card's documentation for details on setting up the microphone.) To record a new file, choose New from the File menu, and click on the Record (microphone) button. You can record up to 60 seconds of sound. When you finish recording, click on the Stop button. Play the sound to be sure that you recorded what you wanted, and then save the sound in a sound file.

You can also record new sounds into an existing sound file. To record into an existing file, open the file and move the slider along the scroll bar to the point at which you want to insert your new sound. Clicking on a scroll arrow moves the slider backward or forward 0.1 second. If you click on the scroll bar, the slider moves backward or forward 1 second. You can also drag the slider. Click on the Record button to start recording. When you finish recording, click on the Stop button, and then play back the sound to be sure that it is correct and that it plays in the position you intended. Now save the modified sound file.

Editing a sound file

Sound Recorder provides a number of ways to edit sounds. You can change the volume or speed of a sound, add special effects, cut part of a sound, insert another sound, and mix in yet another sound. Sound Recorder allows you to creatively experiment with all these methods. And, in case you make some changes to a sound file and don't like the result, Sound Recorder gives you the option of restoring the original contents of the sound file before you save any sound editing changes. Let's look first at the commands on Sound Recorder's Effects menu, shown in Figure 14-66.

Figure 14-66

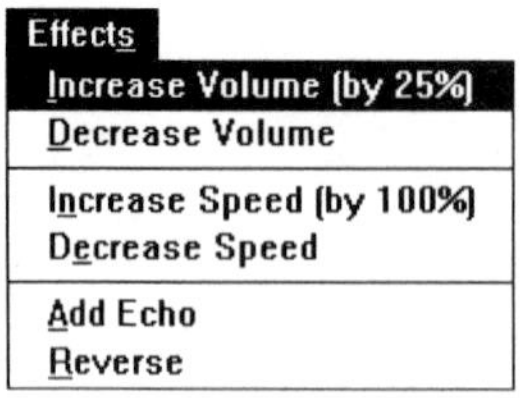

Effects
Increase Volume (by 25%)
Decrease Volume
Increase Speed (by 100%)
Decrease Speed
Add Echo
Reverse

The commands on Sound Recorder's Effects menu let you modify a sound.

You can increase or decrease the volume of a sound by 25%. To make a sound softer, open the sound file, and choose the Decrease Volume command from the Effects menu. Now play the sound to hear the difference in volume. You can return the sound to its normal volume by choosing Increase Volume (by 25%) from the Effects menu. To change the volume permanently, save the file.

To make a sound louder, open the sound file, and then choose Increase Volume (by 25%) from the Effects menu. Play the sound to hear the difference. You can return the sound to its original volume by immediately choosing Decrease Volume from the Effects menu.

Making a sound softer or louder

You can speed up a sound 100%—that is, it will play twice as fast for half as long. You can also slow down a sound by 50% so that it will play half as fast for twice as long. To increase the speed of a sound by 100%, open the sound file, and choose Increase Speed (by 100%) from the Effects menu. If you don't like the speeded-up sound, you can restore the sound to its normal speed by choosing Decrease Speed from the Effects menu.

To decrease the speed of a sound by 50%, open the sound file, and choose Decrease Speed from the Effects menu. Choosing Increase Speed (by 100%) from the Effects menu will return the sound to its original speed. To make either an increase or a decrease in speed permanent, save the sound file.

Slowing down or speeding up a sound

To add an echo to a sound, open the sound file, and then choose the Add Echo command from the Effects menu. To make the added echo permanent, save the sound file. Until you save the file, you can undo the echo by choosing the Revert command from the File menu.

Adding an echo to a sound

Reversing a sound plays it backward. To reverse a sound, open the sound file, and choose the Reverse command from the Effects menu. You can return the sound to the normal playing direction by choosing the Reverse command again. To reverse the sound permanently, save the sound file.

Reversing the sound

You can cut part of a sound before or after the current play position in the sound. To delete from the current play position to the beginning of the sound, open the sound file, and position the slider at the point where you want to start deleting the sound. You can use the Play and Stop buttons, or you can move the slider with the mouse. Click on a scroll arrow to move the slider backward or forward 0.1 second, or click on the scroll bar to move the slider backward or forward 1 second. When the slider is in the correct position, choose Delete Before Current Position from the Edit menu. Choose Yes in the message dialog box that Sound Recorder displays to confirm that you want to delete the beginning of the sound, and Sound Recorder will make the deletion.

Deleting part of a sound file

To delete part of a sound from the current play position to the end of the sound, open the sound file, and position the slider where you want to start cutting. You can position the slider with the Play and Stop buttons, or you can move it with the mouse as described above. Then choose Delete After Current Position from the Edit menu, and choose Yes in the message dialog box to have Sound Recorder complete the deletion.

After a deletion, play the sound to be sure that you deleted the part you wanted to cut. Until you save the file, you can undo a deletion by choosing the Revert command from the File menu.

Inserting another sound file

You can insert the contents of another sound file into the current sound, as long as the total length of the sound does not exceed 60 seconds. To insert a sound into an existing sound file, open the first sound file, and then position the slider where you want to insert the second sound. Choose the Insert File command from the Edit menu, select or type the name of the second sound file in the Insert File dialog box, and click on OK. If you have not yet saved the file, you can undo an insertion with the Revert command from the File menu.

Mixing in another sound file

You can mix the contents of another sound file within the current sound file. The two sound files will blend together and play simultaneously. To mix in one sound file with another, open the first sound file, and then position the slider where you want to begin mixing the sounds. Choose the Mix with File command from the Edit menu. In the Mix with File dialog box, shown in Figure 14-67, select or type the name of the sound file you want to mix into the current sound, and then click on OK. If you don't like the mix when you play the modified sound, you can undo it by choosing the Revert command before you save the file.

Figure 14-67

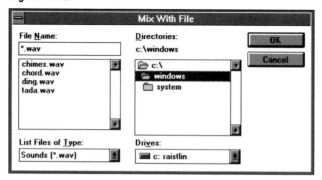

The Mix with File dialog box lets you mix another sound with the current sound.

After you insert, mix, or delete sounds from a sound file, you might decide that you want to start over. For example, you might have deleted the wrong part of the sound or inserted a new sound in the wrong position. You can restore the original contents of a sound file by choosing the Revert command from the File menu. Sound Recorder will display the message dialog box shown in Figure 14-68. Choose Yes in the message dialog box to confirm that you want to discard the changes you've made. After you save a sound file, however, you can't undo any of the changes you've made to the file.

Restoring a
sound file

Figure 14-68

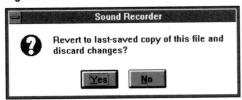

*Sound Recorder asks you to confirm that you want to discard
your changes when you choose the Revert command.*

In this chapter

Playing Games 15

*M*ost of Windows' features are devoted to giving you the tools you need for serious work. But when it comes time for play, Windows doesn't let you down. Windows 3.1 supplies two excellent games: Minesweeper and Solitaire. Whether you're looking for a leisure activity or a stress-reducing break from more serious pursuits, you'll enjoy playing both of these games. (In addition, of course, these games give you a pleasant way to practice and develop your mouse-handling techniques—pointing, clicking, double-clicking, dragging, and choosing commands and options.)

FINDING THE GAMES

The Windows Express Setup program will automatically install both Minesweeper and Solitaire on your hard drive and will create a group window called Games. (Windows Custom Setup also installs both games by default but allows you to omit them if you want.) You can select the Games group window in the Program Manager and then launch either Minesweeper or Solitaire by double-clicking on its icon.

MINESWEEPER

Minesweeper is a mouse skill game that combines some luck with analytical skill and strategy. The game lets you practice pointing and clicking with both mouse buttons, individually and together. Using the mouse, you try to locate mines in a mine field, without setting off any mines. The game board consists of squares on a grid and a scoreboard, as shown in Figure 15-1 on the next page. The mines are buried under some of the squares. The scoreboard reports your progress and the elapsed time.

Figure 15-1

The initial Minesweeper game board for the Beginner skill level is shown here.

The number that appears on the left side of the scoreboard shows the number of mines that are unmarked. (We'll describe marking a little later in the chapter.) At the beginning of the game, this number indicates how many mines are buried in the mine field. The timer, on the right side of the scoreboard, records the elapsed time in seconds since your first click on a square in the mine field. The timer counts up from 0 to 999 seconds, at which point the timer stops. You can continue to play, but your time will be the maximum recordable time. In most Minesweeper games, you will either win or lose long before 1000 seconds (16 minutes and 40 seconds) have passed.

The size of the grid changes for each skill level. For the Beginner skill level (the default level), the grid is 8 by 8 (64) squares and contains 10 mines. By the time you reach the Expert skill level, you will be playing on a grid that is 16 by 30 (480) squares and contains 99 mines.

By default, Minesweeper will appear in color. If you have a monochrome monitor instead of a color monitor, turn off color by selecting and turning off the Color command from the Game menu. You can also play Minesweeper in monochrome (black and white) on a color monitor.

The object of Minesweeper is to uncover all the squares that do not contain mines, without uncovering a square that does contain a mine. To accomplish this, you must locate the mines so that you can avoid uncovering them.

Starting the game

When you double-click on the Minesweeper icon in the Games group window of the Program Manager, the game board appears, ready for you to start playing. The New command on the Game menu allows you to begin a new game at any time. Or you can press [F2], the shortcut key for the New command, to start a new game. The Restart button (the square that contains a "happy face") in the scoreboard area of the game board also restarts the game; just click on it.

Playing Minesweeper is a process of elimination. To start, click on any square on the grid. Minesweeper uncovers the square and starts the timer. (Hold down the mouse button and notice the Restart button.) This first move is a "luck" move. If the square you click on happens to contain a mine, it explodes, you "die," and the game ends. The Restart button will show a sad face, with X's for eyes, as it does in Figure 15-2.

Playing Minesweeper

Figure 15-2

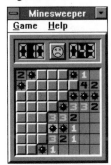

If you uncover a mine, it explodes, all the other mines appear, you "die," and the game is over.

If the first square you uncover contains a number or if it is blank, you're still "alive," and you can continue to play. To continue, click on another square. At this point, analytical skill and strategy come into play. The numbers that appear in the squares tally the number of mines in the immediately adjoining squares, as shown in Figure 15-3.

Figure 15-3

The number in the center square is a tally of the mines contained in the 8 surrounding squares.

A blank square indicates that there are no mines in the 8 surrounding squares. If you are lucky enough to click on a blank square, Minesweeper will also uncover the 8 surrounding squares because none of them contains a mine. If any one of these 8 squares is also blank, Minesweeper will uncover its 8 surrounding squares, too. As you can see in Figure 15-4 on the next page, this can sometimes uncover a large portion of the game board.

This piece of luck helps you develop your strategy for subsequent moves. By analyzing where the visible numbers overlap, you can locate mines and thus avoid them. To avoid a mine permanently, however, you need to mark it.

Figure 15-4

When you click on a blank square, Minesweeper sometimes uncovers a large section of the game board.

Marking a mine

When you've determined that a square contains a mine, you can mark the square with a flag to remind yourself not to click on it. Once you mark a square with a flag, you can't uncover the square until you remove the flag. Clicking the left mouse button on a flagged square has no effect.

To flag a square, point to it and click the *right* mouse button. A flag mark appears on the square. Each time you flag a square, the mine count on the scoreboard decreases by one, even if you erroneously flag a square that doesn't contain a mine.

Minesweeper offers a second mark character, a question mark (?). You can use this alternative mark to mark squares that you suspect contain mines. The question mark does not decrease the mine counter on the scoreboard. In fact, if you replace a flag with a question mark, the mine counter increases by one. Also, the question mark does not prevent you from uncovering the square, as the flag does.

The Marks (?) command on the Game menu controls the availability of the question mark. This command is toggled on by default, making the question mark active. When the Marks (?) command is turned on, clicking once on an unmarked square with the right mouse button marks the square with a flag. A second right mouse button click replaces the flag with a question mark. A third right mouse button click unmarks the square. When you turn off the Marks (?) command (by selecting it again), right mouse button clicks simply mark the square with a flag or remove the flag; the question mark is no longer available. Both the flag mark and the question mark are shown in Figure 15-5.

Figure 15-5

You can mark a square with a flag or a question mark.

You can take a risk and spy on a group of squares. To execute a spy move, point to a square and click *both* mouse buttons at the same time. One of the following scenarios will result:

- Not much happens. If the square you click on is covered, the surrounding squares merely flatten when you press the mouse buttons and then pop back up when you release the buttons. If the square you click on is uncovered and contains a number, the surrounding 8 squares must contain that many flags. If you haven't flagged that many surrounding squares, the squares simply flatten and then pop back up when you release the mouse buttons. Note that the flags do not have to be on mine squares, just on the 8 squares surrounding the square you click on. If all the squares in the surrounding 8 squares are already uncovered or flagged, nothing at all happens.

- The surrounding squares are uncovered, and you "die." If the 8 surrounding squares contain an unflagged mine or a mine marked with a question mark, Minesweeper uncovers the mine, it explodes, you "die," and the game is over. (Remember that using the question mark does not prevent Minesweeper from uncovering squares that contain mines.)

- The surrounding squares are uncovered, and you're still "alive" because you successfully flagged all mines in the 8 surrounding squares.

All three results are illustrated in Figure 15-6. (The mine displayed with an X indicates a flagged square that did not contain a mine.) You'll want to use the spy-click in situations where you think you have correctly analyzed and flagged the mine layout. Remember that the surrounding 8 squares must contain at least as many flags as the uncovered number in the square on which you are spy-clicking.

Figure 15-6

The squares flatten, but then nothing else happens.

A mine is uncovered, and you "die."

You "live" to play on.

When you spy-click (click both mouse buttons at the same time), three results are possible.

Winning the game

When you have uncovered all the squares that don't contain mines, leaving only the squares with mines covered, you win. After a win, notice the Restart button, which is shown in Figure 15-7.

Figure 15-7

When you win, the timer stops, the mine counter shows 0,
and all squares that contain mines are marked with flags.

You don't have to mark the squares that contain mines in order to win. When you win, the timer stops, and Minesweeper marks the rest of the mines for you. If your time equals or beats the best time for the current skill level, Minesweeper displays a message telling you that you have the fastest time for that skill level, as shown in Figure 15-8.

Figure 15-8

When you're the best, Minesweeper asks for your name.

Type your name—which can be serious, legal, outrageous, or nothing at all—in the text box. You can even leave Anonymous as the name. Click on OK to have Minesweeper display the Fastest Mine Sweepers dialog box, shown in Figure 15-9.

Figure 15-9

Minesweeper keeps a record of the fastest mine sweeper at each skill level.

To reset all best time levels to their defaults (999 seconds by Anonymous), click on the Reset Scores button. To view the fastest times at any time, select the Best Times command from the Game menu.

When you have finished playing, select Exit from the Game menu to exit Minesweeper. Note that the Exit command is located on the Game menu because Minesweeper has no File menu.

Exiting
Minesweeper

After you play Minesweeper for a while, you might want to increase the challenge. Minesweeper has three preset skill levels: Beginner, Intermediate, and Expert. To set one of these skill levels, choose the associated command from the Game menu. You have already seen the Beginner game board; Figure 15-10 shows the Intermediate game board, and Figure 15-11 on the next page shows the Expert game board.

**Setting the
skill level**

Figure 15-10

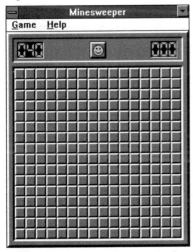

The Intermediate game board is 16 by 16 (256) squares with 40 mines.

Figure 15-11

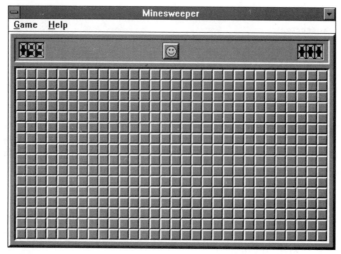

The Expert game board is 16 by 30 (480) squares with 99 mines.

Setting up a custom game

If the preset games aren't challenging enough (or if you want a different challenge), you can set up a custom game by selecting Custom from the Game menu. In the Custom Field dialog box, shown in Figure 15-12, you can set up your own grid by typing in the text boxes how many squares high and how many squares wide your game board should be. You can also type in the number of mines you want the grid to contain.

Figure 15-12

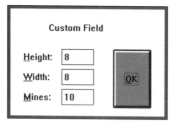

In the Custom Field dialog box, you can set up a custom game board.

When the Custom Field dialog box appears, it shows the height, width, and number of mines from the last game board you viewed. The smallest grid is 8 by 8 (64) squares with at least 10 mines. The largest grid on a VGA monitor is 24 by 30 (720) with a maximum of 667 mines. Minesweeper limits the number of mines that can be contained in specific grids. For example, if you set up a grid with 10 by 10 (100) squares, the maximum number of mines you can set is 81. Even if you type a larger number, such as 99, Minesweeper sets the number at 81 when the grid appears.

Windows 3.1 also includes a Solitaire game. This version of Solitaire is an automated version of Klondike, one of the most popular of the many single-player card games. The graphics of the card faces and backs are impressive, especially on a VGA monitor. And Windows' Solitaire is not only pretty; it's also relaxing to play.

SOLITAIRE

The computer serves as dealer and scorekeeper rather than as your opponent. It takes over all the tedious details of dealing and keeping the rows of cards neatly arranged. It will even keep score, using either a point system or a casino-style betting model, leaving you free to concentrate on just playing the game.

You'll find Solitaire in the Games group window in Windows' Program Manager. Double-click on the Solitaire icon to start the game. In addition to the usual menu bars at the top of the Solitaire window, a status bar will appear at the bottom of the window. By default, a timer in the status bar will indicate the number of seconds elapsed in your game, beginning as soon as you click on a card. (We'll explain later how to use the timer and how to turn it off.) If you activate one of Solitaire's scoring options, your score will also be displayed in the status bar.

To exit Solitaire and close its window, choose the Exit command from the Game menu. Solitaire has no File menu.

Almost anyone who has picked up a deck of cards has played some kind of Solitaire game. Solitaire actually encompasses a whole class of card games, but the game of Klondike (also known as Fascination, Demon, and Patience) is the one most people think of first; and it's the one included with this version of Windows. This computer implementation of Solitaire is faithful to the original card game, and playing it will soon feel completely natural. We'll briefly review the rules. If you are familiar with the game, you may want to skip this section.

The rules of the game

Solitaire uses a single deck of 52 playing cards and deals 28 of those cards into seven piles, arranged in a row across the playing area, as shown in Figure 15-13 on the next page. Starting from the left, the first pile contains one card; the second pile, two cards; and so on, to the last pile, which contains seven cards. The top card in each pile is face-up, and the rest are face-down. We'll refer to these seven piles as the row piles.

The initial deal

Figure 15-13

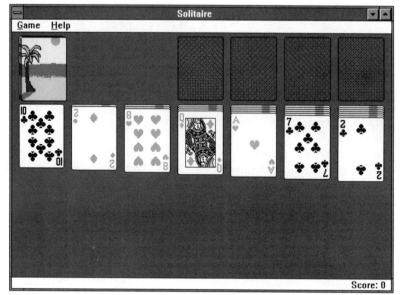

Solitaire deals 28 cards into seven row piles to start the game.

The remaining 24 cards of the deck go face down in the upper-left corner of the window. This is called the stock. You'll draw from the stock and place the cards you draw face up in a pile beside it. Then you can play the top card from this stock pile. The four empty rectangles across the top of the playing area are reserved for the suit stacks.

Building the row piles

Most plays in Solitaire take place on the seven row piles. You build each pile in descending order, alternating red cards (hearts or diamonds) and black cards (spades or clubs). For instance, if the face-up card on one of the piles is a 10 of hearts, you could play either the 9 of spades or the 9 of clubs on it, followed by the 8 of hearts or the 8 of diamonds. The face-up cards in a row pile are cascaded (staggered) down so that an identifiable portion of each card is visible at all times.

You can play face-up cards from one row pile onto the top face-up card of any other row pile. For example, in Figure 15-14, you can play the red jack from the last pile on the black queen in the third pile. In addition, you can play the red 9 in the sixth pile on the black 10 in the fifth pile and can then move both those cards onto the third pile because the black 10 can be played on the red jack. Figure 15-15 shows the results of these moves. When you move the face-up cards from a pile, you'll expose the next face-down card. You can then turn that card face up so that it is available for play.

Figure 15-14

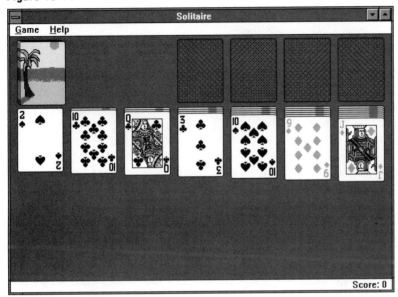

In this example, several plays are available.

Figure 15-15

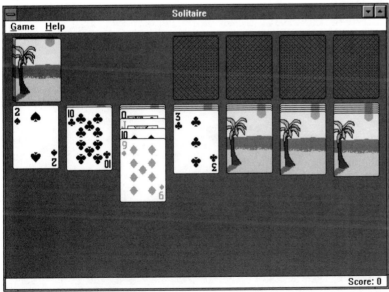

This screen shows the game from the preceding figure after we made the plays described in the text.

Filling empty row piles

If your plays leave a row pile empty (with no more face-down cards), you can move a king into the vacant position. Only a king can fill an empty pile position. If you don't have a king in one of the other piles, the space must remain vacant until a king appears in the draw or until you turn one up in another pile.

Drawing from the stock

When no more plays are available in the row piles, you draw from the stock. Normally, you would draw three cards at a time, place them face up in a pile to the right of the stock, and then play the top card. You can always play any exposed, face-up card.

Once you reach the bottom of the stock, you can turn it over and go through the deck again. You can make multiple passes through the stock if you are not playing a scored game. We'll explain the restrictions imposed by the scoring systems later.

Building the suit stacks

The four empty rectangles across the top of the playing area are the suit stacks. Each suit stack must start with an ace and build in ascending order, by suit. When you expose the first ace, you can move it to one of the four rectangles to start a suit stack. For example, if you turned up the ace of hearts, you could move it to one of the four rectangles to begin the stack of hearts, as shown in Figure 15-16. Then you would play the 2 of hearts (when it appears) on the ace. You can play cards from the row piles or from the stock pile onto the suit stacks.

Figure 15-16

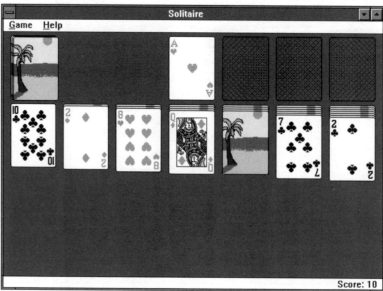

When you expose an ace, you can move it up to the suit stack.

A fast way to move a card to its suit stack is to double-click on the card instead of dragging it. When you double-click on the card, Solitaire moves the card to the proper suit stack.

The object of Solitaire is to move all the cards from the stock and the row piles to the suit stacks. At the completion of a successful game, the entire deck is arranged in four stacks, each containing the ace through king of a suit. Unfortunately, the luck of the draw often blocks this kind of absolute win. Crucial cards can be buried, face down, in the row piles. As alternatives to an all-out win, Solitaire offers two styles of scoring, which we will discuss later.

The object of the game

When you start the program, Solitaire automatically deals the cards and is ready to play. However, you will probably want to maximize the window before you begin moving any cards.

When you start Solitaire for the first time, the program by default sets up a timed game, with a timer display in the status bar. If you want to practice the game without the pressure of time limits, choose the Options command from the Game menu, and turn off the Timed Game check box in the Options dialog box. (We'll explain all the options in this dialog box later in the chapter.)

Starting the game

You can redeal the cards and start a new game at any time—even if the current game isn't complete. Select the Deal command from the Game menu for an immediate redeal.

Beginning a new game

You can pause a Solitaire game at any point by minimizing the window. Click on the Minimize box or select Minimize from the Control menu to reduce Solitaire to an icon on your desktop. Then, to return to your game, simply double-click on the Solitaire icon. Of course, as you can with all Windows applications, you can just open another window over your Solitaire game if you need to perform some other task. Your game will be waiting when you return.

Pausing a game

Most plays in Solitaire involve moving a card from one pile or stack to another. You can play any face-up card, whether it is in the row piles, the stock pile, or the suit stacks. When you expose a face-down card in a pile, you turn it face up so that it can be played. You can draw from the stock pile. If you inadvertently make the wrong move, you can undo it. You accomplish all these plays with a few simple moves of the mouse.

Playing Solitaire

You move cards by dragging them—the same technique you use to reposition and resize windows, rearrange icons on your desktop, or draw in Paintbrush. Begin by positioning the mouse pointer on the card you want to move.

Moving cards

Then press the mouse button to pick up the card, and hold the button down while you move the mouse to drag the card to its destination. Release the mouse button to deposit the card at the end of the move.

You will often need to move all the face-up cards in a pile as a single unit. To move a group of cards, position the pointer on the bottom card. When you drag that card, all the cards on top of it will also move.

You can move cards between piles, from the stock to any of the row piles, or from either the stock or the row piles to the suit stacks. Solitaire will accept only legal moves. If you drag a card to a new position only to have it pop back to its original position when you release the mouse button, you'll know that the move you attempted was not valid and that Solitaire refused it. If this happens often, or if your display is jumpy as you make moves, try activating the outline dragging option (which we'll discuss later).

Turning cards face up

When you move the face-up cards from one pile to another pile, you'll expose the next card in the pile, which is a face-down card. To turn this card face up, simply click on it. Solitaire will reveal the face of the card and make it available for play.

Playing from the stock

To draw from the stock, click on the face-down cards of the stock pile. Solitaire will draw three cards and turn them face up in a pile just to the right of the stock. You can then move the top face-up card to play it on any of the row piles or suit stacks. The next face-up card in the stock pile then becomes available for play. (A variation of the game allows you to draw cards one at a time instead of three at a time.)

After several draws, you will deplete the face-down stock, and all the cards will be in the face-up pile. To continue playing with a traditional deck of cards, you would turn the stock pile over and make another pass through the deck. To turn the stock pile over in Windows' Solitaire, click on the rectangle to the left of the face-up stock pile.

If you use the Vegas scoring option, the rules restrict the number of passes you can make through the stock. Solitaire will put a red X in the stock rectangle to indicate that you may not turn the deck over when you've exhausted your allowed number of passes.

Undoing a move

Sometimes you'll make a mistake. You might draw from the stock before you've played the top card on the stock pile. Or you might move a card and then realize that it's more important to play it somewhere else. For those occasions, Solitaire can reverse the effect of your last draw or move with the Undo command. To use this feature, just select Undo from the Game menu. The computer will cancel your last action.

You win a game of Solitaire when you are able to move all 52 cards to the suit stacks. When you move the final king from the stock or row pile onto its suit stack, Solitaire signals your win by starting a rather flamboyant graphics display. The cards spring from the suit stacks and bounce off the screen one by one, leaving a trail behind them, as shown in Figure 15-17. It's fun to watch, although you will probably get tired of it long before the aces finally bounce away. Click the mouse button or press any key to abort the display.

Winning the game

Figure 15-17

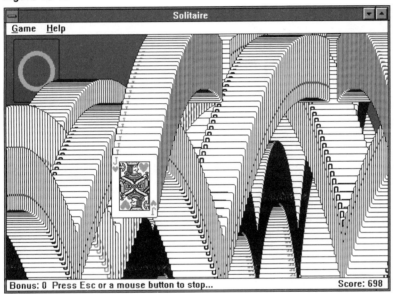

To signal a win, Solitaire puts on a graphics show, bouncing the cards off the screen one by one.

The Game menu contains the Deal command, which lets you start a new game whenever you like; the Undo command, which you can use to cancel your last move or draw; and other commands that allow you to select a deck of cards and to choose various scoring and playing options.

Options

Solitaire includes 12 different designs for the backs of the cards. Initially, Solitaire will randomly choose one of the designs each time it deals. You can choose your favorite design by selecting the Deck command from the Game menu. Solitaire will open a window showing the 12 card-back designs, with the current selection highlighted by an extra outline. Click on the deck you want to use, and then click on the OK button. Once you choose a deck, Solitaire will

Selecting the deck

remember your preference and use it exclusively. Of course, you can always use this procedure to select another deck any time you like. You can even change decks in mid-game, since only the backs of the cards are affected. (The programmers hid a few surprises for the sharp-eyed player in some of the deck designs.)

Drawing

Select the Options command from the Game menu to display Solitaire's Options dialog box, shown in Figure 15-18. In this dialog box, you can designate the drawing and scoring options, hide the status bar, or choose a technique called outline dragging.

Figure 15-18

Solitaire's Options dialog box allows you to select the style of drawing and scoring, hide the status bar, and activate outline dragging.

Solitaire allows you to choose from two variations in the way you draw from the stock. The default is the more traditional method of drawing three cards at a time from the stock and turning them face up in a pile to the right of the stock. As you work through the stock, you see every third card in the deck, and you are allowed at least three passes through the stock. Alternatively, you may choose to draw one card at a time. This way, you see every card in the stock in a single pass. Traditionally, the rules dictate only one pass through the stock if you are using a single-card draw. However, Solitaire does not enforce these limits unless you choose the Vegas scoring option.

The draw options appear in the Draw area in the upper-left portion of the Options dialog box. Click on the radio button beside the option of your choice. If you change the draw option, Solitaire will redeal and start a new game when you choose the OK button and return to the playing window.

Scoring

Because the luck of the draw makes an outright win rare in Solitaire, the program offers two ways to keep score that can add interest to an otherwise "unwinnable" game. The Scoring section in the upper-right portion of the Options dialog box allows you to choose between the Standard and Vegas scoring options or to disable scoring completely.

Standard scoring assigns point values to the significant moves as you play Solitaire. You score points for moving cards from the stock to the row piles and for moving cards to the suit stacks. Solitaire penalizes you for moving cards from the suit stacks down to the row piles and for extra passes through the stock.

Vegas scoring simulates casino-style wagering on Solitaire. In this scoring mode, you ante $52 at the outset of each game. Solitaire automatically assesses the initial wager at the start of the game and gives you an opening score of -$52. The "house" pays $5 for each card you move onto the suit stacks. You'll need to get 11 cards onto the suit stacks before you reach a positive score. The object is to win more than you wager.

The radio buttons in the Scoring section of the Options dialog box indicate which scoring mode is active. To choose another mode, click on its radio button.

The Keep Score check box below the Scoring section works with the Vegas scoring mode. If you select the Keep Score check box, Solitaire will keep a running total of your winnings (or losses) until you close the Solitaire window instead of zeroing the score at the end of each game.

You can't change scoring modes in the middle of a game. Any change you make in the scoring options will force Solitaire to redeal when you return to the playing window.

In Standard scoring, Solitaire assigns the following point values:

- +10 points for each card played onto the suit stacks from either the stock or the row piles

- +5 points for each card played from the stock to any of the row piles

- +5 points for each face-down card in a row pile that is turned face up

- -2 points at each 10-second interval when the Timed Game option is selected

- -15 points penalty for each card played from the suit stacks down to the row piles

- -20 points penalty for each pass through the stock after three passes when the Draw Three option is selected

- -100 points penalty for each pass through the stock after one pass when the Draw One option is selected

Note that under Standard scoring your score will never be less than 0, regardless of the size of the penalty.

The Vegas scoring rules are simple:

- Ante (initial wager) $52; you start with a score of -$52

- Win $5 for each card you play to the suit stacks

- Only one pass through the stock allowed when the Draw One option is selected

- Only three passes through the stock allowed when the Draw Three option is selected

If you select None in the Scoring section of the Options dialog box, Solitaire will not display a score in the status bar at the bottom of the screen. The only real difference between choosing Standard scoring and choosing the None option is the score display. However, if you've chosen Standard scoring but then decide in mid-game that you don't want to see your score, switching to the None option isn't the best idea. Remember that any change in scoring selections will abort the game and force a redeal. If you change your mind about displaying your score in mid-game, a better alternative is to hide the status bar. The Status Bar check box in the Options dialog box controls the status bar at the bottom of the screen, which contains the score display. Turn off the check box to remove or hide the status bar (and the display). You can then return to your game without forcing a redeal.

Outline dragging

The Outline Dragging check box in the Options dialog box allows the system to use a simplified outline to represent the cards you drag. There are two reasons you may want to enable outline dragging.

Dragging a fully detailed graphic of the card across the screen in real time places significant demands on your computer. Fast computers with high-speed displays may handle those demands with ease, but on slower systems, your screen may jump and flicker. Moving a simple outline on the screen as you drag a card lightens the computer's load, resulting in a smoother, faster display.

In addition to faster operation, outline dragging contains a built-in Help feature. As you can see in Figure 15-19, when you drag the outline to a valid destination, the top card in the pile (or the empty rectangle) will change color, making it very easy to recognize legal moves. By dragging the outline across the piles and suit stacks on the screen and noting which piles change color as the outline passes, you can force Solitaire to identify all the potential moves for you.

An X in the Outline Dragging check box indicates that the outline dragging option is active. Click anywhere on the box or its text to change it.

Figure 15-19

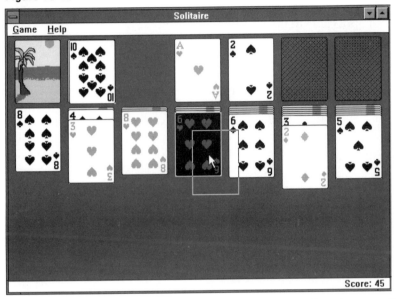

In this example of outline dragging in action, notice that the row pile under the outline changes color to indicate a valid potential move.

The Timed Game check box in the Options dialog box adds a time display to the status bar. The timer starts with your first move and counts in seconds. In the Standard scoring mode, Solitaire reduces your score as time passes, to encourage faster play. If you select this option in the middle of a game, Solitaire will force a redeal.

Timing a game

Like most Windows applications, Solitaire was designed for use with a mouse. In fact, it's one application that you can use without ever touching the keyboard. Pointing and clicking the mouse to draw or turn cards face up and using the mouse to drag cards will soon become second nature, even to people who have not used a mouse before.

Using the keyboard

However, if you are one of those unfortunate few who are struggling along in a graphical user interface minus the requisite supported pointing device (that is, if you are using Windows without a mouse), you can still play Solitaire. You can make all the essential moves with the keyboard. The keyboard equivalents are also a boon to those of you who develop a nervous twitch in your fingers if you don't peck at the keys every few seconds (or to those of you who simply prefer to use the keyboard).

The [Tab] key moves the pointer among the main playing areas: the stock pile, the suit stacks, and the row piles. It automatically skips over any stack or pile that is not applicable to the next move.

Press the ← or → key to move the pointer to the next stack or pile to the left or right. Use the ↑ and ↓ keys in the row piles if you want to select more than the top card in a pile.

Pressing [Spacebar] is roughly equivalent to pressing the mouse button, except that you won't have to hold it down to simulate dragging moves. To move a card or group of cards, first press [Spacebar] to pick up the card at the pointer. Next, press [Tab] or the ← and → keys to move to your destination. Then press [Spacebar] again to release the card and complete the move. To turn a card face up, position the pointer on the card and then press [Spacebar]. To draw, press [Spacebar] while the pointer is on the stock pile.

The other keys and key combinations that access menus and select menu options are the same as in other Windows applications.

Tips

Here are a few tips to help you improve your Solitaire score, although you may find that the score is immaterial. Solitaire is fun to play, regardless of scores and winners.

Take all possible plays

One principle of playing Solitaire is never to miss a play. That goes double when you play with Standard scoring. When you draw a card from the stock that will play directly on a suit stack, look first to see if you can play it on one of the row piles. If you can, Solitaire will award you 5 points for moving the card from the stock to the row pile and then another 10 points for moving it from the row pile to the suit stack, for a total of 15 points. Moving the same card directly from the stock to the suit stacks earns only 10 points. Breaking the move into two parts won't help your chances of getting all the cards to the suit stacks, but it will increase your score under the Standard scoring rules.

"Cheating"

Many of the common ways to cheat at Solitaire (such as shuffling the deck) are simply not allowed by the Solitaire program. However, there are a few loopholes that let you improve your odds of winning or increasing your score.

Traditionally, the rules allow only one pass through the stock if you are drawing one card at a time. As we mentioned, Solitaire does not enforce this rule unless you choose the Vegas scoring option. Making multiple passes through the stock with the Draw One option checked is not strictly legal, but it greatly enhances your chances of winning. Keep in mind that Solitaire discourages the practice by penalizing you 100 points for each extra pass through the stock if Standard scoring is active. When the Draw Three option is selected, Solitaire allows you three passes through the stock before it deducts a smaller penalty of 20 points for each additional pass.

Furthermore, it is customary when you move the face-up cards from one pile to another to move all the face-up cards together in a pile. Solitaire allows you to move any face-up card or cards in a pile. Occasionally, moving a partial pile will help you expose a card of a particular suit that you can then move into the suit stacks.

Tradition dictates that once a card has been moved to the suit stacks, you can't move it back down to the row piles. Windows' implementation of the game permits the move, but it imposes a penalty of 15 points in the Standard scoring mode and subtracts from your winnings in Vegas scoring.

Section 3
Beyond the Basics

In this chapter

Of Modes and Memory **16**

*W*indows 3.1 offers two operating modes, each with its own capabilities and limitations, to accommodate various computer and memory configurations and the demands of different applications. To give you a better understanding of Windows' operating modes and how Windows uses the different kinds of computer memory, this chapter offers brief explanations of some of these often-confusing concepts.

Most computer users understand the difference between the kind of memory provided by a hard drive and the computer's temporary working memory, RAM (random access memory). But when it comes to sorting out the different kinds of RAM, many users get lost in the maze of conventional memory, DOS memory, extended memory, expanded memory, and virtual memory. To make matters worse, much of the computer jargon we must decipher seems to be an alphabet soup of acronyms (MS-DOS, RAM, ROM, EMS, XMS, LIM 3.2, LIM 4.0). Let's start our examination of memory by looking at how memory has evolved in DOS-based computers.

A BRIEF HISTORY OF COMPUTER MEMORY

In the beginning, there was conventional memory. Conventional memory is the name given to the RAM available for applications running under the MS-DOS operating system on computers based on the 8086 and 8088 microprocessors (the IBM PC and compatibles). The 8088 chip can actually address up to 1 MB (1024 KB) of memory, but 384 KB of that is reserved for various hardware and system requirements, leaving 640 KB available for applications. Originally, conventional memory was simply called memory; the term "conventional memory" was coined to differentiate it from the other forms of memory that were subsequently introduced. Conventional memory is also sometimes called DOS memory because it is the memory that DOS-based applications can address directly.

Conventional memory

445

Initially, 640 KB of memory seemed to be more than anyone would ever need in a "personal" computer. Most computers were sold with only about 256 KB installed, and most software ran with room to spare. However, as software grew more complex, machines faster and more powerful, and users more sophisticated and demanding, the "huge" 640 KB capacity of DOS became the "640 KB barrier." New generations of applications offering powerful new features, ease of use, and the ability to manipulate large amounts of data could barely be shoehorned into 640 KB of memory. Nevertheless, the need to maintain compatibility with the installed base of DOS-based computers dictated working within the confines of conventional memory, and the 640 KB barrier became an albatross around the necks of programmers and users alike.

Expanded memory (EMS)

The inevitable eventually happened. Applications expanded to use all the available conventional memory and still needed more—much more! Enter the LIM (Lotus/Intel/Microsoft) expanded memory specification (EMS). EMS memory evolved when hardware and software engineers devised a way to put extra memory on an add-in board and address it by mapping a section of the memory into a special section of conventional memory a "page" at a time. EMS requires special hardware plus a special device driver in your CONFIG.SYS file to tell your system how to find the extra memory. Since DOS can't recognize expanded memory, your applications must request data from the expanded memory manager, which must then locate the data on the EMS memory board and map it into conventional memory where your application can use it.

Expanded memory is an afterthought—an add-on patch designed to allow an 8088-based computer to go beyond its original design specifications and address more memory than is otherwise possible. (EMS memory can also be used with 286- and 386-based computers, but extended memory is a better option for these computers.) Furthermore, applications must be written specifically to take advantage of EMS, and there are major limitations on its usefulness. For instance, under the widely accepted LIM EMS 3.2 specification, applications can store data in EMS memory, but the application itself (its program code) must remain in conventional memory. Consequently, you can create a monstrously large spreadsheet or database file with an application that uses EMS memory, while the 640 KB barrier continues to be an obstacle to multitasking. After all, some larger applications barely fit in 640 KB of memory themselves, much less allow room for another application to simultaneously reside in conventional memory. The LIM EMS 4.0 standard, however, allows newer EMS cards to move programs as well as data into EMS memory. As a result, EMS memory becomes available for multitasking, but it is much slower than directly addressing conventional or extended memory. Still, EMS has been around for years, and many applications will use it to their advantage if it is available.

With the introduction of the 80286 microprocessor (the IBM PC AT and compatibles) came the extended memory specification (XMS, not to be confused with the similarly named expanded memory specification). The 80286 chip can address up to 16 MB of RAM, and there is no physical difference between what we call conventional and extended memory. Some of the memory (usually 1 MB to 4 MB or more) will be on the computer's motherboard. The rest may be installed on an add-in board similar to that used for expanded memory. But unlike the situation with EMS memory, the microprocessor addresses all XMS memory directly, with no special hardware needed to map "pages" of data in and out of conventional memory. You do need an extended memory manager (such as HIMEM.SYS, which is supplied with Windows) to assign blocks of extended memory to different applications.

Extended memory (XMS)

The only difference between conventional and extended memory is a conceptual one imposed by the architecture of DOS. On a 286-, 386-, or 486-based computer, DOS uses the first 640 KB of memory—the conventional memory—just as it does on an 8088-based machine. Any memory past 1 MB in a 286-, 386-, or 486-based machine is called extended memory. While DOS cannot directly access more than 640 KB of memory for applications and data, there is no similar limitation on the amount of memory that can be physically installed in a system running DOS. In other words, your computer can have more memory installed than DOS can use.

Before Windows 3.0, the chief limitation on using XMS memory was the availability of applications that could effectively use extended memory. Typically, XMS memory was used for a RAM disk and perhaps a disk cache, but not much else—hardly optimal use of a vital system resource. Often, XMS memory sat idle while "RAM cram" in conventional memory severely limited your productivity.

An 80386- or 80486-based computer can do everything a 286-based machine can do—and more. The 386DX or 486DX chip, with its 32-bit architecture, dramatically expands the maximum amount of extended memory. (The 386SX version can address only 16 MB of physical memory.) The 386 or 486 chip also has a few more tricks up its sleeve, such as the ability to emulate conventional or expanded memory in extended memory, simulate virtual 8086 microprocessors, and even support virtual memory.

Virtual memory

The 386 or 486 microprocessors support virtual memory by using a section of your hard drive as simulated additional RAM. To an application, the virtual memory appears identical to extended memory. The 386 or 486 microprocessor can swap large blocks of information between the hard drive and XMS memory to make more memory available for data and to run more applications concurrently than would normally fit within your system's combined conventional and extended memory.

As with extended memory, DOS cannot access and control the special features of 386- or 486-based computers without help. Before Windows 3.0, only a few 386 or 486 control programs and specially written applications could take advantage of these powerful features.

REAL MODE VERSUS PROTECTED MODE

Life with an 8088-based computer is simple, if confining. The 8088 chip has only one operating mode and addresses only conventional memory. If you need more than 640 KB of RAM, an expanded memory board is the only option.

Things get a little more interesting with the newer microprocessor chips that have distinct operating modes. The 80286, 80386, and 80486 all maintain full backward compatibility with older computers and DOS software with their "real mode." Real mode simulates the operation of an 8088 microprocessor chip, complete with its limitations. Nearly all DOS-based applications (including versions of Windows earlier than 3.0) were designed to operate in real mode and consequently can't use many of the advanced features of 286-, 386-, and 486-based computers.

The added features of the newer microprocessors are available only in "protected mode." In 286 (16-bit) protected mode, they can address XMS memory; and, in the 386 and 486 microprocessors' 32-bit protected mode, they can play their virtual memory and virtual 8086 microprocessor tricks. However, accessing protected mode requires special software, which is provided as part of Windows 3.0 and 3.1.

WINDOWS' OPERATING MODES

To accommodate the memory configurations of various systems, Windows 3.1 can run in two operating modes. These two operating modes—standard and 386 enhanced—take advantage of the protected modes of 286, 386, and 486 chips to add extended memory management and improved multitasking capabilities to Windows. Windows no longer comes in different versions for different computers. Both operating modes are integrated into a single package, and Windows will automatically sense which mode to use.

Standard mode

In standard mode, Windows applications can break the 640 KB barrier and make full use of XMS memory in 286-, 386-, and 486-based computers. Access to extended memory is especially significant for multitasking since it makes XMS memory as well as conventional memory available for running applications. With enough extended memory installed on your system, you can run several large Windows applications simultaneously. In standard mode, you can multitask Windows applications, but Windows still must suspend DOS-based applications while you are working in the Windows environment and must suspend Windows applications while a DOS-based application is active.

Windows' standard mode is the default on 286-based computers and on 386- and 486-based computers with less than 2 MB of memory. It's an optional operating mode for 386- and 486-based computers with more than 2 MB of memory. In standard mode, Windows can use your computer's full complement of conventional and extended memory but will not use any expanded memory you might have installed. Although Windows itself won't use EMS memory while operating in standard mode, Windows won't interfere with your applications (either Windows-based or DOS-based) using expanded memory if it is available on your system.

Some developers of DOS applications have found ways to break the 640 KB barrier on machines with extended memory by using "DOS extender" technology to access that memory through the processors' protected mode. For example, Lotus 1-2-3 release 3.0 is an application that uses a DOS extender to access extended memory. In standard mode, Windows is compatible with other programs that strictly conform to the VCPI (virtual control program interface) specification for extended memory access. Even if your computer can support Windows' 386 enhanced mode with its advanced features, you'll probably find yourself using standard mode much of the time because of its speed and compatibility with applications that use DOS extender technology.

Windows packs real memory management and multitasking muscle into its 386 enhanced mode. You'll need a 386- or 486-based computer with at least 2 MB of memory to use Windows' 386 enhanced mode. With it, you'll finally be able to realize the potential of your sophisticated system—and do it easily.

386 enhanced mode

In 386 enhanced mode, Windows can use all your system's conventional memory and extended memory and can optionally use a swap file (which we'll explain in the next section) on your hard drive as virtual memory to simulate even more memory for your applications. Windows will not use expanded memory when it operates in 386 enhanced mode, although your expanded memory remains available for applications that request it. If you do not have an expanded memory board installed on your system but do have applications that need EMS memory, Windows can convert a block of extended memory into what appears to be expanded memory. Your DOS-based applications can then access this simulated EMS memory when you run them from Windows.

Windows provides its most powerful multitasking capabilities when it's operating in 386 enhanced mode. In addition to multitasking Windows applications, as it does in standard mode, Windows also can run DOS-based applications simultaneously with Windows applications or other DOS applications. In 386 enhanced mode, Windows can divide your system's processing power between the various running applications and manage contention between the applications for shared resources, such as printers and COM ports. Since 386 enhanced mode uses methods of multitasking that are different from those used in standard mode, you'll have the flexibility to fine-tune the way Windows allocates your system resources to each DOS-based application during multitasking. Windows can allocate a separate section of memory to each application that you launch from Windows in 386 enhanced mode. While the actual location of this memory will likely be in XMS memory, above the 640 KB normally accessed by DOS, Windows takes advantage of the 80386 or 80486 CPU's virtual 8086 mode to make the memory appear to be conventional memory. The 386 or 486 chip's virtual 8086 microprocessor emulation also builds a simulated display and provides a separate copy of the operating system and device drivers for each application so that the application can function as if it were running on a separate computer.

MANAGING SWAP FILES

Windows provides more sophisticated memory management than you'll find in the traditional DOS environment. In the appropriate mode, Windows makes optimal use of your system's memory—in all its various forms. Windows can even provide virtual memory by creating a swap file on your hard drive when you use 386 enhanced mode. In standard mode, Windows automatically creates a temporary swap file to facilitate switching between Windows applications and DOS-based applications. Although this kind of swapping is available within a few DOS-based applications and separate utility programs, Windows provides it automatically for all Windows applications and even for the DOS-based applications you run from Windows.

Temporary swap files

When you launch a DOS-based application while Windows is operating in standard mode, Windows automatically creates a temporary swap file on your hard drive. When you switch back to Windows or to another application, Windows moves (or "swaps") some of the first application out of RAM and stores it in the swap file on your hard drive. Swapping allows you to open more DOS applications from Windows than would normally fit within your system's available memory. This swapping ensures that the maximum amount of memory is available for the next active application. When you exit Windows, Windows deletes the swap file.

Swap files in 386 enhanced mode

In 386 enhanced mode, Windows can use either a temporary or a permanent swap file. The 386 or 486 microprocessor uses the file for virtual memory, thus effectively increasing your system's RAM resources by the size of the swap file. For example, on a 386-based system with 2 MB of XMS and a 5 MB swap file, 386 enhanced mode allows Windows to function as if the computer had 7 MB of extended memory available.

When it operates in 386 enhanced mode, Windows will automatically create a temporary swap file and adjust its size as needed, unless you have created a permanent swap file for Windows' use. The permanent swap file is more efficient but occupies hard-drive space, even when Windows is not running or is running in standard mode. When you install Windows on a 386- or 486-based computer that can use 386 enhanced mode, Setup offers to create a permanent swap file during the installation process. Windows also includes an option through the 386 Enhanced icon in Control Panel that lets you manage swap file setup, including creating, removing, or changing the size of a permanent swap file.

In this chapter

PIFs—Working with Non-Windows Applications 17

*W*indows provides a number of important services to the applications that are designed to run in its environment. In addition to the common user interface, Windows supplies display and printer interfaces and memory management. More important, Windows creates and administers a multitasking environment, ensuring that each application gets its fair share of system resources and mediating the demands of various applications for access to items such as the printer or a COM port. As a result, you can run multiple applications simultaneously, switch quickly between running applications, and share information via Clipboard. These Windows-based applications follow certain rules in the way they request and use system resources. DOS-based applications, however, do not follow the same rules and were not designed to share system resources in a multitasking environment.

The more Windows knows about the way a program operates and what it needs and expects from the computer system, the better job Windows can do of integrating that application into the Windows environment with other applications. Windows-based applications automatically supply Windows with the necessary information, but DOS-based applications do not. To run a DOS-based application, Windows must make certain assumptions about the application's requirements. If the assumptions are correct, the application should run normally. But if they aren't, the application may run poorly or not at all. You might find problems with such details as memory requirements or the display—especially when you switch between the DOS application and your Windows applications.

WHAT IS A PIF?

Fortunately, there is a way to provide Windows with the information it needs to optimize its interaction with your non-Windows applications. You can create a PIF—a program information file—for a non-Windows application to tell Windows how it should run that application. Whenever you start a DOS application under Windows, Windows will look for that application's PIF and will use the information in the PIF instead of its default assumptions about how the application operates. For instance, when you start a DOS application under Windows' 386 enhanced mode, that application's PIF will tell Windows how much memory the application requires, whether to run the application full-screen or in a window, whether to continue running the application in the background when you switch to other applications, and so forth. In other words, a PIF is a file of technical information about a non-Windows application that allows Windows to optimize the way it runs and interacts with that application.

In this chapter, we'll cover PIFs in great detail. We'll explain how to install a PIF and show you how to use the PIF Editor to create and modify PIFs. We'll also explain all the settings you'll find in the PIF Editor for both standard mode and 386 enhanced mode and examine the impact they will have on your applications running under Windows.

INSTALLING A PIF

Microsoft includes in your Windows package predefined PIFs for several popular DOS-based applications. As Windows Setup finds and installs applications during your Windows installation, it automatically installs the predefined PIFs for the non-Windows applications it finds in your Windows directory.

Unfortunately, Windows can't provide predefined PIFs for every DOS application that exists. However, many software manufacturers provide a PIF for their application on the application's program disks (or they will make the PIF available on request). If you're using an application for which the manufacturer has supplied a PIF, you can install that PIF simply by copying it from your program disk to your Windows directory. Once you've copied the PIF to your Windows directory, you can use Windows Setup to install the application, or you can add the application to the Program Manager yourself. (Chapter 5 covers adding applications to the Program Manager.) Then, when you start the application from the Program Manager, Windows automatically looks for and uses the PIF you've copied. You can also explicitly instruct Windows to use a PIF for an application by installing the PIF instead of the application's executable file in the Program Manager.

If neither Windows nor your software manufacturer provides a predefined PIF for your application, don't worry. If Windows can't find a PIF for an application, it will start the application using default PIF settings. For the vast majority of DOS applications, the default PIF settings will work just fine. However, if your application doesn't run properly, or if it doesn't run as you prefer, you might need to create a custom PIF for your application. Similarly, if an application with a predefined PIF isn't working properly, you might need to change some of the settings in that application's PIF—especially if you want to use some of the capabilities of Windows' 386 enhanced mode. When you want to create or modify the settings in a PIF, you must use Windows' PIF Editor.

To start the PIF Editor, open the Accessories group window in the Program Manager, and double-click on the PIF Editor icon. Immediately, Windows will open the PIF Editor window. The PIF Editor is sensitive to Windows' operating mode and displays the appropriate settings for the current mode. If you're running Windows in standard mode, the PIF Editor window will include only the settings that apply to standard mode, as shown in Figure 17-1. If you're running Windows in 386 enhanced mode, the PIF Editor window will have a slightly different set of basic options and will contain an Advanced button that lets you access advanced options available only in 386 enhanced mode. As you do in most Windows applications, you select Exit from the File menu to close the window and leave the PIF Editor.

THE PIF EDITOR

Figure 17-1

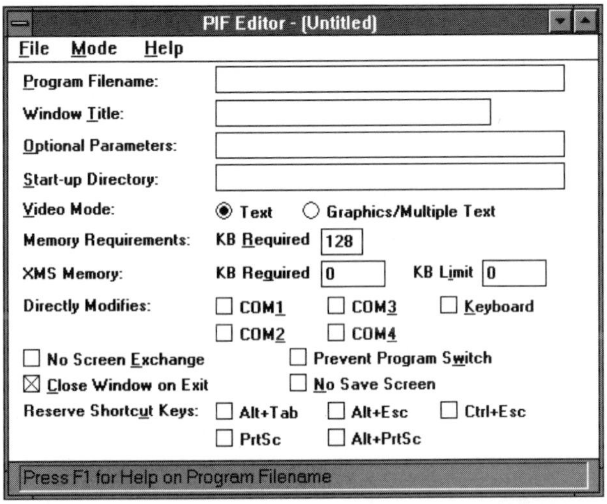

If you're running Windows in standard mode, the PIF Editor window includes these options.

Each PIF contains two sets of options: one for standard mode and one for 386 enhanced mode. The PIF Editor also has two modes—standard and 386 enhanced—for editing the two sets of options. If you plan to run your application under Windows' standard mode, you'll want to run the PIF Editor in standard mode so that you can specify standard mode options. On the other hand, if you plan to run your application under Windows' 386 enhanced mode, you'll want to run the PIF Editor in 386 enhanced mode so that you can specify options for that mode. Notice the difference between the PIF Editor in standard mode, shown in Figure 17-1, and in 386 enhanced mode, shown in Figure 17-2 on the next page.

Figure 17-2

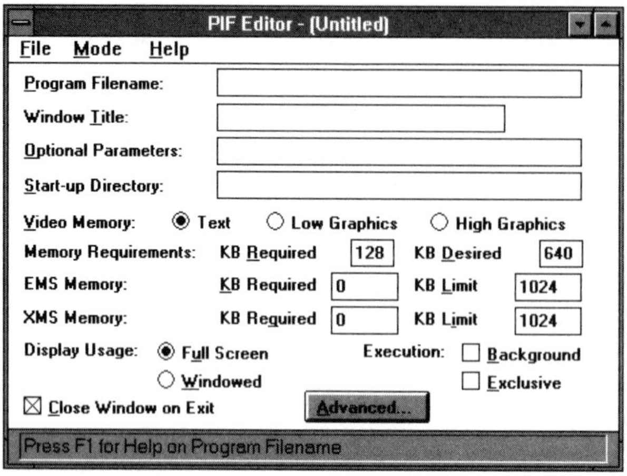

In 386 enhanced mode, the PIF Editor window offers a different set of options, plus a button that allows you to access a dialog box of advanced settings.

By default, the PIF Editor displays the options for the mode in which Windows is currently running. Although this is typically what you'll want, you can use the Mode menu to toggle the PIF options between standard and 386 enhanced modes. For example, if you're running Windows in 386 enhanced mode and you want to create a PIF for a DOS application that will run in standard mode, you'll need to choose the Standard command on the Mode menu before editing that application's PIF. Whenever you use the Mode menu to switch to a mode that differs from Windows' current operating mode, the PIF Editor will display a message box like the one shown in Figure 17-3. When you choose OK in this message box, the PIF Editor will bring up the options for the new mode you selected.

Figure 17-3

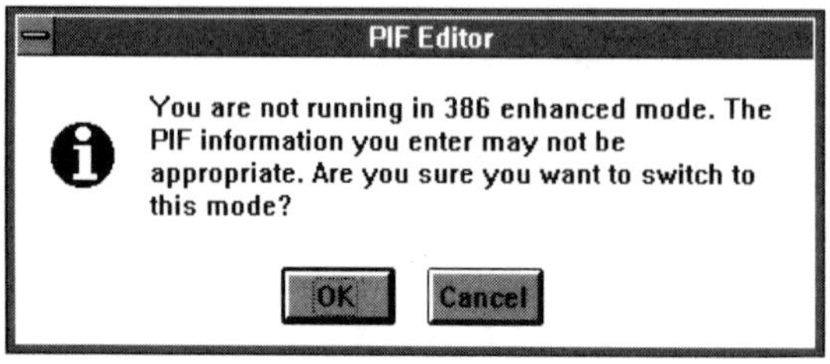

The PIF Editor asks for confirmation when you switch to a different operating mode.

When you first start the PIF Editor, it will create a new, untitled PIF, with all the PIF Editor's default settings. At this point, you can change any of the settings that appear in the PIF Editor window. When you're ready to save the settings on a disk, choose the Save command from the File menu to bring up the familiar Save As dialog box, and then type in the File Name text box the name of the executable file that starts the application. You don't need to supply a file name extension—Windows will automatically append the extension .PIF. Make sure you save the PIF either in your Windows directory or in the same directory as the application whose PIF you're creating. If you use a different name for your .PIF file or store it in another directory, Windows will not automatically find and use the PIF settings when you launch the application. However, you can always launch an application by installing its PIF in the Program Manager instead of the executable file. This technique is handy when you want to use different PIFs to run an application with different configurations.

You can create a new, untitled PIF whenever you want by choosing the New command from the PIF Editor's File menu. Each time you issue the New command, Windows displays the default settings in the PIF Editor window.

To open an existing PIF, choose the Open command from the PIF Editor's File menu. The Open dialog box will appear, with the file name pattern *.PIF in the File Name text box. Windows will display in the File Name list box the names of all the .PIF files in the current directory.

If the name of the PIF you want to open appears in the File Name list box, simply select its name and click on OK. Or, if necessary, use the Drives and Directories list boxes to change to the PIF's drive and directory, and then choose the file name in the File Name list box. As soon as you click on OK, Windows will display the selected file's settings in the PIF Editor window and will place the PIF's name in the PIF Editor window's title bar.

Once you open an existing PIF, you can modify its settings and then use the Save command to save those changes. If you want, you can select the Save As command from the File menu and supply a new name in the File Name text box to save your changes as a new PIF.

The PIF Editor offers numerous options for running DOS-based applications under Windows' standard mode. Most of these options are also available when you are running Windows in 386 enhanced mode. In this section, we'll explain each of the PIF Editor's standard mode options and how they affect your DOS-based applications. You can refer to Figure 17-1 on page 455 to see the location of each option in the PIF Editor window.

Creating new PIFs

Opening PIFs

STANDARD MODE OPTIONS

Program Filename

The Program Filename text box in the PIF Editor stores the full path name of the file that starts your DOS application. This file will have a .COM, .EXE, or .BAT file name extension. Make sure you include the drive and directory path when you specify the Program Filename entry.

For example, suppose that you're creating a PIF for the DOS application Microsoft Word 5.0. You've installed Word in the directory C:\WORD, and the name of the file that starts the application is WORD.COM. In this example, you would enter *C:\WORD\WORD.COM* in the Program Filename text box.

Window Title

The Window Title text box stores the name that should appear in the application window's title bar and also under its icon when the window is minimized. If you leave this text box empty, Windows will use the file name you've entered in the Program Filename text box (without the extension) for the icon name and the window title.

For instance, returning to our Microsoft Word example, if you leave the Window Title text box empty, Windows will use the name *Word* to label the Microsoft Word icon. If you prefer to label the icon with the name *Microsoft Word*, just type that name in the Window Title text box.

Optional Parameters

If you usually type some parameters after the application's file name when you start the application from the MS-DOS prompt, you'll want to type those parameters in the Optional Parameters text box. If you don't need to supply any parameters, just leave this text box empty.

For example, if you normally type *WORD /L* to start Microsoft Word version 5.0 and to automatically load the last file you worked on, type */L* in the Optional Parameters text box. You can specify as many parameters as you like, as long as the total number of characters does not exceed 63. Depending on your application, you might insert a file name for a file you want the application to open automatically or command-line switches that instruct the application to start in a particular mode or perform some automatic function.

You can ask Windows to prompt you for parameters when you start the application. To do this, simply type a question mark (?) in the Optional Parameters text box.

If you specify optional parameters in an application's PIF and later want to start that application with a different set of parameters, you can do so by choosing the Run command from the File menu in the File Manager or the Program Manager. When you use the Run command to start an application, the parameters you supply in the Run dialog box will override those you entered with the PIF Editor.

If you want Windows to make a particular directory the current directory when it starts an application, simply enter the directory name in the Start-up Directory text box. This procedure is roughly equivalent to issuing the CD command at the MS-DOS prompt to change directories before starting an application. Although you can leave this text box empty, you'll probably want to enter the name of the directory containing the application's program files to ensure that the application has access to all the files it will need while running.

For example, if you're creating a PIF for Microsoft Word, and you've installed Word in the directory C:\WORD, you'll want to enter *C:\WORD* in the Start-up Directory text box.

Start-up Directory

The Video Mode options—Text and Graphics/Multiple Text—determine how much memory Windows reserves for your application's display. If your application runs only in text mode, you'll want to choose the Text option, since this mode will leave more memory available for your application. However, if your application takes advantage of your display's graphics mode, you'll need to choose the Graphics/Multiple Text option, which will set aside more memory for storing your application's display. You should also choose this option if your application requires more than one text screen's worth of display memory.

If you aren't sure which video mode your application uses, choose the Graphics/Multiple Text option. Although this option requires more memory, it is the safer option. It will ensure that Windows reserves enough display memory to save the application's display when you switch back to the Program Manager.

Video Mode

The Memory Requirements setting allows you to tell Windows how much memory your application requires. Keep in mind that this setting does not restrict the amount of memory Windows provides for the application—Windows will suspend its own applications and give this application all available conventional memory when you are operating in standard mode. The Memory Requirements setting simply tells Windows the *minimum* amount of memory that must be available before it should even attempt to start the application.

If Windows can't provide the application with at least as much memory as you've specified in the KB Required text box, Windows will display a message dialog box when you attempt to start the application, warning that the available memory is insufficient.

Memory Requirements

The XMS Memory options let you provide extended memory to DOS applications that conform to the Lotus/Intel/Microsoft extended memory specification (XMS). (See Chapter 16 for a discussion of conventional, expanded, and extended memory.) Because a number of newer DOS applications use extended memory, let's consider the two options that relate to XMS memory.

XMS Memory

KB Required

The KB Required setting tells Windows how much extended memory your application requires. The operative word here is "required." Although some applications might be able to use extended memory, very few will *require* it. You'll probably want to leave this setting at 0 since any other KB Required setting will significantly increase the amount of time required to switch to and from the application. Use this setting to tell Windows that the application will not operate without at least the specified amount of XMS memory.

KB Limit

The KB Limit setting specifies the maximum amount of extended memory that Windows should permit the application to use. If you want to prevent the application from using any extended memory, enter 0 in the KB Limit text box. If you want to limit the application to a specific amount of extended memory, enter the appropriate value in the text box. Strangely enough, a value of −1 permits the application to use all the available extended memory.

Directly Modifies

Remember that DOS applications were created under the assumption that each one would be the sole application operating on a computer at any given time and would not be sharing the computer with other applications. Consequently, DOS applications often presume that they have exclusive use of the computer resources and manipulate these resources directly instead of allowing Windows to act as a central clearinghouse.

The five check boxes that appear in the Directly Modifies area of the PIF Editor window allow you to tell Windows that the DOS application will monopolize certain resources. If you select any of these check boxes, Windows will prevent other applications from using that particular resource and will also prevent you from switching to other applications without first quitting the application in question.

As you might expect, you'll use the COM1, COM2, COM3, and COM4 check boxes to tell Windows which communications port(s) the application will monopolize. You'll want to select the Keyboard check box if the application uses the keyboard buffer. If you choose this option, Windows and other applications will not respond to shortcut keys while you are using the application.

No Screen Exchange

Selecting the No Screen Exchange check box prevents you from using the [Print Screen] or [Alt][Print Screen] keys to copy the application's screen to Clipboard. The only reason to choose this option is to provide a small amount of additional memory to the application. The effect of selecting this option is similar to selecting the PrtSc and Alt+PrtSc check boxes in the Reserve Shortcut Keys area of the PIF Editor.

Selecting the Prevent Program Switch check box prevents you from switching to another application or returning to the Windows desktop. Once you've started an application with this option selected, you can use another application only by quitting the first application, as you would if you were working in MS-DOS. The benefit of selecting this option is that it provides a small amount of additional memory to the application.

Prevent Program Switch

By default, the PIF Editor selects the Close Window on Exit check box, which tells Windows to automatically close the application's window when you exit the application. If you want Windows to leave the application's window on the screen even after you exit, turn off the Close Window on Exit check box.

Close Window on Exit

Normally, Windows saves the screen image of your application when you switch to another application. Then, when you return to the first application, Windows can display the correct screen image. Selecting the No Save Screen check box directs Windows not to save the screen image. This allows the application to use the memory Windows would have used for saving the screen image. More memory usually means more speed in an application. The drawback of selecting this option is that when you switch to another application, Windows can't display the correct screen image. You should turn on the No Save Screen check box only if the application itself stores its screen image and also provides a command for refreshing or updating the screen.

No Save Screen

You'll want to use the Reserve Shortcut Keys options if your application uses any of the shortcut keys that Windows normally uses for its own functions. By selecting any of the check boxes in this section of the PIF Editor, you allow your application to respond normally to the selected key combination, and you prevent Windows from intercepting and acting on those keystrokes.

Reserve Shortcut Keys

For instance, your application might insert a tab marker when you press the [Alt][Tab] key combination. Windows, however, uses the same key combination as a shortcut key to switch to another application—a conflict that Windows will win. Windows will intercept the [Alt][Tab] key combination instead of allowing your application to insert a tab marker. But if you select the Alt+Tab check box in the application's PIF, Windows will ignore that key combination, reserving it for the application instead. Then, pressing [Alt][Tab] while your application is in the foreground will insert a tab marker instead of telling Windows to switch to another application.

Keep in mind that the Reserve Shortcut Keys options affect only the application with which the specific PIF is associated. You can still use all of Windows' built-in shortcuts when another application is in the foreground.

For a description of the normal functions of Windows' shortcut keys, refer to the Quick Reference Cards at the end of this book.

386 ENHANCED MODE OPTIONS

In 386 enhanced mode, Windows uses the ability of the 80386 or 80486 microprocessor to create a virtual machine for each DOS-based application you run from Windows. You can exercise considerable control over this simulated machine environment by changing the PIF settings for an application. In 386 enhanced mode, Windows can run some DOS applications in a window alongside the Windows applications on your desktop. It can use multitasking to run DOS applications with Windows applications rather than suspending the Windows applications while each DOS application runs, and vice versa. Windows can simulate conventional or EMS memory by using of XMS memory to provide the appropriate environment for each application and then, when you exit the application, reallocate that memory for the next application. Of course, as you might expect, more control and more options mean more settings to adjust.

If you intend to run your DOS application under Windows' 386 enhanced mode, you'll want to supply the appropriate settings to take advantage of the special capabilities of this mode. If you open the PIF Editor when you are operating in 386 enhanced mode, the PIF Editor window will automatically contain the 386 enhanced mode options. If, on the other hand, you are currently running Windows under standard mode, you can bring up the 386 enhanced settings by choosing the 386 Enhanced command from the PIF Editor's Mode menu. When you choose the 386 Enhanced command when Windows is running in standard mode, Windows will present a message box notifying you that your PIF settings are not appropriate for the current mode. If you choose OK in this message box, the PIF Editor will display the 386 enhanced mode settings, which you can see in Figure 17-2 on page 456.

Most of the basic PIF settings in 386 enhanced mode are the same as their counterparts in standard mode. The Program Filename, Window Title, Optional Parameters, Start-up Directory, and XMS Memory text boxes are all duplicated from the standard mode PIF settings, as is the Close Window on Exit check box. There are also a few changes. Several standard mode options are missing—notably the Directly Modifies, No Screen Exchange, Prevent Program Switch, and No Save Screen check boxes, which are not necessary in 386 enhanced mode. The Reserve Shortcut Keys options are missing from the PIF Editor window in 386 enhanced mode but appear in the Advanced Options dialog box, which is displayed when you click on the Advanced button. Also, standard mode's Video Mode options are replaced in 386 enhanced mode by Video Memory options.

Video Memory

The Video Memory radio buttons tell Windows how much memory to initially set aside for the application's display. Selecting the Text option tells Windows to reserve enough memory to display the application in text mode, which requires the least amount of memory (less than 16 KB).

When the Low Graphics radio button is selected, Windows reserves enough memory to display the application in low-resolution graphics mode, which roughly corresponds to CGA-quality graphics. For most video adapters, CGA graphics require about 32 KB of memory.

When you select the High Graphics option, Windows reserves enough memory to display the application in high-resolution graphics mode, which corresponds to EGA-quality or VGA-quality graphics. This high-resolution graphics mode typically requires about 128 KB of memory—considerably more memory than the other two available modes.

It's important to remember that the Video Memory options specify only how much memory is *initially* reserved for displaying the application. Once the application is running, Windows can adjust the amount of memory used for the application's display. For example, if you start an application in text mode and then choose a function that shifts the application into graphics mode, Windows will provide additional display memory automatically (assuming that the additional memory is available). Similarly, if you're using an application in graphics mode and then switch to text mode, Windows will free up the extra display memory, thus making it available for other applications.

If, while running an application, you switch to a video mode that requires more memory than Windows can provide, you might lose some or all of your display. To avoid this, you can choose the High Graphics radio button and then select the Retain Video Memory check box, which appears in the Advanced Options dialog box.

Memory Requirements

The Memory Requirements options are slightly different from those in standard mode. The Memory Requirements options let you control the amount of *conventional* memory Windows will provide to the application.

KB Required

The KB Required setting is equivalent to the KB Required option in standard mode. This setting does not limit the amount of memory available to the application—it merely tells Windows to be sure that the specified *minimum* amount of memory is available before trying to start the application.

KB Desired

The KB Desired setting specifies the *maximum* amount of memory that Windows will permit the application to use. By default, the PIF Editor supplies a KB Desired setting of 640—the maximum amount of conventional memory any DOS application can use. If you want to limit the amount of conventional memory Windows will provide for the application, simply enter the amount in the KB Desired text box. The only time you might want to enter a value less than 640 is when you want to reserve more memory for other applications.

EMS Memory

As you know, Windows is designed to take advantage of the extended memory you've installed in your machine. Unfortunately, many DOS applications can take advantage of expanded—but not extended—memory. If your DOS application uses expanded memory, you can use the EMS Memory options to tell Windows to simulate expanded memory for that application.

KB Required

The KB Required setting tells Windows the *minimum* amount of expanded memory your application requires. Although many applications can use expanded memory, very few actually *require* it. For this reason, you will probably want to leave this setting at 0.

Like the similar setting for conventional memory, this setting does not limit the amount of expanded memory an application receives—it simply tells Windows to make sure that this amount of expanded memory is available before it attempts to start the application. Once Windows starts the application, that application will receive as much expanded memory as it requests, up to the amount specified by the KB Limit setting.

KB Limit

The KB Limit setting specifies the *maximum* amount of expanded memory that Windows will permit the application to use. By default, the PIF Editor supplies a KB Limit setting of 1024 (1 MB). If you want to prevent the application from using any expanded memory, enter 0 in the KB Limit text box. If you want to grant the application a specific amount of expanded memory, enter the appropriate value in the KB Limit text box.

XMS Memory

The XMS Memory settings are essentially the same as the XMS Memory settings in standard mode. They let Windows provide extended memory to DOS applications that conform to the Lotus/Intel/Microsoft extended memory specification. Unless your DOS application is one that uses extended memory, you will probably not want to change these default settings.

Just as it does for the other memory settings, the KB Required setting here controls the *minimum* extended memory that must be available for Windows to start the application. The KB Limit setting specifies the *maximum* extended memory Windows will allow the application to use.

Display Usage

The PIF Editor's Display Usage options let you tell Windows whether you want to run the application full-screen or in a window. This powerful capability of the 386 enhanced mode allows you to run many of your DOS applications in a window on your desktop, much as you run Windows applications. Not all applications can run in a window, and those that do require more memory than full-screen applications. But running an application in a window makes it easier to switch between multiple applications and to copy and paste information.

By the way, after you start a DOS application, you can easily toggle between a full-screen display and a window by pressing [Alt][Enter].

Execution

The two check boxes in the Execution area of the PIF Editor window determine how the application cooperates with other applications for multitasking. In standard mode, Windows suspends its own applications while a DOS application is running and suspends the DOS application when you switch back to Windows. In 386 enhanced mode, this is no longer necessary—at least not for all DOS applications. Under Windows' control, many DOS applications can run simultaneously with Windows applications and even other DOS applications.

Let's consider each of these check box options. (Notice that these are two independent check boxes—not mutually exclusive radio buttons.)

Background

If you select the Background check box, Windows will allow the application to run in the background while you use another application in the foreground. If you deselect the Background check box, Windows will stop running the application when you switch to another application.

The Background option comes in handy for communications programs. By selecting the Background check box in your communications program's PIF, that program can exchange data with another computer while you use a spreadsheet or word processing application in the foreground.

Exclusive

Selecting the Exclusive check box tells Windows to suspend execution of all other applications while the application controlled by the PIF is running in the foreground—even if the other applications have their Background option selected. The advantage of selecting this option is that it gives the application more memory and processor time.

You should use this option carefully if you have a communications program on your computer. If your communications program is transferring data in the background when you start an application for which you have selected the Exclusive option, the background data transfer job will be suspended, and you will need to redo the transfer.

If you choose the Exclusive option for an application, you should also select the Full Screen option in the Display Usage section. It normally isn't productive to run an exclusive application in a window, since windows are designed to let you load and run multiple applications simultaneously.

ADVANCED OPTIONS FOR 386 ENHANCED MODE

In addition to the basic PIF options we've covered so far, you can control a number of other details in the virtual machine environment Windows creates for each DOS application it runs in 386 enhanced mode. If you click on the Advanced button in the PIF Editor window, Windows will open the Advanced

Options dialog box, which contains advanced options for 386 enhanced mode, as shown in Figure 17-4. Although you probably won't need to modify the options in the Advanced Options dialog box, we'll briefly discuss how each of these options will affect your DOS application.

Figure 17-4

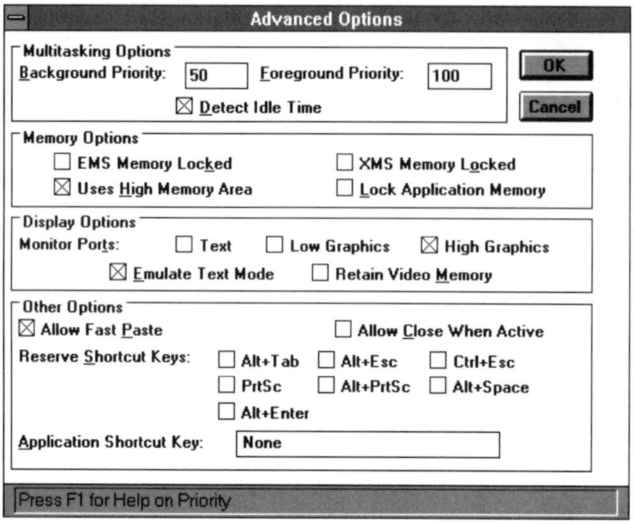

The Advanced Options dialog box lets you choose settings for advanced options in 386 enhanced mode.

Multitasking Options

The Multitasking Options section of this dialog box determines how an application will share processor time with other applications. The values in the Background Priority and Foreground Priority text boxes determine how much processor time the application will receive when it is running in the background or foreground, respectively. Control Panel sets the default background priority to 50 and the foreground priority to 100. These values, which can range from 1 to 10,000, are meaningful only when compared to the corresponding values for other applications. Let's consider an example.

Suppose you're running three applications with the PIF Editor's default priority settings. The application in the foreground has a foreground priority of 100, while the two applications in the background each have a background priority of 50. The total priority value for all three applications is 100 (for the foreground application) plus 2 times 50 (for the background applications), for a total of 200. Each application will get the percentage of processor time equal to its priority value divided by the total priority value. Consequently, the foreground application will get 50 percent (100/200) of the processor's time. Similarly, each background application will get 25 percent (50/200) of the processor's time.

The Detect Idle Time check box tells Windows to give processor time to other applications while an application is idle. In other words, if an application is waiting for your input, Windows will let other applications use its share of the processor's time.

Detect Idle Time

Typically, you'll want to leave this option selected, since it will usually enhance overall system performance. However, if you notice that an application is running unusually slowly, you might deselect that application's Detect Idle Time check box to see if it improves the application's performance.

The Memory Options settings, along with the memory settings in the PIF Editor window, control the way your application uses the computer's memory when it is running under Windows' 386 enhanced mode.

Memory Options

If you select the EMS Memory Locked check box, Windows will not swap to a disk the contents of the expanded memory used by an application. Although selecting this check box will improve the performance of a particular application, it will decrease the overall performance of the system.

EMS Memory Locked

Selecting the Uses High Memory Area check box tells Windows that this application can use your computer's high memory area (HMA), which is the first 64 KB of extended memory. You'll want to keep this option selected for most applications, since it will give your application access to additional memory. To prevent the application from using the HMA, deselect this check box.

Uses High Memory Area

Keep in mind that in order for an application to use the HMA, the HMA must be available when you start Windows. If you run a memory-resident program that uses the HMA before you start Windows, none of your applications will be able to use the HMA.

When you select the XMS Memory Locked check box, you prevent Windows from swapping to a disk the contents of the extended memory used by the application.

XMS Memory Locked

Selecting the Lock Application Memory check box instructs Windows to keep the application running in memory and not to swap it out of RAM and onto a disk. Selecting this option will speed up the application but will slow down the rest of the system.

Lock Application Memory

The Display Options area of the Advanced Options dialog box lets you control how Windows displays your applications and how it manages your display memory.

Display Options

Monitor Ports

The Monitor Ports check boxes help prevent problems that can occur when an application directly interacts with your computer's display adapter. If your application's display functions normally, you should not modify these settings, because this could slow down the application significantly.

However, if the application's display doesn't function properly, select the Monitor Ports check box that corresponds to the display mode in which the application was running when the problem occurred. If that action does not correct the problem, try selecting another Monitor Ports check box until the display functions normally.

Emulate Text Mode

Selecting the Emulate Text Mode check box typically allows the application to display text very quickly. Consequently, you'll want to make sure that this check box is selected for most of your applications. However, if the text in the application's display doesn't appear properly, or if the cursor appears in the wrong place, deselect this option and restart the application.

Retain Video
Memory

As we explained, Windows can adjust the amount of memory used for the application's display while the application is running. This dynamic memory management works fine as long as you don't run out of memory. However, if, while you are running an application, you switch to a video mode that requires more memory than Windows can make available, you might lose some or all of your display. To prevent this situation from occurring, choose the Video Memory radio button (in the PIF Editor window) that corresponds to the highest video mode your application will use, and then select the Retain Video Memory check box in the Advanced Options dialog box. Once you've done this, Windows will not allow any other applications to use the memory reserved for your application's display, even if the application isn't using all of that memory.

Other Options

At the bottom of the Advanced Options dialog box, Windows offers several other PIF options that let you customize the way an application runs under Windows' 386 enhanced mode.

Allow Fast Paste

Selecting the Allow Fast Paste option lets Windows paste text from Clipboard into the application as quickly as possible. Because most applications can accept fast pasting, Windows selects this option by default. If an application cannot accept information at maximum speed, Windows usually detects this and automatically slows down.

Occasionally, Windows may not be able to detect that an application has difficulty with its fast paste. If you're having problems pasting text into an application, deselect the Allow Fast Paste check box and restart the application.

The Allow Close When Active check box affects the way Windows responds when you attempt to exit Windows while the application is running. If you do not select this check box, Windows will not allow you to end your Windows session until you issue the application's Exit command. If you select this check box, however, you can exit your Windows session without having to activate the application and issue its Exit command.

If you want to select the Allow Close When Active check box for your application, first make sure that the application uses standard MS-DOS file handles. If it doesn't, allowing Windows to exit the application automatically could result in data loss. When you select this check box, Windows will warn you that closing an active application could result in a loss of data.

Allow Close When Active

The Reserve Shortcut Keys options operate in the same manner as those in standard mode. In 386 enhanced mode, they appear in the Advanced Options dialog box, rather than in the main PIF Editor window, and include two additional check boxes: Alt+Space and Alt+Enter.

Reserve Shortcut Keys

The last option in this dialog box, Application Shortcut Key, allows you to define a special shortcut key combination for your application. Once you've defined a shortcut key combination for an application, you can press that key combination whenever you want to immediately switch to that application from any other application.

Application Shortcut Key

To define a shortcut key for your application, first click on the Application Shortcut Key text box to activate it. Next, press the key combination you want to define as the shortcut key combination. Acceptable key combinations must include either the [Alt] or [Ctrl] key but cannot include the [Esc], [Enter], [Tab], [Spacebar], [Print Screen], or [Backspace] key. For example, some acceptable key combinations are [Alt]L, [Ctrl][F8], [Alt][Shift]Y, and [Ctrl][Alt]G.

Whenever you press a key while the Application Shortcut Key text box is activated, the name of that key will appear in the text box. If you accidentally press the wrong key, simply use the [Backspace] key to remove it from the text box, and then enter the correct key combination.

To completely remove an entire shortcut key definition, activate the Application Shortcut Key text box and press [Shift][Backspace]. As soon as you do this, Windows will remove the shortcut key definition and will display *None* in the text box.

Keep in mind that once you've started an application with a defined shortcut key, that shortcut key can serve no purpose other than activating that application. No application—including Windows, Windows applications, other DOS applications, or even the associated application itself—will recognize that shortcut key for other functions. For this reason, you should choose your shortcut keys carefully.

For example, imagine that you're editing the PIF for Microsoft Works and that you want to assign the shortcut key combination [Alt][Shift]W to this application. To do this, activate the Application Shortcut Key text box and press the three keys [Alt][Shift]W. Windows will then display *Alt+Shift+W* in the text box. The next time you start Microsoft Works and then switch to another application, you can immediately bring Works back to the foreground simply by pressing [Alt][Shift]W.

CREATING A PIF FOR A BATCH FILE

If you've created a DOS batch file that you want to run under Windows, you'll need to create a PIF for that batch file. To do this, first start the PIF Editor, and then supply the name of the batch file (including the .BAT extension) in the Program Filename text box. Next, specify the appropriate settings in the PIF Editor window. Keep in mind that the PIF settings you specify will be in effect for all applications and utilities that the batch file starts.

Once you've created a PIF for your batch file, you can run that batch file just as you would any other application. Specifically, you can add the batch file's PIF to a Program Manager group and then select it from that group, or you can start the File Manager and then double-click on the PIF's file name.

Section 4
Appendixes

Appendix A
Installing Windows

*I*nstalling Windows 3.1 is a fairly straightforward task. The Setup utility program goes beyond simply copying files onto your hard drive; it configures your computer and Windows to work together, installs printer drivers, and even installs many of your existing applications into Windows. Setup does most of its work automatically, but it doesn't rob you of control. Instead, it keeps you informed of its progress and allows you to make key choices that affect how it installs Windows on your system. The on-screen instructions are generally clear and complete, but if you need more information, Setup provides its own Help system.

DECISIONS, DECISIONS

You'll need to make a few decisions about how you want Windows installed on your system. The first question Setup asks lets you decide whether you want Windows to perform an Express Setup (in which Setup makes most of the decisions for you) or a Custom Setup (in which you are given more control and responsibility). Custom Setup is intended for experienced users.

The next few questions Setup asks pertain to your hardware and system configuration. In most cases, the defaults that Setup offers will be appropriate, and you will simply need to confirm them. In addition to installing Windows, Setup will allow you to set up printers and applications. Exercising these options may require you to supply some additional information. Before you run Setup, be sure you have the information you'll need to complete the installation. The following list will help you anticipate the decisions you might need to make and the information Setup will request.

- Choose Express Setup or Custom Setup.

- Set the drive and path. Before Setup can copy files to your hard drive, you might need to specify the drive and directory where you want Windows installed. The default is C:\WINDOWS.

- Identify hardware. Setup automatically tests your hardware, and it can present for your approval or editing a list of what it finds. It checks the computer type, display, keyboard (including foreign-language keyboard layouts), mouse, and network adapter.

- Modify AUTOEXEC and CONFIG. Setup will propose some changes in your AUTOEXEC.BAT and CONFIG.SYS files. You'll have the opportunity to accept, reject, or edit the suggested changes.

- Set up printers. Setup allows you to specify during installation the printers you'll use with Windows. Printer setup is the most complicated part of installing Windows, primarily because of the variety of printers Windows supports. Printer setup isn't difficult, but you'll need to answer several printer questions. You can always add, delete, or modify printer settings later. Whether you do it now or later, you need to provide information on the brand and model of your printer, the port to which it's attached, and specifics such as font cartridges, memory, resolution, and paper trays. If you choose to wait until later to add printers, be sure to keep your Windows disks handy; you will need them again when you load printer drivers and fonts.

- Install applications. You can ask Setup to scan your hard drive(s) and list the applications it finds. Then you can choose applications from the list and have Setup install them in Windows' Program Manager for you. This step is optional; you can do it later from within Windows, or you can easily change things later if you don't like the way Setup groups your applications in the Program Manager. Setup might not recognize every application that is installed on your system, but this step is a good start toward configuring your computer for operation with Windows.

- Reserve a swap file. You can let Setup create a special file on your hard drive for Windows to use in 386 enhanced mode. This swap file can improve Windows' performance, but it requires space on your hard drive.

INSTALLING WINDOWS

Setup is actually two separate programs that share the task of installing Windows. First, the DOS portion of Express Setup identifies your hardware components, creates a directory on your hard drive for Windows, and copies files from the installation disks. (Custom Setup allows you to confirm or modify Setup's identification of hardware components.) Then, the Windows portion of Setup takes over to complete the installation. It copies more files, modifies your AUTOEXEC.BAT file and CONFIG.SYS file, and automatically goes through the steps needed to configure your Windows environment. To allow you to set up printers and install applications in the Program Manager, Setup uses the same tools that will be available to you within Windows—Setup simply automates the procedures involved and adds helpful instructions.

Running Setup (DOS)

To begin installing Windows on your computer, insert disk 1 from your Windows package into your disk drive. Make that drive the active drive by typing *A:* at the prompt and pressing [Enter]. (If you insert the Windows disk into another drive, substitute that drive designation for *A:* in these instructions.) At the A:\> prompt, type *SETUP* and press [Enter]. This will start the DOS portion of Windows' Setup program.

From this point on, you should simply follow the instructions on the screen. If you need more information than the on-screen instructions provide, press [F1] to activate Setup's built-in Help feature. If you decide to abort your Windows installation before it is complete, you can press [F3] to exit Setup.

We won't attempt to recount every step of the installation in this appendix. Instead, we'll outline the major decision points so that you can change the way Setup installs Windows on your computer.

One of the first and most important decision points occurs when Setup asks whether you want to use Express Setup or Custom Setup. If you are knowledgeable about your computer system and how it works, choose Custom Setup; if you are an inexperienced computer user, choose Express Setup.

If you choose Express Setup and if this is the first time you've installed Windows on your system, Setup begins installing Windows in the C:\WINDOWS directory. Otherwise, Setup asks you for the drive and directory in which you want Windows installed. Setup supplies C:\WINDOWS as the default. (If you have an earlier version of Windows installed on your system, Setup will supply the drive and path of the currently installed version as the default.) To accept the default, just press [Enter]. If you want to install Windows in a different drive or directory, use the [Backspace] key to erase Setup's suggestion, type any valid path name, and then press [Enter]. If the directory doesn't exist, Setup will create it for you and then copy files from Windows' disks to your hard drive.

Next, Setup tests your computer system to evaluate your hardware and its configuration. (Setup might tell you that a newer version of your network

Verifying system information

software is available.) During Custom Setup (but not during Express Setup), Setup will show you a list of its findings and ask for confirmation. Setup checks the following items:

- Computer type. Basically, the choice is between a generic MS-DOS computer and certain other near compatibles. You don't need to distinguish between 286 and 386 models; Windows will do that automatically each time you run it.

- Display. Are your monitor and display adapter a VGA system, an EGA system, or one of the other supported displays?

- Mouse. Which type of mouse do you have? (Of course, you do have a mouse, don't you?)

- Keyboard. Do you have an 84-key, a 101-key, or other keyboard?

- Keyboard layout. The Standard US keyboard is the default, and most people won't need to change it. If you are using a keyboard with a language-specific layout, you will need to tell Windows so that it can properly interpret your keystrokes.

- Language. Windows applications that perform language-specific tasks, such as spell checks and sorting, will refer to the Language setting. The default is American English. If you work in another language, you must change this setting. You can also change this setting later within Windows by using the International dialog box in Control Panel.

- Network. If your computer is attached to a network, make sure this setting is correct so that Windows will be able to address network drives and share files. Otherwise, select No Network Installed.

Below the list of configuration items, a line that reads *The above list matches my computer* will be highlighted in inverse video. If the statement is true, you can simply press [Enter] to confirm the settings.

If you need to change one of the settings, use the arrow keys to move the inverse video highlight bar to the item you want to change, and then press [Enter]. Setup will switch to a screen that lists the options available for that setting. Some of the lists are long, and you'll need to scroll down through them with the arrow keys to see all the options. To make your selection, move the highlight to the proper item on the list and press [Enter]. You can return to the main hardware list without changing the selection by pressing [Esc]. Once you confirm that the list is correct, Setup copies more files onto your hard drive and then automatically runs the Windows portion of Setup.

Because the Windows portion of Setup starts automatically, you won't need to run it as a separate step. Once Setup enters Windows, you will be using standard Windows mouse and keyboard techniques to interact with Setup. In our instructions, we assume that you are using a mouse. To click on an item, position the mouse pointer on it, and press the primary (left) mouse button. See Chapter 2 for more on mouse and keyboard techniques in Windows.

Running Setup (Windows)

Setup asks you to type in your name and company name. Do so, and then click on the Continue button on the screen or press [Enter]. Setup asks you to confirm the information before proceeding.

The Windows Setup screen

In Custom Setup, the next dialog box allows you to select three optional functions for Setup to perform as part of your Windows installation: Set Up Printers, Set Up Applications Already on Hard Disk (that is, add them to the Program Manager), or Set Up Only Windows Components You Select. You can select one or more of these optional functions by clicking on its check box to place an X there; click on the check box again if you want to deselect the option. Normally, you'll want to go ahead and set up your printer and applications while you are installing Windows. After you select the installation options, click on the Continue button on the screen or press [Enter] to proceed.

Options

If you turned on the Set Up Only Windows Components You Select check box during Custom Setup, you will see a Windows Setup dialog box that lists the various types of Windows components—accessories, games, screen savers, and so forth. To install all the files in a component category, leave that category's check box turned on in this dialog box. To exclude all the files in a category, turn off that category's check box. To selectively exclude files in a category, click on the Files button for that category, select the files you don't want to install, click on Remove, and then click on OK.

Installing Windows components

During Custom Setup on a 386 computer with 2 MB or more of total memory, Setup opens a dialog box and proposes reserving a section of your hard drive for Windows' exclusive use as a swap file. In 386 enhanced mode, Windows can use this swap file to simulate additional RAM, noticeably improving Windows' performance—but the price in disk space is high. Depending on your system, the swap file may require several megabytes of storage space on your hard drive. If you have a large, fast hard drive or expect to work with multiple large applications, you may want to use the swap file. Otherwise, you may prefer to live with lower performance from Windows rather than give up so much space on your hard drive. Your decision isn't irrevocable; the 386 Enhanced icon on Control Panel lets you add, delete, or change the size of the swap file.

Creating a swap file

Click on the Continue button in the dialog box to have Setup create the swap file for Windows. If you opt not to create a permanent swap file, click on the Change button, select None from the Type drop-down list box, and then click on Change again.

Copying more files

Setup will start copying the files for the optional Windows components from the Windows disks to your hard drive. (Note that installation of these files is not optional with Express Setup.) Setup informs you of its progress by showing the file names as it copies each file, and it also posts the progress of the copy procedure on a bar chart.

When Setup needs another disk, it asks you to place the disk in a drive—usually drive A. If the disk is in another drive, or if the files are available elsewhere on your system, you can edit the path name. To do so, click on the text box, use the [Backspace] key to erase the default drive designation, and type the appropriate drive and path name. After you place the requested disk in the proper drive, press [Enter] or click on the OK button. Continue to supply disks when Setup requests them.

Modifying your AUTOEXEC.BAT and CONFIG.SYS files

In Custom Setup, Setup proposes modifications to your AUTOEXEC.BAT and CONFIG.SYS files and offers you a choice of three ways to implement the changes: Setup can modify the files automatically, let you edit the proposed changes before it records them, or save the suggested modifications in separate files for you to edit later. When Setup modifies the files, it saves your existing AUTOEXEC.BAT and CONFIG.SYS files with the extension .OOO. In Express Setup, Setup automatically updates the AUTOEXEC.BAT and CONFIG.SYS files.

In most cases, you'll want to review and edit the modifications. In Custom Setup, Setup opens two text boxes with your existing AUTOEXEC.BAT file in the lower box and its proposed changes in the top box. You'll see that Setup inserts the new Windows directory into your PATH statement and assigns an environment variable: *SET TEMP=C:\WINDOWS\TEMP.* You can edit the proposed modifications by clicking on the text and then using the standard editing keys to make your changes. As a convenience, when you use the scroll bars to navigate through the file, the text in both boxes moves together. After you edit the proposed AUTOEXEC.BAT file, click on the Continue button.

Your CONFIG.SYS file will undergo a few more changes. Setup assigns a value of 30 to FILES and sets BUFFERS to 30, unless your configuration was already set to a higher value. It adds device drivers such as HIMEM.SYS and MOUSE.SYS and might disable your existing device drivers by modifying those lines of your CONFIG.SYS file to begin with REM (Remark). Setup does this because your existing device drivers might conflict with Windows 3.1. Later, we'll explain about these device drivers and other measures for optimizing Windows.

For Express Setup, or if you choose to set up printers during Custom Setup, Setup opens the Printers dialog box. With this dialog box, you can install printer drivers, configure port assignments, install fonts, and establish printer-specific preferences. See Chapter 3 for an explanation of setting up printers to work with Windows. After you've installed printers, click on Continue.

Setting up printers

Setup opens the Program Manager window and builds group windows containing the standard Windows accessories and applications so that they will be available when you run Windows.

Setup will search your hard drive for applications to install in the Program Manager. (For Custom Setup, you must specifically choose this option on the opening screen.) This same tool is available as part of the Windows Setup application within Windows (discussed in Chapter 3).

Setting up applications

Setup offers you an opportunity to run the Windows and mouse tutorials. If you have never used the mouse or Windows before, these tutorials can help you. Simply follow the on-screen instructions. You can skip the tutorials if you are already familiar with these operations.

Running the tutorials

Once you've completed the basic installation, you'll need to restart Windows before your newly installed options can take effect. The Exit Windows Setup dialog box lets you choose to reboot the computer, restart Windows, or return to MS-DOS. If you changed your AUTOEXEC.BAT or CONFIG.SYS file during installation, you'll want to select Reboot. (Windows is smart enough to know whether AUTOEXEC.BAT or CONFIG.SYS was changed; if no changes were made, Windows does not present this option.) Click on the appropriate button to end the Windows installation. After you reboot, you should be able to start Windows by typing *WIN* at the MS-DOS prompt.

Exiting Windows Setup

Once Setup has done its job, Windows should be ready to run—at least in its basic configuration. If you opted *not* to allow Setup to modify either your AUTOEXEC.BAT or your CONFIG.SYS file, you will need to edit these files before you reboot your computer and start Windows. And if you didn't set up a printer during installation, you'll need to do so before you can print from Windows or from any Windows-based application. Refer to Chapter 3 for details on working with your printer from Windows.

TWEAKING YOUR INSTALLATION

Windows is a very powerful operating environment with many features and capabilities. However, its power has a price. Windows makes significant demands on your computer hardware. And, since Windows interacts directly with your computer to deliver its impressive performance, it may conflict with third-party software such as RAM disks, disk caching, memory management, and certain Terminate-and-Stay-Resident (TSR) programs.

Optimizing your system

Windows can't perform at its best if your system isn't performing at its best. You'll need to take a few steps to optimize the speed, capacity, and available disk space of your system. Although the steps we outline below are not normally required to get Windows up and running, they often can improve performance significantly. These steps require varying degrees of technical knowledge about your computer system. Don't feel intimidated. Remember, the steps are optional performance enhancements, not required parts of the installation.

Hard-drive housecleaning

The first step in optimizing your system is cleaning up your hard drive. Get rid of those old, unneeded files cluttering up your drive. If the files are obsolete, delete them. If they are still valuable but infrequently used, save them on floppy disks where they'll be available when you need them, but don't tie up valuable space on your hard drive. If you don't plan to use all the Windows accessories, you can delete the program and help files for the applications you won't need.

If your system crashes, locks up, or otherwise exits applications unexpectedly, you may find temporary files left on your disk that would normally have been deleted automatically. It's a good idea to check for and delete any stray temporary files after an application aborts unexpectedly.

The MS-DOS command CHKDSK is a valuable tool for hard-drive maintenance. You should use it regularly, in addition to running it after any system crash. But do *not* run CHKDSK from within Windows! Exit Windows first, and then type *CHKDSK /F* at the MS-DOS prompt and press [Enter]. CHKDSK will scan your disk for lost chunks of data that it can't identify as part of a file. If it finds any, CHKDSK will offer to convert the lost data to files. Unless you are highly skilled in these matters, you should answer *N* at the prompt, allowing CHKDSK to simply delete the lost data. Reconstructing files from lost data chains is a job best left to experts. Others should rely on backup files or resort to re-installing applications and re-entering information (depending on what files were damaged).

As you create, delete, and modify files, MS-DOS stores the data on your hard drive. It doesn't necessarily save a file in one contiguous string—a single file may be fragmented into bits and pieces scattered across your disk. MS-DOS keeps track of where it puts all the pieces of a file and can reassemble the file on demand. However, hard-drive performance suffers noticeably when the disk heads must move to multiple locations to read each file.

Several good utility programs on the market can restore order to the disjointed files on your hard drive. They are called defragmentation utilities, disk compression programs, or disk compaction programs, and the major brands all work well. We recommend you purchase one and use it regularly. Just don't attempt to use it from within Windows, and, for safety, always have a current backup.

Conventional memory is your most precious system resource. The small device drivers and memory-resident utilities that need only "a couple of KB" each can add up and consume memory that your applications desperately need.

You'll want to examine your AUTOEXEC.BAT and CONFIG.SYS files and strip out anything that might unnecessarily eat up RAM. (Use Windows' Notepad to edit and save the files, and then exit Windows and reboot your system in order to use the edited version of the files.) You can deactivate a device driver in your CONFIG.SYS file or a command in your AUTOEXEC.BAT file by typing *REM* followed by a space at the beginning of the line containing the device driver. This causes MS-DOS to treat that line as a remark. (It may also cause a harmless error message such as *Unrecognized command in CONFIG.SYS.*)

Windows incorporates a built-in mouse interface and doesn't require a separate device driver (at least for the Microsoft Mouse and most compatibles). Windows includes a version of the MOUSE.SYS device driver that you should use instead of your old device driver for the Microsoft Mouse. (This is one of the changes Setup automatically makes in your CONFIG.SYS file.)

There are other device drivers commonly found in your CONFIG.SYS file that you should remove or replace with the drivers supplied with Windows. We'll outline the purpose of each of these device drivers in a moment. Setup automatically installs most of the device drivers, but it's a good idea to check for yourself. Generally, you should use the driver supplied with Windows if one is available. Otherwise, consider removing the device driver if it's not essential to your system. If you are running MS-DOS 5.0, consider using DEVICEHIGH in CONFIG.SYS to move as many drivers as possible into high memory. (See the MS-DOS 5.0 manual for more information.)

In addition to device drivers, Country settings, and the like, your CONFIG.SYS file will contain FILES and BUFFERS statements. FILES should be set at 30 unless you expect to run applications that require a higher value. A lower setting won't save any memory and may cause problems for Windows, while a higher setting will use more RAM. A setting of 20 is normally adequate for BUFFERS, and you can often save some memory by reducing it to 10 if you use the SMARTDrive disk cache driver that is supplied with Windows. (Note that Windows 3.1 will add *BUFFERS=30* to CONFIG.SYS and a line that will load SMARTDrive to AUTOEXEC.BAT if those parameters do not already exist.)

After you've scrutinized your CONFIG.SYS file for unnecessary uses of memory, turn your attention to AUTOEXEC.BAT. The AUTOEXEC.BAT file is often home to many small TSRs and pop-up accessories. Because these are installed in memory when you start your system, they will be available at any time. Some, such as network interfaces, are vital parts of your system and should remain. Others are unnecessary and inappropriate on a system operating under

Windows. They can conflict with Windows and create serious problems, or they might simply be useless in the Windows environment and represent a waste of precious system memory. Be ruthlessly objective in evaluating TSRs, and remove any that are not essential to your system.

If a particular application requires a TSR to run, consider moving the TSR to a batch file that loads the TSR, runs the application, and then removes the TSR when you exit the application. (See Chapter 17 for more information on using batch files to run DOS-based applications from within Windows.)

During installation, Setup adds a line to your AUTOEXEC.BAT file that tells Windows where to store temporary files. Usually, the line will read *Set TEMP = C:\WINDOWS\TEMP.* You might change it to any convenient directory, such as C:\TEMP. If you have a RAM disk installed in extended or expanded memory, you can use it for the temporary files. For example, if your RAM drive is E, change the line in your AUTOEXEC.BAT file to read *Set TEMP = E:\.* Reading and writing temporary files into fast memory instead of a slow disk drive noticeably improves the performance of applications that use temporary files extensively.

Windows' device drivers

Device drivers are a special class of memory-resident programs that, once installed, effectively become extensions of your operating system. Device drivers provide an interface between your computer and a peripheral device or another feature (such as extended memory management) that is not included in the MS-DOS operating system. You install device drivers by including a statement such as *DEVICE = pathname\driver.SYS* in your CONFIG.SYS file.

Microsoft provides several device drivers with Windows that were created especially to maximize Windows' capabilities. Whenever possible, you should use the device drivers supplied with Windows since other device drivers intended to perform similar functions may conflict with Windows. You may need some, none, or all of the device drivers supplied with Windows, depending on your computer hardware, Windows' operating mode, and your applications.

HIMEM.SYS

HIMEM.SYS, which is Windows' extended (XMS) memory manager, assigns blocks of extended memory to your various applications and makes sure one application doesn't use another application's memory during multitasking operations. MS-DOS versions earlier than 5.0 perform similar functions within conventional memory but can't manage the extended memory addressed by your 286 or 386 computer's protected mode; MS-DOS 5.0 also provides HIMEM.SYS to perform the same functions in a non-Windows environment.

HIMEM adds one unusual capability to its repertoire. In addition to managing extended memory, HIMEM can effectively increase conventional memory by making the first 64 KB of extended memory available for use as conventional memory. It's like having 704 KB of conventional memory.

Setup automatically copies HIMEM.SYS to your hard drive. Be sure that you use the version of HIMEM.SYS supplied with Windows 3.1 rather than an older version from a previous Windows or MS-DOS installation.

SMARTDrive is a disk-cache utility that uses extended or expanded memory to improve your system's disk access speed. SMARTDrive, like other disk-cache programs, stores in memory a copy of the latest information read from your hard drive. Then, when your application requests the same information again (as often happens), SMARTDrive can supply the information from memory much faster than reading it from a disk again. Unlike other disk-cache programs, this version of SMARTDrive allows Windows to automatically reduce the memory allocated to the disk cache and use that memory for applications.

SMARTDRV.EXE

If Setup detects the necessary memory available on your system, it will automatically copy SMARTDRV.EXE to your hard drive and will install it in your AUTOEXEC.BAT file during installation. You might want to experiment with different settings for the maximum and minimum cache sizes to find the optimum settings for your system and the applications you use.

A RAM disk is a section of memory that your computer system can use as a hard drive. The advantage of a RAM disk is that moving information to and from memory is much faster than reading and writing the same information to a physical disk. The disadvantage of a RAM disk is that you will lose the information when you turn the computer off since it is stored in volatile RAM instead of on the magnetic media of a physical disk.

RAMDRIVE.SYS

A RAM disk has many uses, but perhaps the most appropriate is to store temporary files. Applications that create and use temporary files extensively will benefit greatly from the speed of the RAM disk, and the impermanent nature of the RAM disk is not a negative factor since temporary files are normally deleted when you exit an application.

RAMDrive is the RAM disk that is supplied with Windows. Setup copies the RAMDRIVE.SYS file to your Windows directory during installation but does not install RAMDrive in your CONFIG.SYS file. You can configure a RAM disk of any size in conventional memory (not recommended), expanded memory, or extended memory. However, you should remember that any memory devoted to a RAM disk will not be available for your applications. (See your Windows manual for more information about RAMDrive.)

EMM386 is an expanded memory emulator for 386-based systems. It can configure a block of extended memory on a 386- or 486-based computer to simulate LIM EMS 4.0 expanded memory. In 386 enhanced mode, Windows can simulate EMS memory for the applications that need it, without any help from a

EMM386.EXE

separate EMS emulator. You'll need EMM386 only if you expect to run applications that require EMS memory outside Windows. In many cases, the capabilities of Windows' 386 enhanced mode will eliminate the need for any other expanded memory manager. You can simply run your DOS applications that need EMS memory from Windows. Setup copies EMM386.EXE to your Windows directory but does not install it in your CONFIG.SYS file.

EGA.SYS

If you have an EGA display, Windows needs EGA.SYS to help manage the video display for DOS applications you run from Windows in standard mode. If your system includes an EGA monitor, make sure that your CONFIG.SYS file includes the line *DEVICE = C:\WINDOWS\EGA.SYS*. (Window's Custom Setup will not copy EGA.SYS to the Windows directory unless you choose or confirm EGA as your display during Setup.)

MOUSE.SYS

For users of the Microsoft Mouse and compatibles, Microsoft includes an updated version of the MOUSE.SYS device driver with Windows. This version is specially modified to be compatible with Windows and the other Windows device drivers. Be sure to use this version of MOUSE.SYS in your Windows directory rather than your original mouse driver. If you use your mouse only in Windows, you may not need a mouse driver at all. Windows includes a built-in mouse interface (at least for the Microsoft Mouse and compatibles) that doesn't require a separate mouse driver or MOUSE.COM program.

Managing swap files

Windows creates and uses one of three kinds of swap files. In standard mode, Windows uses application swap files to store the inactive application when switching between Windows and a DOS application. In 386 enhanced mode, Windows uses a swap file on your hard drive as virtual memory. Windows can create a temporary swap file each time you enter 386 enhanced mode, or you can create a permanent swap file for Windows to use as virtual memory.

Application swap files

In standard mode, Windows uses application swap files to facilitate task switching between Windows and DOS applications. When you execute a DOS application from within Windows, Windows first suspends your Windows applications and swaps them from memory to a file on your hard drive, thus freeing your memory for the DOS application. At the same time, Windows creates a temporary application swap file for the DOS application. If you switch back to Windows (or another DOS application) without first exiting the DOS application, Windows will suspend the DOS application, swap it to its application swap file on a disk, and restore Windows to memory from the swap file. When you exit an application, Windows deletes the application swap file it created for that application.

Application swap files are temporary files that Windows automatically creates and deletes. They are hidden files that are normally stored in your Windows directory; their names begin with ~WOA. If you suspect that an abnormal exit from an application or from Windows left application swap files lingering on your disk, use the File Manager to find and delete them. See Chapter 6 for instructions on how to view hidden files with the File Manager.

In 386 enhanced mode, Windows doesn't use application swap files; it uses a different kind of swap file known as virtual memory. Virtual memory is a special section of your hard drive that the 386 processor can treat as additional RAM. The processor can swap large blocks of information between your hard drive and extended memory to make more memory available for data and to run more applications concurrently than would normally fit within your system's combined conventional and extended memory.

386 enhanced mode swap files

Windows can create a temporary swap file each time you start Windows in 386 enhanced mode and automatically adjust its size depending on the applications you run and your available disk space. Windows names the temporary swap file WIN386.SWP and normally creates it in your Windows directory. The temporary swap file has the advantage of being only as large as needed under the current circumstances and, since Windows automatically deletes it at the end of your Windows session, the swap file doesn't tie up hard-drive space when you use Windows in standard mode or work outside the Windows environment entirely. The disadvantages of a temporary swap file are that it is slower than a permanent swap file, it doesn't work well if your disk is fragmented, and it doesn't offer large contiguous blocks of disk space.

As an alternative to a temporary swap file, you can create a permanent swap file on your hard drive for Windows to use as virtual memory. Using a permanent swap file is faster and more efficient than using a temporary swap file. The permanent swap file creates a section of your hard drive for Windows' exclusive use, but that space is unavailable when you use Windows in standard mode or work outside the Windows environment.

Setup automatically offers to create a permanent swap file on your hard drive if your system will support it (a 386-based computer with 2 MB of memory and sufficient hard-drive space). You can also create, delete, or change the size of your permanent swap file at a later time by using the 386 Enhanced settings available through Control Panel.

Choosing the Virtual Memory button in the 386 Enhanced dialog box in Control Panel will allow you to manipulate a permanent swap file that Windows can use as virtual memory when it operates in 386 enhanced mode. With virtual memory, you can create a new permanent swap file, change its size, or delete it.

Virtual memory

You'll need a large contiguous block of hard-drive space for the permanent swap file, so you should compact your hard drive before attempting to create a permanent swap file. Virtual memory has only a few options and is fairly easy to use.

A word of warning: Be sure to use *only* virtual memory to manipulate your permanent swap file. Do not attempt to manipulate the 386SPART.PAR and SPART.PAR files with the File Manager or with MS-DOS commands.

Windows' startup files

Each time you start Windows, it refers to its initialization files for information about your system configuration and preferences. Windows finds this information in the WIN.INI, SYSTEM.INI, CONTROL.INI, and PROGMAN.INI files, as we'll explain in this section.

WIN.INI

The WIN.INI file contains a wealth of information about your Windows environment and how you have customized it for your own system and working preferences. The WIN.INI file records your preferences for everything from printer ports and the file name extensions associated with certain applications to the defaults for installed applications such as Word for Windows. Although you often had to edit the WIN.INI file to exercise various options in early versions of Windows, that is no longer the case. Now, you can control nearly every aspect of your Windows environment with Control Panel and the built-in control features of the other Windows applications. Windows will record your changes in the WIN.INI file; you won't need to edit it yourself.

Even though it isn't usually necessary, you can edit the WIN.INI file with Windows' Notepad accessory (or any ASCII text editor). You can also use Notepad to read the WININI.WRI file, which lists the purpose and correct syntax for each setting in the WIN.INI file.

The LOAD and RUN settings in the WIN.INI file are worth mentioning despite the fact that using them requires manually editing the WIN.INI file. With these settings, you can instruct Windows to set up your desktop automatically with the applications and files you normally use, as an alternative to placing them in the StartUp group window.

By default, the *LOAD=* and *RUN=* lines at the top of the WIN.INI file are blank. You can add a list of applications and files to these lines to have Windows automatically start the applications and open the specified files when you start Windows. The LOAD and RUN settings take effect before the StartUp group in the Program Manager. The LOAD and RUN settings are very similar in that both automatically start the applications you list. The difference is that LOAD minimizes each application to an icon on your desktop, while RUN runs the application in a window.

For example, consider the following lines from a WIN.INI file:

load=winfile.exe   mci-mail.trm
run=schedule.cal

As you can see in the first line, you can list more than one item for Windows to load, with the items separated by a space. If you list the file name for an application, Windows will load that application as an icon on the desktop. (WINFILE.EXE is the executable file for the File Manager.) If you list a data file that is associated with an application (in this case, MCI-MAIL.TRM is a file that contains the settings for Terminal to use with MCI Mail), Windows will load the associated application and open the data file. The RUN setting on the next line causes Windows to run the Calendar application and load the associated Calendar data file SCHEDULE.CAL.

Unless you have a special reason to run an application before Windows starts the applications specified in the StartUp group, you should not need to use the LOAD or RUN setting.

SYSTEM.INI

The SYSTEM.INI file is Windows' other major file of initialization information. It contains hardware configuration information, such as the display and keyboard drivers, and the location of the temporary swap file. As you can with the WIN.INI file, you can control nearly all the SYSTEM.INI options from within Windows with Windows Setup and Control Panel. You can edit the SYSTEM.INI file with Notepad (or any ASCII text editor), although it should rarely be necessary. The SYSINI.WRI file contains a list of the SYSTEM.INI settings and their correct syntax. Study the information in the SYSINI.WRI file carefully before attempting to edit the SYSTEM.INI file.

PROGMAN.INI

When Windows is loaded, it reads the PROGMAN.INI file to determine which group windows to display, where on the screen the Program Manager window should be placed, and the order in which each group window is chosen when you cycle through the group windows. Changes made to the Program Manager window are saved in this file if Save Settings on Exit is active.

CONTROL.INI

Windows provides a set of default values for color schemes, custom colors, and patterns for Control Panel's Desktop and Color functions. Any changes to Desktop or Color are saved in this file. As printers are installed, printer driver names are also added to this file.

Customizing Windows

The true power of a product such as Windows lies in its ability to help you work in a more natural, intuitive fashion. To take full advantage of Windows, you need to customize it to reflect *your* preferences and style. Chapter 3 discusses Control Panel, which allows you to change everything from printers and ports to the color and pattern of Windows' desktop and window borders.

To use Windows as a true operating environment from which you launch applications, you'll need to add your applications to the Program Manager as icons. If you instructed Setup to search your hard drive, you should be well on your way. Although it will find most major Windows-based applications and many others as well, Setup probably won't recognize all your applications. You'll need to add some of them to the Program Manager yourself, as discussed in Chapter 5. You may need to create or edit PIF files for some of your DOS applications before they will run optimally with Windows 3.1; see Chapter 17 for information on using the PIF Editor.

Networking Windows

If you are installing Windows in a network environment, you'll first need to decide whether to install it on an individual work station or as a shared resource on the network server. The installation procedures for these two situations are quite different; we discuss both in Chapter 8. Chapter 8 also covers using network printers with the Print Manager and connecting to network drives.

Appendix B
Glossary

386 enhanced mode
386 enhanced mode is one of Windows' operating modes. It takes advantage of a 386- or 486-based computer's protected mode to offer advanced memory management and multitasking.

accelerator key
An accelerator key, a keyboard shortcut for a command, is commonly a function key such as [F5] or a combination of [Alt] or [Ctrl] with another typing or function key.

active window
The active window, identified by its colored title bar, is the window on the desktop currently operating in the foreground. It's the window that is currently selected or the one in which you are working.

alert message
An alert message is a dialog box with a graphic and a critical, warning, confirmation, or information message. It is also called a message dialog box or a message box.

alignment icons
In Write, the alignment icons (left-align, centered, right-align, and justified) allow you to change a paragraph's formatting.

ANSI
ANSI, which stands for the American National Standards Institute, is the set of codes Windows uses to define characters you enter into documents and other types of files. The ANSI character set is the standard across all Windows applications and includes the 128 characters in the ASCII (American Standard Code for Information Interchange) set. The ASCII character set defines all the letters, numbers, punctuation marks, and symbols on your keyboard, as well as special instructions such as carriage returns, line feeds, and tabs. In addition to the ASCII characters, the ANSI set also includes foreign-language characters.

application window	An application window is a type of window that furnishes menus of commands and a work area for your data. All Windows applications run in application windows. An application window can contain multiple document windows.
arrow keys	The arrow keys, which are marked ↑, ↓, ←, and →, typically control cursor movement.
arrow pointer	The arrow pointer, the "mouse" pointer for all Windows applications, is used for selecting commands, activating applications, and moving windows.
background operation	A background operation refers to a task performed by one application while another application is running in the active window (the foreground). For example, while you are editing a document in Write, the Print Manager can print a Paintbrush drawing in the background.
Calculator	Calculator is an application packaged with Windows to provide standard and scientific versions of a calculator.
Calendar	Calendar, which is packaged with Windows, is an electronic appointment book that keeps track of your appointments by date and time.
Cardfile	Cardfile, which is packaged with Windows, is a simple database that has two fields and sorts on one of them (the index line).
cascading	Cascading is a process in which windows are stacked diagonally so that their title bars show. Choose the Cascade command from the Window menu, select the Cascade button in the Task List dialog box, or press [Shift][F5].
cascading menus	Cascading menus branch from a command on a superior menu. Windows indicates that an entry on a menu is attached to a cascading menu by displaying a small triangle pointer next to the menu selection. When you click on a cascading menu command, another menu of commands appears next to the current drop-down menu.
Character Map	Character Map is a Windows accessory that you can use to insert special characters into many Windows applications through Clipboard. The Character Map window provides a wide range of foreign-language characters, extended characters, symbols, and fonts.
check box	A check box lets you turn a particular dialog box option on or off. When it is selected (the option is turned on), a check box contains an X.

clicking
Clicking is a mouse action that selects an item or activates a command. To click, you press a mouse button once and immediately release it.

Clipboard
Clipboard is a Windows utility that provides a conduit for transporting data between applications running in Windows. The Cut, Copy, and Paste commands found in Windows applications use Clipboard to store and retrieve data. The Clipboard Viewer window allows you to view the current contents of Clipboard.

Clock
Clock is an application packaged with Windows that displays the time of day with either a traditional analog clock face or a digital number face.

color scheme
A color scheme is a set of colors for the desktop. Windows comes with a set of preformatted color schemes but also allows you to create your own.

command buttons
Command buttons are the large, gray, rectangular buttons that appear in dialog boxes. The command associated with the button appears in black letters in the center of an active button and in gray letters on an inactive button.

confirmation message
Windows presents a dialog box asking you to confirm that you want certain actions performed, such as deleting a file in the File Manager. You can turn confirmation messages off if you so desire.

Control menu
Windows displays the Control menu of a window when you click on the box containing the dash in the upper-left corner of an application window (or press [Alt][Spacebar]) or when you click on the box containing the hyphen in the upper-left corner of a document window (or press [Alt]-). The Control menu provides keyboard access to many window manipulations that otherwise require a mouse (for example, moving or sizing the window).

Control Panel
Control Panel is a built-in Windows application that modifies your WIN.INI and CONTROL.INI files to customize your Windows environment. For example, you can use Control Panel to change screen colors and install printers.

Copy
Copy is a command that duplicates selected text or graphics in the work area and places the copy in Clipboard. You can retrieve the text or graphics with the Paste command.

critical message
Windows presents a dialog box with a red stop sign and a message to tell you that a critical error has occurred. Some critical messages also suggest a way to recover from the error.

crosshair pointer

Whenever you work with graphics, you'll see the crosshair pointer or a variation of it. This pointer is often found in Windows' drawing application, Paintbrush.

cursor

The cursor is a blinking vertical line that appears in an active desktop element in which you can enter text. The cursor is sometimes referred to as the insertion point marker.

Cut

Cut is a command that removes selected text or graphics from the work area and places it in Clipboard. You can retrieve the text or graphics with the Paste command.

DDE

DDE, Dynamic Data Exchange, is a protocol that enables Windows to dynamically update data in one application with data from another application. The two applications issue the commands, and Windows provides the path for the flow of data.

desktop

The desktop is the screen area in which all Windows operations take place. The desktop fills the entire screen, and all windows and icons appear on top of it.

desktop pattern

A desktop pattern is a bit map that fills your desktop, adding a decorative accent to Windows. Windows comes with several patterns and also allows you to create your own patterns.

dialog box

A dialog box is a Windows element that you use to define parameters or options before implementing a command. A dialog box is made up of a framed box, a title bar, a Control menu, and various elements such as radio buttons and text boxes that allow you to set options. A menu item or command button with an ellipsis (...) after its name indicates that a dialog box will appear before Windows processes the command.

directory contents pane

A directory contents pane, which is a pane of a directory window in the File Manager, displays the subdirectories and files located in a selected directory. When you click on a directory icon in the directory tree pane or double-click on a subdirectory icon in the directory contents pane, the File Manager displays the contents of the selected directory.

directory tree pane

A directory tree pane, a pane of a directory window in the File Manager, contains a visual representation of the directories on a floppy disk, a hard drive, a CD-ROM drive, a RAM disk, or a network drive.

directory window

A directory window is a window of the File Manager. It can contain both a directory tree pane and a directory contents pane, one listing directories on the current drive and the other listing files and subdirectories of the current directory. When you start the File Manager, it displays a directory window for the current directory; when you activate a different drive or directory icon, the directory window changes to show the files and subdirectories in the new drive or directory.

display box

A display box provides a sample picture of the results produced by one or more options in a dialog box.

dithered color

A dithered color uses a composite of two colors to form a third color. For example, light yellow is a combination of yellow and white.

document window

A document window is a type of window that partitions the work area of an application window, allowing you to display and work with more than one data file at once. However, not all Windows applications are designed to use document windows.

double-clicking

A double-click refers to pressing a mouse button twice in quick succession. Double-clicking activates icons, chooses items from lists, and can open a file.

draft quality

If you choose to print a file with draft quality, Windows will print the file quickly (faster than printing at the highest resolution) but won't include all the details that the advanced features of your printer can provide.

dragging

Dragging is a mouse technique in which you point to a desktop element (such as an icon), press a mouse button to select the element, and then hold down the mouse button while you move the mouse. As long as you hold down the mouse button, Windows will move the desktop element or enlarge your selection in accordance with your mouse movement. When you want to release the element or finish selecting, release the mouse button.

drop-down list box

Drop-down list boxes allow you to choose a single option from a large list. Their lists are not immediately visible in dialog boxes. When you open a dialog box, you see only a text box containing the drop-down list box's current setting. To display the list, click on the drop-down arrow. After you make a selection, the list will disappear.

drop-down menu

A drop-down menu refers to a menu that appears below its title on a menu bar. When you click on the title of the menu, a list of commands drops down.

embedded object	An embedded object is data created by an OLE source application that is then inserted and stored in a data file of the receiving application. To edit an embedded object, double-click on the object or choose the object's name from the Edit menu.
File Manager	The File Manager is a built-in Windows application that you can use to manage all your MS-DOS files. The File Manager creates a multiple-window environment that provides file management capabilities based on, but exceeding, those of MS-DOS.
font	Fonts are typefaces that determine the shape, size, and spacing of characters both on your screen and on the printed page.
full-screen window	By default, Windows sets up a full-screen window for a non-Windows application when you launch it from the Program Manager or the File Manager. A full-screen window looks like an MS-DOS screen.
granularity	Granularity refers to the invisible guidelines on the desktop that Windows uses to arrange windows and icons. You can use Control Panel to vary the spacing of this invisible grid.
graphics mode	Graphics mode is a setting in an application's PIF informing Windows that the application can display images as well as text. (The opposite of graphics mode is text mode, in which an application can display only text.)
group box	A group box organizes dialog box elements by function so that an option is easier to find. The group box doesn't set an option itself but simply frames a number of different options under one main heading.
group window	A group window, a variant of a document window, groups icons inside the Program Manager.
guideline	Windows uses guidelines to represent the outline of a window or graphic when you resize or move it. The guidelines appear only as you drag the window or graphic.
hand pointer	While in the Help application, you use the hand pointer to jump between Help topics.

Help Help is an on-line information application packaged with Windows. You can use Help from any application that is packaged with Windows to find out more about that application's keyboard, menu, and procedures. You can also get help for Help.

HIMEM.SYS HIMEM.SYS is an extended memory manager (actually a device driver for memory) that assigns blocks of extended memory to different applications. Windows uses this facility extensively.

hot link A hot link is a dynamic relationship, created with DDE commands, between two files in different applications. In a hot link, the source application automatically updates data in the receiving application whenever linked data changes.

hourglass pointer The hourglass pointer indicates that Windows is working to complete the command you issued. While the hourglass is on the desktop, you can't issue any other commands or select desktop elements within that application, but you can switch to another Windows application to perform a different task. This switching leaves the first task running in the background. When the pointer returns to its previous shape, you can go on to the next task in that application.

I-beam pointer The default arrow pointer changes into an I-beam shape whenever you point to an area in which you can enter text.

icon An icon is a graphic with a title that represents an application, directory, file, or minimized window. You can usually select an icon by clicking on it. Double-clicking on it causes the action associated with that icon to occur. For example, double-clicking on an application icon launches the application, while double-clicking on a minimized window icon restores the window to its previous size.

inactive window An inactive window is any window on the desktop other than the active window. Any application running in the background has an inactive window.

increment box An increment box is a text box that will accept numbers only. Windows adds a pair of arrows to the increment box so that you can scroll through the range of values for an option.

information message An information message appears in a dialog box with a lowercase *i* in a blue circle and informs you about an aspect of the command you just issued.

key repeat rate The key repeat rate is the speed at which a key will type or repeat characters while you hold down the key.

link   A link is a connection between data files. Links can be hot (the data in a source file automatically updates the linked data in a receiving file) or warm (the data in the receiving file is updated only when you request or confirm updating).

list box   A list box lets you choose a single option from a group of options. List boxes use scroll bars when a long list of options is available.

macro   A macro is a sequence of keystrokes and mouse movements that Windows repeats when you issue a command or type a key combination. You use the Recorder application, which is packaged with Windows, to record and play macros.

maximize   Maximizing an application window expands it to fill the desktop. Maximizing a document window expands it to fill its application window. To maximize a window, click on the Maximize box in the window's upper-right corner, or issue the Maximize command on the window's Control menu. To restore a maximized window to its previous size, click on the box displaying up and down arrows (the Restore box) in the window's upper-right corner, or issue the Restore command on the window's Control menu.

Media Player   Media Player is a Windows accessory that allows you to play animation, sound, and MIDI sequencer files and to control hardware such as CD-ROM drives and videodisc players.

menu bar   The menu bar, located below the title bar in an application window, contains a series of menus listed by title (for example, the File menu).

minimize   Minimizing a window reduces the window to an icon. To minimize a window, click on the Minimize box in the window's upper-right corner, or issue the Minimize command on the window's Control menu. To restore a minimized window to its previous size, select the window's icon and then choose the Restore command from its Control menu, or simply double-click on the icon.

move pointer   The move pointer appears when you issue the Move command from a window's Control menu. After you see the move pointer, which includes arrows pointing in all four directions, you can use the arrow keys on your keyboard to move the window on the desktop. As you press arrow keys, Windows will move an outline of the window but will not reposition the actual window until you press [Enter].

MS-DOS Prompt The MS-DOS Prompt is a utility that starts a second copy of the MS-DOS command interpreter, which appears as a normal MS-DOS session. You can then run non-Windows applications or MS-DOS utilities in the session, switch to Windows or another application, and even run the MS-DOS session in a window.

Notepad Notepad is a simple word processor that works only with ASCII-based text and is packaged with Windows. Notepad is handy for creating and editing MS-DOS batch files, electronic mail messages, and date-and-time logs.

object An object is data from one application that is inserted into a file of another application, using Microsoft Object Linking and Embedding (OLE) functions. Object editing takes place in a window of the source application. Objects can be embedded (stored in a file of the receiving application) or linked (stored in a file of the source application).

Object Linking and Embedding (OLE) OLE is the Microsoft architecture for sharing data between Windows applications in a way that makes it easy to insert and edit data from another application without manually switching applications. Also, by being able to edit data in its source application, you add that application's full functionality to the application that receives the data without having to add all those functions to the receiving program itself.

Object Packager Object Packager is an OLE application that gives you a way to insert into a file an icon that represents a link to data or to an application.

Paintbrush Paintbrush, which is packaged with Windows, is a graphics application for "paint"-style drawing (bit map editing).

palette A palette refers to a range of colors provided by Windows. Control Panel's Color dialog box and the Paintbrush application both provide palettes.

Paste Paste is a command that copies selected text or graphics from Clipboard into an application's work area.

PIF A PIF (program information file) contains technical information about a non-Windows application that enables Windows to optimize the way the application runs when you launch it from Windows. You can create your own PIFs or modify existing PIFs with the PIF Editor.

PIF Editor

The PIF Editor is an application packaged with Windows that helps you customize the way a non-Windows application is launched and how it uses Windows' capabilities and features, including memory and multitasking.

pixel

A pixel is one dot on your screen. The detail of an image shown on your screen depends on the number of pixels your monitor can display in an area.

pointer

The pointer is a floating graphic on your screen that represents the actions of your mouse. It changes shape to reflect changes in your mouse's capabilities. For example, when you move the default arrow pointer over a word processor's document, the pointer turns into an I-beam, indicating that you can work with text.

prevent pointer

The prevent pointer, which looks like a circle with a slanted line through it, indicates that you can't relocate a desktop element where you're pointing.

primary mouse button

The primary mouse button is the one you use to make most of your selections and perform most mouse actions. By default, it's the left button on a Microsoft mouse. You can use Control Panel to make the right button the primary button.

printer driver

A printer driver is a device driver that tells Windows how to format data for a particular type of printer.

Print Manager

The Print Manager is a Windows application that controls printing for all Windows applications. The Print Manager, Windows' print spooler, allows you to work with applications while you print.

processor time

Processor time refers to the way the computer's microprocessor splits its time between different applications running simultaneously. If you're running Windows in 386 enhanced mode, you can define the size of the timeslice (the microprocessor's basic time unit) with Control Panel.

Program Manager

The Program Manager is a built-in Windows application that is a program execution shell—that is, it's an application devoted to launching other programs. The Program Manager presents each application as an icon. You can launch the application by double-clicking on the icon.

proof quality

If you choose to print your file with proof quality, Windows will use all the advanced features of your printer to produce the highest-quality image.

protected mode   Protected mode is the operating mode of the computer's 80286, 80386, or 80486 microprocessor chip that enables extended memory management and other advanced features.

push button   A command button with two chevrons (>>) next to the command name is called a push button. Push buttons expand a dialog box to include more options.

queue   A queue is a list or a waiting line. In Windows, a queue keeps track of which file is next in line for a printer in the Print Manager.

radio button   Radio buttons allow you to choose a single option from a group of options, much as you'd choose one answer to a question on a multiple-choice exam. A radio button looks like a small circle. When the button is selected, a dot appears inside the circle.

ReadMe   ReadMe is a Write document containing Windows information not found in the Windows manual.

Recorder   Recorder is a Windows application that records keystrokes and mouse movements as a macro and plays them back when you type the macro's name or a key combination.

restore   When you restore a window, you return it to its previous size. You can restore an icon representing a minimized window or restore a maximized window to its smaller size on the desktop.

scaling   Scaling refers to enlarging or reducing an image. You can vary scaling when you set up certain types of printers.

screen capture   A screen capture is a graphic image (bit map) of your computer's screen. In Windows, you can capture the entire desktop by pressing [Print Screen] to copy it to Clipboard. If you press [Alt][Print Screen], you'll capture only the active desktop element, such as a window or dialog box. The captured graphic can be pasted from Clipboard into an application or modified by Paintbrush.

scroll bar   A scroll bar is the vertical or horizontal bar located at the right or the bottom of a window that lets you navigate within the window. If you click on the arrows at the ends of a scroll bar, you'll move one line at a time. You can drag the slider to move more quickly.

shell
A shell is a variation of an application window from which you can launch other applications. The Program Manager and the File Manager are both shells.

shortcut key
A shortcut key is a keystroke or sequence of keystrokes that activates a command or a Recorder macro. Accelerator keys are also shortcut keys.

sizing pointers
Sizing pointers let you adjust the size of a window on the desktop by dragging the window's frame.

slider
A slider is the square on a scroll bar that indicates the cursor's or the selection's current location in a document or in a list. You can drag the slider to change its position.

SMARTDrive
SMARTDrive is a disk-cache utility that uses extended or expanded memory to improve your system's speed by storing, in RAM, the latest information read from your disk drives.

Sound Recorder
Sound Recorder is a Windows accessory that allows you to play, record, and edit sound files if you have a sound card installed in your computer.

standard mode
Standard mode is one of Windows' two operating modes. It uses a 286-based computer's protected mode to address extended memory.

swap file
A swap file is a portion of your hard drive that Windows sets aside when it installs its files. Windows uses this part of your hard drive for temporary storage when RAM fills up. In 386 enhanced mode, Windows can treat the swap file as if it were RAM (virtual memory).

SYSTEM.INI
The SYSTEM.INI file stores your Windows system information, some of which is supplied with the Windows Setup application. This information includes the type of monitor, keyboard, mouse, computer, network, and so on.

Task Manager
The Task Manager is a Windows utility that manages multiple applications on the desktop and provides access to them with the Task List dialog box. You can open the Task List dialog box by pressing [Ctrl][Esc] or by double-clicking on the desktop outside all application windows.

Terminal
Terminal is a communications application packaged with Windows.

text box
Text boxes allow you to answer a dialog box's "fill in the blank" questions by typing characters in the text box.

text mode   If your non-Windows application runs only in text mode (as specified in its PIF), it displays only character information and does not display any graphic images.

tile   If you use the Tile command on the Window menu or select the Tile button in the Task List dialog box to tile a series of windows, Windows will divide the available space for windows (either the desktop or an application's window) among all the windows so that you can see the work area of each window. You can also press [Shift][F4] to tile windows.

title bar   The title bar, which is a line of information appearing at the top of every window, presents the name of the application and the file it's working with (if applicable). The color of the title bar tells you whether the window is active or inactive. By default, an active window has a blue title bar, and an inactive window has a white title bar.

tracking speed   Tracking speed refers to the pace of Windows' effort to keep up with you when you drag the mouse.

Tutorial   Tutorial is a Windows application that teaches you how to use the mouse to move and resize windows, choose commands from menus, launch applications, and perform other Windows tasks. Choose the Windows Tutorial command from the Program Manager's Help menu to access the tutorial.

Undo   Undo is a command that reverses the effect of your previous action (and only that action).

wallpaper   Wallpaper is a Paintbrush image that you can use to decorate your desktop. It can fill all or part of your screen. Windows supplies a number of wallpaper images, and you can also create your own.

warm link   DDE links data between applications. In a warm link, the source application updates data in the receiving application only when the receiving application (or user) approves the transfer.

warning message   A warning message appears in a dialog box containing an exclamation mark in a yellow circle and cautions you that a command will permanently change the status of a file. For example, the File Manager will present a warning message before it lets you delete a file. If Windows needs more information to complete the operation you began, it will present a dialog box with a question mark inside a green circle and a message to warn you and ask for additional information.

window	A window is a framed area in which Windows runs an application, displays a document, or performs a task. Windows provides several types of windows, but the two you will use most often are application and document windows.
Windows Setup	Windows Setup is an application packaged with Windows that lets you change your installed hardware specifications. Windows Setup then stores your settings in the SYSTEM.INI, PROGMAN.INI, and WIN.INI files.
WIN.INI	The WIN.INI file stores your Windows environment preferences, such as wall-paper choices or installed printers, most of which are set with Control Panel.
WinPopup	WinPopup is an application supplied as part of Microsoft LAN Manager that allows you to send messages to other Windows users on the network.
work area	The work area is the space in a window in which you can enter and manipulate information. For example, when you use Cardfile, you can open multiple cards, each of which has its own work area for data. In the File Manager, you can open multiple windows, each of which has its own work area.
workspace	The workspace is the part of an application window in which you can place additional windows and icons representing data. Each window you open on the workspace has its own work area in which you can manipulate data.
Write	Write is a word processing application packaged with Windows.

Index

Page numbers in *italics* indicate figures or tables.

Lori L. Lorenz

A graduate of Carleton College in Minnesota, Lori L. Lorenz worked as an information center consultant at Westinghouse Materials Company and Honeywell, Inc., before joining The Cobb Group as an author and as assistant editor of *Inside Microsoft Windows*, The Cobb Group's monthly publication for Windows users. She is currently employed at Capital Holding Corporation in the end-user computing services department.

R. Michael O'Mara

R. Michael O'Mara wrote technical manuals and served as vice president of presentation services for Kinetic Corporation before joining The Cobb Group as an author. His background includes specialties in computer graphics, business communications, and design. Mike is a graduate of Morehead State University in Kentucky.

Russell E. Borland

Russell E. Borland earned a bachelor of arts degree from Whitworth College, a master of arts degree from Portland State University, and a Ph.D. degree from the University of Washington. He has been a technical writer at Microsoft Corporation for 12 years and currently resides near Sauk, Washington. He is the author of *Working with Word for Windows, Running Word for Windows, Microsoft WordBasic Primer,* and *Microsoft WordBasic Handbook,* all published by Microsoft Press.

The manuscript for this book was prepared and submitted to Microsoft Press in electronic form. Text files were processed using Microsoft Word and formatted using Aldus PageMaker.

Principal proofreader: Kathleen Atkins
Principal typographer: Connie Little
Principal illustrator: Connie Little
Color insert designer: Peggy Herman
Color insert screenshots: AppART, Seattle
Color insert separator: Color Control
Cover designer: Rebecca Johnson
Color cover separator: Color Service

Text composition by Electronic Publishing Services, Edmonds, in ITC Garamond Light with display type in Helvetica Condensed, using Aldus PageMaker and the Linotronic 300 laser imagesetter.

Windows 3.1 Companion Quick Reference

Windows Keys

Keystroke(s)	Function
[Alt][Spacebar]	Opens Control menu for application window
[Alt]- (hyphen)	Opens Control menu for document window
[Alt][F4]	Closes active window or dialog box
[Alt][Esc]	Cycles through application windows and icons
[Alt][Tab]	Switches to next application window, restoring applications that are running as icons
[Alt][Enter]	Switches non-Windows application between running in a window and running full-screen
↑, ↓, ←, →	Moves window when you have chosen Move from Control menu, or changes size of window when you have chosen Size
[Ctrl][Tab]	Cycles through document windows and icons
[Ctrl][Esc]	Switches to Task List dialog box
[Print Screen]	Copies image of screen contents to Clipboard
[Alt][Print Screen]	Copies image of active window to Clipboard
[Ctrl][F4]	Closes active document window
[F1]	Displays Help contents for an application; displays Contents for How to Use Help when a Help window is open
[Shift][F1]	Changes pointer to question mark to access Help on specific command, screen element, or key

Dialog Box Keys

Keystroke(s)	Function
[Tab]	Moves to next item
[Shift][Tab]	Moves to previous item
[Alt]n	Moves to item whose title contains underlined letter n
↑, ↓, ←, →	Moves between options in group box, or moves cursor up or down in list or left or right in text box
[Home]	Moves to top item in list box or first character in text box
[End]	Moves to last item in list box or last character in text box
[Page Up] or [Page Down]	Scrolls up or down one boxful of data in list box
[Alt]↓	Opens drop-down list box
↑ or ↓	Selects item in drop-down list box
[Spacebar]	Selects or cancels highlighted item in list box or check box
[Ctrl] / (slash)	Selects all items in list box
[Ctrl]\ (backslash)	Cancels all selections in list box except active item
[Shift]↑ or [Shift]↓	Extends list box highlight in direction of arrow
[Shift][Home]	Extends text box highlight to first character
[Shift][End]	Extends text box highlight to last character
[Backspace]	Deletes one character from left of cursor
[Enter]	Selects highlighted item (if any) and executes active command button
[Esc] or [Alt][F4]	Closes or exits dialog box without completing any commands

Menu Keys

Keystroke(s)	Function
[Alt] or [F10]	Selects first menu on menu bar
[Alt]n	Opens menu whose underlined letter matches n
n	Chooses menu or command whose underlined letter matches n
←, →	Moves among menus
↑, ↓	Moves among menu items
[Enter]	Chooses selected menu item
[Esc]	Cancels selected menu

Cursor Movement Keys

Press this	To move
↑	Up one line
↓	Down one line
←	Left one character
→	Right one character
[Ctrl]←	Left one word
[Ctrl]→	Right one word
[Home]	To beginning of line
[End]	To end of line
[Page Up]	Up one window
[Page Down]	Down one window
[Goto]←	To previous sentence
([Goto] is 5 on numeric keypad)	
[Goto]→	To next sentence
[Goto]↑	To previous paragraph
[Goto]↓	To next paragraph
[Goto][Page Up]	To previous numbered page
[Goto][Page Down]	To next numbered page
[Ctrl][Home]	To beginning of document
[Ctrl][End]	To end of document
[Ctrl][Page Up]	To top of window
[Ctrl][Page Down]	To bottom of window

Text Selection Keys

Press this	To select
[Shift]← or [Shift]→	One character left or right
[Shift]↑ or [Shift]↓	One line of text up or down
[Shift][Page Up]	Text up one window
[Shift][Page Down]	Text down one window
[Shift][Home]	Text to beginning of line
[Shift][End]	Text to end of line
[Ctrl][Shift]←	Previous word
[Ctrl][Shift]→	Next word
[Ctrl][Shift][Home]	Text to beginning of document
[Ctrl][Shift][End]	Text to end of document

Editing Keys

Keystroke(s)	Function
[Backspace]	Deletes character to left of cursor; also deletes selected text
[Delete]	Deletes character to right of cursor; also deletes selected text
[Ctrl]Z	Undoes previous editing command or function
[Ctrl]X	Deletes selected text and places it in Clipboard
[Ctrl]C	Copies selected text to Clipboard
[Ctrl]V	Inserts, or pastes, text from Clipboard into document at cursor

Clipboard Keys

Keystroke(s)	Function
[Shift][Delete]	Cuts highlighted selection and places it in Clipboard
[Ctrl][Insert]	Copies highlighted selection and places it in Clipboard
[Shift][Insert]	Pastes selection from Clipboard into document at cursor
[Delete]	Clears contents of Clipboard
[Print Screen]	Copies entire screen to Clipboard
[Alt][Print Screen]	Copies active window to Clipboard

Program Manager Keys

Keystroke(s)	Function
↑, ↓, ←, →	Moves among items in group window
[Ctrl][F6] or [Ctrl][Tab]	Moves among group windows
[Alt][Spacebar]	Opens Control menu
[Alt]	Closes Control menu
[Enter]	Starts highlighted program
[Shift][F4]	Tiles open windows
[Shift][F5]	Cascades open windows
[Ctrl][F4]	Closes active group window
[Alt][F4]	Exits Windows

Windows 3.1 Companion Quick Reference

File Manager Keys

Keystroke(s)	Function
In directory tree panes:	
[Home]	Selects root directory
[End]	Selects last listed directory
← or [Backspace]	Selects parent directory of selected directory
→	Selects first subdirectory of selected directory
[Page Up]	Selects first directory in current or previous window
[Page Down]	Selects last directory in current or next window
[Ctrl]↑	Selects previous directory in same level
[Ctrl]↓	Selects next directory in same level
n	Selects next directory whose name starts with n
[Ctrl]n	Selects and activates disk drive n
- (hyphen)	Collapses selected directory
+ (plus)	Expands selected directory
* (asterisk)	Expands entire branch of selected directory
[Ctrl]* (asterisk)	Expands all directory branches
[Tab] or [F6]	Moves to contents pane
[Delete]	Deletes selected directory
In directory contents panes:	
↑	Selects file or directory above current one
↓	Selects file or directory below current one
[Home]	Selects first file or directory in list
[End]	Selects last file or directory in list
[Page Up]	Selects first file or directory in current or previous window
[Page Down]	Selects last file or directory in current or next window
n	Selects next file or directory whose name starts with n
[Ctrl]/ (slash)	Selects all files and directories in list
[Ctrl]\ (backslash)	Deselects all files and directories in list
[Shift][F8]	Begins selecting files or directories out of sequence and ends selection
[Backspace]	Selects parent directory of current directory
[Delete]	Deletes selected files and directories
[Spacebar]	Selects or deselects file or directory during out-of-sequence selection

File Manager Keys, continued

Keystroke(s)	Function
In File Manager:	
[Enter]	Opens selected directory or file
[F7]	Issues Move command
[F8]	Issues Copy command
[Delete]	Issues Delete command
[Shift][F5]	Cascades all directory windows
[Shift][F4]	Tiles all directory windows
[F5]	Issues Refresh command
[Ctrl][Tab] or [Ctrl][F6]	Moves between directory windows

Print Manager Keys

Keystroke(s)	Function
[Ctrl]↑	Moves selected file up in print queue
[Ctrl]↓	Moves selected file down in print queue
[Alt]D	Deletes selected file from print queue
[Alt]P	Pauses printing
[Alt]R	Resumes printing

Write Keys

Keystroke(s)	Function
[Ctrl][Shift]- (hyphen)	Inserts optional hyphen
[Ctrl][Enter]	Inserts manual page break
[F3]	Issues Repeat Last Find command
[Alt][F6]	Switches between document and Page Header or Page Footer dialog box
[F5]	Selects Regular style
[Ctrl]B	Selects Bold style
[Ctrl]I	Selects Italic style
[Ctrl]U	Selects Underlined style
[Ctrl]Z	Undoes last command

Paintbrush Keys

Keystroke(s)	Function
[Insert]	Same as clicking left mouse button
[Delete]	Same as clicking right mouse button
[F9][Insert]	Same as double-clicking left mouse button
[F9][Delete]	Same as double-clicking right mouse button
[Shift]↑	Moves up one line
[Shift]↓	Moves down one line
[Home]	Moves to top
[End]	Moves to bottom
[Page Up]	Moves up one screen
[Page Down]	Moves down one screen
[Shift][Home]	Moves to left edge
[Shift][End]	Moves to right edge
[Shift]←	Moves left one space
[Shift]→	Moves right one space
[Shift][Page Up]	Moves left one screen
[Shift][Page Down]	Moves right one screen
[Tab] or [Shift][Tab]	Moves pointer counterclockwise or clockwise among Toolbox, Linesize box, Palette, and drawing areas
[Ctrl]B	Selects Bold style for text
[Ctrl]I	Selects Italic style for text
[Ctrl]U	Selects Underlined style for text

Terminal Keys

Keystroke(s)	Function
[Ctrl][Insert]	Copies selection to Clipboard
[Shift][Insert]	Sends Clipboard contents to remote system
[Ctrl][Shift][Insert]	Sends selected text to remote system
[Ctrl][Alt][F1]-[F8]	Executes one of 32 user-defined commands

Recorder Keys

Keystroke(s)	Function
[Ctrl][Break]	Halts recording or replaying of macro

Notepad Keys

Keystroke(s)	Function
[F3]	Issues Find Next command
[F5]	Issues Time/Date command

Calendar Keys

Keystroke(s)	Function
In day view:	
[F4]	Shows date
[F5]	Sets alarm
[F6]	Marks
[F7]	Adds special time slot
[F9]	Displays month view
[Ctrl][Page Up]	Shows previous day
[Ctrl][Page Down]	Shows next day
↑	Moves to time slot above
↓ or [Enter]	Moves to time slot below
[Page Up]	Moves to previous screen
[Page Down]	Moves to next screen
[Ctrl][Home]	Moves to starting time
[Ctrl][End]	Moves to 12 hours after starting time
[Tab]	Moves between appointment area and scratch pad
In month view:	
[F4]	Shows date
[F6]	Marks
[F8]	Displays day view
[Ctrl][Page Up]	Shows previous month
[Ctrl][Page Down]	Shows next month
↑, ↓	Moves to week above or below
[Page Up]	Moves to previous month
[Page Down]	Moves to next month
[Tab]	Moves between date and scratch pad
[Enter]	Changes to day view

Windows 3.1 Companion Quick Reference

Cardfile Keys

Keystroke(s)	Function
[Page Up]	Scrolls backward one card
[Page Down]	Scrolls forward one card
↑, ↓	Scrolls backward or forward one card (list view)
[Ctrl][Home]	Brings first card in file to front
[Ctrl][End]	Brings last card in file to front
[Ctrl]*n*	Displays first card whose index line begins with *n* (list view)
[F3]	Repeats search
[F4]	Accesses specific card
[F5]	Sets up autodial
[F6]	Adds text to index line
[F7]	Adds new card

Calculator Keys

Keystroke(s)	Function
+, -, *, /	Adds, Subtracts, Multiplies, Divides
[F9]	Applies positive or negative sign
. (period) or , (comma)	Inserts decimal point
%	Calculates percentage
= or [Enter]	Calculates or Equals
R	Calculates reciprocal
[Backspace] or ←	Deletes last number entered
[Esc]	Clears calculation
[Delete]	Clears last function or displayed number
[Ctrl]P	Adds displayed number to value in memory
[Ctrl]L	Clears memory
[Ctrl]R	Recalls value from memory
[Ctrl]M	Stores value in memory
@	Takes square root of displayed number

Media Player Keys

Keystroke(s)	Function
[Tab]	Moves from button to button (left to right)
[Shift][Tab]	Moves from button to button (right to left)
[Spacebar]	Selects button
←	Moves playing position backward when scroll bar is selected
→	Moves playing position forward when scroll bar is selected

Sound Recorder Keys

Keystroke(s)	Function
[Spacebar]	Selects button
[Tab]	Moves from button to button (left to right)
[Shift][Tab]	Moves from button to button (right to left)
[Page Up]	Moves backward 1 second when scroll bar is selected
[Page Down]	Moves forward 1 second when scroll bar is selected
[Home]	Moves to beginning of sound when scroll bar is selected
[End]	Moves to end of sound when scroll bar is selected

Great Resources for Windows™ 3.1 Users

LEARNING & RUNNING WINDOWS™ 3.1
Includes *Microsoft® Productivity Pack for Windows 3.1* **and** *Running Windows 3.1, 3rd ed.*

Microsoft Corporation and Craig Stinson

This is the ideal blending of software and book instruction for users of all levels of experience. If you want to be up and running with Windows 3.1 quickly and easily, this is the place to start. The *Microsoft Productivity Pack for Windows 3.1* (regularly $59.95) combines disk-based lessons with hands-on exercises. Guided practice sessions and concise explanations help you master the basics of Windows. RUNNING WINDOWS 3.1 (regularly $27.95) will continue to answer your day-to-day questions about Windows long after you've learned the basics from the software tutorial. An unbeatable package at an unbeatable price. Sold separately for $87.90.
608 pages, softcover with one 5^1/$_2$-inch (HD) disk $39.95 ($54.95 Canada)

RUNNING WINDOWS™ 3.1, 3rd ed.

Craig Stinson

Build your confidence and enhance your productivity with Microsoft Windows, quickly and easily, using this hands-on introduction. This Microsoft-authorized edition—for new as well as experienced Windows users—is completely updated and expanded to cover all the new exciting features of version 3.1. You'll find a successful combination of step-by-step tutorials, helpful screen illustrations, expert tips, and real-world examples. Learn how to install and start using Windows 3.1, use applications with Windows, and maximize Windows performance.
608 pages, softcover $27.95 ($37.95 Canada)

CONCISE GUIDE TO MICROSOFT® WINDOWS™ 3.1

Kris Jamsa

Instant answers to your Windows 3.1 questions! Clear, concise information on all the key Microsoft Windows 3.1 features; covering everything from installation to customization. For beginning to intermediate users. Great complement to *Windows 3.1 Companion.*
192 pages, softcover   6 x 9 $12.95 ($17.95 Canada)

CONCISE GUIDE TO MICROSOFT® WORKS FOR WINDOWS™

JoAnne Woodcock

This handy guide—for beginning to intermediate users—offers a clear overview of the significant features of each Microsoft Works for Windows application; the word processor, spreadsheet, and database. Arranged by topic and features readable, down-to-earth text.
224 pages, softcover   6 x 9 $12.95 ($17.95 Canada)

Microsoft Press books are available wherever quality computer books are sold.
Or call **1-800-MSPRESS** *for ordering information or placing credit card orders.*
Please refer to **BBK** *when placing your order. Prices subject to change.*

* In Canada, contact Macmillan Canada, Attn: Microsoft Press Dept., 164 Commander Blvd., Agincourt, Ontario, Canada M1S 3C7, or call (416) 293-8141.
In the U.K., contact Microsoft Press, 27 Wrights Lane, London W8 5TZ.